GENEALOGICAL NOTES,

OR

Contributions to the Family History

OF SOME OF THE

FIRST SETTLERS OF CONNECTICUT AND MASSACHUSETTS.

BY THE LATE

NATHANIEL GOODWIN.

Baltimore
GENEALOGICAL PUBLISHING CO., INC.
1987

Originally published: Hartford, Connecticut, 1856
Reprinted: Genealogical Publishing Co., Inc.
Baltimore, 1969, 1978, 1982, 1987
Library of Congress Catalogue Card Number 75-76817
International Standard Book Number 0-8063-0159-7
Made in the United States of America

PREFACE.

THE following pages contain a selection from the Genealogical Notes made by my uncle, NATHANIEL GOODWIN,
from time to time after his appointment to the office of
Judge of Probate for the district of Hartford, in 1833, and
prepared for publication by him during the last three or four
of the latter years of his life. They were not designed by
him to be complete genealogies even of the families which
are treated of, but, as the title indicates, genealogical notes
to assist others in tracing out their family histories. Mr.
Goodwin had begun to print the work, making his final cor-
rections as the proof-sheets were brought to him, and had
proceeded as far as page 68, when the printing was suspend-
ed, as he hoped temporarily, by a severe attack of disease,
but as the event proved, finally, so far as he was concerned,
by his death. At his request, made a few days before his
death, and the desire of his executors, the manuscripts
were placed in the hands of HENRY BARNARD, LL. D.,
President of the Connecticut Historical Society, who had
rendered my uncle similar aid in his former publications, to
see through the press; but the pressure of his engagements
obliged him, after the supervision of some fifty pages, to
relinquish all further care of the work, beyond preparing a

memoir of the author's life, and the immediate charge of the publication devolved on CHARLES J. HOADLY, Esq., late Librarian of Trinity College, and now State Librarian.

It is difficult for one man to enter into the labors of another in matters of this kind, and to harmonize memoranda differing sometimes in date and substance with regard to the same facts, particularly when the original sources whence the information was gathered are not indicated. Probably many of the blanks in the following genealogies would have been filled out, had Mr. Goodwin lived to finish the work himself, but no pains have been spared, to supply missing dates from the large mass of manuscript notes left by my uncle, and to add some from other reliable sources.

The undersigned would, in conclusion, express his thanks, and the thanks, he doubts not, of many others interested in inquiries of this sort, to both of the gentlemen above named, for their coöperation in carrying this work through the press, as another, although imperfect, contribution to this department of literature, from one who had devoted many years to its preparation.

DANIEL GOODWIN.

HARTFORD, CONN., May 15th, 1856.

CONTENTS.

APPENDIX.

*** The Editors would acknowledge their obligations to James Savage, LL. D., President of the Massachusetts Historical Society, for many valuable suggestions.

MEMOIR

OF

NATHANIEL GOODWIN.

NATHANIEL GOODWIN,—whose accurate contributions to the genealogical literature of New England entitle him to an honorable remembrance, not only among professed antiquarians, but by all who desire to see the restless habits of our people corrected by a stronger infusion of family and local attachments, which genealogical studies are calculated to foster—was born in Hartford, Connecticut, on the 5th of March, 1782; the youngest child of Nathaniel Goodwin, and Anna [Sheldon] Goodwin, the daughter of Deacon Isaac Sheldon.

His ancestor on the father's side, was of the old New England Puritan stock—the names of the brothers William and Ozias Goodwin, being inscribed* on the stone monument erected to the memory of the early settlers of Hartford, in the ancient burying-ground of the First Church in Connecticut, where Mr. Thomas Hooker, "the light of the Western Churches," first ministered; Ozias Goodwin, and his elder brother William Goodwin, were of that "goodly company" of men, women, and children, who in June, 1635 or 1636, left Newtown, New Cambridge, and other settlements in the seaboard of Massachusetts, to plant a new colony on the "delightful banks" of the Connecticut. Mr. William Goodwin was a man of mark in his day. He was admitted a freeman of Massachusetts, at Cambridge, in November, 1632, and was a member of the first General Court in that

---

* See list of names in Goodwin's " *Descendants of Thomas Olcott.*" p. XII.

province at which delegates attended, held in May, 1634. Gov.
Winthrop in his journal speaks of him as "a very reverend and
godly man, being an elder in the congregation of Newtown"—in
Cambridge. In 1636, he was commissioned with Mr. Samuel
Stone, to negotiate for the grant of the land where Hartford now
stands, from Sunckquasson, Sachem of Suckiauge, and grand pro-
prietor of the lands of this region. He was one of the trustees
of Gov. Hopkins' will—and in the dissensions about church
membership, baptism, and discipline which convulsed the church
of Hartford and Wethersfield, in 1659, he sided with the Rev.
Mr. Russell, of the church at the latter place; and with Gov.
Webster, Mr. Whiting, Mr. Culick, Mr. Barnard and others,
removed to Hadley, and founded there a church of which he became ruling elder, as he had previously been in the church at
Hartford. He subsequently removed to Farmington, where he
died in 1673, leaving one daughter who married John Crow, of
Hartford. Mr. Goodwin's homestead, in the original distribution
of the town of Hartford among the settlers, in 1639, embraced
three acres—"abutting on the highway, lying at the North side
of the *Riveret*, leading from the palisado to Sentinel Hill"—and
included the site on which Wadsworth Atheneum, with the
Library of the Connecticut Historical Society, now stands.

Mr. Ozias Goodwin did not sympathize with his brother in his
peculiar views as to church membership, and discipline, so far
as to feel constrained to go out from his brethren in the church at
Hartford, but continued to reside there, where he became the
progenitor* of most of the name now in this section of the State.
His home-lot was located on the west side of what is now Trumbull street, and on both sides of Church street as since laid out.

Nathaniel Goodwin, the father of the subject of this memoir,
was a merchant in Hartford, and died in 1782, a few weeks before
this son was born. The children were placed under the guardian-
ship of Capt. Ebenezer Barnard, at that time a resident of Berlin,
but who afterwards removed to Hartford, where he died in 1827.
The guardian appears to have aimed to secure a good education for
his wards—both Nathaniel and his older brother James, having

---

* See Genealogical Notes of Ozias Goodwin, page xv. These Notes were not intended by
Judge Goodwin to form a part of this volume, and are therefore, not so complete as he
would have made them, had he lived.

been sent to the Academy at Plainfield, at that time second to none other in Connecticut. From a specimen copy, executed by young Goodwin, and dated April 30, 1792, we should judge that the scholars of that school made one valuable acquisition—that of a handwriting, which has even now, the rare merit of legibility.

After leaving school, Nathaniel served an apprenticeship in the art of printing; for two years with Mr. Obrient, in New Haven, and for three in the office of Charles R. and George Webster, in Albany. From a letter written by E. W. Skinner, Esq., Librarian of the New York State Library, dated Albany, April 17, 1856, and who was an apprentice in the same office at the time, it appears that Mr. Goodwin exhibited early in youth those traits of character and manners which distinguished him in after life. " During his residence in this city, he was diligent, exemplary and faithful in the discharge of all his duties ; kind and affectionate to his associates, and respectful and obedient to his instructors. His habits were good, and seemed based upon fixed moral principle. Practical good sense was predominant in his character, assisted and aided by study and observation. He was plain and unostentatious, and somewhat antiquated in manner and habit ; so much so, indeed, was this peculiarity observable, as to give to him the appearance of more mature age. Yet there were times in which he would indulge in mirthful sports and playfulness of mind ; and particularly in manly adventure and ingenious strategy."

On leaving the Messrs. Webster in 1803, they addressed to his guardian a kind letter, from which the following passages are taken.

" Your ward Nathaniel Goodwin, had previously given us notice, that his apprenticeship would expire on the 5th day of the present month ; and that he had been requested by Mr. Barber, to enter into his employment as foreman or superintendent of his printing office, at very handsome wages. To this we most cheerfully give our approbation, as we have no urgent business, and Mr. Barber is very much pressed in getting forward the journal of the legislature and other public printing.

" We embrace this occasion, Sir, to acquaint you how perfectly satisfied we have been with the general good conduct and demeanor of N. Goodwin while with us, and that in our opinion this conduct is indicative of intrinsic goodness of heart, and evidences in a perspicuous manner how anxious he has been, by a suitable

B

and becoming behavior toward us, to render his amiable mother happy and give entire satisfaction to his respected guardian.

" Permit us to add, (and we feel a pleasure in doing it,) that he leaves us a master of the art of printing—acquired by assiduous attention to business during his apprenticeship—a young man of handsome talent, pleasing manners, and correct morality. That his future life may be happy and prosperous is our most sincere prayer."

For this gratifying exhibition of conduct and character, much is due to the watchful interest taken by his guardian, Capt. Barnard, in the moral and intellectual improvement of his ward. His letters addressed to him while at Plainfield and Albany, are full of urgent and judicious advice as to the employment of his time and the formation of good habits.

" So important do I deem a right improvement of your time and talents, that you must accept from me a frequent repetition of advice on these points. * * Let my years and experience, as well as duty and inclination advise you, not to be deterred by rain, nor snow, nor hail, nor wind, nor frown, nor flattery, nor false amusements, nor ideal pleasures, for a day, from laying a virtuous foundation in youth on a rock which can not be shaken." " Yours is the seed-time of life, if you sleep now, you can have no harvest." " Practice beneficence, resolution, perseverance, and self-denial. Fly from the vices you are inclined to, and hold fast to the virtues you would make your own."

Mr. Goodwin did not pursue the business of printing, for which he had served an apprenticeship, but devoted himself to teaching and occasionally to commerce, in connection with his brother James. In 1814 he was appointed deputy collector of the revenue for the fourth collection district of Connecticut; and in 1833 received a commission from the Surveyor General of Connecticut, as deputy surveyor for Hartford county. He had been for years a practical land surveyor, which he had mastered by himself; and had assisted Mr. Daniel St. John in making a survey and map of the city of Hartford, which was published in 1824.

Mr. Goodwin held many important public trusts, which he discharged with exemplary fidelity and to the universal acceptance of his fellow-citizens. He was elected Treasurer of the City of Hartford, in March, 1818, and annually thereafter for thirty-five years, till April, 1853, when he declined a re-election. In 1835 he was elected Town Treasurer, and held the office till he declined a re-nomination in 1854; and in 1833 he was appointed County Treasurer, and held the office till 1854, when he resigned the place, and declined all further appointments. From 1832 to 1833, he held the office of Judge of Probate for the probate district of Hartford, and for several years afterwards served as clerk; and in addition to the regular duties of the office, he performed a great public service in arranging, and classifying the papers of the office, in making out full alphabetical indexes, and in copying out partially obliterated pages, and other ways contributing to the preservation and convenient consultation of these important documents. In the mean time and from a very early period, he had been employed as administrator in settling intestate estates, until probably no individual in the community had had so much to do with the business of the probate office, and with the city, town and county records. He was thus prepared for the prosecution of genealogical inquiries, and it is to be regretted that he did not at an earlier day, determine on preparing his memoranda of individual and family histories for publication.

In 1845 he published in pamphlet form his first contribution to genealogical literature, under the title of the "*Descendants of Thomas Olcott, one of the first settlers of Hartford,*" which he dedicated to the Connecticut Historical Society. In 1849, he published "*The Foote Family: or the Descendants of Nathaniel Foote, one of the first settlers of Wethersfield.*" And from the date of the last publication projected the plan of a series of works of a similar character, in connection with a history of the towns of Hartford, Wethersfield, and Windsor, in the preparation of which the author of this memoir was to be associated, as he had previously been in preparing the introduction and notes to the above mentioned genealogies. Warned by some premonitory symptoms of a serious malady, which might terminate his labors before the history could be prepared, he determined on making a selection from his memoranda, and publishing them under the title of "GENEALOGICAL NOTES, or CONTRIBUTIONS *to the Family History of some of the First Settlers of Connecticut and Massachusetts.*" He accordingly selected enough as he thought to make a volume of four or five hundred pages, and after a thorough revision commenced their publication, but had not proceeded far when he was obliged to suspend his labors, by an attack of sickness from which he never recovered.

After lingering for many months in his sick-room, with periods of great suffering, which he bore with exemplary patience, and with intervals too of assured hope that he might again resume his favorite studies, he died on the 29th of May, 1855, in the 74th year of his age. His funeral was attended by a large concourse of his fellow citizens, who entertained for him the highest respect for the exemplary diligence and fidelity with which he had discharged important public trusts, and for his industrious, useful and upright life.

In an article published in the Connecticut Courant on the day following his funeral, Mrs. Sigourney presents the following discriminating estimate of the character of Mr. Goodwin :

" All his services for the public were discharged with incorruptible fidelity, and a diligence and punctuality seldom equalled. Neither is it slight praise that in the intercourse growing out of them, with people of varying rank and occupation, he should have been enabled to ever preserve his self-command, and steadfastly to regard the rights of the humblest, and to treat with respect the opinions of those from whom he differed.

" Antiquarian tastes had the predominance in his mind, and the genealogical works he has been induced to give to the press, are models of persevering research and accurate arrangement. Even his chirography might seem correctly to symbolize his character— plain, neat, upright, perfect in punctuation, rejecting all factitious flourish, and as legible as the clearest typography.

" In his household, as well as in the community, his judgment was revered, and the authority of his example invariably upheld useful employment, and solid comfort, as opposed to vain ostentation or the sway of fickle fashion. His whole life was marked by that avoidance of display ; that freedom from the pride of wealth; that regard for honest industry, which ought to take high rank among the virtues of a republic, interwoven as they are with its stability and health. He was conspicuous for " a sound mind in a sound body;" for the love of order and the spirit of peace.

" Venerable neighbor and friend, we lay thee in thy grave at this last vernal sunset, not without sorrow. Thou wert one of the few representatives of a race rapidly vanishing away, who illustrated the virtues and the manners of the olden time : Peace to thy stainless memory. We think of thee now, as with that Saviour, to whom in truth and humility thou didst commit thine everlasting trust."

Mr. Goodwin was one of the original incorporators of the Connecticut Historical Society, although he seldom met with its members. He was at the time of his death a Vice-President of the New England Historic-Genealogical Society—whose appreciation of the deceased was expressed in the following preamble and resolutions.

"At a meeting of the New England Historic-Genealogical Society, held August 1st, 1855, the following preamble and resolutions were unanimously adopted.

"WHEREAS we have heard of the decease of Hon. NATHANIEL GOODWIN, of Hartford, Conn., one of the Vice-Presidents of the Society. Therefore,

"*Resolved*, That we deeply regret the loss the Society has sustained in the death of a most useful, active and valuable member, and we heartily sympathise with the family and relatives in their severe affliction.

"*Resolved*, That the Corresponding Secretary request the family to furnish for the use of the Society, or for publication in the Genealogical Register, the leading facts and incidents of his life.

"*Resolved*, That the Secretary be requested to forward a copy of these proceedings to the family of the departed.

" CHARLES MAYO,

"*Recording Secretary.*"

Mr. Goodwin, from his habits of patient and persevering industry, from his official familiarity with early records, and from his grateful admiration of the character and services of the early settlers of Connecticut, was admirably fitted for his work. In the introduction to his genealogy of the " Foote Family," he thus expresses himself as to the rewards and ultimate aims of his labors.

" To the author, the labor of looking through the dusty and fast perishing records of the past, has carried along with it, its own sweet reward. Every step in his investigations, has been on some fragment of reverend history which has exalted his admiration of the sufferings and services,—of the far-sighted policy, the religious devotion and public spirit of the founders of our own little State : and he will feel amply honored, if his labors shall prove in any measure successful in chiseling deeper the inscriptions on their tombstones—in renewing the memory of their virtues from oblivion, and in brightening the links which connect the present generation with the first generation of New England, and thereby infusing a larger spirit of patriotism into the life of to-day.

"Our researches into the past will fail of their true import, unless the living are instructed by its experience, warned by its trials, and quickened by its example."

OZIAS GOODWIN.

OZIAS GOODWIN, one of the first settlers of Hartford, Conn., was born about 1596, as in 1674, in a deposition, Ozias Goodwin calls himself aged 78 years. He was a brother of elder William Goodwin, also one of the first settlers of Hartford.

Ozias Goodwin died about April, 1683.

Children.

I. William,	born	1629.
II. Nathaniel,	born about	1637.
III. Hannah,	born	Married William Pitkin, Esq., of Hartford. He died December, 1694, aged 59. His widow survived him, and died at a great age.

DESCENDANTS IN THE LINE OF WILLIAM GOODWIN, SON OF OZIAS GOODWIN, THE SETTLER.

SECOND GENERATION.

I.

WILLIAM GOODWIN married Susanna ———, who after the death of Mr. Goodwin, married ——— Shepard.

William Goodwin died in 1689. (His will is dated June 25, 1689, and his inventory, October 15, 1689.)

Children.

4 William,	born about	1658.
5 Nathaniel,	born	Married Mehitabel, daughter of Samuel Porter, of Hadley. He was a deacon in the church, and died in November, 1747. His wife was born September 15, 1673, and died February 6, 1726, aged 52. *Children*,—Hezekiah, died January 14, 1776, aged 87; Isaac, died December 28, 1773, aged 82; Abraham; Stephen; Eleazer, married Hannah, daughter of Jonathan Easton; Mehitabel, married Joseph Goodrich, December 23, 1714; Benedict, married Jacob Goodrich, September 12, 1717; Joanna; Ruth, married ——— Bird; Alice, married ——— Cadwell.
6 Susanna,	born	Married John Pratt, Jun. She died July 22, 1718.

THIRD GENERATION.

4.

WILLIAM GOODWIN married ———.

Children.

7 Elizabeth,	born April	24, 1681.	Died August 21, 1702.
8 Sarah,	born April	1, 1683.	Married May 9, 1710.
9 Mary,	born December	8, 1685.	Married March 21, 1711.
10 Susanna,	born February	24, 1689.	Died November 12, 1703.
11 Rebecca,	born January	15, 1691.	
12 Hannah,	born April	10, 1695.	Died May 12, 1695.
13 Violetta,	born October	18, 1696.	Died October, 1776.
14 William,	born July	9, 1699.	
15 Rachel,	born January	18, 1702.	Died January 25, 1702.
16 Susanna,	born August	12, 1704.	Died February, 1793.

FOURTH GENERATION.

14.

WILLIAM GOODWIN married Elizabeth Collyer, who was born August 9, 1707.

William Goodwin died May 19, 1774.

His widow, Mrs. Elizabeth Goodwin, died October 11, 1776.

Children.

17 William,	born November	10, 1733.	
18 Thankful,	bap. March	21, 1736.	
19 John,	born August	26, 1739.	Married Martha Spencer, December 14, 1769.

FIFTH GENERATION.

17.

WILLIAM GOODWIN married Margaret Cook, daughter of John Cook, August 5, 1756.

William Goodwin died May 26, 1805.

Children.

20 Allyn,	born December,	1756.	
21 Moses,	born March	5, 1759.	

DESCENDANTS IN THE LINE OF NATHANIEL GOODWIN SON OF OZIAS GOODWIN, THE SETTLER.

SECOND GENERATION.

II.

NATHANIEL GOODWIN married 1. about 1664, Sarah, daughter of John Cowles, of Farmington, Conn., afterwards of Hadley, Mass. She was born in 1646, and died May 8, 1676. 2. Elizabeth, daughter of Daniel Pratt.

Nathaniel Goodwin died 1714.

His widow, Mrs. Elizabeth Goodwin, died ————.

Children,—by his first wife.

22 Nathaniel,	born July,	1665.	
23 Sarah,	born April,	1668.	
24 John,	bap. May	19, 1672.	

Children,—by his second wife.

25 Samuel,	bap. August	22, 1682.	
26 Hannah,	bap. December	6, 1685.	Died January, 1693.
27 Ozias,	bap. June	26, 1689.	Married Martha Williamson, June 6, 1723; was a deacon in the church, and died January 14, 1776, aged 87. His wife died February 9, 1777, aged 75.
28 Mary,	bap. October	14, 1691.	

29 Elizabeth, born 1691. Married John Cole, of Hartford, and raised a family of children ; she died December 28, 1773, aged 82. Mr. Cole died September 8, 1760.

THIRD GENERATION.

22.

NATHANIEL GOODWIN married 1. Lois, only daughter of Deacon Thomas Porter, of Farmington; she died June 15, 1697, aged 27. 2. Sarah Easton, daughter of John Easton, of Hartford, September 14, 1699.

Ensign Nathaniel Goodwin died March 12, 1746, aged 79. [Gravestone.]

Mrs. Sarah Goodwin died January 2, 1740, aged about 60. [Gravestone.]

Children,—by his first wife.

30 Nathaniel,	born February	20, 1691.	Died February 25, 1696.
31 Thomas,	born May	3, 1692.	Died in 1695.
32 Lois,	born September	10, 1694.	Married Josiah Hart, of Farmington, February 22, 1738.
33 Eunice,	born	1697.	

Children,—by his second wife.

34 Timothy,	born January	14, 1700.	Died young.
35 Thankful,	born April	29, 1703.	Died young.
36 Daniel,	born January	15, 1705.	
37 Timothy,	bap. January	19, 1707.	
38 Thankful,	bap. February	23, 1709.	
39 Sarah,	born	1711.	
40 Daughter,	born	1713.	
41 Rachel,	bap. January	22, 1715.	Married Moses Seymour, of Litchfield, March 14, 1738.
42 Elizabeth,	bap. July	5, 1719.	

24.

JOHN GOODWIN, son of Nathaniel Goodwin, and grandson of Ozias Goodwin, was twice married. 1. To Sarah ——— ; she died May, 1735. 2. To Mary Olmsted, widow of Nicholas Olmsted, of Hartford. Her maiden name was Mary Hosmer.

Deacon John Goodwin died February 6, 1758, aged 86.

His widow, Mrs. Mary Goodwin, alias Olmsted, died March 2, 1760, aged 77.

Children.

43 Damaris,	bap. February	11, 1699.	Married a Forbes ; she died August, 1723, aged 24.
44 Mary,	born		Married Joseph Cowles, of East Hartford.
45 John,	bap. August	11, 1706.	Married Dorothy Pitkin. Died September 14, 1793, aged 87.
46 William,	born	1709.	Died February 18, 1745, aged 36.
47 Joseph,	born	1711.	Died February 28, 1838, aged 27.
48 Caleb,	born	1712.	Never was married, or if married, had no issue. [See Probate Records.] Died April 12, 1769, aged 57.
49 Richard,	born	1719.	Died March 3, 1745, aged 26.
50 Hannah,	born		Married ——— Porter, by whom she had children,—Aaron, Caleb, Damaris, and Hannah.

25.

SAMUEL GOODWIN, married 1708, Mary or Sarah Steele, of Hartford. Samuel Goodwin died 1712, aged 30.

His widow, Mrs. Sarah Goodwin, died ———.

C

Children.

51 Abigail,   bap. December   19, 1708. Married March 23, 1738, Nathaniel Eggles-
                                          ton.
52 Samuel,   bap. October   15, 1710.

FOURTH GENERATION.

36.

DANIEL GOODWIN, married 1. Dorothy Cole; she died October 7, 1746, aged 26. 2. November 6, 1748, Mrs. Abigail Bigelow, widow of Timothy Bigelow, and daughter of John Olcott, of Hartford.

Capt. Daniel Goodwin died January 6, 1772, is his 67th year.

His widow, Mrs. Abigail Goodwin, died December 26, 1776, in her 73d year.

Children.

53 Dorothy,   born   1742. Married John McLean, son of Doct. Neil
                                     McLean, of Hartford.
54 Nathaniel,   born about   1743.
55 Daniel,   born   1745.
56 Sarah,   born   1747.

45.

JOHN GOODWIN, of East Hartford, was married to Dorothy Pitkin, daughter of ———— Pitkin, of the same town.

Mrs. Dorothy Goodwin died August 17, 1789, aged 72.

Deacon John Goodwin died September 14, 1793, aged 87.

Children.

57 Damaris,   born   1738. Died October 18, 1773, aged 35.
58 John,   born   1741. Died 1784, aged 43.
59 Joseph,   born May   9, 1743. Died November 13, 1809, aged 66.
60 William,   born   1745. Died March 20, 1785, aged 40.
61 Sarah,   born   1750. Married John Wyles, of East Hartford.
62 Richard,   born   1753. Died August 15, 1821, aged 68.
63 Thankful,   born   1754. Died December 13, 1771, aged 17.
64 Levi,   born   1757. Married Jerusha Drake, of East Windsor.
                                     Died April 24, 1830, aged 78.
65 Hannah,   born   Married Deacon Moses Smith.
66 Mary,   born   Married Doctor Timothy Hall, his second
                                     wife. [No issue.]
67 Anna,   born   1762. Died January 14, 1780, aged 18.
68 Dolly,   born   Married Benjamin Roberts, Jun., of East
                                     Hartford.
69 Caleb,   born

52.

SAMUEL GOODWIN married 1. Abigail ————, who died September 16, 1748, aged 32. 2. Leodamia ————.

Samuel Goodwin died September 30, 1776, aged 66.

Mrs. Leodamia Goodwin died May 1790, aged 61.

Children.

70 Samuel,   born   1752.
71 James,   born December   5, 1754. Married Hannah Mather; she was born
                                     March 20, 1761, and died February 22,
                                     1805. He died June 24, 1822. Father of
                                     James M. Goodwin, Esq., of Hartford.
72 George,   born January   7, 1756. Married Mary, daughter of Richard Ed-
                                     wards, Esq., December 2, 1779.
73 Abigail,   born   1759. Married James Anderson.
74 David,   born   1761. Married Susanna, daughter of Joseph Pratt,
                                     of Hartford. He died ————. She died
                                     1855; without children.
75 Theodore,   born   1764.
76 Russell,   born   1766.
77 Mary,   born   1769. Died May, 1783, aged 14.
78 Mary,   born   1771.

FIFTH GENERATION.

54.

NATHANIEL GOODWIN married Anne, daughter of Isaac Sheldon.
Nathaniel Goodwin died February 20, 1782.
Mrs. Anne Goodwin died February 4, 1823, aged 73.

Children.

79 Sarah,	born November	12, 1769.	Died May 1, 1811.
80 Anna,	born May	22, 1771.	Died same day.
81 Nathaniel,	born March	18, 1772.	Died same day.
82 Elizabeth,	born July	27, 1773.	Married Jesse Hopkins. Died February 14, 1799.
83 Dorothy,	born April	20, 1775.	Died September 20, 1776.
84 Daniel,	born March	24, 1777.	Married Lucretia, daughter of Major Robert Davis, of Boston, December 19, 1798. He died of the yellow fever, on his passage from Monserrat to Charleston, S. C., August 16, 1807, aged 29. *Children,*—Lucretia Ann, Daniel. [After the death of Mr. Goodwin, his widow married Hon. Elisha Colt, by whom she had four children.] Mrs. Lucretia Colt, alias Goodwin, died October 30, 1820, aged 40.
85 James,	born October	24, 1779.	Died October 12, 1843, unmarried.
86 NATHANIEL,	born March	5, 1782.	Died May 29, 1855, unmarried.

59.

JOSEPH GOODWIN, of East Hartford, was married to Hannah Olmsted, daughter of ———— Olmsted, June 3, 1773.
Mr. Joseph Goodwin, died November 13, 1809, aged 66.
His widow, Mrs. Hannah Goodwin, died July 1, 1814, aged 67.

Children.

87 Joseph,	born June	2, 1776.	
88 Caleb,	born November	3, 1778.	Married Harriet Williams, of Wethersfield. *Children,*—Elizabeth, William, Henry M., Caleb, and Lewis.
89 Hannah,	born July	4, 1781.	Married John, son of Charles Reynolds, of East Hartford. *Children,*—Francis, Clarissa, John, Mary, George, Joseph, Frederick, Charles and Julia.
90 Clarissa,	born March	20, 1784.	Died November 8, 1824, aged 40.
91 Sally,	born October	12, 1786.	Died July 16, 1836, aged 50.
92 Hezekiah,	born September	21, 1789.	Married Emily Pratt, of East Hartford. *Children,*—Frances P., Emily, Horace E., Frederick L. and Edwin Olmsted.

SIXTH GENERATION.

87.

JOSEPH GOODWIN was thrice married. 1. To Abigail Smith, daughter of ———— Smith, 1800; she died January 10, 1801, aged 21. 2. To Eleanor Olcott, daughter of Jedediah Olcott, of Windsor, September 9, 1802; she died December 26, 1831, aged 55. 3. To Olive J. Gaylord, widow of ———— Gaylord, June 25, 1836. Her maiden name was Olive J. Johnson.

Child,—by his first wife.

93 Joseph Smith, born January	1, 1801.	Died October 29, 1829, in his 29th year.

Children,—by his second wife.

94 George Olcott, born June	11, 1803.	Married Harriet Fairchild, of East Hartford. Died August 28, 1831, aged 28. *Chil-*

dren,—Harriet and Julia. She removed to Indiana, and married again.

95 Abigail, born October 5, 1805. Died April 13, 1816, in her 11th year.

96 Eliza Eme-
line, born May 2, 1807.

97 Edward Scott, born September 29, 1809. Married Jane Treat Roberts, daughter of —— Roberts, September 24, 1835.

98 Eleanor Lord, born January 13, 1812. Married Samuel P. Robinson, of Canterbury, Conn.

99 Jedediah
Ashley, born March 18, 1814. Died May 20, 1814.

100 James Cad-
well, born September 4, 1815. Married Abigail Judd, of Hartford.

101 Abigail Ash-
ley, born January 18, 1819. Married Barnabas Haskell, of East Hartford.

REV. ADAM BLAKEMAN,

ONE OF THE

FIRST SETTLERS OF STRATFORD, CONN.

Rev. ADAM BLAKEMAN, of Stratford, Conn., and first Minister of that town, was married to Jane ———.
Rev. Adam Blakeman died in 1665.*
His widow, Mrs. Jane Blakeman, died in 1674.†

FIRST GENERATION.

Children of Rev. Adam Blakeman.

I. John,	born	
II. James,	born	
III. Samuel,	born	
IV. Deliverance,	born	He, probably, died unmarried.
V. Benjamin,	born	Harvard College, 1663. Preacher at Malden, Mass., 1675. Married to Rebecca Scottow, daughter of Joshua Scottow, of Boston, April 1, 1675. "Mrs. Rebecca Blakeman, wife to yᵉ Rev. Mr. Benjamin Blakeman, aged about 60 years, died March yᵉ 20th, 1715." Grave Stone, Copp's Hill burying ground, Boston. By records he appears to have had children, but I do not find their names.‡

* Rev. Adam Blakeman left a Will, dated 1st mo: 16, 1665, [March 16, 1665.] The following extract from that instrument contains an important historical reference to the form of Church Discipline approved by the Reverend Elders and brethren of the Colony of Connecticut, and of the Bay in 1649, and set forth by Rev. Thomas Hooker, first minister of Hartford, in his elaborate work entitled "*The Survey of Church Discipline.*"

" *Item.* Because many of God's servants have been falsely accused concerning the judgment of the kinglike power of Christ; though I have cause to bewail my great ignorance and weakness in acting, yet I do and hope I shall, through the strength of Christ, to my dying day, adhere to that form of Church Discipline agreed on by the Rev. Elders and brethren in the year 49, now in print.   And to the truth of God concerning that point, left on record by that famous and Rev. servant of God, of blessed memory, Mr. Thomas Hooker, in his elaborate work called '*The Survey of Church Discipline,*' to which most in all the churches of Christ then gathered in this colony gave their consent, as appears in the Rev. author's epistle, so at Milford, New Haven, Guilford, and those in the Bay, who could be come at in that stress of time.   And, I being one who, in the name of our church, subscribed that copy, could never, (through the grace of Christ,) see cause to receive any other judgment nor fall from those principles so soundly backed with Scripture, and arguments which none yet could overturn."

† Mrs. Blakeman's Will, which will be found recorded on Fairfield Probate Records, is dated September 20, 1671.   Her inventory bears date January 23, 1673-4.

‡ *Extract from the Will of Rev. Adam Blakeman.* " Concerning my books, which I intended for my son Benjamin, seeing his thoughts are after another course of life, that his thoughts be not to attend the work of Christ in the ministry, my wish is that my son

1

VI. Mary,   born   Was twice married, 1. To Joshua Atwater, Esq., of Connecticut, afterwards of
Boston, Mass., merchant, May 6, 1651.
He died May 16, 1676.   2. To Rev.
John Higginson, sixth minister of Salem, Mass., formerly of Guilford, Conn.,
about 1677.* He died December 9,
1708. She died March 9, 1709. She
was his second wife. His first wife was
daughter of Rev. Henry Whitfield, first
minister of Guilford. Children by her
first husband,—Ann; Samuel, born
June 20, 1654; Joshua, born April 10,
1658; Mary, born 1659, and perhaps
others.

DESCENDANTS IN THE LINE OF JOHN BLAKEMAN, SON OF REV. ADAM BLAKEMAN.

SECOND GENERATION.

I.

JOHN BLAKEMAN, of Stratford, Conn., was married to Dorathy Smith, daughter of Rev. Henry Smith, the first ordained minister of Wethersfield, Conn., about 1653. [After his death, she was married, 1. To Francis Hall, of Stratford, October 31, 1665. She

---

Atwater, make his son Joshua a scholar, and fit him for that work, I give unto him all my Latin Books; but if not, they shall be put into my estate and disposed of as my wife and my overseers shall think fit." [After the date of his father's Will the Rev. Benjamin Blakeman was educated for the ministry, at Harvard College, and subsequently became a preacher of the Gospel.]

* The following statement of Rev. John Higginson, which I find recorded on the Land Records of the town of Stratford, informs us that ' *the Meeting House at Hartford*, (I suppose the reader may infer the first Meeting House,) *was not buylded in the beginning of the year* 1638.' " Being desired to express what I remember concerning the transactions between the English at Connecticut and the Indians along the coast from Quilipoke to the Manatoes about the land, the substance I can say is briefly this: That in the beginning of the year 1638, the last week of March, Mr. Hopkins and Mr. Goodwin being employed to treat with Indians and make sure of that whole tract of land in order to prevent the Dutch, and to accommodate the English who might after come to inhabit here, I was sent with them as an interpreter, (for want of a better.) We having an Indian with us for a guide, acquainted the Indians as we passed, with our purpose, and went as far as about Narwoke before we stayed ; coming tither on the sixth day we gave notice to the Sachem and the Indians to meet there on the second day that we might treat with them all-together about the business; accordingly on the second day there was a full meeting, (as themselves said) of all the Sachems, old men and Captaynes from about Milford to Hudson's River: after they had understood the cause of our coming and had consulted with us and amongst themselves, and that in as solemn a manner as Indians use to do in such cases, they did with an unanimous consent express their desire of the English friendship, their willingness the English should come to dwell amongst them and proofs that they did give and surrender up all their land to the English Sachems at Connecticut, and hereupon presented us with two parcels of wampum, the lesser they would give us for our message. the greater they would send us a present to the Sachems at Connecticut, it being not long after the Indian conquest, and the fear of the English being then upon them ; it being moved amongst them which of them would go up with us to signify this agreement and to present their wampum to the Sachems at Connecticut, at last, Wauwhan and Wouwequsrkpeanast offered themselves and were much applauded by the rest for it ; accordingly these two Indians went up with us to Hartford ; not long after there was a committee in Mr. Hooker's barn, the meeting house then not buylded. where they two did appear and presented their wampum, and I remember I went out and attended the business no farther ; so that what was further done or what writings there were about the business I cannot now say, but I suppose if search be made, something of the business may be found in the (contents, minutes or) papers of the Court; and I suppose if Mr. Goodwin be enquired of, he can say the same for substance as I have, and William Cornwall at Saybrook, who was there. Mr. Nicholas Knell testifies the same with Mr. Higginson as respecting the Indians giving the land to the English, and mentions the payment of money to the Indians as a gratuity for the gift. Taken this 3d April, '71.

Milford, May 25, 1659.   JOHN HIGGINSON."

was his second wife. He died in 1689. 2. To Mark Sension, of Norwalk, Conn. She was his second wife. He died in 1693. 3. To Deacon Isaac Moore, of Farmington, Conn.] Mr. John Blakeman died in 1662.*

Mrs. Dorathy Blackman, alias Hall, alias Sension, alias Moore, died at Farmington, in 1706.†

Children.

7 John,   born
8 Ebenezer,   born
9 Joseph,   born

THIRD GENERATION.

7.

JOHN BLAKEMAN, of Fairfield, Conn., was married to Mary Curtis, daughter of Widow Hannah Curtis, of Stratford.

Mr. John Blackman died in 1706.‡

Mrs. Mary Blackman died ———.

Child, one only.

10 Abraham, born October 25, 1694. Married Elizabeth Barlow, February 27, 1718.

8.

EBENEZER BLAKEMAN, of Stratford, Conn., was twice married. 1. To Patience Willcoxson, daughter of John Willcoxson, of Stratford, by his second wife, Elizabeth Welles, widow of John Welles, deceased, of the same town, October 4, 1681. She was born February 1, 1663, and died ———. 2. To Abigail Curtis, daughter of Widow Hannah Curtis, of Stratford, November 3, 1692.

Mr. Ebenezer Blackman died in 1715.

His widow, Mrs. Abigail Blackman, died ———.

Children,—by his first wife.

11 Dorathy, born March   18, 1683. Married Daniel Foote, of Stratford, January 2, 1705.

12 John,   born April   4, 1685.

---

* Mr. John Blakeman left a Will, in which " Son Joseph. if he conducts himself dutifully towards his mother, he shall have ten pounds more than the rest." Will dated 11 mo: 19, 1661. [January 19, 1661.] Exhibited into Court, November 26, 1662.

† The following extract from the Will of the Rev. Adam Blakeman, should be read in connection with the annexed order of the Particular Court, held Oct. 10, 1665, having reference to the "unsuccessful suit" of one John Thomas, for the hand of the Widow Blakeman, whose many virtues caused her to be much sought after, she having been married three times after the death of her first husband.

"I give to my daughter Blakeman, if she marry not John Thomas, and shall take her friends' consent in the matter, or continue a widow, five pounds." [Daughter Widow Blakeman here referred to, was Dorathy Blakeman, widow of John Blakeman, (son of Rev. Adam Blakeman,) who died in 1662. She was daughter of Rev. Henry Smith, the first ordained minister of Wethersfield, Conn.]

At a particular Court held at Hartford, October 10, 1665. "The Magistrates do order, that in case John Thomas and the Widow Blakeman do not issue their difference by reference now concluded on, that the said Thomas shall make good his claim to that woman at the next Court held at Fairfield, otherwise, the widow shall have liberty to marry."

‡ Left a Will, which was probated November 6, 1706, in which he devises his estate to his only son Abraham; and in case of his death, to John Blakeman, son of his brother Ebenezer.

13 Elizabeth, born February 18, 1688. Married Edward Fairchild, of Strat-
                                                   ford, January 25, 1711.
14 Ebenezer, born August   9, 1690.

Children,—by his second wife.

15 Jonathan, born April   24, 1696. Married Mary Beecher, December 20,
                                                   1722.
16 David,   born January   6, 1698. Died March, 1703.
17 Abigail, born November 20, 1700. Died March, 1703.
18 Nathan,   born September 29, 1702.
19 Sarah,   born April   3, 1705.

9.

JOSEPH BLAKEMAN, of ———, Conn., was twice married. 1.
To Hannah Hall, of Stratford, July 4, 1674. She died ———.
2. To Esther Wheeler, January 29, 1705.
   Mr. Joseph Blakeman died ———.
   His widow, Mrs. Esther Blakeman, alias Wheeler, died ———.

Children,—by his first wife.

20 Joseph, born April   30, 1675. Married Elizabeth Seeley, September
                                                   14, 1697.
21 John,   born   Married Jemima Hollibut, April 29,
                                                   1701.
22 Samuel, born
23 Abigail, born   Married William Smith, of ———,
                                                   November 6, 1701.
24 Rebecca, born   Married William Curtis, of Stratford,
                                                   December 1, 1708.

Children,—by his second wife, none.

FOURTH GENERATION.

12.

NATHAN BLAKEMAN, first of Stratford, Conn., and after 1744,
of Munroe, Conn., was married to Sarah Welles, daughter of Samuel Welles, of Stratford, December 31, 1732.
   Mr. Nathan Blakeman died in 1789, aged 87.
   His widow, Mrs. Sarah Blakeman, died ———.

Children.

25 Eunice, born October   8, 1733.
26 Sarah,   bap. July   1735.
27 Ephraim, born March   9, 1746.
28 David,   born   1748. And others, whose names I have not
                                         found

FIFTH GENERATION.

27.

EPHRAIM BLAKEMAN, of Munroe, Conn., was married to Sarah
Wilcoxson, daughter of John Wilcoxson, 1777. She was born
February 10, 1757.
   Ephraim Blakeman, Esq., died in 1811, aged 65.
   His widow, Mrs. Sarah Blakeman, died in 1828, aged 71.

Children.

29 Agur,	born July	27, 1778.
30 Sarah,	born February	18, 1780.
31 Samuel,	born October	5, 1781.
32 John,	born December	1, 1783.
33 Eli,	born April	14, 1788.
34 Philo,	born September	13, 1790.
35 Ira,	born October	30, 1792.
36 Rufus,	born January	12, 1795.

Rufus Blackman, M. D., my much esteemed friend, while he has earned a high reputation as a skillful and learned physician, has found time to indulge his taste for antiquarian research, and has been frequently called upon by his fellow-citizens of the town of Fairfield to represent them in the General Assembly of the State. He has been President and annual orator of the Connecticut Medical Society.

37 Anna Maria,	born July	3, 1798.
38 Eli Wilcoxson,	born November	27, 1800.

DESCENDANTS IN THE LINE OF JAMES BLAKEMAN, SON OF THE REV. ADAM BLAKEMAN.

SECOND GENERATION.

II.

JAMES BLAKEMAN, of Orange Society, Stratford, Conn., was married to Meriam Wheeler, daughter of Moses Wheeler, of Stratford, 1657.

Mr. James Blakeman died in 1689.*

His widow, Mrs. Meriam Blakeman, died ———.

Children.

39 Sarah,	born April	25, 1658.
40 Mary,	born April	21, 1661.
41 Hannah,	born January	21, 1665.
42 Jane,	born October	26, 1668.
43 Meriam,	born February	8, 1671.
44 Zechariah,	born May	26, 1678.
45 Adam,	born January	1, 1683.
46 James,	born December	4, 1686.

DESCENDANTS IN THE LINE OF SAMUEL BLAKEMAN, SON OF REV. ADAM BLAKEMAN.

SECOND GENERATION.

III.

SAMUEL BLAKEMAN, of Stratford, or Huntington, Conn., was married to Elizabeth Wheeler, daughter of Moses Wheeler, of Stratford, "the latter end of November, 1660." [After his death,

---

* Will dated July 18, 1689. Probated November 7, 1689.

she was married to Jacob Walker, of Stratford, December 6, 1670, by whom she had, Samuel, born November 6, 1671; John, born October 29, 1674; Mary, born January 6, 1679; Mercy, born March 11, 1682.]

Mr. Samuel Blakeman died November 27, 1668.

Mrs. Elizabeth Blakeman, alias Walker, died ———.

Children.

47 Son,	born January	1661.	Died March 11, 1661.
48 Abigail,	born December 11, 1663.		
49 Adam,	born September 4, 1665.		Supposed to have died in early life.
50 Joanna,	born December 4, 1667.		Said to have married David Watkins, of Stratford.

48.

ABIGAIL BLAKEMAN was married to Hezekiah Dickinson, first of Stratford, Conn., then of Hatfield, Mass.; then of Hadley, Mass.; and then of Springfield, in the same State, December 4, 1679. He was son of Nathaniel Dickinson, one of the first settlers of Wethersfield, Conn., where he was born "the last of February, 1645."*

Mr. Hezekiah Dickinson died in Springfield, June 14, 1707, in his 63d year.

Mrs. Abigail Dickinson, alias Ingersoll, died ———.

Children.

51 Joanna,	born February	2, 1684, in Hatfield.
52 Jonathan,	born April	22, 1688, in Hatfield.†

* In 1659, Nathaniel Dickinson, the father of Hezekiah Dickinson, removed with his minister, Rev. John Russell, Jun., from Wethersfield to Hadley, Mass., and there continued to reside until his death, which occurred June 16, 1676. All his children, nine sons and one daughter, went with him.

† Rev. Jonathan Dickinson, son of Hezekiah Dickinson, and grandson of Nathaniel Dickinson, the settler, was pastor of the church in Elizabethtown, N. J., and subsequently President of the College of New Jersey, which was located in Elizabethtown, but afterwards removed to Newark, New Jersey, and finally to Princeton, N. J. He died in Elizabethtown, October 7, 1747, aged 59, leaving surviving of eight children, three daughters, the rest having died young. " As he lived a devout and useful life, and was a bright ornament of his profession, he died universally lamented."

One of the daughters of President Dickinson was married to Jonathan Sargeant, Esq., of Princeton, being his second wife, by whom he had two children, a son and daughter. The son was Jonathan Dickinson Sargeant, born in 1746, afterwards counsellor at law, Philadelphia.

Jonathan Dickinson Sargeant, Esq., married a daughter of Rev. Dr. Elihu Spencer, successor in the ministry to Rev. Jonathan Dickinson, at Elizabethtown, and subsequently Pastor of Trenton, N. J.

Rev. Dr. Spencer was a native of East Haddam, Conn., and descendant of Jared Spencer, who, in 1634, was one of the proprietors of land in " The New Town," now Cambridge, Mass., was admitted a freeman of Massachusetts, in 1637, removed from Cambridge to Lynn, in the same State, in 1637, had the ferry of Lynn, granted to him in 1638, removed to and was admitted an inhabitant of Hartford, Conn., in 1660, and in the same year, removed from Hartford to Haddam, Conn., where he continued to reside until his death, which took place in 1685.

Jonathan Dickinson Sargeant, Esq., died in 1793, in the 47th year of his age, leaving ten children.

The third child of Jonathan Dickinson Sargeant was John Sargeant, born about 1780, and died ———. He long occupied an eminent position at the Philadelphia bar, and was candidate for Vice President of the United States in 1832.

Sarah Sargeant, the second child of Jonathan Dickinson Sargeant, was born January 1, 1778, and in 1801, was married to Rev. Dr. Samuel Miller, now [1848] of Princeton College, having been 47 years his wife. This venerable and beloved minister died January 7, 1850. aged 80. From a letter dated December 4, 1848, addressed by Dr. Miller to a brother in the ministry, the compiler of these notes has been permitted to transcribe the following sentence.

53 Abigail,   born December   8, 1690, in Hadley.
54 Elizabeth, born March   9, 1693, in Hadley.
54 Moses,   born December 12, 1695, in Springfield.*
55 Adam,   born February   5, 1702, in Springfield.

" I am ashamed, my dear Sir, that the business of genealogy, has, in times past, engaged so little of my attention ; and that now, when I see so much of its real value, a great deal, truly interesting to me, has irrecoverably gone."

[I am indebted to Rev. Richard Webster, of Mauch Chunk, Penn., a descendant of John Webster, one of the first settlers of Hartford, Conn., and Hadley, Mass., and fifth Governor of the Colony of Connecticut, for much of the information contained in the above note.]

* Rev. Moses Dickinson, son of Hezekiah Dickinson, and grandson of Nathaniel Dickinson, the settler, was called from Maidenhead, N. J., and installed Pastor of the Congregational Church, at Norwalk, Conn. The following is the inscription on his monument : " Beneath this monumental stone lies interred the body of the Revd. Moses Dickinson, late pastor of the first Church of Christ in Norwalk, who departed this life May 1, 1778, in the 83d year of his age, and 51st of his ministry in said Church. A man of good understanding, well informed by study, chearful in temper, prudent in conduct, he came to his grave in full age like as a shock of corn cometh in his season." His widow, Mrs. Hannah Dickinson, died at Plymouth, Conn., June 16, 1803, in the 99th year of her age.

LEONARD CHESTER,

ONE OF THE

FIRST SETTLERS OF WETHERSFIELD, CONN.

LEONARD CHESTER, one of the first settlers of Wethersfield, Conn., was married to Mary ———, of England, about 1634.*
[After his death, she was married about 1655, to Hon. Richard Russell, of Charlestown, Mass. She was his second wife. Mrs. Maud Russell, first wife of Hon. Richard Russell, died in 1652. He died May 14, 1676, in the 65th year of his age.]
Leonard Chester, Esq., died December 11, 1648, aged 39.†

---

* In Genealogical Notes relating to the Chester family, shown me by George Brinley, Jun., Esq., of this city, is the following: "Leonard Chester came from England. He married Mary Wade, widow, daughter of Mr. Nicholas Sharpe."

† Leonard Chester was son of John Chester, of the parish of Blaby, in the county of Leicester, England, and of Dorathy, his wife, daughter of Thomas Hooker, of England, and sister of Rev. Thomas Hooker, one of the first settlers, and the first minister of Hartford, Conn., as I was informed by Sylvester Judd, Esq., of Northampton, Mass., about twelve years ago, and who told me this information was communicated to him several years previous, by a member of the family of Stephen Chester, Esq., of Wethersfield.

The following is a Copy of the last Will and Testament of Leonard Chester.—" Memor. Whereas I have some years since drawn up the frame of my thoughts and desires into a writing, and committed it to the keeping of my uncle Thomas Hooker. now deceased; which writing, for the present, I cannot well come at: and further, because in the writing, I have not, so far as I remember, made any provision for my younger children, which have been born since: I do therefore hereby declare, that whatever provision is therein made for my younger children that were then born, the same provision I do appoint to be made for my younger children born since, so that they may all have their portions alike, equal one to another, except my eldest son to whom I have bequeathed and do still bequeath a double portion. And whereas in that my will, I have entreated Mr. J. Webster* and my cousin Newton† to be my Executors, I do hereby make known that my desire is to ease them of the trouble, and do constitute and appoint my loving wife to be my sole and alone Executrix. And lastly, because I have taken no order in that writing for the dispose of what estate I have remaining still in Old England, I do therefore hereby bequeath all that estate, whether in annuity, goods or otherwise, which either is or shall be of right appertaining unto me or my heirs; and in particular, one annuity of thirty quarters of barley issuing out of the estate of Nicholas Sharpe, deceased, and by his will bequeathed unto me and my heirs, for the selling whereof, I have sent over a letter of attorney to my father Wade: all this with whatever else will be coming to me out of Old England, I do give to my wife during her life, with all the profits that shall accrue therefrom; and after her decease, I do give and bequeath it to my children, viz.: to my eldest son, a double portion,—and to the rest, to every one an equal portion. That this is my full mind and final resolution and will, I do hereby, in testimony hereof, set my hand and seal, this 2d day of August, 1648.

LEONARD CHESTER. ⟨ C. L. M. ⟩

" In the presence of us,
    HE: SMITH,
    WILLIAM SMITH,
    THOMAS HANCHETT.

---

* John Webster, one of the first settlers of Hartford, Conn.
† Rev. Roger Newton, first minister of Farmington, Conn., and afterwards, second minister of Milford, Conn. He married Mary Hooker, daughter of Rev. Thomas Hooker, first minister of Hartford, Conn.

Mrs. Mary Chester, alias Russell, died at Charlestown, November 30, 1688, aged about 80.* [Charlestown Records.]

FIRST GENERATION.

Children of Leonard Chester, and of Mary his wife.

I. John, born August, 3, 1635, at Watertown, Mass. [Watertown Rec.]
II. Dorcas, born November 5, 1637, at Wethersfield.
III. Stephen, born March 3, 1639, at Wethersfield. Died, unmarried, at Hartford, Conn., April 23, 1705.

My desire is to add something further to my within mentioned will, *viz.*:

1. In case my annuity in Old England shall not be sold, and so shall fall by law, upon my eldest son, that then whatever I have given to my eldest son by my will, *viz.*: that double portion of goods, shall be translated from him to my other children, to mend their portions.

2. In case any of my children shall prove undutiful and stubborn to their mother, that it shall be in the power of their mother to take away the one half of that portion I have bequeathed to that child, and to give it to such of the rest as shall be more dutiful to her.

These things, though in a rude and indigested manner, I desire for the present thus to set down,—intending, if God spare my life, to reduce all into one entire writing. This 2d of Aug: 1648. LEONARD CHESTER.

* *The following is a copy of her last will and testament as recorded on Middlesex Co.* (*Mass.*) *Probate Records.*—"In the name of God, Amen. I Mary Russell, widow of the late Richard Russell, of Charlestown, in his Majesty's territory and dominion, in New England, [formerly Mary Chester, wife of Leonard Chester, late of Wethersfield, in the Colony of Connecticut, deceased,] being often weakly in body, but of reasonable good understanding and memory; and forasmuch as I know not how soon it may please God to take me out of this world, by death, I account it my duty, to resign up myself, soul and body to the good will and pleasure of the Lord of life and death,—hoping and trusting, that after this temporal life is ended, to receive everlasting happiness through the only merits of Jesus Christ my Lord and only Saviour. And as concerning what temporal estate it hath pleased God in his goodness to give unto me, I do, by this last will and testament, give and bequeath the same in manner as followeth.

"Imprimis. After my just debts shall be paid, and my decent funeral charges defrayed, I give and bequeath unto my eldest son, Capt. John Chester, of Wethersfield, in the aforesaid territory and dominion in New England, the sum of thirty pounds.

"Item. I give and devise to my daughter, Mrs. Dorcas Whiting, of Billerica, in the aforesaid territory, the sum of thirty pounds, and also, my wearing apparel, and that household stuff which I shall have remaining unwilled to any other; and to her husband, the Rev. Mr. Samuel Whiting, my son-in-law, ten pounds.

"Item. I give and bequeath to my grand-daughter Elizabeth Whiting, my bed and bedstead, bolsters, blanket and rugg. More: I give to said Elizabeth the trunk which is in the chamber, and what is in it. More: I give to her my brass andirons, and silver tankards.

"Item. I give and bequeath to my second son, Stephen Chester, of the aforesaid Wethersfield, merchant, the sum of forty pounds,—one chest of drawers, and a painted carpet.

"I give and bequeath unto my daughter Prudence Russell's orphans, *viz.*, my grandson, Thomas Russell, my brick house, with four feet front on the wharf, which I bought of my son Mr. Daniel Russell: and to my two grand-daughters, Mary Russell and Prudence Russell, fifteen pounds to each one of them. More, I give to my grand-daughter, Mary Russell,

I.

my silver wine cup marked M. D., and one silver spoon. More. I give to my grand-daughter, Prudence Russell aforesaid, my silver plate with the Chester arms on it. Also, I give unto the said Orphans, all that debt of thirty and two pounds due to me on the Book of Accounts. Further, it is my will, that the house and land where Thomas Rand lives, with the yard room, situated and lying in the aforesaid Charlestown, be equally given between the said Mary and Prudence Russell. Further, it is my mind and will that the small house and yard room where John Guppy at present lives, and the leanto rising up against Dr. Chickering's, with the privilege of water at the well, be given unto my daughter, Mrs. Dorcas Whiting aforesaid.

"Item. I give unto my son-in-law, James Russell, Esq., the sum of five pounds.

"Item. I give unto my son-in-law, Capt. Richard Sprague, the sum of five pounds.

"Item. I give and bequeath unto my old servant, Jno Coultman, of Wethersfield, if then living, twenty shillings.

"And further it is my will, that if my estate should fall short of the aforesaid legacies, then, that there be a proportionable abatement on every legatee.

"And further, I constitute and ordain my beloved sons, Mr. Samuel Whiting and Mr. Stephen Chester abovesaid, to be Executors of this my last will and testament. And in confirmation whereof, I have hereunto set my hand and seal, this 20th day of November, A. D. 1688. MARY RUSSELL, L. S."

"In presence of
"EDWARD WILLSON,
"JNO: NEWELL, Senr."

2

IV. Mary,   born January   15, 1641, at Wethersfield. Supposed to have died
                                        in early life, as she is not named in
                                        her sister Mercy's will, nor can a
                                        trace of her be found.
V. Prudence, born February 16, 1643, at Wethersfield.
VI. Eunice,   born January   15, 1645, at Wethersfield.
VII. Mercy,   born February   1647, at Wethersfield. Died in Charlestown,
                                        Mass., September 15, 1669, leaving
                                        a will. Gave her estate to her
                                        three sisters, Dorcas Whiting, of
                                        Billerica, and Prudence Chester and
                                        Eunice Chester, both of Charles-
                                        town, and her brother, Stephen
                                        Chester, of Charlestown, 'to be
                                        divided to them in such proportion
                                        as Testator's dear mother, Mrs.
                                        Mary Russell, shall prescribe.'

DESCENDANTS IN THE LINE OF JOHN CHESTER, SON OF LEONARD CHESTER, THE SETTLER.

SECOND GENERATION.

I.

JOHN CHESTER, of Wethersfield, Conn., was married to Sarah
Welles, daughter of Thomas Welles, one of the first settlers of
Hartford, Conn., and of Wethersfield, and fourth Governor of the
Colony of Connecticut, February, 1653.

"The worshipful Capt. John Chester, Esq.," died February 23,
1698, in the 63d year of his age.

His widow, Mrs. Sarah Chester, died December 12, 1698, aged
"about 67."

Children.

8 Mary,   born December 23, 1654.
9 John,   born June   10, 1656.
10 Sarah,   born November,   1657.
11 Stephen, born May   26, 1660.
12 Thomas,   born March   23, 1662.
13 Samuel,   born May   23, 1664.   Died May 12, 1689, unmarried.
14 Prudence, born December 10, 1666.
15 Eunice,   born May   17, 1668.

THIRD GENERATION.

8.

MARY CHESTER was married to John Wolcott, of Windsor,
Conn., son of Henry Wolcott, one of the first settlers of that town,
February 14, 1677. [After her death, Mr. Wolcott was married
to Hannah Nichols, of Stamford, Conn., June 22, 1692.]

Mrs. Mary Wolcott died July 10, 1689, aged 34.

Mr. John Wolcott died January 3, 1712, aged 68.

Children.

16 John,   born November 20, 1677. Died August 20, 1750.
17 Henry,   born August   7, 1679.
18 Charles, born September 3, 1681.
19 George,   born October   20, 1683.
20 Benjamin, born

21 Mary,   born   Was married to John Eliot, Esq., of
Windsor, Conn., December 19, 1706.
She was his second wife. His first
wife, to whom he was married Octo
ber 31, 1699, was Elizabeth Mackman, widow of James Mackman,
deceased, of Windsor, and daughter
of Thomas Stoughton, of the same
town. She died November 24, 1702.

9.

JOHN CHESTER, Esq., of Wethersfield, Conn., was married to
Hannah Talcott, daughter of Hon. Samuel Talcott, of Wethersfield, son of the Worshipful John Talcott, one of the first settlers
of Hartford, Conn., November 25, 1686.

Major John Chester died December 14, 1711, aged 55.

His widow, Mrs. Hannah Chester, died July 23, 1741, in the
77th year of her age.

Children.

22 Penelope, born October   21, 1687. Died April 1, 1688.
23 Mehitabel, born January   29, 1689.
24 Mary,   born March   8, 1691.
25 Penelope, born November 18, 1693.
26 Hannah,   born May   15, 1696.
27 Prudence, born March   4, 1699.
28 Eunice,   born May   11, 1701.
29 John,   born June   30, 1703.
30 Sarah,   born July   1, 1707.
31 Thomas,   born August   31, 1711. Died May 29, 1712.

10.

SARAH CHESTER was married to Simon Wolcott, of Windsor,
Conn., son of Simon Wolcott, of Windsor, and grandson of Henry
Wolcott, one of the first settlers of that town, December 5, 1689.

Mrs. Sarah Wolcott died August 3, 1723, in the 67th year of
her age.

Mr. Simon Wolcott died August 3, 1732, in the 66th year of
his age.

Children.

32 Sarah,   born   1690. Was married to Samuel Treat, of
Wethersfield, Conn., November 22,
1716. He died March 5, 1733, aged
63. She died April 16, 1743, in the
53d year of her age. *Children,—*
Sarah, born April 26, 1718, and died
March 5, 1733. Samuel, born December 26, 1723, and died February 26,
1756.

33 Martha, born   1692. Was married to William Stoughton, of
Windsor, (east side.) He died May
18, 1750, aged 64. She died May 15,
1751, aged 59.

34 Simon,   born   1694. Died July 26, 1742.
35 Christo-
    pher,   born   1696. Died October 9, 1727.
36 Eunice, born September 24, 1697. Died February 18, 1725.
37 James,   born   1700. Died February 16, 1748.

11.

STEPHEN CHESTER, of Wethersfield, Conn., was married to Jemima Treat, daughter of Lieut. James Treat, of the same town, December 17, 1691. She was born March 15, 1668.

Mr. Stephen Chester died February 9, 1698, in the 38th year of his age.

His widow, Mrs. Jemima Chester, died October 5, 1755, in the 87th year of her age. Her grave is in Newington Society burying ground.

Children.

38 Dorathy,   born September 5, 1692.
39 Sarah,   born March   5, 1694.
40 Mercy,   born October   26, 1696.
41 Stephen
   John,   born February 14, 1698, (posthumous.) Died June 8, 1725.

12.

THOMAS CHESTER, of Wethersfield, Conn., was married to Mary Treat, daughter of Richard Treat, Esq., of Wethersfield, Conn., December 10, 1684.

Mr. Thomas Chester died December 4, 1712, in the 53d year of his age.

His widow, Mrs. Mary Chester, died January 1, 1748, aged 81.

Children.

42 Eunice,   born November 22, 1685.
43 Samuel,   born September 29, 1696. Died March 17, 1710.
44 John,   born December 17, 1699. Died December 14, 1700.
45 Mary,   born January   6, 1706.

14.

PRUDENCE CHESTER was married to James Treat, Jun., of Wethersfield, Conn., December 17, 1691.

Mrs. Prudence Treat died May 25, 1727, in the 61st year of her age. [After her death, Mr. Treat was married to Hannah Boardman, widow of Daniel Boardman, deceased, of Wethersfield, and daughter of —— Wright, of the same town, by whom he had no issue. She died February 25, 1746, aged 83.]

Mr. James Treat died February 18, 1742, in the 76th year of his age.

Children.

46 Abigail,   born December 6, 1692. Was married to David Boardman, of Wethersfield, December 6, 1717. Died October 4.

47 Charles, born January 29, 1695. Died October 4.
48 Prudence, born April   23, 1697.
49 Eunice,   born January 26, 1699. Was married to David Buck, son of David Buck, of Wethersfield, December 19, 1723.

50 James,   born September 2, 1701. Was married to Mary Crane, daughter of Abraham Crane, of Wethersfield, August 11, 1731.

51 Oliver,   born May   31, 1705.
52 Jerusha, born March 14, 1707. Was married to Wait Welles, of Wethersfield.

15.

EUNICE CHESTER was married to Rev. Timothy Stevens, Pastor of the Congregational Church at Glastenbury, Conn., May 17, 1694, being his birth-day. He was son of Timothy Stevens, of Roxbury, Mass., and was born at Roxbury, May 17, 1665. [After her death, Rev. Mr. Stevens was married at Cambridge, Mass., on the 19th of May, 1701, to Allice Whiting, widow of Rev. John Whiting, deceased, second minister of Lancaster, Mass., and daughter of Joseph Cook, Esq., of Cambridge, by whom he had eight children, *viz.:* John, born September 13, 1702, and died August 30, 1717. Eunice, born September 14, 1704, and died September 19, 1704. Martha, born September 6, 1705, and died November 7, 1717. Two sons, born September 8, 1707, and died the night following. Timothy, born July 9, 1709. Joseph, born August 15, 1711. Benjamin, born March, 1714. She died March 10, 1714, aged 40.]

Mrs. Eunice Stevens died June 16, 1698, aged 30.
Rev. Timothy Stevens died April 14, 1726, aged 61, nearly.

Children.

53	Timothy,	born March	23, 1695.	Died April 1, 1695.
54	Sarah,	born March	19, 1696.	Died September 25, 1717.
55	John,	born June	4, 1698.	Died June 27, 1698.

FOURTH GENERATION.

23.

MEHITABEL CHESTER was married to Nathaniel Burnham, of Wethersfield, Conn., May 1, 1714.
Mr. Nathaniel Burnham died December 16, 1754, aged —.
His widow, Mrs. Mehitabel Burnham, died March 18, 1773, aged 84.

Children.

56	Nathaniel,	born January	16, 1719.
57	Mehitabel,	born December	15, 1720.
58	Peter,	born March	22, 1723.
59	Jeremiah,	born July	24, 1725.

24.

MARY CHESTER was married to Jonathan Burnham, of Wethersfield, Conn., January 1, 1718.
Mr. Jonathan Burnham died January 24, 1752, aged 60.
His widow, Mrs. Mary Burnham, died April 19, 1766, aged 75.

Children.

60	Jonathan,	born November	7, 1718.	Died March 15, 1740.
61	Elizur,	born March	21, 1722.	Died December 25, 1724.
62	Abigail,	born August	17, 1727.	
63	Prudence,	born December	1, 1729.	Died June 27, 1730.
64	Elizur,	born June	24, 1733.	
65	Mary,	born August	9, 1735.	

25.

PENELOPE CHESTER was married to Rev. Ebenezer Williams, first minister of Pomfret, Conn., May 24, 1716. Ordained October 26, 1715. He was son of Deacon Samuel Williams, of Roxbury, Mass., and grandson of Robert Williams, one of the first settlers of that town.

Rev. Ebenezer Williams died March 28, 1753, in the 63d year of his age.

His widow, Mrs. Penelope Williams, died June 27, 1764, in the 77th year of her age.

Children.

66 Samuel,   born May   27, 1717. Died July 17, 1717.
67 Chester,   born June   29, 1718. Was minister of Hadley, Mass., and was married to Sarah Porter, daughter of Hon. Eleazur Porter, of Hadley, August 23, 1744. He died October 13, 1753, aged 36. She died February 5, 1774, aged 48. They had 5 children.

68 Ebenezer,   born May   26, 1720. Died June 11, 1720.
69 Nehemiah,   born September 15, 1721. Died March 17, 1739.
70 Ebenezer,   born November 22, 1723. Settled in Pomfret. Was married to Jerusha Porter, daughter of Hon. Eleazur Porter, of Hadley, 1749. Col. Ebenezer Williams died August 22, 1780, aged 57. He was a distinguished man. His widow, Mrs. Jerusha Williams, died September 23, 1805, aged 71. They had 13 children; among them, Elisha, their 12th child, was born August 29, 1773. He studied law, settled in Hudson, N. Y., in 1799, and "he became a few years after a very successful and eminent advocate at the bar, and rose rapidly and brilliantly in his profession." [Judge Kent.]

71 Hannah,   born July   3, 1762. Was married to Jabez Huntington, Esq., of Norwich, Conn., July 10, 1740. She was his second wife. His first wife, to whom he was married January 20, 1742, was Elizabeth Backus, of Norwich. She died July 1, 1745.* He died October 5, 1786. She died ——. *Children*,—Joshua, born August, 1751. Hannah, born July 5, 1753. Ebenezer, born December 26, 1754, was a General.† Eliza_

---

* By this wife, he had 2 children,—1. Jedediah, born August 4, 1743. Harvard College, 1763. Was a Brigadier-General in the army of the Revolution. His first wife, daughter of Governor Trumbull, died at Dedham, Mass., in 1775, while he was on his way to join the army at Cambridge. His second wife was sister of Bishop Moore, of Virginia. She died in March, 1831. "With the courage of the soldier, he combined the humble graces of the Christian." He died September 25, 1818, aged 75. 2. Andrew, born June 22, 1745.

† General Ebenezer Huntington was twice married, 1. To Sarah Isham, daughter of Joseph Isham, of Colchester, December 10, 1791. She was born in December, 1771, and died ——. 2. To Lucretia May McLellen, of Woodstock, Conn., October 7, 1795. Mrs. Lucretia M. Huntington died November 5, 1819. General Ebenezer Huntington died ——. *Child, by his first wife, one only,*—Alfred, born June 2, 1793. *Children, by his second wife,*—Wolcott, born August 20, 1796. Louisa Mary, born February 20, 1798. George Washington, born November 22, 1799. Emily, born August 6, 1801. Nancy, born April 6, 1803. Walter, born November 4, 1804. Sarah J., born May 1, 1806. Elizabeth M., born August 24, 1808. Maria H., born December 13, 1810.

beth, born February 9, 1757. Mary,
born March 24, 1760. Zechariah,
born November 2, 1764,‡ General.

26.

HANNAH CHESTER was married to Gideon Welles, of Wethersfield, Conn., November 30, 1716.

Gideon Welles, Esq., died March 28, 1740, aged 48.

His widow, Mrs. Hannah Welles, died May 29, 1749, aged 53.

Children.

72 Chester,	born October	8, 1718.	Died November 15, 1718.
73 Solomon,	born October	6, 1721.	
74 Eunice,	born August	6, 1723.	
75 Sarah,	born December	23, 1725.	
76 Gideon,	born May	26, 1735.	

27.

PRUDENCE CHESTER was married to Col. John Stoddard, of Northampton, Mass., December 13, 1713.

Col. John Stoddard died at Boston, Mass., June 19, 1748, aged 66. His remains were interred at Northampton.

His widow, Mrs. Prudence Stoddard, died September 11, 1780, aged 81.

Children.

77 Mary, born November 27, 1732. Was married to John Worthington, Esq., of Springfield, Mass., December 7, 1768. She was his second wife. [His first wife, to whom he was married January 10, 1759, was Hannah Hopkins, daughter of Rev. Samuel Hopkins, second Pastor of the first church at West Springfield, Mass. She died November 15, 1766, in the 36th year of her age.] Hon. John Worthington, L.L. D., died April 25, 1800, in the 81st year of his age. His widow, Mrs. Mary Worthington, died July 12, 1812, in the 80th year of her age. *Child,—by his second marriage,*—one only, John, born April 22, 1770, and died August 11, 1770.

78 Prudence, born May 28, 1734. Was married to Ezekiel Williams, of Wethersfield, Conn., November 6, 1760. Ezekiel Williams, Esq., died 1818, aged 86. His widow died ——. *Children,*—Emily, born June 9, 1761, married Samuel W. Williams. John, born September 11, 1762, was twice married, 1. To Sophia Worthington, daughter of the Hon. John Worthington, of Springfield, Mass., 1799. She died ——. 2. To Mary Silliman, widow of the Rev. Ebenezer Silliman, of Amsterdam, N. Y., and daughter

‡ Zechariah Huntington, of Norwich, was married to Hannah Mumford, of Norwich, March 23, 1786. Children, Thomas Mumford, born December 28, 1786. Jabez Williams, born November 8, 1788, was United States Senator. Elizabeth, born October 5, 1793.

of Col. Thomas Dyer, of Windham, Conn., 1817. John Williams, Esq., died 1840, aged 78. Harriet, born June 26, 1764, was married to Rev. Dr. David Parsons, of Amherst, Mass.;—was the father of Hon. Francis Parsons, of Hartford, Conn. Ezekiel, born December 29, 1765, Prudence, born October 2, 1767, was married to Rev. Mr. Howard, of Springfield, Mass. Mary, born August 14, 1769, was married to John Salter, of Mansfield, Conn. Esther, born April 14, 1771. Solomon Stoddard,. born October 10, 1773. Christina, born September 22, 1775. Thomas Scott, born June 22, 1777, was twice married, 1. To Delia Ellsworth, daughter of Hon. Oliver Ellsworth, of Windsor, Conn., and after her death, to Martha M. Coit. Samuel Porter, born February, 1779, was twice married, 1. To Mary H. Webb, and after her death, to Sarah Tyler. He lived in Mansfield, and afterwards in Newburyport, Mass.

79 Solomon, born May   29, 1736. Settled in Northampton, Mass., was twice married. 1. To Martha Partridge, of Hatfield, Mass., November 21, 1765. She died October 20, 1772, aged 33. 2. To Eunice Parsons, of Amherst, Mass. Mrs. Eunice Stoddard died January 22, 1797. Solomon Stoddard, Esq., died December 19, 1787, aged 51. He had 3 children by each wife.

80 Israel,   born April   28, 1741. Settled in Pittsfield, Mass. Was married to Eunice Williams, of Hatfield, Mass. He died June 27, 1782, aged 41.

81 Hannah,   born October 13, 1742. Died August 1, 1843.

28.

EUNICE CHESTER was married to Col. Joseph Pitkin, of East Hartford, Conn. She was his second wife. [Col. Pitkin was thrice married. His first wife, to whom he was married February 20, 1724, and by whom he had all his children, six in number, was Mary Lord, daughter of Richard Lord, of Hartford, Conn. She died October 10, 1740, aged 38. His third wife was Eunice Law, widow of Governor Jonathan Law, deceased, of Milford, Conn., alias Eunice Andrew, widow of Samuel Andrew, Esq., of Milford, son of Rev. Samuel Andrew, minister of that town. She was the only daughter of the Hon. John Hall, of Wallingford, Conn., and aunt to Lyman Hall, one of the signers of the Declaration of Independence from Georgia. She died at New Haven, Conn., June 23, 1774, aged 75.] Col. Joseph Pitkin died November 3, 1762, aged 67. His second wife, Mrs. Eunice Pitkin, died June 25, 1756, aged 55.

Children,—none.

29.

JOHN CHESTER, of Wethersfield, Conn., was married to Sarah Noyes, daughter of Rev. Joseph Noyes, pastor of the first Congregational church at New Haven, Conn., November 19, 1747. Hon. John Chester died September 11, 1771, aged 68. His widow, Mrs. Sarah Chester, died January 25, 1797, aged 75.

Children.

82 John, born January 18, 1749. Settled in Wethersfield. Was married to Elizabeth Huntington, daughter of the Hon. Jabez Huntington, of Norwich, Conn., November 25, 1773. Hon. John Chester died November 4, 1809, in the 61st year of his age.* His widow, Mrs. Elizabeth Chester, died July 1, 1834, aged 77. *Children,* Elizabeth, born November 10, 1774, married Eleazer F. Backus, of Albany, June 8, 1807. Mary, born April 20, 1779, married Ebenezer Welles, of Brattleboro, Vt., June 8, 1806. Hannah, born October 27, 1781, married Charles Chauncey, Esq., of Philadelphia. Sarah, born June 17, 1783. John, born August 17, 1785, Yale College, 1804, Pastor of the Congregational church, now Rev. Dr. Sprague's, Albany, N. Y. Rev. Dr. Chester died at Philadelphia, January 12, 1829, leaving surviving his wife, Rebecca Ralston, daughter of Robert Ralston, of Philadelphia, but no children. As a preacher, he was considered one of the most able and useful, affectionately esteemed by his people, and highly respected by the community at large. Charlotte, born March 20, 1787. Henry, born October 3, 1790, died March 1, 1791. Julia, born March 15, 1792, married Matthew C. Ralston, of Philadelphia, April 2, 1816. Henry, born December 22, 1793, Lawyer, Settled in Philadelphia. William, born November 20, 1795, a Clergyman. George, born June 14, 1798, died in early life.

83 Leonard, born September 18, 1750. Settled in Wethersfield. Was married to Sarah Williams, daughter of Col. William Williams, of Pittsfield, Mass., by his second wife, Miss Welles, September 12, 1776. He died August 17, 1803, aged 53. She died May 3, 1835, aged 76. *Children,—* Leonard William Pepperell, born December 20, 1777. Sarah, born August 8, 1779. Henrietta, Sophia, twins, born March 8, 1781. John

---

* Hon. John Chester was a Colonel in the army of the Revolution, and distinguished himself by his bravery at the battle of Bunker Hill. He sustained several important civil offices, the duties of which he performed with great fidelity. In all the private relations of life, he was much esteemed and beloved for his amiableness, sincerity, hospitality and benevolence. He was a sincere and pious Christian.

3

Noyes, born March 20, 1783. Sally Williams, born November 2, 1784. William Williams, born July 13, 1786. James D., and Abigail.

84 Sarah, born August 12, 1752. Was married to Thomas Coit, of Norwich, Conn., about 1795.

85 Abigail, born May 27, 1754. Was married to Joseph Webb, of Wethersfield, Conn., November 22, 1774. They had 12 children, John Haynes, their seventh child, born December 8, 1786, settled in Albany, N. Y., was a merchant. Died at Hartford, Conn.

86 Stephen, born October 28, 1761. Married Elizabeth Mitchell, daughter of Chief Justice Stephen Mix Mitchell, of Wethersfield. He died December 6, 1835, aged 74. She died December 22, 1852, aged 82. They had several children.

87 Thomas, born January 7, 1764. Settled in Wethersfield, but afterwards removed to Hartford. Was attorney at law. Married to Esther M. Bull, daughter of Joseph Bull, of Hartford, March, 1795. He died October 2, 1831, aged 67. She died June 22, 1844, aged 67. Several children, among them, the wife of James M. Bunce, of the city of Hartford.

30.

SARAH CHESTER was married to Israel Williams, of Hatfield, Mass., about 1731.

Mrs. Sarah Williams died September 18, (8 on grave-stone,) 1770, aged 63.

Hon. Israel Williams died June (January on grave-stone) 10, 1788, in the 79th year of his age.

Children.

88 John, born May 26, 1632. Harvard College, 1751. Died same year.

89 William, born 1734. Was in public business until the Revolution.

90 Israel, born Died unmarried.

91 Sarah, born Was married to Doct. Perez Marsh, of Dalton, Mass.

92 Eunice, born Was married to Major Israel Stoddard, (of Northampton, probably.)

93 Jerusha, born Was married to Elisha Billings, Esq., of Conway, Mass.

94 Lucretia, born Was married to John Chandler Williams, Esq., of Pittsfield, Mass.

38.

DORATHY CHESTER was married to Martin Kellogg, of Wethersfield, Conn., January 13, 1716. He dwelt in the Society of Newington, in that town, several of the last years of his life.

Capt. Martin Kellogg died November 13, 1753, in the 68th year of his age.

His widow, Dorathy Chester, died Sept. 26, 1754, aged 62.

Children.

95 Dorathy,	born December	4, 1716.	
96 Martin,	born August	2, 1718.	
97 Anna,	born February	19, 1720.	
98 Jemima,	born August	24, 1723.	
99 Mary,	born October	19, 1725.	
100 Sarah,	born August	22, 1727.	
101 Stephen,	born September	24, 1729.	
102 Joseph,	born October	9, 1736.	

42.

EUNICE CHESTER was married to Rev. Elisha Williams, first Pastor of the Congregational Church in Newington Society, Wethersfield, Conn., but subsequently President of Yale College, and afterwards a Judge of the Superior Court of Connecticut, February 23, 1714.

[After her death, being in England, Mr. Williams was there married to Elizabeth Scott, only daughter of the Rev. Thomas Scott, of Norwich, England; surviving whom, she was married to the Hon. William Smith, of the city of New-York, May 12, 1761, at Wethersfield, upon whose decease she returned to Wethersfield, where she resided at Mr. Sheriff Williams's until her death, June 13, 1776, aged 68.]

Mrs. Eunice Williams died May 31, 1750, aged —.

Rev. Elisha Williams died July 25, 1755, aged 61.

Children.

103 Eunice,	born February	3, 1716.	Died September 26, 1741.
104 Elisha,	born January	31, 1718.	Settled in Wethersfield. Was a magistrate.*
105 Samuel,	born August	16, 1720.	Died November 14, 1740.
106 William,	born November	20, 1722.	Died October 28, 1741.
107 Mary,	born August	5, 1725.	
108 Anna,	born April	30, 1731.	at New Haven, and died at Wethersfield, February 23, 1750.

---

* He appears to have been of the Committee of Inspection of the Association entered into by the inhabitants of Wethersfield in 1775, for denying themselves the use of tea, but granting permits for its use in certain cases, which permits were addressed to "Mr. Leonard Chester, Merchant." The following are copies of two of those permits:

"Mr.—Leonard Chester, Merchant, Sir,—Mrs. Welles is desirous of getting some tea; and *as she relates her case to me,* I do consent that you let her have half a pound.

I am yours, &c.,

ELISHA WILLIAMS.

"WETHERSFIELD, July 6, 1775."

Mr. Leonard Chester, Merchant, Sir,—If you will let the Bearer have one-quarter of a pound of tea, it being, as she informs me, *for a woman who is necessitated for some,* you have the consent of Yours, &c.,

ELISHA WILLIAMS.

"June 29, 1775."

45.

MARY CHESTER was married to Thomas Welles, Jun., of Wethersfield, Conn., June 14, 1738.

Mr. Thomas Welles, Jun., died ————.

His widow, Mrs. Mary Welles, died ————.

Children.

109 Chester,	born March	22, 1739.
110 Thomas,	born June	12, 1741.
111 Samuel,	born April	25, 1744.
112 Bille,	born April	26, 1747.

DESCENDANTS IN THE LINE OF DORCAS CHESTER, DAUGHTER OF LEONARD CHESTER, THE SETTLER.

SECOND GENERATION.

II.

DORCAS CHESTER was married to Rev. Samuel Whiting, first minister of Billerica, Mass., November 12, 1656. ["Rev. Mr. Whiting was born in England in 1633, and was son of Rev. Samuel Whiting, first minister of Lynn, Mass., and of Elizabeth his second wife, daughter of the Right Hon. Oliver St. John, of England. He came into New England with his father, and arrived at Boston, May 26, 1636. He was graduated at Harvard College in 1653, settled in Billerica, 1658, and was ordained there November 11, 1663."]

Mrs. Dorcas Whiting died February 16, 1713, aged 76.

Rev. Samuel Whiting died February 28, 1713, aged 80.

Children.

113 Elizabeth, born October 6, 1660. Was married to Rev. Thomas Clark, second minister of Chelmsford, Mass., 1702, by whom she had no children. She was his second wife.

114 Samuel, born December 19, 1662. Was married to Elizabeth ————. He was a cornet in the troop. He died February 8, 1714, leaving children,— Leonard, born July 12, 1693. Joseph, born December 14, 1795,—and probably others.

115 John, born July 1, 1664. Harvard College, 1685. Was second minister of Lancaster, Mass., where he was ordained December 3, 1691. He was married to Allice Cook, daughter of Joseph Cook, of Cambridge, Mass., about 1694. [After his death, she was married on the 19th of May, 1701, to Rev. Timothy Stevens, Pastor of the Congregational Church at Glastenbury, Conn.,

by whom she had 8 children, 6 sons and 2 daughters.] Rev. Mr. John Whiting was shot and scalped about noon, September 11, 1697, by the Indians, aged 33. Mrs. Allice Whiting, alias Stevens, died at Glastenbury, March 10, 1714, aged 40. *Children of Rev. John and Allice Whiting,*— Allice, born December, 1694, and died at Cambridge, October 19, 1697. Eunice, born 1696, and died at Cambridge, November 4, 1697. A gravestone, standing at the graves of these children in the old burying-ground at Cambridge, Mass., has on it the following inscription, *viz.:* "Here lyes yᵉ children of John & Alice Whiteing. Alice Whiteing Aged 2 years & 10 Mᵒ. Died October 19, 1697. Eunice Whiteing Aged 1 year Died November 4 1697."

| 116 Oliver, | born October | 8, 1665. | Was married to Anna Danforth, daughter of Capt. Jonathan Danforth, of Billerica, December 22, 1689, "before Rev. Samuel Whiting, and Jonathan Danforth, senior." Oliver Whiting, Esq., died December 22, 1736, aged 71, "having been many years a magistrate." They had 9 children,—6 sons and 3 daughters. |

117 Mary,	born April	28, 1667.	
118 Dorathy,	born August	23, 1668.	
119 Joseph,	born January	7, 1670.	Died August 6, 1701.
120 James,	born July	20, 1671.	Died August 1, 1671.
121 Eunice,	born August	6, 1672.	Died August 20, 1672.
122 Benjamin,	born August	26, 1675.	Died September 18, 1675.
123 Benjamin,	born October	5, 1682.	Died October 20, 1682.

DESCENDANTS IN THE LINE OF PRUDENCE CHESTER, DAUGHTER OF LEONARD CHESTER, THE SETTLER.

SECOND GENERATION.

V.

PRUDENCE CHESTER was married to Capt. Thomas Russell, of Charlestown, Mass., December 30, 1669.

Capt. Thomas Russell died October 21, 1676, aged 35.

His widow, Mrs. Prudence Russell, died October 21, 1678, aged 35.

Children.

124 Mary,	born September 27, 1670.	Married John Watkins.
125 Thomas,	born March 30, 1672.	
126 Prudence,	(no date in Record.)	Married a Mr. Dole, of Charlestown.

DESCENDANTS IN THE LINE OF EUNICE CHESTER, DAUGHTER OF LEONARD CHESTER, THE SETTLER.

SECOND GENERATION.

VI.

EUNICE CHESTER was married to Capt. Richard Sprague, of Charlestown, Mass., son of Mr. Ralph Sprague, one of the first settlers of that town, February 1, 1672. [After her death, Capt. Sprague was married to Catharine Anderson, widow, by whom he had no children.]

Mrs. Eunice Sprague died May 27, 1676, aged 31.

Capt. Richard Sprague died October 7, 1703, aged 78.

Children,—none.

DANIEL CLARK,

ONE OF THE

FIRST SETTLERS OF WINDSOR, CONN.*

DANIEL CLARK, one of the first settlers of Windsor, Conn., was twice married. 1. To Mary Newberry, of Windsor, daughter of Thomas Newberry,† June 13, 1644. She died August 29, 1688. 2. To Martha Wolcott, widow of Simon Wolcott, deceased, of the same town, and sister of William Pitkin, Esq., one of the early settlers of Hartford, Conn.

Hon. Daniel Clark died August 12, 1710, "in the 88th year of his age, or thereabouts." [Windsor Records.] He was an Attorney at Law, and, during his long life, was generally in public office.‡

Mrs. Martha Clark, alias Wolcott, died October 13, 1719, aged —. [Grave-stone East Windsor burying-ground, where several of her children rest.]

FIRST GENERATION.

Children of Daniel Clark,—by his first wife.

I. Mary,	born April	4,	1645.	Died in childhood.
II. Josiah,	born January	21,	1648.	
III. Elizabeth,	born October	28,	1651.	
IV. Daniel,	born April	5,	1654.	
V. John,	born April	10,	1656.	
VI. Mary,	born September	22,	1658.	
VII. Samuel,	born July	6,	1661.	
VIII. Sarah,	born August	7,	1663.	
IX. Hannah,	born August	25,	1665.	Died in early life.
X. Nathaniel,	born September	8,	1666.	

Children,—by his second wife,—none.

---

* The principal part of this paper was prepared from statistics collected in 1851 and 1852.

† Mr. Thomas Newberry died at Dorchester, Mass., not long after his arrival in New England. He left a will, which is of record in Suffolk County Probate Court.

‡ For the use of their Magistrates, the town of Windsor appropriated a particular pew in their Meeting House and in addition to the ordinary finish, ordered it to be "wainscotted." On the elevation of Mr. Clark to the Magistracy, the Town, in Town meeting assembled, passed the following vote:"
"May 5, 1651. At a meeting of the Towne, Mr. Clark was appointed to sitt in the greate pew."

DESCENDANTS IN THE LINE OF JOSIAH CLARK, SON OF DANIEL CLARK, THE SETTLER.

SECOND GENERATION.

II.

JOSIAH CLARK, of Windsor, Conn., was married to Mary Crow, widow of Christopher Crow, deceased, of Windsor, and daughter of Benjamin Burr, of Hartford, Conn., one of the first settlers of that town.

Child,—recorded on Windsor Records,—one only.

11 Josiah,   born January   13, 1682.

DESCENDANTS IN THE LINE OF ELIZABETH CLARK, DAUGHTER OF DANIEL CLARK, THE SETTLER.

SECOND GENERATION.

III.

ELIZABETH CLARK was twice married. 1. To Moses Cooke, of Warronoke, [Westfield,] Mass., son of Captain Aaron Cooke, one of the first settlers of Windsor, Conn., afterwards of Northampton, Mass., November 25, 1669. He was slain by the Indians at Westfield, aged —. 2. To Lieut. Job Drake, of Windsor, son of Job Drake, of that town, September 13, 1677.

Lieut. Job Drake died December 19, 1711, in the 60th year of his age.

Mrs. Elizabeth Drake, alias Cook, died December 22, 1729, aged 78.

Children,—by her first husband.

12 Elizabeth, born August   25, 1673, in Westfield. Married to Benjamin Griswold, of Windsor, Conn., by whom she had a numerous family of children, among them, Moses, born July 10, 1714, and married Mary Nichols, daughter of Cyprian Nichols, of Hartford.

13 Moses,   born April   17, 1675, in Windsor.

Children,—by her second husband.

14 Job,   born   1678. Died unmarried, October 15, 1712.
15 Mary,   born April   29, 1680. Married to John Porter, of Windsor, September 23, 1697. *Children,—* John, born March 7, 1699. Mary, born July 10, 1703. Anna, born April 2, 1706. Catharine, born September 14, 1707. Lydia, born May 4, 1711. Ann, born October 13, 1714.

16 Jacob,   born January   29, 1683. Dwelt in Wintonbury Parish, Windsor. He died January 29, 1762, aged 80 nearly. Had 5 chldren, among them, Job, his 4th child, born November 6, 1714, in whose line descended Richard G. Drake, Esq., of the city of Hartford, attorney at law.

17 Sarah, born May 10, 1686. Married December 3, 1702, to Hon. Roger Wolcott, of Windsor, Conn. He became Major General and second in command at the taking of Louisburg, in 1745, and was Lieut. Governor of the Colony of Connecticut, from 1741 to 1750, and Governor from 1750 to 1754. He died May 17, 1767, aged 89. They had 11 children.*

DESCENDANTS IN THE LINE OF DANIEL CLARK, SON OF DANIEL CLARK, THE SETTLER.

SECOND GENERATION.

IV.

DANIEL CLARK, first of Windsor, Conn., then of Hartford, Conn., after about 1710, of Colchester, Conn., was married to Hannah Pratt, daughter of Daniel Pratt, of Hartford, 1678.

Mr. Daniel Clark died ———.

His widow, Mrs. Hannah Clark, died ———.

18 Daniel, born 1679.
19 Moses, born 1683.
20 John, born 1685.
21 Aaron, bap. November 13, 1687, at Hartford.
22 Nathaniel, bap. March 26, 1693, at Hartford.
23 Abraham, bap. November 10, 1695, at Hartford.
24 Noah, bap. April 25, 1697, at Hartford.

THIRD GENERATION.

18.

DANIEL CLARK, of Colchester, Conn., was married to Elizabeth Butler, daughter of Daniel Butler, of Hartford, Conn., and of Mabel Butler, his wife, December 14, 1704.

Mr. Daniel Clark died September 14, 1762, in the 83d year of his age.

His widow, Mrs. Elizabeth Clark, died April 11, 1763, aged 77.

Children.

25 Hannah, born June 30, 1706.
26 Elizabeth, born June 29, 1708.
27 Son, (not
  named,) born July 17, 1710. Died same day.

---

* Oliver, the youngest of the eleven, was born in 1723, and filled many State offices ; was a Brigadier General during the war of the Revolution ; member of the Continental Congress, and Signer of the Declaration of Independence ; Lieut. Governor from 1786 to 1796, and Governor, 1797. He married Laura Collins, of Guilford, Conn., by whom he had four children, two sons and two daughters. He died December 1, 1797, aged 71. Oliver, one of the sons, was born January 11, 1760 : Yale College, 1778 : admitted to the Bar in 1781 : was appointed one of the Committee of Pay-table at Hartford, January, 1782 : Joint Commissioner to settle Accounts with the United States, May, 1784 : Sole Commissioner, May, 1787 : Comptroller of Public Accounts of the State, May, 1788 : Auditor of the Treasury of the United States, September 12, 1789 ; Comptroller of the same, June 17, 1791, and Secretary of U. S. Treasury, February 2, 1795, which office he resigned in 1800 : a Judge of the Second Circuit of the United States, February 20, 1801 : Governor of Connecticut from 1817 to 1827. Died June 1, 1833. Gov. Wolcott was married in 1785, to Elizabeth Stoughton, only daughter of John Stoughton, of Windsor, Conn., by whom he had several children.

28 Daniel,   born September 28, 1711.
29 Josiah,   born December 19, 1713.
30 Roger,   born December 24, 1715.
31 Alexander, born November 6, 1717.
32 Zerviah,   born March   14, 1719.
33 Darius,   born February   2, 1720.
34 Mabel,   born October   7, 1721.
35 Uriah,   born November   2, 1722.
36 Rebecca,   born June   16, 1726.

19.*

MOSES CLARK, of Lebanon, Conn., was married to Elizabeth Huntington, daughter of Samuel Huntington, of Lebanon, February 23, 1710. She was born April 24, 1689.

Mr. Moses Clark died September 18, 1749, in the 67th year of his age.†

His widow, Mrs. Elizabeth Clark, died December 27, 1761, in the 73d year of her age.‡

Children.

37 Mary,   born January   22, 1717.
38 Moses,   born September   2, 1720.
39 Anna,   born January   26, 1723.
40 Elizabeth, born January   25, 1725.
41 John,   born January   7, 1728.
42 James,   born September 15, 1730.§

24.

NOAH CLARK, of Colchester, Conn., was married to Sarah Taintor, daughter of Michael Taintor, of Colchester, Conn., and of Mabel Taintor, his second wife, widow of Daniel Butler, of Hartford, Conn., and daughter of Nicholas Olmsted, of the same town, June 10, 1719. She was born November 19, 1698.

Mr. Noah Clark died June 1, 1749, aged 52.

His widow, Mrs. Sarah Clark, died ———.

Children.

43 Sarah,   born February 19, 1719. Died in infancy.
44 Sarah,   born March   9, 1721.
45 Noah,   born August   24, 1722. Married Eunice Quitterfield, December 5, 1751.
46 Jerusha,   born February 28, 1724.
47 Ezra,   born November   8, 1725. Died at Colchester, June 7, 1797, aged 71.
48 Elihu,   born November   8, 1727. Married Elizabeth Kellogg, May 9, 1750.
49 Esther,   born October   14, 1729.

---

* Several of the grandsons of Hon. Daniel Clark, and a family of the name of Clark from Saybrook, Conn., settled in Lebanon at an early date. Gov. Myron H. Clark, of Canandaigua, N. Y., is a descendant of these Clarks, but of which family we have not ascertained.

† Here lye Inter⁴ the Remains of Moses Clark, who was of a Sober, charityble, virtuous disposition, Who having serued His generation faithfully, departed this Life in hope of Life Eternal, Sept the 18th, 1749, in the 67th year of his age. [Grave-Stone.]

‡ Here lies the Body of Mrs Elisabeth Clark, ye wife of Mr. Moses Clark, who Recommended herselfe and religion to ye world by Piety and Good works ; a midwife who feared God, skilful and greatly useful in the art of healing, who to ye Public loss and grief, was Suddenly called to a better hope Decr 27, 1761, in the 73d year of her age. [Grave-Stone.]

§ Col. James Clark died December 29, 1826, aged 96. Col. Clark was a Captain in the Army of the Revolution, and fought at the battle of Bunker Hill, and was the oldest man in the town of Lebanon at the time of his decease. [*Lebanon Records.*]

FOURTH GENERATION.

41.

JOHN CLARK, of Lebanon, Conn., was married to Jerusha Hunt-ington, daughter of Jabez Huntington, Esq., of Windham, Conn., and of Elizabeth, his wife, daughter of Rev. Timothy Edwards, Pastor of the Congregational Church, at East Windsor, Conn., and sister of the first President Edwards, November 7, 1751.

Doct. John Clark died at Utica, N. Y., December 23, 1822, aged 94 years, nearly. [Yale College, 1749.]

His widow, Mrs. Jerusha Clark, died at Utica, N. Y., December 14, 1823, aged 92.

Children.

50	John,	born June	13, 1752, O. S.	
51	Jabez,	born November	2, 1753.	
52	Israhiah,	born May	16, 1755.	Died June 1, 1755.
53	Jerusha,	born May	7, 1756.	Died, unmarried, at Utica, N. Y., July 8, 1840.
54	Hezekiah,	born December	19, 1757.	
55	Tryphena,	born February	10, 1760.	
56	Deodatus,	born July	27, 1762.	
57	Hannah,	born May	19, 1764.	
58	Henry,	born May	4, 1766.	
59	Erastus,	born May	11, 1768.	
60	Thaddeus,	born February	12, 1770.	
61	Elizabeth,	born February	2, 1772.	

FIFTH GENERATION.

50.

DOCT. JOHN CLARK, first of Windham, Conn., afterwards of Lebanon, Madison county, N. Y., was married to Abigail Moseley, daughter of the Rev. Samuel Moseley, second Pastor of the second Congregational Church in that part of Windham now called Hampton, and sister of the late William Moseley, of Hartford, Conn., December 13, 1781.

Mrs. Abigail Clark died January 28, 1833, aged 76.

Doct. John Clark died April 21, 1847, aged 95 nearly.

Children.

62	Sophia,	born September	24, 1782.	
63	Tryphena,	born May	17, 1786.	
64	John Mose-ley,	born July	2, 1788.	Died October 2, 1788.
65	Nabby,	born November	30, 1789.	Died August 22, 1807.
66	Mary,	born June	17, 1792.	Died June 17, 1828.
67	Amanda,	born October	12, 1794.	
68	Hannah,	born September	10, 1797.	
69	William Moseley,	born March	23, 1803.	Residence, Gilbert's-ville, N. Y.

51.

JABEZ CLARK, of Windham, Conn., was married to Amie El-derkin, daughter of Jedediah Elderkin, of that town, April 4, 1787.

Hon. Jabez Clark died November 11, 1836, aged 83.*

His widow, Mrs. Amie Clark, died July 1, 1838, aged 77.

Children.

70 Charles,	born March	6, 1788.	Died October 22, 1798.
71 Elizabeth,	born October	29, 1789.	Married Walter King, Esq., of Utica, N. Y. She died September, 1812, aged 22, nearly.
72 Anna,	born April	6, 1792.	Married Edward Vernon, formerly of Utica, N. Y., now of the city of New York.
73 Jerusha,	born March	26, 1794.	Married Jesse W. Doolittle, of Utica, N. Y.
74 Edwards,	born February	24, 1796.	An Attorney at Law, Windham, Conn. Married Hannah Perkins, May 28, 1823.
75 Charlotte Edwards,	born October	20, 1798.	Married Samuel Perkins, of Philadelphia. She died January 18, 1823.

54.

Doct. Hezekiah Clark, of Pompey, N. Y., was married to Lucy Bliss, daughter of Hon. Moses Bliss, of Springfield, Mass., June 2, 1785. She was born June 19, 1766.

Doct. Hezekiah Clark died at Pompey, N. Y., March 4, 1826, aged 68.

His widow, Mrs. Lucy Clark, died at Syracuse, N. Y., January 19, 1850, aged 83.

Children.

76 Henry,	born January	20, 1787.	Died, by drowning, September 29, 1788.
77 Henry,	born January	25, 1789.	Was a Lawyer. Served as an officer in the war of 1812, and died, unmarried, at Ithaca, N. Y., February 19, 1817, aged 28.
78 Harriet,	born April	14, 1791.	
79 Charles,	born April	12, 1793.	
80 Lucy,	born April	23, 1795.	Died August 2, 1796.
81 Lucy,	born October	27, 1796.	Died, unmarried, at Syracuse, N. Y., July 29, 1846.
82 John H.,	born July	28, 1798.	Dwells in Pompey, N. Y., unmarried. He is a Farmer.
83 William Metcalf,	born April	3, 1800.	
84 Moses Bliss,	born November	28, 1803.	
85 Theodore Edwards,	born January	25, 1806.	Dwells in Baldwin's Ville, Onondaga Co., N. Y., and is unmarried.

55.

Tryphena Clark was married to Ebenezer Bushnell, Jun., of Lebanon, Conn., August 14, 1780, by her father.

---

* Jabez Clark, Esq., was an upright, brave and honorable man. He served through the Revolutionary War, in the Quarter Master General's Department, in good reputation, and subsequently held the honorable office of Chief Justice of Windham County Court.

Mrs. Tryphena Bushnell died October 12, 1785, in the 24th year of her age.

Mr. Ebenezer Bushnell died ————.

Child,—one only.

86 Hezekiah, born September 27, 1782. Residence, Susquehanna County, Penn.

56.

DOCT. DEODATES CLARK, first of Cambridge, Washington County, N. Y.,—then of New Lebanon Springs, N. Y.,—then of Clinton, Oneida County, N. Y.,—then of Pompey Hill, Onondaga County, N. Y., and afterwards of the City of Oswego, N. Y., where he continued to reside until his death, was married on the 2d of February, 1794, while residing in Clinton, to Nancy Dunham, eldest daughter of Deacon Daniel Dunham, of Lebanon Crank, Columbia, Conn., grand-daughter by her mother's side of Rev. Samuel Moseley, Pastor of the Congregational Church at Hampton, Conn., and sister of the late Col. Josiah Dunham, formerly of Windsor, Ver., but more recently of Lexington, Ken.

Mrs. Nancy Clark died May 6, 1821, in the 48th year of her age.

Doct. Deodatus Clark died June 10, 1848, aged 85 years, nearly.

Children.

87 John,	born December	3, 1794.	
88 Julia,	born November	10, 1796.	
89 Nancy,	born April	27, 1798.	Died May 21, 1818.
90 Laura,	born December	22, 1799.	Died September 20, 1808.
91 Edwin W.,	born September	10, 1801.	
92 Julius,	born September	30, 1802.	
93 Sidney,	born December	20, 1803.	
94 Lucien,	born May	26, 1806.	Died May 31, 1806.
95 Nabby,	born August	12, 1808.	Died September 6, 1808.
96 Ossian,	born July	5, 1813.	

57.

HANNAH CLARK was married to Hon. George Bliss, of Springfield, Mass., May 22, 1789. [After her death, Mr. Bliss was twice married. 1. To Mary Lathrop, daughter of John Lathrop, of New Haven, Conn., May 29, 1799, by whom he had no children. She was born March 25, 1757, and died May 1, 1803, aged 36. 2. To Abigail Rowland, daughter of Rev. David Sherman Rowland, Pastor of the Congregational Church at Windsor, Conn., November 15, 1804, by whom he had 3 children,—Delia, born April 7, 1806. Abigail, born December 8, 1807, married Samuel Reynolds, 1831, died May 27, 1832, no children. Richard, born May 12, 1811, married Sarah Eastman, 1837, and had children, Richard, born May 26, 1842, Abigail, born January 4, 1846.]

Mrs. Hannah Bliss died September 19, 1795, aged 32.

Hon. George Bliss, LL. D., died March 8, 1830, aged 65. [Grave-Stone.]

Children.

97 Delia
 Bliss,   born April   16, 1790.   Died January 31, 1805, in her 15th
98 Caroline   year.
 Bliss,   born December 28, 1791.   Married Hon. Oliver B. Morris, of
                                    Springfield, Mass., September 15,
                                    1813. She died February 9, 1842.
                                    Their children,—*Henry Morris*, born
                                    June 16, 1814, married Mary War-
                                    riner, May 16, 1837, by whom he has
                                    children,—Mary, born June 29, 1839.
                                    Edward, born January 16, 1841.
                                    Henry Oliver, born July 9, 1844, and
                                    died May 3, 1845. Charles Henry,
                                    born April 5, 1846. William Frede-
                                    rick and Frederick William, twins,
                                    born May 2, 1850. *Henry Bliss
                                    Morris*, born November 12, 1818,
                                    married Elizabeth Lathrop, August
                                    23, 1842, by whom he has chil-
                                    dren,—George Bliss, born Novem-
                                    ber 5, 1843. Robert Oliver, born
                                    October 18, 1846. Caroline, born
                                    September 18, 1848.
99 George
 Bliss,   born November 16, 1793. Residence, Springfield, Mass. Married
                                    Mary S. Dwight, 1825. Children,—
                                    Sarah, born June 3, 1826, married
                                    George Walker, 1849. *George*, born
                                    May 3, 1830. *Mary*, born April 5,
                                    1832, and died in infancy.
100 Hannah
 Clark
 Bliss,   born September 5, 1795. Married Rev. Joseph Brockett, 1822.
                                    She died November 16, 1826, at Rush-
                                    ville, N. Y., aged 31, leaving 2 chil-
                                    dren,—George Bliss Brockett and
                                    Henry Martyn Bliss.

58.

HENRY CLARK, first of Pompey, N. Y., and then of Manlius,
N. Y., was married to Mary Ann Elderkin, daughter of Capt.
Vine Elderkin, of Windham, Conn., February 1, 1796. She was
born December 18, 1771. After the death of Mr. Clark, she was
married to Doct. James Jackson, whom, she also, at this date,
[July 20, 1851,] survives.
Mr. Henry Clark died in 1810, aged 44.

Children.

101 Augustus, born November,   1796, in Pompey, N. Y. Died in 1821, at New
                                                      Orleans, unmarried.
102 Hannah,   born July   28, 1798, in Pompey, N. Y.
103 Harriet, born July   31, 1799, in Pompey, N. Y.
104 Henry,   born   1803, in Pompey, N. Y.
105 Mary
 Anna,   born July   6, 1804, in Pompey, N. Y.
106 Louisa
 Elizabeth, born April   7, 1808, in Manlius, N. Y.

59.

ERASTUS CLARK, of Utica, N. Y., was twice married. 1. To Sophia Porter, of Lebanon, Conn. She died in Utica, N. Y., 1810. 2. To Sophia Flint, daughter of Royal Flint, and niece to Rev. Abel Flint, Pastor of the second Congregational Church at Hartford, Conn., July 1, 1812. Erastus Clark, Esq., died November 6, 1825, aged 57. His widow, Mrs. Sophia Clark, is still living. [January 26, 1851.]

Children by his first wife,—none.

Children by his second wife.

107	Sophia,	born June	1, 1813.
108	Elizabeth,	born November	1, 1815.
109	Erastus,	born November	20, 1818.
110	James,	born	1820. Died at the age of 5 months.

60.

THADDEUS CLARK, of New-Brighton, Penn., was married to Deborah Baker, daughter of Doct. Joseph Baker, of Brooklyn, Conn., March 24, 1802. Her mother's name was Lucy Devotion, daughter of Rev. Ebenezer Devotion, first Pastor of the third Congregational Church in Windham, Conn., who was a descendant of the Rev. Edward Devotion, who fled from the persecutions in France, and settled in Roxbury, Mass.

Doct. Thaddeus Clark died February 22, 1854, aged 84.

Children.

111 Delia Adelaide, born December 25, 1804, in Connecticut. Died October 6, 1826.
112 Joseph Baker, born October 23, 1806, in Connecticut.
113 Frederick Julian, born September 10, 1808, in Connecticut.
114 Sophia Elizabeth, born October 22, 1810, in Connecticut.
115 Albert Henry, born March 19, 1813, in Connecticut. Died February 28, 1823.
116 Charles Edwards, born September 17, 1815, in Connecticut.
117 Rufus Lathrop Baker, born June 4, 1817, in Connecticut.
118 William Edwin, born February 22, 1819, in Connecticut.
119 Lucy Caroline, born May 8, 1821, in Connecticut.
120 Sarah Jane, born September 28, 1823, in Pompey, N. Y. Extensively and favorably known as a writer, over the signature of "Grace Greenwood." Married at New-Brighton, Penn., October 17, 1853, to Mr. Lippencott, of Washington City, D. C.
121 Albert Henry, born May 22, 1826, in Pompey, N. Y.

61.

ELIZABETH CLARK was married to Rev. Ludovicus Weld, Pastor of the Congregational Church, in Hampton, Conn., November 11, 1795.

Rev. Ludovicus Weld died October 9, 1844, aged 78.

His widow, Mrs. Elizabeth Weld, died at Belleville, N. Y., August 31, 1854, aged 81.*

Children.

122 Lewis,	born October	17, 1796.	Yale College, 1818. Was married to Mary Austin Cogswell, daughter of Mason F. Cogswell, M. D., of Hartford, Conn., May 7, 1828. Died, sustained by the hope of the Christian, and by the consolations of that gospel which he had so long cherished as his choicest treasure, December 30, 1853.† *Children,*—Mason Cogswell Weld, born February 18, 1829. Charles Theodore Weld, born March 21, 1831. Lewis Ledyard Weld, born May 13, 1833. Mary Elizabeth Weld, born October 1, 1835. Alice Cogswell Weld, born December 4, 1837.
123 Charles Huntington,	born April	26, 1799.	Residence,—Belleville, N. Y.
124 Ezra Greenleaf,	born October	26, 1801.	Residence,—Cazenovia, N. Y.
125 Theodore Dwight,	born November	23, 1803.	Residence,—Belleville, N. Y.
126 Caroline Elizabeth,	born June	28, 1809.	Residence,—Belleville, N. Y.

SIXTH GENERATION.

78.

HARRIET CLARK was married to Daniel Gilbert, Esq., now of Cold Water, Branch County, Mich., September 6, 1817.

Children.

127 Henry Clarke,	born July	14, 1818.	Married Harriet Champion, of Michigan, February, 1844. He is a Lawyer.

---

* Great integrity, cheerfulness, frankness, sincerity, a strong and instinctive sense of justice, truthfulness that recoiled from a shadow of deception, and a deep reverence for God and sacred things, were the marked characteristics of her life.

† On the resignation of the first Principal of the American Asylum at Hartford for the Education and Instruction of the Deaf and Dumb, (Rev. Thomas H. Gallaudet,) about twenty-three years since, Mr. Weld was appointed his successor; and for this long period he discharged the duties of the office with dignity and ability. In all his arrangements and matters of business, he was remarkably punctual and systematic; careful to do everything in proper time and in due order. In his intercourse with his pupils, his chief aim and most earnest endeavour was to do them good, not merely by cultivating their intellects, but by improving their characters; by imbuing their minds with worthy sentiments and correct views. While solicitous to prepare them for usefulness and happiness in this present life, he was still more anxious to secure for them a blessed inheritance in the life to come. We doubt not, that in the great day of final revision, he will rejoice in the results of his labors and prayers. [*Rev. William W. Turner.*]

128 James
   William,   born July   13, 1820.   Married Celia H. Gaston, of Michigan,
                                           November, 1846. He is a Lawyer.
129 Margaret
   A.,   born September 22, 1822.
130 Harriet
   Adelaide, born October   12, 1824.   Married L. T. Wilson, of Michigan,
                                           April, 1847.

79.

CHARLES CLARKE was twice married. 1. To Olly Ostrander,
daughter of Peter Ostrander, of Pompey, N. Y., April 12, 1815.
She died July 1, 1833, in the 39th year of her age. 2. To Clarissa
Carlisle, daughter of Daniel Carlisle, a native of Massachusetts,
February 26, 1846.

Children,—by his first wife.

131 Charles
   Fordham, born
132 Catharine
   Emily,   born
133 Henry
   Hezekiah, born

Children,—by his second wife.

134 Son,   born

83.

WILLIAM METCALF CLARK, of Syracuse, N. Y., was married
to Clara Catlin Tyler, daughter of John Tyler, of Harford,
Susquehanna County, Penn., June 7, 1836.

Children.

135 Henry
   Wadsworth, born November 6, 1837.
136 Frances
   Aurelia, born December   6, 1839.

84.

MOSES BLISS CLARK, of Pompey, N. Y., was married to Lucy
Dana, January 26, 1837.

Child,—one only.

137 Lucy Ade-
   laide,   born March   6, 1838.

87.

JOHN CLARK, of Oswego, N. Y., was married to Olive Jackson,
daughter (and 19th child) of Col. Giles Jackson, of Tyringham,
Mass., October 24, 1826.

Children.

138 Julia
   Brewster, born September 5, 1827, at Cohocton, N. Y.
139 James
   Jackson, born September 30, 1833, at Oswego, N. Y.

   5

88.

JULIA CLARKE was married to Doct. Sardius Brewster, of Mexico, N. Y., youngest son of Deacon Brewster, of Columbia, Conn., October 1, 1822.

Mrs. Julia Brewster died February 5, 1826, aged 39.

Child,—one only.

140 Julia
    Clarke, born June   7, 1823.

91.

EDWIN W. CLARK was married to Charlotte Ambler, fourth daughter of David Ambler, Esq., of Augusta, Oneida county, N. Y., January 16, 1833.

Children.

141 Frederick
    Oberlin, born December 20, 1834.
142 Marshall S.
    Bidwell, born November 8, 1836.
143 Edwin
    Ambler, born June   8, 1839.
144 Florence, born May   13, 1843.
145 Eugene
    Clarence, born February 3, 1848.

92.

JULIUS CLARK was married at St. Louis, Mo., to Hannah Weeks, daughter of ——— Weeks, Esq., of Salisbury, Ver., May 31, 1842.

Mr. Julius Clark died June 7, 1845, aged 42.

Child,—one only.

146 Josiah
    Dunham, born October   1843, at Lexington, Ken.

93.

SIDNEY CLARK was married to Olive Jackson, daughter of Artemas Jackson, and grand-daughter of Col. Giles Jackson, of Tyringham, Mass., January 14, 1814.

Children.

147 Charles
    Lucien, born August   14, 1842, at Oswego, N. Y.
148 Julius
    Wendell, born January   1, 1844. Died March 28, 1851.
149 Edward
    Huntington, born January 22, 1846.
150 Sarah
    Danforth, born August   22, 1848.

96.

OSSIAN CLARK, of Oswego, N. Y., was married to Nancy Squires, daughter of Mr. William Squires, of Oswego, March 25, 1839.

Children.

151 Oscar,   born December 5, 1839, in Oswego.
152 Nancy,   born November 11, 1841, in Oswego.
153 Harriet,   born March   26, 1843, in Oswego.

102.

HANNAH CLARK was twice married. 1. To Giles Jackson, (the half-brother of her mother's husband,) January 12, 1818, at Manlius, N. Y. He died February 14, 1820. 2. To David Lewis Roberts, June 2, 1830, at Utica, N. Y., June 3, 1830.

Children,—by her first husband,—one only.

154 Sarah
    Atwood
    Jackson,   born October   4, 1819, at Lyons, N. Y. Died August 23, 1832.
                                A remarkable child,—an invalid from
                                the cradle,—whose memoirs have
                                been published.

Children,—by her second husband.

155 Mary
    Anna,   born June   7, 1831, at Boonville, N. Y.
156 Jane,   born February 28, 1833, at Boonville, N. Y. Died March 31,
                                1834.
157 Ellen Otte-
    line,   born May   6, 1835, at Boonville, N. Y.
158 Roderick
    Roberts,   born June   23, 1837, at Juliet, Ill. Died June 21, 1840.
159 Glendower, born October   23, 1841, at Chicago, Ill. Died October 2, 1842.

103.

HARRIET CLARK was married to Elias Brewster, of Mexico, Oswego county, N. Y., August 8, 1826.

Children.

160 Henry A.,   born June   8, 1827.
161 Elias P.,   born April   24, 1829.
162 Harriet H., born May   14, 1831.
163 Sardius C., born October   23, 1833.
164 Elliott P., born December   27, 1836. Died April 15, 1838.
165 Mary Jane, born January   3, 1839.
166 Roderick
    P.,   born December   6, 1842.

104.

HENRY CLARK, of Oswego, N. Y., was married to Olive Hawks, April 22, 1824, at Oswego.

Children.

167 Charlotte
    M.,   born May   24, 1825. Married to Salem Town, March 19,
                                1845.
168 Augustus, born   1827.
169 Mary Ann, born [no date.]   Dead.
170 Maria,   born [no date.]
171 Henry,   born [no date.]   Dead.

105.

MARY ANNA CLARK was married to David Lewis Roberts, of Rosa-fawr, in the Parish of Laurhaish, Denbighshire, North Wales, April 10, 1828.

Mrs. Mary Ann Roberts died at Utica, N. Y., November 19, 1829, aged 25.

Child,—one only.

172 Clark,   born November 12, 1829.

106.

LOUISA ELIZABETH CLARK was married to Ephraim Reed, of Oswego, N. Y., November 25, 1825.

Mrs. Louisa Elizabeth Reed died May 20, 1837, aged 29.

Children.

173 Helen
    Amelia, born   1830, at Oswego. Died in infancy.
174 Mary
    Louisa,   born November 20, 1832.

DESCENDANTS IN THE LINE OF JOHN CLARKE, SON OF DANIEL CLARKE, THE SETTLER.

SECOND GENERATION.

V.

JOHN CLARK, first of Simsbury, Conn., where he was admitted an inhabitant, December 24, 1686, and after 1698, of Windsor, Conn., was married to Mary Crow, daughter of Christopher Crow, of Windsor, and of his wife Mary, daughter of Benjamin Burr, of Hartford, Conn., 1685. She was born in October, 1665. After his death, she was married to William Randall, of Enfield, then under the jurisdiction of Massachusetts, now under that of Connecticut, about 1720.

Mr. John Clark died September, 1715, in the 60th year of his age.

Mrs. Mary Clark, alias Randall, died ———.

Children.

175 Hannah,   born August   6, 1686, in Simsbury. Married to Thomas Gillett, of ———, February 26, 1705.
176 John,   born [no date.]   in Simsbury. Died March 7, 1709.
177 Mary,   born [no date.]   in Simsbury. Married Samuel Cooley, of Springfield, Mass., October 24, 1711.
178 Jemima,   born [no date.]   in Simsbury. Married a Cooley.
179 Martha,   born March   19, 1697, in Windsor. Married James Eggleston, of Windsor, August 28, 1718. She died May 25, 1728.
180 Solomon,   born May   20, 1699, in Windsor. Married to Ann Eggleston, of Windsor, February 24, 1720.
181 Elizabeth, born May   16, 1701, in Windsor.
182 Sarah,   born October   28, 1702, in Windsor. Died young.

183 Daniel,   born December 31, 1704, in Windsor.
184 Ann,   born January   12, 1707, in Windsor. Died August 13, 1716.
185 Benoni,   born October   21, 1708, in Windsor. Died at Enfield, January
                                 16, ——.

DESCENDANTS IN THE LINE OF MARY CLARK, DAUGHTER OF DANIEL CLARK, THE SETTLER.

SECOND GENERATION.

VI.

MARY CLARK was twice married. 1. To John Gaylord, jun., of Windsor, Conn., son of John Gaylord, of that town, December 13, 1683. He died April 29, 1699, aged 32, nearly. 2. To Jedediah Watson, of Windsor, son of Robert Watson, of that place, about 1700.

Mrs. Mary Watson, alias Gaylord, died April 14, 1738, in the 81st year of her age.

Mr. Jedediah Watson died December 13, 1741, in the 76th year of his age.

Children,—by her first husband.

186 John,   born
187 Mary,   born   Married Ebenezer Bliss, senior, of Springfield, Mass., 1707.
188 Ann,   born   Died before she came of age. Her portion of her father's estate was distributed to her brother John and sister Mary, by Order of Court, dated February, 1710.

Children,—by her last husband,—none.

DESCENDANTS IN THE LINE OF SAMUEL CLARK, SON OF DANIEL CLARK, THE SETTLER.

SECOND GENERATION.

VII.

SAMUEL CLARK, of Windsor, Conn., was married to Mehitabel Thrall, daughter of Timothy Thrall, of the same town, 1687. She was born in March, 1664.

Mrs. Mehitabel Clark died August 15, 1723, aged 59.

Mr. Samuel Clark died ———.

Children, found on Record.

189 Samuel,   born November 10, 1688.
190 David,   born April   7, 1696.
191 Joseph,   born July   13, 1697.
192 Nathaniel, born October 11, 1699.

THIRD GENERATION.

189.

SAMUEL CLARK, of Simsbury, Conn., was married to Abigail Owen, daughter of Josiah Owen, of Simsbury. She was born December 8, 1681.

Mrs. Abigail Clark died ———.

Sargeant Samuel Clark died November 6, 1749, aged 61, nearly. His grave is in Turkey Hills burying-ground.

Children.

193 Joel,	born March	19, 1717.	
194 Abigail,	born May	5, 1719.	
195 Samuel,	born December	15, 1720.	Settled in Northampton, Mass.
196 Hannah,	born May	5, 1723.	
197 David,	born July	17, 1725.	
198 Ann,	born July	1, 1729.	Died January 5, 1741.

FOURTH GENERATION.

193.

JOEL CLARK, of Simsbury, Conn., was married to Lydia Forbes, April 7, 1742.

Joel Clark, Esq., died October 15, 1777, in the 61st year of his age. [Grave-Stone.]

His widow, Mrs. Lydia Clark, died November 5, 1796, aged 96. [Grave-Stone.]

Children.

199 Joel,	born	1747, and four others, as is said; but I do not find their names on record. Joel was married to Martha Pinney. He died October 17, 1808, aged 61. She died January 29, 1808, aged 60.

197.

DAVID CLARK, of Simsbury, Conn., was married to Rachel Moore, about 1749. They lived together 64 years and 5 months, and had 20 children, one only at a birth, five of which died in infancy. He was grandfather of Mr. David Clark, of East Granby, Conn.

Mrs. Rachel Clark died October 9, 1814, aged 83.

Mr. David Clark died October 26, 1819, aged 94.

Children.

200 Rachel,	born December	1, 1750.
201 Anna,	born February	29, 1752.
202 Roseanna,	born May	14, 1753.
203 David,	born August	6, 1754.
204 Mary,	born September	16, 1756.
205 Jesse,	born May	1, 1758.
206 Joseph,	born September	17, 1760.
207 Levi,	born September	26, 1762.
208 Sophronia,	born July	26, 1763.
209 Cephas,	born November	6, 1764.

210 Russel,	born		1766. Lived in Windsor, Poquonnoc Society.
211 Annis,	born		1768. Married William Rockwell. Died May 4, 1811.
212 Philander,	born		1771. Died July 24, 1824.
213 Huldah,	born		1773. Married Reuben Winchel. Died August 17, 1827.
214 Abial,	born October,		1775. Died at Sackett's Harbor, N. Y., 1815.

DESCENDANTS IN THE LINE OF SARAH CLARK, DAUGHTER OF DANIEL CLARK, THE SETTLER.

SECOND GENERATION.

VIII.

SARAH CLARK was twice married. 1. To Isaac Pinney, of Windsor, Conn., son of Humphrey Pinney, one of the first settlers of that town, about 1685. He was born February, 1663. "Sargeant Isaac Pinney died on board the vessel, coming from Albany, October, 1709." [Windsor Records.] 2. To ———— Marsh or Nash, of Hadley, Mass.

Mr. ———— Marsh, or Nash, died ————.

Mrs. Sarah Marsh, or Nash, died ————.

Children,—by her first husband.

215 Isaac,	born January	17, 1686.	
216 Jonathan,	born October	23, 1688.	
217 Mary,	born March	4, 1690.	
218 Sarah,	born March	7, 1692.	Died, unmarried, 1748.
219 Humphrey,	born September	5, 1694.	
220 Elizabeth,	born January	6, 1697.	
221 Noah,	born January	24, 1703.	
222 Hannah,	born [no date.]		
223 Daniel,	born [no date.]		

DESCENDANTS IN THE LINE OF NATHANIEL CLARK, SON OF DANIEL CLARK, THE SETTLER.

SECOND GENERATION.

X.

Children,—none.

NATHANIEL CLARK did not marry. He was slain by the enemy, [Indians,] 1690. He left a will, which is dated April 29, 1690, and was exhibited into Court of Probate, and approved July 31, 1690. Its opening clause is as follows, *viz.*: "Whereas, I Nathaniel Clarke, of Windsor, in the county of Hartford, am by the providence of God, called to goe out against the common enemie, for his Maties service and the defence of the country; and considering the peril and hazard of such an undertaking, and being now of good understanding and memory, I count it my duty to settle that estate God hath of his mercy bestowed upon me, in manner following."

JOHN DWIGHT,

FIRST SETTLERS OF DEDHAM, MASS.

JOHN DWIGHT, one of the first settlers of Dedham, Mass., was twice married. 1. To Hannah ———. She died September 5, 1656. 2. To Elizabeth Ripley, January 20, 1658. Mrs. Elizabeth Dwight died July 17, 1660. Mr. John Dwight died January 24, 1661.

FIRST GENERATION.

Children of John Dwight, named in his will,—by his first wife.

I. Timothy,	born			
II. Hannah,	born			
III. Mary,	born July	25, 1635.	Married Henry Phillips.
IV. Sarah,	born June	17, 1638.	Married Nathaniel Reynolds.

Children,—by his second wife, none.

DESCENDANTS IN THE LINE OF TIMOTHY DWIGHT, SON OF JOHN DWIGHT, THE SETTLER.

SECOND GENERATION.

I.

TIMOTHY DWIGHT, of Dedham, Mass., was married six times. 1. To Sarah Perman, November 11, 1651. She died in 1652. 2. To Sarah Powell, daughter of Michael Powell, of Dedham, who kept the Ordinary in that town, May 3, 1653.* She died June 27, 1664. 3. To Anna Flint, of Braintree, January 9, 1665. She died January 29, 1685. 4. To Mrs. Mary Endwind, of Reading, January 7, 1686. She died August 30, 1688. 5. To Esther Fisher, daughter of Daniel Fisher, of Dedham,† July 31,

---

* Michael Powell was representative from Dedham in 1641 and 1648. He removed to Boston, and taught, without ordination, in the second church of Boston, previous to the settlement of its first minister, Increase Mather. [Farmar.]

† The following honorable mention of this gentleman is taken from an Historical Address delivered before the citizens of Dedham, Mass., September 21, 1836, by Samuel F. Haven, Esq. " Then follows the third remarkable period in the history of American resistance to arbitary power. The charter was dissolved in 1686, and soon after Sir Edmund Andros was appointed Governor. His administration was grievous oppression. In 1689, an indirect rumor having arrived, by the way of Virginia, of the landing of the Prince of Orange in England, and the consequent revolution in the government there, the people without waiting for a confirmation, determined to take its truth for granted, and simultaneously set about

1690. She died January 30, 1691. 6. To Bethia Morse, February 1, 1692.

Mr. Timothy Dwight died January 31, 1718, aged 88.*

Mrs. Bethia Dwight died February 6, 1718.

Child, by his first wife,—one only.

5 Child, (not named,) born   1652. Died in infancy.

Children,—by his second wife.

6 Timothy,	born November 26, 1654.	Goldsmith in Boston. Said to have left no children.
7 Sarah,	born April 2, 1657.	Died February 9, 1659.
8 John,	born May 31, 1661.	Said to have left no children.
9 Sarah,	born June 25, 1664.	Died July 10, 1668.

Children,—by his third wife.

10 Josiah,	born October 8, 1665.	Died in infancy.
11 Nathaniel,	born November 20, 1666.	Settled at Hatfield, Mass., but subsequently removed to Northampton, Mass., where he was a trader and inn-keeper. Married Mahetabel Partridge, daughter of Capt. Samuel Partridge, of Hatfield, Mass., December 9, 1693. He died at West Springfield, Mass., November 7, 1711.
12 Samuel,	born December 2, 1668.	
13 Josiah,	born February 8, 1670.	Harvard University, 1687. Minister of Woodstock, Conn. Ordained 1690. Dismissed September 3, 1726, and afterwards was installed, June 4, 1735, over the third Parish Church in Dedham, Mass. Married Mary Partridge, daughter of Col. Samuel Partridge, of Hatfield, Mass.. December 4, 1695. They had 13 children.
14 Seth,	born July 25, 1673.	
15 Anna,	born August 12, 1675.	Died October 15, 1675.
16 Henry,	born December 10, 1676.	Merchant in Hatfield, Mass., and ancestor of the rich family of his name, Springfield, Mass.
17 Michael,	born January 10, 1679.	
18 Daniel,	born September 23, 1681.	Said to have left no children.
19 Jabez,	born September 1, 1684.	Died June 15, 1685.

Children, by his fourth, fifth and sixth wives,—none.

---

accomplishing a revolution of their own. On the morning of the 18th of April, the town of Boston was in arms. The Governor and Council were seized and confined, and the old magistrates reinstated. The country people came into town in such rage and heat as made all tremble to think what would follow. Nothing would satisfy them but that the Governor must be bound in chains or cords and put in a more secure place, and for their quiet the was guarded by them to the Fort. Whose hand was on the collar of that prisoner, leading him through the excited crowd, at once securing him from escape and guarding him from outrage? It was the hand of DANIEL FISHER, of Dedham ; aye ' a *second* Daniel *come* to JUDGMENT,' a son of the former, and heir of his energetic ardor in the cause of freedom.''

The expulsion of His Excellency Gov. Andros from New England, so graphically described by Mr. Haven, was of a very different character from his reception into Boston, as noted by Judge Sewell in his "*Interleaved Almanack.*" "On December 19, 1686. Arrived at Nantaskit, his Excellency Sir Edmund Andross, His Majesties Generall Governour, of his Territory and Dominion in America. He landed at Boston, on the Monday following, and was received wth general Acclamation of Joy.''

* He was a child when his father brought him to Dedham, in 1635, and he is described as one of an excellent spirit, peaceable, generous, charitable, and a promoter of the true interests of the church and town. [Farmar.]

THIRD GENERATION.

II.

NATHANIEL DWIGHT, first of Hatfield, Mass., afterwards of Northampton, in the same State, was married December 9, 1693, to Mehitabel Partridge, daughter of Col. Samuel Partridge, of Hatfield, and Mehitabel, his wife, daughter of John Crow, one of the first settlers of Hartford, Conn., and Hadley, Mass., and Elizabeth his wife, daughter of Elder William Goodwin, one of the first settlers, likewise, of Hartford and Hadley, December 9, 1693. She was born May 1, 1674.

Mr. Nathaniel Dwight died at Springfield, Mass., November 7, 1711, aged 46.

His widow, Mrs. Mehitabel Dwight, died at Northampton, October 19, 1756, aged 82.

Children.

20 Timothy, born October 19, 1694, in Hatfield.
21 Samuel, born June 28, 1696, in Northampton, married Mary Lyman. Lived in Suffield, Conn., and in Middletown, Conn., some years in each place, but finally settled in Somers, Conn.
32 Mehitabel, born November 11, 1697, in Northampton. Died December 22, 1697.
23 Daniel, born April 29, 1699, in Hatfield. Yale College, 1721. Was Episcopal Clergyman, located near Charlestown, S. C., at St. Johns. Married 1. Christina, daughter of Gov. Boughton. She died without issue. 2. Esther Cordis, by whom he had 5 children.
24 Seth, born March 3, 1702, in Northampton. Died September 12, 1703.
25 Elihu, } twins. born February 17, 1704, in Northampton. Died in Philadelphia, in 1728, without children. Is called cordwainer.
26 Abia, } born February 17, 1704, in Northampton. Married Samuel Kent, of Suffield, Conn., February 28, 1722.
27 Mehitabel, born November 2, 1705, in Northampton. Married Abraham Burbank, of Suffield, January 31, 1728.
28 Jonathan, born March 14, 1708, in Northampton. Married Mary Lane. Settled at Boston. Had children. Died at Halifax, N. S.
29 Anna, born July 2, 1710, in Northampton. Married Abel Caldwell.
30 Nathaniel, born June 20, 1712, (posthumous,) in Northampton. Lived in Belchertown, Mass. Was a Surveyor, &c. Married Mary Lyman.

16.

HENRY DWIGHT, of Hatfield, Mass., was married to Lydia Hawley, daughter of Capt. Joseph Hawley, of Northampton, Mass., August 27, 1702.

Henry Dwight, Esq., died March 20, 1732, in the 56th year of his age.

His widow, Mrs. Lydia Dwight, died April 27, 1748, in the 68th year of her age.

Children.

31 Joseph,	born October	16, 1703.	Died June 9, 1764.
32 Seth,	born August	18, 1707.	Died June 7, 1774.
33 Dorathy,	born September	17, 1709.	Died July 12, 1745.
34 Lydia,	born April	25, 1712.	
35 Annas,	born August	14, 1714.	Died same month.
36 Josiah,	born October	23, 1715.	Died September 28, 1768. Was a wealthy Springfield merchant; the richest man, it is said, in the old county of Hampshire, at the time of his death.
37 Edmund,	born January	10, 1717.	Died October 28, 1755.
38 Simeon,	born February	18, 1719.	Died February 21, 1778.
39 Elisha,	born May	25, 1722.	Died in 1803.
40 Anna,	born September	2, 1724.	Died December 22, 1802.

FOURTH GENERATION.

20.

TIMOTHY DWIGHT, of Northampton, Mass., was married to Experience King, daughter of the second John King, of Northampton, in 1716. He was a Surveyor, a Magistrate, Judge of Probate, &c., and usually called Col. Dwight.

Mrs. Experience Dwight died December 15, 1763, in the 71st year of her age.

Col. Timothy Dwight died April 30, 1771, aged 76.

Children.

41 Eleanor,	born	1717.	Married Phineas Lyman, of Suffield, Conn., afterwards Gen. Lyman.
42 Gamaliel,	born	1718.	Died in infancy.
43 Gamaliel,	born	1720.	Died young.
44 Timothy,	born	1726.	

31.

JOSEPH DWIGHT, of Brookfield, Mass., afterwards of Great Barrington, in the same State, was twice married. 1. To Mary Pynchon, daughter of Col. John Pynchon, of Springfield, Mass., August 11, 1726. She died March 29, 1751, aged —. 2. To Abigail Sargeant, widow of Rev. John Sargeant, deceased, of Stockbridge, and daughter of Col. Ephraim Williams, of Stockbridge, about 1752.

Hon. General Joseph Dwight died June 9, 1765, aged 62.*

Mrs. Abigail Dwight, alias Sargeant, died February 15, 1791, aged 69.

Children,—by his first wife.

45 Mary,	born June	22, 1727. Died July 10, 1734.
46 Dorathy,	born November	13, 1729. Married Hon. Jedediah Foster, of Brookfield, Mass.

---

* He was Lieutenant-Colonel in the Militia,—Brigadier-General in the expedition to Louisburg, in 1745,—many years a member of the Council,—Speaker of the House of Representatives,— Judge of the Court of Common Pleas for the County of Worcester, from 1743 to 1750,—and after his removal to Great Barrington, was appointed in 1761, Judge of the County Court and Judge of Probate for that County.

47 Lydia,	born January	3, 1732.	Married Rev. Dr. J. Willard, of Sheffield, Mass.
48 Henry,	born December	22, 1733.	Died February 28, 1756.
49 Mary,	born January	26, 1736.	Married Capt. John Lock. Died at Deerfield, Mass.
50 Bathsheba,	born March	12, 1738.	Died January 11, 1761.
51 Elijah,	born April	23, 1740.	
52 Moses,	born October	29, 1742.	Died May 22, 1764.
53 Joseph,	born January	23, 1745.	Settled at Great Barrington, Mass. Was Col. in the Militia, Senator, Judge of Court of Common Pleas, for Berkshire county. Married Anna Williams, by whom he had seven children.

Children,—by his second wife.

54 Pamelia,	born June	26, 1753.	Married Hon. Theodore Sedgwick, of Stockbridge, being his second wife.
55 Henry, Williams,	born September 15, 1757.		

FIFTH GENERATION.

44.

TIMOTHY DWIGHT, of Northampton, Mass., was married to Mary Edwards, daughter of the Rev. Jonathan Edwards, Pastor of the Church at Northampton, afterwards President of the College in New Jersey, November 8, 1750.

Timothy Dwight, Esq., died at Natchez, June 10, 1772, aged 52.

His widow, Mrs. Mary Dwight, died at Northampton, February 28, 1807, in the 73d year of her age.

Children.

56 Timothy,	born May	3, 1752,	O. S. D. D., LL.D.,Yale College, 1769. Ordained Pastor over the Church and Congregation in the Parish of Greenfield, in Fairfield County, November 12, 1783. Inaugurated President of Yale College, 1795, Married Mary Woolsey, daughter of Benjamin Woolsey, Esq., of Dorsous, L. I., by whom he had 8 sons. He died January 11, 1817, aged 64.
57 Sereno Edwards.	born December	10, 1754.	Married Cynthia Pomeroy.
58 Erastus,	born September	13, 1756.	Died unmarried, in 1825.
59 Jonathan,	born January	29, 1759.	Married a Wright.
60 Sarah,	born May	29, 1761.	Married a Storrs.
61 Mary,	born January	9, 1763.	
62 Theodore,	born December	16, 1764.	Married Abby Alsop, of Middletown, Conn. He was an eminent lawyer. Settled in Hartford, Conn., but subsequently removed to the City of New York, where he died in 1846.
63 Maurice William,	born December	15, 1766.	
64 Fidelia,	born August	7, 1768.	Married Jonathan Edwards Porter, of Hadley, Mass., January 16, 1793.
65 Nathaniel,	born January	31, 1770.	Married Rebecca Robbins, daughter of Appleton Robbins, Esq., of Wethersfield, Conn., June 20, 1798. Doct. Nathaniel Dwight died June 11, 1831, aged 61. Mrs. Rebecca Dwight died April 28, 1848, aged 77. They had a family of children.

66 Elizabeth, born January   29, 1772.
67 Cecil,   born June   20, 1770.   Married Mary Clapp.
68 Henry Ed-
    win,   born September 20, 1770.   Married Electa Centre.

55.

HENRY WILLIAMS DWIGHT, of Stockbridge, Mass., was married to Abigail Welles, daughter of Ashbel Welles, of West Hartford, Conn., June 8, 1796.   She was born December 19, 1762.

Henry Williams Dwight,, Esq., died September 15, 1804, aged 50.

His widow, Mrs. Abigail Dwight, died May 31, 1840, aged 77.

Children.

69 Henry W., born February,   1788.   Hon. Col. Henry W. Dwight.
70 Edwin
   Welles,   born November,   1789.   Rev. Edwin W. Dwight.   Was for several years, Pastor of the Church in Richmond, Mass.   Died at Stockbridge, February 25, 1841.
71 Louis,   born March,   1793.   Rev. Louis Dwight died July 12, 1854, at Boston, aged 61.   He was Secretary of the Prison Discipline Society, from its original formation in 1825.   " Though the life of Mr. Dwight was not prolonged beyond its grand climacteric, yet it has been a long life when estimated by the ' great end ' it answered." [Puritan Recorder, July 20, 1854.]   Mr. Dwight was married May 20, 1824, to Louisa H. Willis, daughter of Deacon Nathaniel Willis, of Boston.   She died April 6, 1849.   Mr. Dwight leaves three children, one of whom is the wife of Rev. William T. Eustis, of New Haven, Conn.

DESCENDANTS IN THE LINE OF HANNAH DWIGHT, DAUGHTER OF JOHN DWIGHT, THE SETTLER.

SECOND GENERATION.

II.

HANNAH DWIGHT was married to Nathaniel Whiting, of Dedham, Mass., March 4, 1643.

Mr. Nathaniel Whiting died January 15, 1682.*

His widow, Mrs. Hannah Whiting, died November 4, 1714, aged 89.

Children.

72 Nathaniel, born September   7, 1644.
73 John,   born September 29, 1646.   Died in early life.
74 John,   born October   9, 1647.   Died in infancy.

---

* The first mention we find of Nathaniel Whiting is, that he had a grant of ten acres of land in Lynn, in 1638.   The next notice of him appears in Dedham, where he joined the Church on the 30th of July, 1641, and where he continued to reside until his death.

75 Samuel,	born November	20, 1649.	
76 Hannah,	born February	17, 1651.	
77 Timothy,	born January	5, 1653.	
78 Mary,	born July	8, 1656.	Died in infancy.
79 Mary,	born October	.12, 1658.	
80 Sarah,	born December	3, 1660.	
81 Abigail,	born June	7, 1663.	
82 John,	born July	19, 1665.	
83 Jonathan,	born October	9, 1667.	
84 Judah,	born March	30, 1670.	
85 Anna,	born February	25, 1672.	

THIRD GENERATION.

82.

JOHN WHITING, of Wrentham, Mass., was married to Mary Billings, of Wrentham, December 24, 1688.

Mrs. Mary Whiting died January 4, 1728.

Mr. John Whiting died in 1732.

Children,—several,—one of them.

86 Nathaniel, born February   2, 1691.

FOURTH GENERATION.

86.

NATHANIEL WHITING, of what was then Medfield, now the Factory Village, in Medway, Mass., was married to Margaret Man, daughter of Rev. Samuel Man, of Wrentham, April 18, 1711. She was born December 21, 1691.

Mrs. Margaret Whiting died January 11, 1775, in her 84th year.

Mr. Nathaniel Whiting died September 4, 1779, aged 87.

Children,—several,—among them.

87 Nathan,   born December 22, 1725.

FIFTH GENERATION.

87.

NATHAN WHITING, of the West Parish of Medway, Mass., was married to Mary Metcalf, daughter of John Metcalf, of Bellingham. She was sister of Judge Stephen Metcalf, of Bellingham, and was born October 16, 1728.

Lieut. Nathan Whiting died May 9, 1790, aged 64.

His widow, Mrs. Mary Whiting, died in, or about 1798.

Children,—several,—among them.

88 Timothy,   born August   5, 1767.

SIXTH GENERATION.

88.

TIMOTHY WHITING, of Medway, Mass., was married to Rhoda Bullard, daughter of Timothy Bullard, of Medway, April 20, 1796. She was born December 25, 1771. In 1815, Mr. Whiting removed to Washington County, Me., where he owned a tract of land, and where the town of Whiting, in that County, was named after him.

Mrs. Rhoda Whiting died August 15, 1805, aged 33.

Children,—several,—among them.

89 Nathaniel, born   Is Nathaniel Whiting, Esq., of Watertown, Mass.

WILLIAM EDWARDS,

FIRST SETTLERS OF HARTFORD, CONN.

————————

WILLIAM EDWARDS, of Hartford, Conn., and one of the first settlers of that town, was married to Agnes Spencer, widow of William Spencer, who also was one of the first settlers of Hartford, about 1645.

Mr. William Edwards died before 1672.*

Mrs. Agnes Edwards, alias Spencer, died ————.

FIRST GENERATION.

Child of William Edwards, and of Agnes Edwards, his wife,—one only.

1 Richard, born May, 1647.

———————————————

*Mrs. Ann Edwards, the mother of Mr. William Edwards, was married in England to her second husband, Mr. James Cole, who, together with her son William Edwards, then a young man, and Abigail Cole, daughter of said James Cole, by his first wife, came early into New England, and were among the first settlers of Hartford.

Mr. James Cole died in 1652, leaving a will, of which the following is a copy :—

"I, James Cole, of Hartford, upon the river of Connecticut, being of perfect memory and soundness of minde, doe, according to my duty, (knowing the frailty of my body and uncertainty of my life, for the preventing of distractions to myselfe while I live, and differency in my family when I am gathered to my Fathers,) make and ordaine this, my last Will and Testament, and doe dispose of that outward estate wherewith the Lord hath of his abundant mercy blessed me in manner following.

" Impri: I, give to my deare and well-beloved sonn and daughter Daniel and Abigail Sullavane, my new dwelling-house in Hartford, with all other outhousings, orchard, garden, homelott, with all appertinances thereto belonging with one peice of land, being about five acres more or less, lying at penny wise within Wethersfield bounds ; as alsoe, one parcel of upland, being about fowre acres more or less, lying about the Wolfe pound, all wᶜʰ forementioned lands and housing I give to them, and ther heires for ever, provided that my sonn Daniel and daughter Abigail, pay yearly to my deare and Well beloved wife Ann Cole, the just and full summ of three pounds in good current pay during her naturall life. further my Will is, That my wife should have an upper roome at the South end of my new dwelling-house during her widowhood with free liberty of egress and regress without molestation. further, my Will is, that shee my wife Ann Cole, should have the use of their firering for her owne comfort in any respect ; as also any fruit or herbes in the orchard or garden for her owne particular spending ; as also the use of the well belonging to the house. further if my wife desires to keep a cow, or a hogg, or some poultry for her perticular use, she providing meat for them, my will is, that she shall have yard roome for Them wher my Sonn Daniels Cattel are usually yarded.

" Item. I give all my Cooper Tooles equally to be divided between my well-beloved sonn William Edwards, and my Loving Cousen Henry Cole. Item. I give to my deare and well beloved wife Ann Cole, all my household stuff of every kind undisposed of, with all my Cattell and Crop of Corne now one the ground with all my debts owing to me, provided that shee pays all my just debts and defray all that charge wᶜʰ shall be thought necessary by the overseers of this my will, for my christian buriall. also, I doe desire and appoint my trusty and well beloved Friends, Mr. John Webster, and William ,Gibbons overseers of this my will, and. further, I doe appoint my deare and well-beloved Ann Cole, to be my sole executrix of this my last Will and Testament.   JAMES COLE."

" Witnesses,
" JOHN WHITE,
" THOMAS HOSMER."

DESCENDANTS IN THE LINE OF RICHARD EDWARDS, SON OF WILLIAM EDWARDS, THE SETTLER.

SECOND GENERATION.

I.

RICHARD EDWARDS, of Hartford, Conn., was twice married. 1. To Elizabeth Tuthill, daughter of William Tuthill, of New Haven, in the same State, November 19, 1667. She died ———. 2. To Mary Talcott, daughter of Lieutenant-Colonel John Talcott, of Hartford, by his first wife, Helena Wakeman, daughter of Rev. John Wakeman, of New Haven, about 1692.

Richard Edwards, Esq., died April 20, 1718, in his 71st year.

His widow, Mrs. Mary Edwards, died April 19, 1723, aged 62.

Children,—by his first wife.

2 Mary,	born	1668.	No trace of her to be found.
3 Timothy,	born May	14, 1669.	
4 Abigail,	born	1671.	
5 Elizabeth,	born	1675.	
6 Ann,	born	1678.	
7 Mabel,	bap. December	13, 1685.	
8 Child, (un-named,)	born [no date.]		

Children,—by his second wife.

9 Jonathan,	born January	20, 1693.	Died March 21, 1693.
10 John,	born February	27, 1694.	
11 Hannah,	born January	3, 1696.	
12 Richard,	born January	5, 1698.	Died May 20, 1713.
13 Daniel,	born April	11, 1701.	
14 Samuel,	born November	1, 1702.	

THIRD GENERATION.

3.

Rev. TIMOTHY EDWARDS, of East Windsor, Conn., and Pastor of the Church in that town, was married to Esther Stoddard, daughter of the Rev. Solomon Stoddard, Pastor of the Church in Northampton, Mass., November 6, 1694. Mr. Edwards was graduated at Harvard University in 1691, and ordained Pastor of the Church of Christ in East Windsor, May, 1694.

Rev. Timothy Edwards died January 27, 1758, in the 89th year of his age.

Mrs. Ann Cole; alias Ann Edwards, died February 20, 1679. A short time before her decease; she made a verbal disposition of her estate, which, as entered on the Records of the Court of Probate for the District of Hartford, is as follows, *viz.:*

" Mrs. Cole declaring that it was her minde, that after her decease, her home and Land should be to her son William Edwards, he only to have the use & Improvement for himselfe & wife during their naturall life, & then it should return to her Grandson Richard Edwards & to his heires forever, and the like dispose she made of the other part of her estate, as appeares by the Testimony of Mr. Saul Willy, Mr. Jonathan Gilbert, and Wm. Edwards, which the Court approves of & confirmes, & this Court Granted Administration upon the estate to Richard Edwards, who accepted the same in Court."

His widow, Mrs. Esther Edwards, died January 19, 1771, in the 99th year of her age.

Children.

15 Esther,	born August	6, 1695.	
16 Elizabeth,	born April	14, 1697.	
17 Ann,	born April	28, 1699.	
18 Mary,	born February	11, 1701.	Died in East Windsor, September 17, 1776, unmarried.
19 Jonathan,	born October	5, 1703.	
20 Eunice,	born August	20, 1705.	
21 Abigail,	born December	25, 1707.	
22 Jerusha,	born May	30, 1710.	Died December 22, 1729.
23 Hannah,	born February	8, 1713.	
24 Lucy,	born May	25, 1715.	Died August 21, 1736.
25 Martha,	born January	5, 1718.	

4.

ABIGAIL EDWARDS was twice married. 1. To Benjamin Lathrop, 1689. He died 1690. 2. To Capt. Thomas Stoughton, of East Windsor, Conn., May 19, 1697. She was his second wife. [His first wife, to whom he was married December 31, 1691, was Dorathy Talcott, daughter of Lieutenant-Colonel John Talcott, of Hartford, Conn. She died March 28, 1696, aged 31. By her, Mr. Stoughton had one child only, a daughter Mary, born January 4, 1693, married Pelaliah Allyn, of Windsor.] Capt. Thomas Stoughton died January 14, 1749, in the 87th year of his age.

Mrs. Abigail Stoughton, alias Lathrop, died January 23, 1754, aged 82.

Children,—by her first husband,—none.

Children,—by her second husband.

26 Thomas,	born April	9, 1698.	
27 Daniel,	born August	13, 1699.	
28 Benjamin,	born April	28, 1701.	
29 Timothy,	born June	27, 1703.	
30 Abigail,	born December	21, 1704.	
31 David,	born September	9, 1706.	
32 Mabel,	born August	19, 1708.	
33 Jonathan,	born October	21, 1710.	Died August 10, 1733, unmarried.
34 Elizabeth,	born December	20, 1712.	
35 Isaac,	born November	2, 1714.	

5.

ELIZABETH EDWARDS was twice married. 1. To Jacob Deming, of Hartford, Conn., March 14, 1695. He died ———. 2. To ——— Hinckley, of Kingston, R. I. ——— Hinckley died ———.
Mrs. Elizabeth Hinckley, alias Deming, died ———.

Children,—by her first husband.

36 Jacob,	born March,	1696.	
37 Timothy,	bap. March	26, 1698.	
38 Abigail,	born January	21, 1700.	
39 Lemuel,	born	1702.	

Children,—by her second husband,—if any, their names not found.

6.

ANN EDWARDS was twice married. 1. To Jonathan Richardson, of Stonington, Conn., 1696. He died May 7, 1700. 2. To William Davenport, first of Hartford, Conn., then of Stonington, Conn., and afterwards, of Coventry, Conn., 1702. She was his second wife. His first wife was Elizabeth Nichols, daughter of Cyprian Nichols, of Hartford. She died February 19, 1697, aged 27. By her he had one child only, William.

Mr. William Davenport died in Coventry, June 29, 1742, in the 77th year of his age.

Mrs. Ann Davenport, alias Richardson, died in Coventry, May, 1764, aged about 86.

Children,—by her first husband.

40 Jonathan, bap. November 21, 1697, at Hartford. Settled in Stonington, married Anna Treat, daughter of Rev. Salmon Treat, minister of Preston, Conn., October 25, 1721. Three children are recorded to them.

41 Amos, born June 23, 1700, at Hartford. Settled in Coventry. Married Rachel Yarrington, of Long Island. He died in 1779. They had 14 children.

Children,—by her second husband.

42 Humphrey, born 1703. Settled in Coventry. Married Hannah Fitch, May 9, 1737. He died January 19, 1750, aged 47. They had no children.

43 Ann, bap. August 26, 1705, at Hartford. Married Habakuk Turner, of Coventry. She died November, 1780, aged 75. He died January, 1792, in the 87th year of his age.

44 Elizabeth, born Married Nathaniel Gove, of Coventry. He died December, 1763. She died September, 1783.

45 Rachel, born

46 Richard, born 1716. Settled in Coventry. Married Allice ———. She died February, 1772. He died October 16, 1803, aged 87. They had 6 children.

7.

MABEL EDWARDS was married to Jonathan Bigelow, of Hartford, Conn., December 14, 1699.

Mr. Jonathan Bigelow died July 29, 1749, aged 75.

His widow, Mrs. Mabel Bigelow, died May 16, 1765, in the 80th year of her age.

Children.

47 Timothy, born June 20, 1702. Married Abigail Olcott, daughter of John Olcott, of Hartford, 1727. After his death, she was married to Capt. Daniel Goodwin, of Hartford, November 6, 1748, being his second wife. Mr. Timothy Bigelow died in June, 1747. Mrs. Abigail Goodwin, alias Bigelow, died December 26, 1776, aged 73. Seven children are recorded to Timothy and Abigail Bigelow.

48 Mabel,   bap. November 6, 1703.   Married Daniel Seymour, Jun., of
                                           Hartford. She died November 10,
                                           1757. He died September 21, 1769.
                                           Four children are recorded to them.
49 Rebecca,   bap. November 5, 1708.   Died, unmarried, January 8, 1754.
50 Irena,   bap. November 4, 1711.   Married Daniel Marsh, of Oxford
                                           Society, East Hartford, Conn. She
                                           died March 27, 1790, in the 79th
                                           year of her age. He died Novem-
                                           ber 6, 1795, in the 85th year of his
                                           age. They had children.
51 Jonathan,   bap. June   27, 1714.   Married Tabitha Coleman, of Hart-
                                           ford, Conn. He died January 23,
                                           1779, in the 65th year of his age.
                                           She died September 17, 1785, aged
                                           70. They had 7 children, among
                                           them Hannah, born in 1738, married
                                           Captain John Barnard, of Hartford.
                                           She died March 13, 1800, aged 62.
                                           He died in December, 1813. They
                                           were the grand-parents of Hon.
                                           Henry Barnard, LL. D., Superintend-
                                           ent of the Public Schools of Connecti-
                                           cut, and President of the Connecticut
                                           Historical Society. [After her death,
                                           Mr. John Barnard was married to
                                           Martha Stanley, widow of Frederick
                                           Stanley, of Hartford, and sister of his
                                           first wife, by whom he had no issue.
                                           She died November 11, 1823, aged
                                           71.]
52 Jerusha,   born   1717.   Married Elisha Butler, of Hartford.
                                           She died August 17, 1777, aged 60.
                                           He died April 27, 1780, aged 65.
                                           They had no children.

10.

JOHN EDWARDS, of Hartford, Conn., was married to Christian
Williamson, supposed sister of Caleb Williamson, of Hartford,
formerly of Barnstable, Mass., December 14, 1719.

Mrs. Christian Edwards died January 18, 1769, aged —.
Deacon John Edwards died May 16, 1769, aged 75.

Children.

53 Mary,   born August   20, 1721.
54 Richard,   born October   26, 1723.
55 Christian,   bap. September 25, 1726.
56 Sarah,   ⎱ twins bap. February 9, 1729. ⎱ Died in childhood.
57 Abigail, ⎰   ⎰
58 Jerusha,   bap. May   30, 1731.   Died in early life.
59 John,   bap. February   3, 1734.   Died in early life.

11.

HANNAH EDWARDS was married to Joseph Backus, Jun., of
Norwich, Conn., afterwards of Hartford, in the same State, and
subsequently of Norwich, March 1, 1722.

Mrs. Hannah Backus died in Hartford, October, 1747, aged 51.
Mr. Joseph Backus died in Norwich.

Children.

60 William,   born April   20, 1723, in Norwich.
61 Mary,   bap. October   31, 1725, in Hartford.
62 Hannah,   bap. April   21, 1728, in Hartford.
63 Joseph,   bap. August   22, 1731, in Hartford.

13.

DANIEL EDWARDS, of Hartford, Conn., was married to Sarah Hooker, daughter of Nathaniel Hooker, of Hartford, and granddaughter of the Rev. Samuel Hooker, Pastor of the Church in Farmington, in the same State, 1728.

Hon. Daniel Edwards died at New Haven, Conn., September 6, 1765, in the 65th year of his age.

His widow, Mrs. Sarah Edwards, died July 31, 1775, aged 70.

Children,—several,—all which died in infancy, except,

64 Sarah,	born	1739.	
65 Daniel,	bap. May	23, 1746.	Died in childhood.

14.

SAMUEL EDWARDS, of Hartford, Conn., was married to Jerusha Pitkin, daughter of William Pitkin, of Hartford, east side, and grand-daughter of Hon. William Pitkin, one of the early settlers of Hartford, 1731. [After the death of Mr. Edwards, she was married to Rev. Ashbel Woodbridge, Pastor of the Church in Glastenbury, Conn., November 17, 1739. He died August 6, 1758, in the 55th year of his age. He was son of Rev. Timothy Woodbridge, 6th minister of the First Church in Hartford.]

Mr. Samuel Edwards died November 4, 1732, aged 30.

Mrs. Jerusha Edwards, alias Woodbridge, died July 31, 1799, in the 89th year of her age.

Child,—one only.

66 Jerusha,	bap. October	1, 1732.	Married John Welles, of Glastenbury, son of the Hon. Thomas Welles, of the same town, March 7, 1753.

FOURTH GENERATION.

15.

ESTHER EDWARDS was married to Rev. Samuel Hopkins, second Pastor of the First Church in West-Springfield, Mass., June 28, 1727.

Rev. Mr. Samuel Hopkins died October 5, 1755, in the 62d year of his age.

His widow, Mrs. Esther Hopkins, died June 17, 1766, in the 72d year of her age.

Children.

67 Timothy,	bap. June	23, 1728.	Married Dinah Miller, of West-Springfield, Mass., December 9, 1756.
68 Samuel,	bap. October	20, 1729.	Minister of Hadley, Mass. Was twice married. 1. To Sarah Williams, widow of Rev. Chester Williams, his predecessor in the ministry at Hadley, and daughter of Hon. Eleazur Porter, of Hadley, 1756. She died February 5, 1774, aged 48. 2. To Margaret Stoddard, of Chelmsford, Mass., October, 1776. She died Oc-

tober 3, 1796, aged 66.   He died March 8, 1811, aged 81.   9 children, all by his first wife.

69 Hannah,   bap. January   29, 1731.   Married Hon. John Worthington, of Springfield, Mass., January 10, 1759. She was his first wife. She died November 25, 1766, in her 36th year. Hon. John Worthington died ———.

70 Esther,   bap. July   21, 1733.   Died March 23, 1740.

16.

ELIZABETH EDWARDS was married to Jabez Huntington, Esq., of Windham, Conn., June 30, 1724.

Mrs. Elizabeth Huntington died September 21, 1733, aged 36.*

Col. Jabez Huntington died September 26, 1752, aged 60.

Children.

71 Elizabeth,† born November   1, 1725.   Married Abraham Davenport, Esq., of Stamford, Conn., November 1, 1750.

72 Sarah,‡   born June   20, 1727.   Married twice. 1. Hezekiah Wetmore, Esq., of Middletown, Conn., August 22, 1748, and after his death, 2. Samuel Beers, Esq., of Stratford, Conn., February 19, 1758.

73 Tryphena, born August   27, 1729.   Died in East Windsor, Conn., August 19, 1745, at the house of her grand father, Rev. Timothy Edwards.

74 Jerusha,   born August   24, 1731.   Married Doct. John Clark, of Lebanon, Conn.

17.

ANN EDWARDS was married to Capt. John Ellsworth, of East-Windsor, Conn., May 8, 1784.

Capt. John Ellsworth died January 4, 1784, in the 87th year of his age.

His widow, Mrs. Ann Ellsworth, died April 11, 1790, aged 91 years, wanting 16 days.

Children.

75 John,   born August   24, 1735.
76 Solomon,   born April   30, 1737.§

---

* After her death, Jabez Huntington, Esq., was married to Sarah Wetmore, widow, May 21, 1735. She died at Norwich, Conn., March 21, 1783, in the 83d year of her age. By this wife, he had children, *Hannah*, born July 22, 1736. Married Gideon Tomlinson, Esq., of Stratford, Conn., January 17, 1760. She died December 26, 1762, aged 26. He died January 19, 1766, in his 35th year. He was an officer in the army, and fought in the battle of the Narrows, and was at the taking of Ticonderoga, Crown Point, and Montreal. They had one child only, a son, Jabez H., born December 24, 1760, married Rebecca Lewis, daughter of Joseph Lewis, of Stratford, by whom he had four children, of whom, Gideon, born December 31, 1780, was Governor of Connecticut, from 1827 to 1831, both years inclusive. Mrs. Rebecca Tomlinson died January 1, 1823. Jabez H. Tomlinson, Esq., died in 1849, aged 88. *Jabez*, born April 15, 1738. Married Judith Elderkin, daughter of Jedediah Elderkin, of Windham, August 6, 1760. She was born in Norwich, March 2, 1743. He died November 24, 1782. She died September 24, 1786. They had 6 or more children. *Anna*, born January 20, 1740. Married Hon. Benjamin Huntington, of Norwich, May 3, 1765. He died at Rome, N. Y., October 6, 1800, aged 64. She died at Norwich, October 6, 1790, aged 50. *Samuel*, born October 19, 1742. Died January 15, 1743. *Lucy*, born June 16, 1744. Married Col. Experience Storrs, of Mansfield, Conn. She died February 6, 1801. He died July 22, 1801, in his 67th year. They had several children.

† See No. 71 of Appendix to Notes on Edwards Family.

‡ See No. 72 of Appendix to Notes on Edwards Family.

§ See No. 76 of Appendix to Notes on Edwards Family.

77 Frederick, born October   20, 1738.   Married Anna Thompson, widow of
                                       Capt. Hugh Thompson, deceased, of
                                       East-Windsor, and daughter of Na-
                                       thaniel Stoughton, of the same town.
                                       He died February 20, 1799, aged 60.
                                       She died August 5, 1820, aged 79.
                                       They had no children.
78 Ann,   born January   23, 1741.*

19.

Rev. JONATHAN EDWARDS, colleague Pastor of the Church in Northampton, Mass., was married to Sarah Pierpont, daughter of Rev. James Pierpont, fourth Pastor of the First Church in New Haven, Conn., and of Mary, his third wife, daughter of Rev. Samuel Hooker, second Pastor of the First Church in Farmington, Conn., and grand-daughter of Rev. Thomas Hooker, first minister of Hartford, in the same State, July 28, 1727.

Rev. Jonathan Edwards died at Princeton, N. Y., March 22, 1758, in the 55th year of his age.

His widow, Mrs. Sarah Edwards, died at Philadelphia, October 2, 1758, in the 49th year of her age.

Children.

79 Sarah,   born August   25, 1728.
80 Jerusha,   born April   26, 1730.   Died February 14, 1747.
81 Esther,   born February   13, 1732.
82 Mary,   born April   7, 1734.
83 Lucy,   born August   31, 1736.
84 Timothy,   born July   25, 1738.
85 Susanna,   born June   20, 1740.
86 Eunice,   born May   9, 1743.
87 Jonathan,   born May   26, 1745.
88 Elizabeth,   born May   6, 1747.   Died at Northampton, January 1, 1762.
89 Pierpont,   born April   8, 1750.

20.

EUNICE EDWARDS was married to Rev. Simon Backus, Pastor of the Church in Newington Society, Wethersfield, Conn., October 1, 1729, " by Rev. Timothy Edwards, Minister."

Rev. Simon Backus died at Louisburg, Island of Cape Breton, (" having gone there as Chaplain of the Army of the New England Colonies,") February 2, 1746, aged 45. He was son of Joseph Backus, of Norwich, Conn., and was born February 11, 1701.†

His widow, Mrs. Eunice Backus, died at East Windsor, Conn., June 1, 1788, aged 83.

---

* See No. 78 of Appendix to Notes on Edwards Family.

† General Assembly, May Session, 1746. Petition of Eunice Backus, stating that her late husband, the Rev. Mr. Backus, in compliance with public desire and order, was induced to leave his family and ministerial charge at Newington, and to repair to Louisburg, there to reside in quality of Chaplain to the troops from this Colony, in garrison there. That not long after his arrival there, it pleased God so to dispose, that he, in the general mortality, was conveyed to the place of silence. He left seven children, which are generally young. She asks for pecuniary relief. £300 granted her, in bills of credit of the old tenor.—*Records of Connecticut.*

Children.

90	Clorinda,	born October	31, 1730.*	
91	Eunice,	born January	14, 1733.	Died in East-Windsor, 1808, unmarried.
92	Elizabeth,	born May	19, 1734.†	
93	Simon,	born February	13, 1738.‡	
94	Esther,	born November	19, 1739.§	
95	Joseph,	born May	30, 1741.	Died in 1742, about the 1st of January.
96	Jerusha,	born January	13, 1743.‖	
97	Mary,	born March	24, 1745.	Died in East-Windsor, December 27, 1751.

21.

ABIGAIL EDWARDS was married to William Metcalf, of Lebanon, Conn., October 25, 1737.

Mrs. Abigail Metcalf died September 24, 1764, in the 57th year of her age.

William Metcalf, Esq., died June 15, 1773, in the 65th year of his age.

Children.

98	Abigail,	born April	2, 1739.	
99	William,	born June	14, 1742.	Died July 5, 1750.
100	Eliphalet,	born July	10, 1744.	Died May, 1745.
101	Lucy,	born May	25, 1746.	
102	Eliphalet,	born November	25, 1747.	

23.

HANNAH EDWARDS was married to Seth Wetmore, Esq., of Middletown, Conn., January 15, 1746. She was his third wife.¶
Mrs. Hannah Wetmore died June 7, 1773, aged 61.

---

* See Appendix to Notes on Edwards Family.
† See Appendix to Notes on Edwards Family.
‡ See No. 93 of Appendix to Notes on Edwards Family.
§ See No. 94 of Appendix to Notes on Edwards Family.
‖ See No. 96 of Appendix to Notes on Edwards Family.

¶ The first wife of Seth Wetmore, Esq., to whom he was married September 30, 1730, was Margaret Gaylord, widow of Samuel Gaylord, of Middletown, and daughter of William Southmayd, of that town, by his second wife, Margaret Allyn, daughter of Hon. Lieut. Colonel John Allyn, of Hartford. She died November 6, 1730, soon after her marriage to Mr. Wetmore.

His second wife was Hannah Wetmore, daughter of Deacon Beriah and Margaret Wetmore, of Middletown. She was born March 2, 1703, and died May 1, 1744.

Children,—by his second wife.

1	Jerusha,	born	1741.	Died June, 1749, in her 9th year.
2	Seth,	born October	9, 1743.	

2.

Seth Wetmore, of Middletown, Conn., son of Seth Wetmore, of that town, was twice married. 1. To Mary Wright, daughter of Joseph Wright, of Middletown, November 14, 1768. She died December 24, 1790, aged 45. 2. To Lucretia Scott, widow of John Scott, deceased, of Middletown, March 27, 1791. She was daughter of Stephen Warner, of Middletown, and of his wife, Mary, daughter of Samuel Starr, of the same town, and was born September 23, 1752. Mr. John Scott died March 14, 1787.

Capt. Seth Wetmore died April 15, 1810, in the 67th year of his age.
Mrs. Lucretia Wetmore, alias Warner, died May 18, 1820, aged 67.

Children,—by his first wife.

3	Seth,	born September	10, 1769.
4	William,	born September	16, 1771.
5	Hannah,	born May	28, 1773.
6	Samuel,	born October	5, 1775.
7	Mary,	born September	14, 1777.

Seth Wetmore, Esq., died of small pox, April 12, 1778, aged 78.*

Children.

103	Lucy,†	born April	10, 1748.
104	Oliver,‡	born May	24, 1752.
105	Hannah,	born	1754. Died July, 1756.

25.

MARTHA EDWARDS was married to Rev. Moses Tuthill, of Granville, Mass., and first Pastor of the Church in that town, 1746. He was the son of John Tuthill, of New Haven, Conn., and was born June 25, 1715.

Rev. Moses Tuthill died at Southold, L. I., October, 1785, aged 70.§

His widow, Mrs. Martha Tuthill, died in Wapping Society, East-Windsor, Conn., February, 1794, aged 77 years, nearly.

Children.

| 106 | Martha, | born | 1747, in Bedford Society, Granville, Mass. Died unmarried in Wapping Society, East-Windsor, March 15, 1837, aged 90. |
| 107 | Hannah, | born | 1750, in Bedford. Died unmarried, in Wapping Society, East-Windsor, December 11, 1831, aged 81. |

8	Willard Wright,	born October	13, 1779.
9	Titus,	born July	16, 1781.
10	Josiah,	born July	21, 1783.
11	Lucy,	born April	6, 1786.
12	Nathaniel Downing,	born October	30, 1790.

Children,—by his second wife.

| 13 | Julia, | born January | 21, 1792. |
| 14 | Harriet, | born September | 22, 1794. Married Henry S. Ward, of Middletown, and died there March 1, 1823. |

13.

Julia Wetmore, daughter of Seth Wetmore, Jun., and of Lucretia Wetmore, his second wife, was married to John C. Bush, of New-Haven, Conn., now of Ogdensburgh, N. Y., December 3, 1812.

Children.

| 15 | Robert Wasson, | born November | 18, 1813, in New-Haven. |
| 16 | Harriet Wetmore, | born April | 25, 1815, in Middletown, Conn. Married E. W. N. Starr, Esq., Adjutant-General of the Militia of Connecticut, May 27, 1840. |

Stephen Warner, above named, died at the Bay of Honduras, August 3, 1752. His widow, Mary Warner, was married to Stephen Van Overwyk, of Middletown, October 8, 1761, by whom she had one child only, a daughter Sally, born May 27, 1763. Mr. Van Overwyk died June 6, 1764. Mrs. Mary Van Overwyk, alias Warner, died May 30, 1811, aged 83.

* Formed for public usefulness, improved in various stations of civil life,—an able lawyer, a just judge,—an affectionate head of his family, a faithful friend,—having outlived most of his acquaintance of early life, was gathered to his fathers in a good old age. [Grave-Stone, Middletown west burying ground.]

† See No. 103 of Appendix to Notes on Edwards Family.

‡ See No. 104 of Appendix to Notes on Edwards Family.

§ Mr. Tuthill was graduated at Yale College, 1745, and ordained Pastor of the First Church in Granville, about 1747, and was the first Pastor of the Church. He was dismissed in 1753. "Mr. Tuthill was an orthodox and faithful minister, and his short ministry of six years in Granville, was blessed with prosperity and peace. The good man, after his dismission, preached in various places, and died in peace, in a good old age.—[Rev. Dr. Timothy M. Cooley, the present Pastor of said Church.]

8

108 Ruth,	born	1753, in New-Haven, Conn. Died unmarried, in Wapping Society, in East-Windsor, 1805, aged 52.
109 Esther,	born	1756, in Kent, Penn. Married Amos Cady, first of Tolland, Conn., afterwards of Vernon, Conn., December, 1789, being his second wife. He died August 3, 1843, aged 96 years and 11 months. His widow, Mrs. Esther Cady, was living in Vernon on the 4th of October, 1850, and was cared for by her son-in-law, Russell Cady, Esq., of that town. They had 4 children. Mr. Amos Cady's first wife, to whom he was married July 16, 1770, was Hannah Kingsbury, daughter of Simon Kingsbury, of Ellington, Conn. She died November 7, 1786, aged about 35. By her, he had 7 children; among them, Russell, above named, born June 12, 1777, and lives on the old family farm in Vernon.

53.

MARY EDWARDS was married to Caleb Ely, of West-Spring-field, Mass., May 21, 1740.

Caleb Ely, Esq., died May 16, 1764, in the 40th year of his age.

His widow, Mrs. Mary Ely, died March 7, 1783, in the 62d year of her age.

Children.

110 Caleb,	born April	1, 1741.
111 William,	born June	15, 1743.
112 John Edwards,	born April	21, 1745.
113 Mary,	born February	23, 1747.
114 Martin,	born July	14, 1751.

54.

RICHARD EDWARDS, of Hartford, Conn., was married to Mary Butler, daughter of Jonathan Butler, of the same town, February 21, 1750.

Richard Edwards, Esq., died May 5, 1770, in the 47th year of his age.

His widow, Mrs. Mary Edwards, died September 20, 1795, aged 77.

Children.

115 Mary,	born August	14, 1750.	Died in infancy.
116 Richard,	born December	3, 1755.	Died in childhood.
117 John,	born July	31, 1757.	Died August 29, 1759.
118 Mary,	born October	3, 1759.	Married George Goodwin, of Hartford.

55.

CHRISTIAN EDWARDS was married to Hezekiah Marsh, of Hartford, Conn., December 15, 1743. [After her death, he was twice married. 1. To Elizabeth Jones, widow of Levi Jones, of Hartford, who was blown up in the School House, May 23, 1766.

She was daughter of Aaron Cooke, of Harwinton, Conn., formerly of Hartford, was born in Hartford, 1722, and was married to Mr. Jones, June 10, 1742. She died October 24, 1788, aged 66. 2. To Hannah Tiley, widow of Samuel Tiley, deceased, of Hartford, 1789. After his death, she was married to Captain John Cooke, of Hartford, being his second wife.]

Mrs. Christian Marsh died June 16, 1770, in the 44th year of her age.

Capt. Hezekiah Marsh died April 18, 1791, aged 71.

Children.

119 Jerusha,	born August	28, 1744.	Married Joseph Wadsworth, Jun., of Hartford, Conn., September 22, 1768.
120 John,	born November	6, 1749.	Died in infancy.
121 Abigail,	born November	29, 1750.	Married Theodore Skinner, of Hartford, Conn. He died April 28, 1796, aged 49. She died July 5, 1808, aged 57. They had 5 children.
122 John,	born October	4, 1753.	Married Susan Bunce, daughter of Timothy Bunce, of Hartford, 1783. He died July 28, 1815, in his 62d year. She died June 14, 1787, aged 62. They were the parents of John and Edward Marsh, of the Neck, Hartford, farmers.
123 Christian,	born August	8, 1755.	Married Charles Merrill, of Hartford. She died November 8, 1778, aged 23. Child, one only, Christian, who married a Root, lawyer, of Western New York.
124 Son, (unnamed,)	born January	4, 1759.	Died March 16, 1759.
125 Anna,	born June	10, 1761.	Was married to a Bunce, and after his death, to John Packard. No children by either husband.
126 Hezekiah,	born March	2, 1763.	Married Sarah Burnham, daughter of Asahel Burnham, of Hartford, 1790. He died May 4, 1819, aged 56. She died August 7, 1849, aged 82. They were the parents of William and Hezekiah Marsh, of the Neck, Hartford, farmers.

57.

ABIGAIL EDWARDS was married to Timothy Phelps, of Hartford, Conn., July 25, 1751.

Mr. Timothy Phelps died June 21, 1776, aged 51.

His widow, Mrs. Abigail Phelps, died April 9, 1786, aged 57.

Children.

127 Abigail,	bap. May	10, 1752.	
128 Richard,	bap. March	24, 1754.	Died September 30, 1765.
129 Sarah,	bap. August	22, 1756.	
130 Timothy,	bap. October	15, 1758.	
131 Anna,	bap. March	29, 1761.	
132 Daniel,	bap. December	26, 1762.	
133 Jerusha,	bap. September	22, 1765.	
134 Esther,	bap. October	2, 1768.	

64.

SARAH EDWARDS was married to George Lord, of Hartford, Conn., son of Richard Lord, of Wethersfield, Conn., and of Ruth, his wife, daughter of Hezekiah Wyllys, of Hartford, in the same State, December 14, 1758.

Mrs. Sarah Lord died October 11, 1764, in the 25th year of her age.

Mr. George Lord died October 19, 1765, aged 28.

Children.

135 George,   bap. December   2, 1759. Died in infancy.
136 Daniel Ed-
    wards,   bap. July   5, 1761. Died September 14, 1762.

66.

JERUSHA EDWARDS was married to John Welles, of Glastenbury, Conn., March 7, 1753.

Mr. John Welles died April 16, 1764, aged 35.

His widow, Mrs. Jerusha Welles, died August 15, 1778, in the 46th year of her age.

Children.

137 John,   born September   2, 1754.
138 George,   born February   13, 1756.
139 Jerusha,   born October   2, 1757.
140 Daniel,   born April   7, 1760. Died April 10, 1760.
141 Isaac,   born April   17, 1761.
142 Ashbel,   born April   27, 1763.

FIFTH GENERATION.

79.

SARAH EDWARDS was married to Elihu Parsons, of Northampton, Mass., but subsequently, of Stockbridge, in the same State, June 11, 1750.

Elihu Parsons, Esq., died at Stockbridge, Mass., August 22, 1785, aged 66.

His widow, Mrs. Sarah Parsons, died at Goshen, Mass., May 15, 1805, aged 76.

Children.

143 Ebenezer,   born [no date.]   Died in infancy.
144 Esther,   born May   29, 1752. Died in Stockbridge, November 17, 1774.
145 Elihu,   born December   9, 1753. Married Lydia Hinsdale, of Lenox, Mass. She was the first white child born in that town. After the birth of his last child, he removed from Stockbridge, to Goshen, Mass., where he died August 25, 1804, aged 50. Had 6 children.
146 Eliphalet, born June   18, 1756. Married Martha Young, of Long Island. Died at Chenango, N. Y., 1813. Five children.
147 Lydia,   born June   15, 1757. Married Aaron Ingersoll, of Lee, Mass.
148 Lucretia,   born August   11, 1759. Married Rev. Justin Parsons, of Pittsfield, Vermont, February 9, 1786. She died at Goshen, Mass., December, 1786, leaving 1 child only. After

her death, he was again married, and by his second wife, had, among other children, son Levi, born July 18, 1792, who was Missionary to Palestine.

149 Sarah,	born September	8, 1760.	Married Deacon David Ingersoll, of Lee, Mass., December 13, 1781. They had 13 children.
150 Lucy,	born September	8, 1762.	Married Joshua Ketchum, of Victor, N. Y.
151 Jonathan,	born [no date.]		Died in infancy.
152 Jerusha,	born March	1, 1765.	Died in infancy.
153 Jerusha,	bap. June	1, 1766.	Married Ira Seymour, of Stockbridge, Mass., afterwards of Victor, N. Y.

81.

ESTHER EDWARDS was married to Rev. Aaron Burr, Pastor of the Church, at Newark, N. J., and afterwards President of the College at Princeton, in the same State, June 29, 1752. Rev. Mr. Burr was son of Daniel Burr, of Fairfield, Conn., grandson of John Burr, of the same town, and great-grandson of Jehu Burr, one of the first settlers of Springfield, Mass., and Fairfield, and was born in 1714, baptized March 4, 1716.

Rev. Aaron Burr died at Princeton, September 24, 1757, in the 43d year of his age.*

His widow, Mrs. Esther Burr, died at Princeton, April 7, 1758, aged 26.

Children.

| 154 Sarah, | born May | 3, 1754. | Married Hon. Tapping Reeve, of Litchfield, Conn., June 24, 1772. Mrs. Sarah Reeve died March 30, 1797, in the 43d year of her age. Chief Justice Tapping Reeve died December 13, 1823, aged 79. *Child,*—one only,—Aaron Burr Reeve, born October 3, 1780. Yale College, 1802. Was married in Litchfield, to Arabella Shedden, November 21, 1808, and died at Troy, N. Y., (where he had established himself in his profession of an attorney and counsellor at law,) September 1, 1809. His widow (who was born in New York, of Scotch parents, November, 1837) subsequently married David J. Burr, a native of New Haven, and went to Richmond, Virginia, where she died early in the year 1839. The only child of Aaron Burr Reeve, and his wife Arabella, was Tapping Reeve Burr, who was born at Troy, August 16, 1809, and died in Litchfield, Au- |

---

* " Can you imagine to yourself a person modest in prosperity, prudent in difficulty, in business indefatigable, magnanimous in danger, easy in his manners, of exquisite judgment, of profound learning, catholic in sentiment, of the purest morals, and great even in the minutest things,—Can you imagine so accomplished a person, without recollecting the idea of the late PRESIDENT BURR?

" Though a person of a slender and delicate make to encounter fatigue, he had a heart of steel; in the Sacred Scriptures he was a perfect Apollos; his piety eclipsed all his other accomplishments." *Funeral Eulogium of Rev. Mr. Burr, by William Livingston, Esq.*

gust 28, 1829, while a member of
Yale College,—the last descendant of
Judge Reeve. [After the death of
his wife Sarah, Judge Reeve was
married to Betsy Thompson, daughter of Zachariah Thompson, of Bethlem, Conn., April 30, 1798. She was
born February 14, 1774, in Bethlem,
and died in Litchfield, December 8,
1842, in the 68th year of her age.
No issue by this wife.

155 Aaron,   born February   6, 1756.   Vice-President of the U. S. Married
Theodosia Prevost of the City of
New York, July 2, 1782, daughter of
Col. Prevost of the British Army.
They had one child only,—a daugh-
ter, Theodosia, who married Hon.
Gen. Joseph Allston, of Charleston,
S. C., afterwards Governor of the
State. She was lost at sea, on her
passage from Charlestown to New
York, in 1812. Gov. Allston died at
Charleston, September 10, 1816,
aged 38.

82.

MARY EDWARDS was married to Timothy Dwight, of Northampton, Mass., November 8, 1750.

Timothy Dwight, Esq., died at Natchez, June 10, 1772, aged
52.

His widow, Mrs. Mary Dwight, died at Northampton, February
28, 1807, in the 73d year of her age.

Children.

156 Timothy,   born May   3, 1752, O. S.   Pastor of the Church at Green-
field Hill, Fairfield, Conn. Presi-
dent of Yale College. Married Mary
Woolsey, daughter of Benjamin
Woolsey, Esq., of Dorsous, L. I.
Died January 11, 1817, aged 64.

157 Sereno Ed-
wards,   born December 10, 1754.   Married Cynthia Pomeroy.
158 Erastus,   born September 13, 1756.   Died, unmarried, in 1825.
159 Jonathan, born January   29, 1759.   Married a Wright.
160 Sarah,   born May   29, 1761.   Married a Storrs.
161 Mary,   born January   9, 1763.
162 Theodorus, born December 15, 1764.   Married Abby Alsop, of Middletown,
Conn. He was an eminent lawyer.
Settled in Hartford, Conn., but subsequently removed to the city of
New York, where he died, in 1846.

163 Maurice
William,   born December 15, 1766.
164 Fidelia,   born August   7, 1768.   Married Jonathan Edwards Porter, of
Hadley, Mass., January 16, 1793.

165 Nathaniel, born January   31, 1770.   Married Rebecca Robbins, daughter of
Appleton Robbins, Esq., of Wethers-
field, Conn., June 20, 1798. Doct.
Nathaniel Dwight died June 11, 1831,
aged 61. Mrs. Rebecca Dwight died
April 28, 1848, aged 77. Had a
family of children.

166 Elizabeth, born January   29, 1772.

167 Cecil,   born June   10, 1774.   Married Mary Clapp.
168 Henry
    Edwin,   born September 20, 1776.   Married Electa Center.

83.

LUCY EDWARDS was married to Jahleel Woodbridge, of Stock-
bridge, Mass., June 7, 1764. [After her death he was married to
Hannah Rebecca Keep, widow of Rev. John Keep, of Sheffield,
Mass., and daughter of the Rev. Philemon Robbins, of Branford,
Conn., by whom he had no children.]
    Mrs. Lucy Woodbridge died September 18, 1786, aged 51.
    Hon. Jahleel·Woodbridge, died August 13, 1796, aged 58.

Children.

169 Stephen,   born March   12, 1765.   Married Rachel Welles, daughter of
                                              Ashbel Welles, of West Hartford,
                                              Conn. He died in Youngstown, O.,
                                              August 7, 1836. She died in Stock-
                                              bridge, November 7, 1833, aged 66.
170 Jonathan, born January   24, 1767.   Married Sarah Meech, of Worthington,
                                              Mass. Was a Lawyer. He died in
                                              Worthington in 1808, leaving five
                                              children, *viz.*: Lucy Edwards Wood-
                                              bridge, who married Mr. E. S. Her-
                                              rick, of Albany; Mary Ann Wood-
                                              bridge, who married Mr. Calvin
                                              Walker, of Brockport, N. Y.; Abby
                                              D. Woodbridge, a teacher in the Al-
                                              bany Female Academy, Rev. Jona-
                                              than Edwards Woodbridge, late
                                              Editor of the Puritan Recorder, Bos-
                                              ton, and Rev. George Woodbridge, of
                                              Richmond, Va.
171 Lucy,   born April   14, 1769.   Married her cousin, Jonathan Edwards,
                                              son of Hon. Timothy Edwards, of
                                              Stockbridge.
172 Joseph,   born July   22, 1771.   Married Louisa Hopkins, daughter of
                                              Col. Mark Hopkins, of Great Barring-
                                              ton, Mass., May 20, 1800. He was a
                                              Lawyer, and for a number of years,
                                              Clerk of the Court. She died Febru-
                                              ary 9, 1819, aged 44. He died April
                                              23, 1829, in his 58th year. *Children*,
                                              Catharine, Henry, Joseph, William.
173 Elizabeth, born July   1, 1773.   Married Elisha Brown, first of Stock-
                                              bridge, Mass., afterwards of Dayton,
                                              O., where he died in February, 1853.
174 Sarah Ed-
    wards,   born June   7, 1775.   Married Moses Lester, of Griswold,
                                              Conn., November 2, 1807. She was
                                              his second wife. He died in 1815.
                                              She died in Constantia, N. Y.,
                                              December 11, 1837. She was the
                                              mother of C. Edwards Lester, the
                                              author.
175 John Eliot, born June   24, 1777.   Married. Place of residence unknown
                                              to me.
176 Ann,   born November   6, 1779.   Died at the age of about 9 years.
177 Timothy,   born November 23, 1783.   Rev. Timothy Woodbridge, D. D., of
                                              Green River, N. Y. Married Cynthia
                                              Phelps, of Green River, N. Y. "Rev.
                                              Dr. Woodbridge lost his sight while
                                              preparing for the ministry, but com-

pleted his studies, and after preaching in New York and other places, settled in Green River, from which place he afterwards removed to Spencertown, in the same county. In 1852, he retired from the pastoral office, but preaches, as stated supply, much of the time, devoting his leisure chiefly to writing." [*Miss Electa F. Jones' History of Stockbridge.*]

84.

TIMOTHY EDWARDS, of Elizabethtown, N. J., until 1771, and after that year, of Stockbridge, Mass., was married to Rhoda Ogden, daughter of Robert Ogden, of Elizabethtown, September 25, 1760.

Hon. Timothy Edwards died October 27, 1813, aged 75.[*]

His widow, Mrs. Rhoda Edwards, died at Litchfield, Conn., November 2, 1822, aged 80. Her remains were interred at Stockbridge.

Children.

178 Sarah, born July 11, 1761, in Elizabethtown, N. J. Married Benjamin Chaplin, of Mansfield, Conn., June 5, 1783, and after his death, a Mr. Tyler of Brookfield, Conn., father of Frederick Tyler, of Hartford, Conn., merchant.

179 Edward, born January 20, 1763, in Elizabethtown, N. J. Married Mary.

180 Jonathan, born October 16, 1764, in Elizabethtown, N. J. Married Lucy Woodbridge, daughter of Jahleel Woodbridge, Esq., of Stockbridge, November 20, 1778. Lived some time in Berkshire, N. Y.

181 Richard, born March 5, 1764, in Elizabethtown, N. J.

182 Phebe, born November 4, 1768, in Elizabethtown, N. J. Married Rev. Asahel Hooker, of Goshen, Conn., June 11, 1792, and after his death, Samuel Farrar, Esq., of Andover, Mass., Treasurer and Financial Agent of Andover Theological Seminary, October 30, 1814. She died January 22, 1848. One of her daughters by the Rev. Mr. Hooker, married Rev. Dr. Elias Cornelius, who died in Hartford, Conn., February 12, 1832, aged 37.

183 William, born November 11, 1770, in Elizabethtown, N. J. Resided some time in Hunter, N. Y. Died, suddenly, at Brooklyn, N. Y., December 29, 1851. Was Colonel.

184 Robert Ogden, born September 30, 1772, in Stockbridge, Mass. Married Miss Pomroy, of Northampton, who, after his death, married John Tappan, of Boston.

---

[*] Mr. Edwards was graduated at Princeton College, 1757. Was a merchant in Elizabethtown, and opened the first store in Stockbridge in 1772. From 1775 to 1780, Mr. Edwards was a Member of the Council of Massachusetts: from 1778 to 1787, Judge of Probate, and Member of the County Congress, July 6, 1774, and one of the Committee to consider of the consumption of English goods. He was, also, a Deacon in the Congregational Church, Stockbridge.

185 Timothy, born July 12, 1774, in Stockbridge, Mass.
186 Mary Og-
   den, born April 9, 1776.
187 Rhodas, born May 7, 1778, in Stockbridge. Married Josiah Dwight, March 3, 1798. Had 1 son, Robert Ogden Dwight, Missionary to India. She is the mother of Mrs. Charles Sedgwick, of Lenox, Mass.
188 Eliza-
   beth, } twins. born October 11, 1780, in Stockbridge.
189 Mary, } Married Mason Whiting, attorney at Law, of Chenango Point, formerly of Great Barrington, Mass., April 25, 1800.
190 Anna, born February 2, 1784, in Stockbridge. Married Deacon Ashley Williams, of Dalton, Mass. He died in Hadley, in the same State.
191 Robert
   Burr, born September 14, 1787, in Stockbridge. Deceased.

85.

SUSANNA EDWARDS was married to Eleazur Porter, Esq., of Hadley, Mass., September 17, 1761. She was his second wife.

Hon. Eleazur Porter died May 27, 1797, aged 69.

His widow, Mrs. Susanna Porter, died May 2, 1803, in the 63d year of her age.

Children.

192 Eleazur, born June 14, 1762.
193 William, born December 9, 1763.
194 Jonathan
   Edwards, born May 17, 1766.
195 Moses, born September 19, 1768.
196 John, born July 27, 1772. Died August 7, 1772.
197 Pierpont, born June 12, 1775.

86.

EUNICE EDWARDS was twice married. 1. To Thomas Pollock, Esq., of Newbern, N. C., January, 1764. He died in 1777. 2. To Robert Hunt, Esq., of Elizabethtown, N. J., about 1780.

Robert Hunt, Esq., died in March, 1816.

Mrs. Eunice Hunt, alias Pollock, died in Newbern, N. C., September 9, 1822, aged 79.

Children,—by her first husband.

198 Elizabeth, born Married —— Williams.
199 Hester, born Died young.
200 Thomas, born Died at Leghorn, in 1803.
201 Frances, born Married John P. Devereux, Esq., of Newbern, N. C., 1790.
202 George, born 1772. Died on his plantation in North Carolina, by a fall from a horse, in the spring of 1839.

Child,—by her second husband,—one only that survived childhood.

203 Sarah
   Pierpont, born May 9, 1789. Married John Fanning Burgwyn, Esq., of the Hermitage, Wilmington, N. C., August 30, 1800, at Saratoga Springs, N. Y. He was son of John Bur-

gwyn, of Wilmington, N. C., Esq.,
deceased, and was born in Thornburg, in Glocester county, England,
March 14, 1783. Mrs. Sarah P. Burgwyn died March 22, 1823, in the 34th
year of her age. Children of John F.
and Sarah P. Burgwyn,—Julia Theodosia, born September 30, 1807.
George Pollock Alvestone, born June
11, 1810, died February 25, 1829.
Henry King, born January 7, 1813.
Thomas Pollock, born December 3,
1814. John Collinson, born September 7, 1816, died November 9, 1842.
Edwards Devereux, born March 22,
1819, died September 7, 1822. William Bush, born March 22, 1821, died
September 3, 1822. Sarah Emily,
born February 24, 1823.

87.

Rev. Jonathan Edwards was twice married. 1. To Mary
Porter, daughter of Eleazur Porter, senior, of Hadley, Mass., and
of Sarah his wife, October 4, 1770. She was born at Hartford,
East Side, September 16, 1748, and was accidentally drowned in
Sabin's Mill Pond, New Haven, Conn., June 10, 1782, in the 34th
year of her age. 2. To Mercy Sabin, daughter of Col. Hezekiah
Sabin, of New Haven, December 18, 1783.

Rev. Dr. Jonathan Edwards, President of Union College, died
in Schenectady, N. Y., August 1, 1801, in the 45th year of his
age.

His widow, Mrs. Mary Sabin, died in Lenox, Mass., February
23, 1823, in the 65th year of her age.

Children,—by his first wife.

204 Jonathan
Walter, born January   5, 1772. Married Elizabeth Tryon, daughter of
Moses Tryon, Esq., of Wethersfield,
Conn., a Captain in the Navy of the
United States. He died April 3,
1831, aged 59. *Children,*—Jonathan,
Residence, Troy, N. Y., Lawyer,
and Mayor of that city. Mary Porter, died in early life. Walter, residence, City of New York, Lawyer.
Elizabeth Tryon, deceased. John
Erskine, Minister. Tryon, D.D.,
Pastor of Congregational Church,
New London, Conn. George William,
minister. Sarah Pierpont. Catharine Agnes. Eugene, lawyer.

205 Mary,   born June   22, 1773. Married James Jauncey Hait, Esq., of
Schenectady, N. Y., merchant, son of
the Rev. Benjamin Hait, of Connecticut Farms, New Jersey. He died at
Colebrook, Conn., September 30,
1812, aged 42. Widow, Mrs. Mary
Hait, is now living in the City of
New York, with her son, William
Hait, merchant. *Children,*—Jonathan Edwards, William, James, died

206 Jerusha, born January 30, 1776. in Wethersfield, Conn., by drowning. Benjamin, died unmarried. Married Rev. Calvin Chapin, Pastor of the Congregational Church in Stepney Society, Wethersfield, February 2, 1795. Mrs. Jerusha Chapin died December 5, 1847, in her 72d year. Rev. Dr. Calvin Chapin died March 16, 1851, aged 87. *Children*,—Jerusha, born February 12, 1796, died March 1, 1796. Eliza, born April 4, 1797, married Asher Robbins, Esq., of Wethersfield. Edward, born February 19, 1799, married Sarah Mc Grath, of York, Penn., where he resides. He is a lawyer. Jerusha, born April 2, 1802.

Children,—by his second wife,—none.

89.

PIERPONT EDWARDS, of New Haven, Conn., was married to Frances Ogden, second daughter of Moses Ogden, of Elizabethtown, N. J., May, 1769.

Mrs. Frances Edwards died at New Haven, July 7, 1800, in the 51st year of her age.

Hon. Pierpont Edwards died at Bridgeport, Conn., April 5, 1826, aged 76 years—wanting 3 days.

Children.

207 Susan, born December 24, 1771. Married Samuel W. Johnson, Esq., of Stratford, Conn.

208 John
Starke, born August, 1777. Married a daughter of Governeur Morris. After his death, she was married to General M'Clure. Col. John Starke Edwards, Esq., died at Huron, O., February 22, 1813, after an illness of five days, aged 35.

209 Henry
Waggerman, born October, 1779. Married Lydia Miller, daughter of John and Lydia Miller. *Children*,—John Miller, Henry Pierpont, Alfred H. P., Frances Ogden, Henry Whiting.

210 Ogden, born August, 1781. Married Harriet Penfield.

211 Alfred
Pierpont, born September, 1784. Married Deborah Glover.

212 Henrietta
Frances, born June, 1786. Married Eli Whitney, Esq., of the City of New Haven. Conn., the celebrated inventor of the cotton gin. He was born at Westborough, Mass., December 8, 1765, and died January 8, 1825. For inventive power and a persevering spirit which never relinquished an undertaking until it was accomplished, Mr. Whitney had scarcely a parallel. His name will be ranked with the names of Fulton, Arkwright and Watt. *Children*,—Frances Edwards, married Charles L. Cheplain, of Cunbridge, Maryland,

December 1, 1842. Elizabeth Fay.
Eli, married Sarah P. Dallibie, of
Utica, N. Y., June, 1845.

118.

MARY EDWARDS was married to George Goodwin, of Hartford, Conn., December 2, 1779.

Mrs. Mary Goodwin died July 24, 1828, in the 69th year of her age.

George Goodwin, Esq., died May 13, 1844, aged 87.

Children.

213 Elizabeth,	born September	2, 1781.	Died October, 1826.
214 Richard E.,	born December	9, 1782.	Died February, 18, 1838.
215 Oliver,	born October	10, 1784.	Died August 14, 1855.
216 George,	born April	23, 1786.	
217 Jason,	born January	18, 1788.	Died in childhood.
218 Jason,	born January	22, 1789.	Died in childhood.
219 Charles,	born January	13, 1791.	
220 Henry,	born November	16, 1793.	
221 Jeremiah,	born January	3, 1795.	Died in childhood.
222 Jason,	born August	13, 1796.	Died May 1, 1823.
223 Edward,	born December	7, 1800.	

[For other particulars respecting the Edwards Family, *see* Appendix.]

WILLIAM GOODRICH,

ONE OF THE

FIRST SETTLERS OF WETHERSFIELD, CONN.

ENSIGN WILLIAM GOODRICH, one of the first settlers* of Wethersfield, Conn., was married to Sarah Marvin, of Hartford, Conn., October 4, 1648, at Hartford. [After his death, she was married to Capt. William Curtis, Esq., of Stratford, Conn., son of John Curtis, one of the first settlers of that town, by whom she had no children. She was his second wife. Capt. William Curtis, Esq., died December 21, 1702.]

Ensign William Goodrich died 1676, aged —.

Mrs. Sarah Goodrich, alias Curtis, died at Stratford, near the close of the year 1702. She left a will, which is dated October 21, 1697, and was exhibited into, and approved by the Court of Probate, January 7, 1702-3.

FIRST GENERATION.

Children of Ensign William Goodrich, and Sarah, his wife.

I. William,	born August	8, 1649.	Died in childhood.
II. John,	born May	20, 1653.	
III. Elizabeth,	born	1658.	
IV. William,	born February	8, 1661.	
V. Ephraim,	born June	2, 1663.	
VI. David,	born May	4, 1667.	
VII. Sarah,	born		
VIII. Mary,	born		
IX. Abigail,	born		

* On coming into New-England, the first settlers of Wethersfield, (among whom were William Goodrich and his brother John Goodrich,) located themselves at Watertown, Mass., with a view of making that place their permanent residence. In a "Record of the Grants and the Possessions of the Lands" in that town we find recorded to William Goodrich, six several tracts of Land, viz:

" 1. An homstall of 5 acres.
2. Three acres of remote meadow.
3. Ten acres and half of upland beyond the further plain.
4. Twenty-five acres of upland in the fourth division.
5. Three acres of plow-land on the further plain.
6. One acre of meadow at Beaver Brook."

In or about the year 1636, the Watertown Company, or the largest portion of them, including the brothers Goodrich, removed from Watertown to Wethersfield, Conn., and there planted themselves anew, and in the distribution of the town among the settlers, William Goodrich had assigned to him several lots.

It is not known from what part of England the Goodrich brothers emigrated. Enquirers on this point may derive aid from the following facts, viz:

DESCENDANTS IN THE LINE OF JOHN GOODRICH, SON OF WILLIAM GOODRICH, THE SETTLER.

SECOND GENERATION.

II.

JOHN GOODRICH, of Wethersfield, Conn., was married to Rebecca Allen, daughter of Capt. John Allen, of Charlestown, Mass., mariner,* March 28, 1678, at Charlestown, by Mr. Danforth.

Children.

10 Sarah,	born April 10, 1679.	Was married to Abraham Kilbourn, of Wethersfield, October 26, 1699. He died March 9, 1713, aged 38. She died ———. *Children,*—Samuel,· born January 25, 1701. Sarah, born May 6, 1702. Abraham, born April 12, 1708.
11 Rebecca,	born November 11, 1680.	Was married to David Wright, of Wethersfield, December 28, 1699. [After her death Mr. Wright was married to Mary Belden, daughter of Lieut. Jonathan Belden, of Wethersfield, June 8, 1710. She died January 9, 1769, in the 88th year of her age.] *Children* of David and Rebecca Wright, Anna, born December 19, 1700. Mrs. Rebecca Wright died April 10, 1703, aged 22. David, born April 10, 1703. Mr. David Wright died September 6, 1752.
12 Mary,	born September 4, 1682.	Was married to Thomas Curtis, of Wethersfield, December 30, 1703. [After i her death, Mr. Curtis was married to Rachel Morgan, daughter of John Morgan, of Groton, Conn., March 17, 1715.] Mrs. Mary Curtis died ———. Mr. Thomas Curtis died ———. *Child* of Thomas and Mary Curtis, one only is recorded

In 1678, there died in Hedgesset, Suffolk county, England, childless, Rev. William Goodrich, a minister of the established Church, leaving a will, in which he bequeathed certain specified real and personal estate to his wife, Rebecca Goodrich, during her natural life, with remainder to one of the sons of his brother, John Goodrich, and one of the sons of his brother, William Goodrich, naming them.

Mrs. Rebecca Goodrich, widow of Rev. William Goodrich, died in November, 1698, and was buried on the 18th day of the same month, after which Jonathan Goodrich and John Goodrich, the former son of said John, and the latter son of said William Goodrich, were entitled to receive, and did, I believe, receive under the will aforesaid, about two hundred pounds sterling, each. Soon after the death of his aunt, Jonathan Goodrich took steps to possess himself of his devised estate.

Rev. William Goodrich's will is dated May 12, 1677. In it he appoints his wife Rebecca, sole executor, and his "kinsman," Henry Bull, senior, of Bury, in the county of Suffolk, and his "cousin," John Goodrich, eldest son now living of his "cousin," Robert Goodrich, of Haughley, overseers of the same.

I suppose Rev. William Goodrich, married a sister of John and William Goodrich, brothers, and hence entitles them his brothers.

In a letter written by said Henry Bull, of Bury, to John Goodrich, of Wethersfield, and dated July 16, 1678, to inform him of the death of Rev. William Goodrich, the writer says, "My wife, who was Jane Coates, and is your cousin, desires to be kindly remembered to you."

* Capt. Allen had but two children, both daughters, Rebecca and Elizabeth. The latter was married to Nathaniel Blagrove, of Bristol, in the county of Bristol, Mass.

13 Samuel, born May 24, 1684.

14 Abigail, born April 27, 1686.

15 John, born June 9, 1688.

16 Allen, born November 13, 1690.

17 Ann, born September 1, 1692.

18 Jacob, born [no date.]

to them on Wethersfield Records, viz., Rebecca, born April 28, 1705.

Died May 7, 1706, aged near 22.

Was married to David Curtis, of Wethersfield, April 25, 1706. *Children*, recorded to them on Wethersfield Records,—Allen, born May 18, 1708. Anna, born July 18, 1710.

Was married to Mary Tillotson, formerly of Saybrook, Conn., June 15, 1712, supposed daughter of John Tillotson, of that town. She died May 31, 1740. He died ———. *Children*, recorded to them on Wethersfield Records,—Samuel, born July 26, 1713, and died in July, 1714. Abraham, born November 3, 1715. Mary, born May 20, 1718.

Was married to Elizabeth Goodrich, daughter of Capt. David Goodrich, of Wethersfield, December 29, 1709. He settled in Wethersfield, but afterward removed to Farmington. She died at Farmington, August 25, 1726. *Children*, recorded to them on Wethersfield Records,—Elizabeth, born October 19, 1710. Elisha, born September 22, 1712. After the death of Elizabeth, his wife, he was married to ———, by whom he had children. Abigail, born December 13, 1714. Jedediah, born July 24, 1717. Samuel, born April 23, 1720. Allen, born August 18, 1726, recorded in Farmington.

Was married to Benedict Goodwin, daughter of Nathaniel Goodwin, of Hartford, Conn., September 12, 1717. He died 1746, at Windsor, Conn. *Children*, recorded to them on Wethersfield Records,—Hannah born August 31, 1719. Rebecca, born April 14, 1721. Elijah, born July 3, 1724. Settled in Windsor, Conn. Married Margaret Gillett, of Windsor, August 20, 1752. Nine children are recorded to them on Windsor Records. Ruth, born 1727. Stephen, born January 21, 1731. Married Rachel Gillett, of Windsor, Conn., where he settled, January 3, 1754. He died in August, 1758, leaving one child, Jacob, born February 5, 1755, and perhaps another. Sarah, born October 31, 1733.

DESCENDANTS IN THE LINE OF ELIZABETH GOODRICH, DAUGHTER OF WILLIAM GOODRICH, THE SETTLER.

SECOND GENERATION.

III.

ELIZABETH GOODRICH, was married to Capt. Robert Welles, of Wethersfield, Conn., June 9, 1675, "by Capt. Welles, Commissioner." He was son of John Welles, of Stratford, Conn., and grandson of Thomas Welles, one of the first settlers of Hartford, Conn., and Wethersfield, and one of the early Governors of the Colony of Connecticut. [After her death, Capt. Welles was married to Mary ———, who survived him, by whom he had no issue. Mrs. Elizabeth Welles died February 17, 1698, aged about 40. Capt. Robert Welles died June 22, 1714, aged 66.

Children.

19 Thomas, born May, 1676. Settled in Wethersfield. Was twice married. 1. To Hannah Warner, daughter of Capt. William Warner, of Wethersfield, September 28, 1699. She died September 18, 1738, aged 60. 2. To Sarah Robbins, widow of Capt. Joshua Robbins, and daughter of ———, May 3, 1739. Capt. Thomas Welles died September 21, 1741, aged 65. Mrs. Sarah Welles, alias Robbins, died December 3, 1744, aged 62. *Children,*—by his first wife,—Thomas, born December 26, 1700, and died July 5, 1708, "being drowned in the great river." Elizabeth, born August 24, 1702. Thomas, born July 7, 1712.

20 John, born June, 1678.
21 Joseph, born September, 1680. Settled in Wethersfield. Was married to Hannah Robbins, daughter of Joshua Robbins, of Wethersfield, January 6, 1709.

22 Prudence, born Was married to Rev. Anthony Stoddard, second Pastor of the Congregational Church, at Woodbury, Conn., son of Rev. Solomon Stoddard, of Northampton, Mass. [After her death, Rev. Mr. Stoddard married Mary Sherman, January 31, 1720, by whom he had no issue. She died ———.] Mrs. Prudence Stoddard died May, 1714, aged —. Rev. Solomon Stoddard died September 6, 1760, aged 82. *Children,*— Mary, born June 19, 1702. Solomon, born October 12, 1703, and died " of the Great Fever," May 23, 1727. Eliakim, born April 3, 1705, married Joanna Curtis. Elisha, born November 24, 1706, married Rebecca Sherman. Israel, born August 7, 1708, and died May 30, 1727. John, born

March 2, 1710. Prudence, born October 12, 1711. Gideon, born May 27, 1714, married Olive Curtis, 1734. Esther, born October 11, 1716, married Preserved Strong. Abijah, born February 28, 1718, married Eunice Curtis, April 4, 1739. Elizabeth, born November 15, 1719, married Daniel Munn.

23 Robert, born Settled in Wethersfield. Was married to Sarah Wolcott, daughter of Samuel Wolcott, of Wethersfield, and of Judith, his wife, daughter of the Worshipful Samuel Appleton, of Ipswich, Mass., December 12, 1706. *Children,*—Sarah, born February 1, 1709. Married to Jonathan Robbins, of Wethersfield, November 21, 1728. Robert, born September 7, 1710. Settled in Newington Parish, Wethersfield, where he died February 3, 1786, aged 76. Appleton, born February 4, 1712. Abigail, born October 9, 1715. Elizabeth, born March 18, 1717. Mary, born June 3, 1719. Josiah, born March 9, 1721. Christopher, born May 29, 1724. Hezekiah, born December 9, 1725. Martha, born August 29, 1729. Judith, born March 4, 1731.

24 Gideon, born 1692. Settled in Wethersfield. Was married to Hannah Chester, daughter of Major John Chester, of Wethersfield, November 30, 1716. Gideon Welles, Esq., died March 28, 1740, aged 48. His widow, Mrs. Hannah Welles, died May 29, 1749, aged 53. *Children,*—Chester, born October 8, 1718. Solomon, born October 6, 1721. Eunice, born December 23, 1725. Gideon, born May 26, 1735. He was the great grandfather of Gen. Leonard R. Welles, of Wethersfield, Conn., late warden of the State Prison of Connecticut.

DESCENDANTS IN THE LINE OF WILLIAM GOODRICH, SON OF WILLIAM GOODRICH, THE SETTLER.

SECOND GENERATION.

IV.

WILLIAM GOODRICH, of Wethersfield, Conn., was twice married. 1. To Grace Riley, daughter of —— Riley, of Wethersfield, November 22, 1680. She died October 23, 1712, aged 51. 2. To Mary Ann Ayrault, widow of Doct. Nicholas Ayrault, of Wethersfield, deceased. [Doct. Ayrault died March 4, 1706, "aged 50. His age not exactly found." Wethersfield Records. He left 3 children,—Esther, born March 5, 1699. Peter, born December 4, 1702. Nicholas, born October 2, 1705.]
Lieut. William Goodrich died 1737, aged 76.

10

Mrs. Mary Ann Goodrich, alias Ayrault, died August 27, 1741, in the 60th year of her age.

Children,—by his first wife.

25 William,	born August	3, 1681.	Died November 16, 1681.
26 William,	born July	2, 1686.	Settled in Litchfield, Conn., but subsequently removed to Sharon, in the same State.
27 Benjamin,	born September 29, 1688.		Settled in Wethersfield. Was married to Grace Kilbourn, daughter of Ebenezer Kilbourn, of Glastenbury, Conn., March 7, 1716. He died May 11, 1742, aged 54. His grave is in Newington Society burying ground. She died November 26, 1764, aged 71. His estate distributed January 10, 1751, to his wife Grace, and children, Benjamin, Ebenezer, Timothy, who settled in Farmington, Daniel, Waitstill, who dwelt in Woodbury, Conn., in 1760, and Sarah, who died, unmarried, in 1758.
28 Joseph,	born February 29, 1691.		Settled in Wethersfield. Was married to Mehitabel Goodwin, daughter of Nathaniel Goodwin, of Hartford, Conn., December 23, 1714. Lieut. Joseph Goodrich died January 31, 1768, in the 77th year of his age.
29 Isaac,	born August 18, 1693.		Settled in Wethersfield. Was married to Mary Butler, daughter of Samuel Butler, of Southold, L. I., formerly of Wethersfield, November 9, 1718. He died in December, 1737.
30 Ann,	born March 25, 1697.		Was married to Robert Powell, of Wethersfield, February 3, 1717. He died De——. She died December 28, 1783, aged 86. They had several children.
31 Ephraim,	born September 12, 1699.		Settled in Wethersfield. Was married to Susannah Hooker, daughter of Doct. Daniel Hooker, of Wethersfield, Conn., October 25, 1726. He died in 1728.
32 Ethan,	born June 3, 1702.		He is supposed to have died in early life, as he is not mentioned in the Court proceedings on the settlement of his father's estate.

Children,—by his second wife.

33 Elizabeth,	born
34 Lucenia,	born
35 Eunice,	born

DESCENDANTS IN THE LINE OF EPHRAIM GOODRICH, SON OF WILLIAM GOODRICH, THE SETTLER.

SECOND GENERATION.

V.

EPHRAIM GOODRICH, of Wethersfield, Conn., was twice married. 1. To Sarah Treat, daughter of Richard Treat, Esq., of Wethersfield, May 20, 1684, by Samuel Talcott, Commissioner.

She died January 26, 1712, in the 48th year of her age. 2. To Jerusha Welles, widow of Capt. Thomas Welles, of Wethersfield, deceased, and daughter of Capt. James Treat, of the same town, December 25, 1712, by Capt. Robert Welles, Justice.

Capt. Ephraim Goodrich died February 27, 1739, aged 76.

Mrs. Jerusha Goodrich, alias Welles, died January 15, 1754, in the 76th year of her age.

Children,—by his first wife.

36 Richard,	born February 27, 1685.	Settled in Glastenbury, Conn., but by deed from him to Thomas Welles, of Glastenbury, dated in 1725, it appears that he was then residing in Middletown, Conn., (probably in Middletown, Upper Houses, so called.) Was married to Hannah Bulckley, daughter of Doct. Charles Bulckley, of New London, Conn., son of Rev. Gershom Bulckley, May 18, 1709. She died September 23, 1720, aged 30. *Children,*—Ann, born March 6, 1710. Richard, born July 13, 1712, and died September 1, 1714. Sarah, born July 6, 1715. Gershom, born May 5, 1717. Richard, born July 23, 1719.
37 Sarah,	born	1698.	Married Richard Butler, of Wethersfield, Rocky Hill, December 15, 1725. He died October 27, 1757, aged —. She died May 6, 1795, in the 98th year of her age.
38 Ephraim,	born		Settled in Glastenbury, Conn. Was married to Hannah Steele, daughter of James Steele, of Wethersfield, and of Ann, his wife, daughter of Capt. Samuel Welles, of that town, July 10, 1715. She was born March 18, 1697. *Children,* recorded to them on Glastenbury Records,— Abigail, born July 10, 1716. James, born January 21, 1718. Charles, born November 9, 1720. Ephraim, born December 9, 1722. Hannah, born May 16, 1725.
39 William,	born	1701.	Settled in Glastenbury, Conn. Was married to Rachel Savage, daughter of Capt. Thomas Savage, of ———, April 4, 1728. She died September 20, 1787, aged 84. He died December 16, 1787, aged 86. *Children,* recorded to them on Glastenbury Records,—William, born January 20, 1729. Stephen, born May 2, 1732. Elisha, born May 27, 1734. Jehiel and Jemima, twins, born September 16, 1741. Mary, born November 18, 1745.
40 David,	born	1705.	Settled in Glastenbury. Was married to Sarah Edwards, daughter of ——— Edwards, February 13, 1729. He died June 7, 1779, in the 74th year

of his age.* She died May 11, 1799, in the 80th year of her age. *Children*, recorded to them on Glastenbury Records,—John, born June 16, 1730. David, born May 22, 1732. Wait, born February 8, 1736. Lucy, born February 24, 1738. Rhoda, born December 17, 1739. Isaac, born May 2, 1743. Elizur, born August 8, 1745. Sarah, born June 20, 1747. Honor, born April 8, 1749. George, born August 13, 1751. Prudence, born April 14, 1754.

41 Thomas, born Settled in Glastenbury. Was married to Hannah Reynolds, daughter of John Reynolds, of Wethersfield, November 26, 1719.

42 Gideon, born Settled at Wethersfield, Rocky Hill, where he resided some time, and then removed to Middletown, Upper Houses. He was married to Sarah ———, June 29, 1718. *Children*, recorded to them on Wethersfield Rocky Hill Church Records,—Elijah, bap. 1726. Lois, bap. April 13, 1728. Caleb, bap. September 5, 1731. Ebenezer, bap. March 18, 1733. Eunice, bap. April 6, 1735. Joshua, bap. May 21, 1738. Wait, bap. January 20, 1740. Levi, bap. June 10, 1750.

Children,—by his second wife.

43 Oliver, born September 14, 1714. Settled in Wethersfield, Rocky Hill. Was married to Temperance Wright, daughter of ——— Wright, of Wethersfield, June 26, 1740. He died September 23, 1780, in the 66th year of his age. She died October 4, 1803, in the 80th year of her age. *Children*, recorded to them on Rocky Hill Church Records,—Roger, born October 18, 1741. Sarah, born July 31, 1743. Prudence, born August 11, 1745. Temperance, born October 11, 1747. Oliver, born October 8, 1749. Milletta, born November 3, 1751. Millescent, born September 29, 1754. Pollicena, born May 15, 1757. Ezekiel, born April 22, 1759. Lucretia, born May 8, 1761.

44 Gurdon, born December 29, 1717. Settled in Wethersfield, Rocky Hill. Was married to Abigail Belden, daughter of ——— Belden, of Wethersfield, June 7, 1739. She died February 22, 1787, in the 66th year of her age. He died ———. *Children*, recorded to them on Rocky Hill Church Records,—Gurdon, born August 31, 1740, and died October 2, 1741. Jerusha, born July 26, 1741. Experience, born September 25, 1743, and died July 24, 1746. Gur-

---

* Deacon David Goodrich, who, on the 7th of June, 1779, at his evening prayer, fell down in an instant, and never saw to make any motion after,—being in the 74th year of his age. [Gravestone.]

don, born January 12, 1745. Elizabeth, born August 16, 1747. Abigail,
born November 12, 1749. Ephraim,
born January 26, 1752. Jemima,
born April 7, 1754. Elizur, born
September 10, 1756. Ichabod, born
September 10, 1758.

DESCENDANTS IN THE LINE OF DAVID GOODRICH, SON OF WILLIAM GOODRICH, THE SETTLER.

SECOND GENERATION.

VI.

DAVID GOODRICH, of Wethersfield, Conn., was twice married.
1. To Hannah Wright, daughter of Thomas Wright, of Wethersfield, March 7, 1689. She was born March 10, 1671, and died
April 27, 1698, aged 28, nearly. 2. To Prudence Churchill,
daughter of Benjamin Churchill, of Wethersfield, December 1,
1698. She was born July 2, 1678.

Mrs. Prudence Goodrich died May 9, 1752, in the 74th year of
her age.

Col. David Goodrich died January 23, 1755, in the 88th year
of his age. He was a Lieut. Colonel in the Old French War.

Children,—by his first wife.

45 Josiah,	born June	15, 1690.	Settled in Wethersfield, but subsequently removed to Tolland, Conn. He was twice married. 1. To Sarah Porter, daughter of Samuel Porter, Esq., of Hadley, Mass., December 5, 1711. She died at Wethersfield, July, 1726, aged 34. 2. To Sarah Mix, daughter of Rev. Stephen Mix, of Wethersfield, about 1727. Josiah Goodrich, Esq., died at Tolland, in 1731, aged 41. His widow, Mrs. Sarah Goodrich, died at Wethersfield, 1748. *Children*, by his first wife,— Josiah, born August 22, 1717. Aaron, born 1719. Samuel, born 1721, and died. *Children*, by his second wife,— John, born 1728. David, born 1729.
46 Elizabeth,	born November	19, 1691.	Married to Allen Goodrich, son of John Goodrich, all of Wethersfield, December 29, 1709. He afterward removed to Farmington, Conn., where she died August 25, 1746, aged 55.
47 Elizur,	born March	30, 1693.	Settled in Wethersfield. Was married to Anna Talcott, daughter of Cornet Samuel Talcott, of Wethersfield, April 22, 1714. Col. Elizur Goodrich died April 4, 1774, aged 81. His widow, Mrs. Anna Goodrich, died January 3, 1776, aged 83.
48 David,	born December	8, 1694.	
49 Abigail,	born April	2, 1697.	Died September 23, 1712.

Children,—by his second wife.

50 Hezekiah, born January 28, 1700. Settled in Wethersfield. Was married to Honor Deming, daughter of Samuel Deming, deceased, of Wethersfield, October 16, 1729. He died 1732. After his death, she was married to Dr. Thomas Perrin, of Wethersfield, July 5, 1733. *Children* of Hezekiah Goodrich, and of Honor, his wife,—Elizur, born 1730. Honor, born 1732, was twice married. 1. To Charles Whiting, of Norwich, Conn., May 18, 1749, by whom she had 6 children,—and after his death, 2. To Rev. Joshua Belden, of Wethersfield, Newington Society, November 14, 1774. She was his second wife. Anna, his first wife, died October 29, 1773, in her 47th year. Mrs. Honor Belden, alias Whiting, died August 21, 1801, in her 70th year. Rev. Joshua Belden died July 23, 1813, aged 89. *Child*, by her second husband, one only,—Hezekiah, born February 17, 1778, died March 22, 1849, being, at the time of his death, Clerk of the Town of Wethersfield.

51 Prudence, born June 18, 1701. Married David Hubbard, Esq., of Eastbury Society, Glastenbury, and after his death, Judah Holcomb, Esq. David Hubbard, Esq., died October 13, 1760, in the 63d year of his age. Mrs. Prudence Hubbard, alias Holcomb, died November 29, 1783, in the 83d year of her age. By this marriage, David Hubbard, Esq., had a number of children, among them, Elizur Hubbard, born in 1736, married Lois Wright, daughter of James Wright, of Wethersfield. She died September 15, 1794, aged 49. After her death he was married to Huldah ———. She died April 26, 1807, aged 55. Capt. Elizur Hubbard died September 14, 1818, aged 82. By his first wife, Capt. Hubbard had several children, among them, David E. Hubbard, bap. March 15, 1778, and married to Pamelia Hollister, daughter of Elisha and Penelope Hollister, of Glastenbury, October 6, 1799. She was baptized April 26, 1781.

52 Sarah, born March 12, 1703.
53 Mary, born December 15, 1704.
54 Hannah, born August 2, 1707.
55 Jeremiah, born September 9, 1709. Settled in Wethersfield. Was married to Ruth Kimberly, daughter of Thomas Kimberly, Esq., of Glastenbury, July 6, 1732.

56 Ann, born February 14, 1712.
57 Zebulon, born November 22, 1713.
58 Benjamin, born November 13, 1715.
59 Abigail, born January 18, 1718.
60 Charles, born August 7, 1720. Settled in Wethersfield. Married

61 Millescent, born January 23, 1723.

Mary ———, (supposed Mary Belden, daughter of Samuel Belden.) Died 1752, leaving children,—David, born 1746. Abigail, born 1748. Dorcas, born 1750. Mary, born May, 1742.

THIRD GENERATION.

48.

DAVID GOODRICH, of Wethersfield, Conn., Rocky Hill Society, was married to Hepzibah Boardman, daughter of Ensign Jonathan Boardman, deceased, of Wethersfield, and of Mary, his wife, daughter of John Hubbard, of Hatfield, Mass., December 21, 1721. She was born February 16, 1702.

Deacon David Goodrich died July 15, 1785, in the 91st year of his age, 46 years a deacon. [Gravestone, Rocky Hill buryingground.]

His widow, Mrs. Hepzibah Goodrich, died December 9, 1785, in the 84th year of her age. [Gravestone, Rocky Hill buryingground.]

Children.

62 Abigail,	born October	11, 1722.	Died November 10, 1723.
63 David,	born September	2, 1724.	
64 Alpheus,	born March	4, 1727.	
65 Josiah,	born May	5, 1731.	
66 Hezekiah,	born April	9, 1733.	Died November 21, 1788.
67 Elizur,	born October	18, 1734.	
68 Hepzibah,	born January	19, 1737.	
69 Abigail,	born March	8, 1739.	
70 Mercy,	born June	17, 1741.	
71 Hannah,	born August	29, 1743.	

50.

HEZEKIAH BELDEN, of Wethersfield, Conn., was married to Honor Deming, daughter of Samuel Deming, deceased, of Wethersfield, October 16, 1729. [After his death, she was married to Doct. Thomas Perrin, of Wethersfield, July 5, 1733. He died ———.]
Mr. Hezekiah Goodrich, died ———.
Mrs. Honor Goodrich, alias Perrin, died ———.

Children.

72 Elizur,	born	1730.
73 Honor,	born	1732.

DESCENDANTS IN THE LINE OF SARAH GOODRICH, DAUGHTER OF WILLIAM GOODRICH, THE SETTLER.

SECOND GENERATION.

VII.

SARAH GOODRICH was married to John Hollister, Jun., of that part of ancient Wethersfield, Conn., now called Glastenbury, son of John Hollister, one of the first settlers of Wethersfield, November 20, 1667. Mrs. Sarah Hollister died about 1700. Sergeant John Hollister died November 24, 1711.

Children.

74 John, born August 9, 1669. Settled in Glastenbury. Was twice married. 1. To his cousin, Ahiah Hollister, daughter of Lieut. Thomas Hollister, of Wethersfield, 1693. She died August 28, 1717, aged 47. 2. To Susannah ——, of Wethersfield. Mr. John Hollister died December 13, 1741, in the 73d year of his age. Mrs. Susannah Hollister died ——. *Children,*—by his first wife,—Benjamin, born February 5, 1694. Jeremiah, born October 21, 1696. Sarah, born January 6, 1699. Abigail, born August 11, 1701, and died November 17, 1712. Abraham, born May 5, 1705. Prudence, born March 3, 1707. Mehitabel, born February 4, 1709, and died December, 1728. Martha, born March 20, 1712. Abigail, born January 26, 1713. Elizabeth, born December 5, 1715, and died February 19, 1737. *Children,*—by his second wife,—none.

75 Thomas, born January 14, 1672. Settled in Glastenbury. Was married to Dorathy Hill, daughter of Joseph Hill, of Glastenbury, 1696. Mrs. Dorathy Hollister died October 5, 1741, in the 64th year of her age. Mr. Thomas Hollister died October 12, 1741, in the 70th year of his age. *Children,*—Josiah, born June 7, 1696. Dorathy, born October 17, 1697. Gideon, born September 23, 1699. Charles, born July 26, 1701. Elizabeth, born December 17, 1703. Hannah, born December 26, 1705, and died October 12, 1712. Thomas, born January 13, 1707. Ruth, born October 13, 1710. Rachel, born July 27, 1712. Hannah, born February 16, 1714.

76 Joseph, born July 8, 1674. Settled in Glastenbury. Was married to Ann ——, November 27, 1694. Mrs. Ann Hollister died October 5, 1712, in the 34th year of her age. Mr. Joseph Hollister died July 9, 1746, in the 72d year of his age. *Children,*—Joseph, born December

26, 1696. Was married to Mary White, daughter of Joseph White, of Middletown, Conn., December 28, 1721. He died October 8, 1746. William, born July 8, 1699, and died in early life. Mary, born August 29, 1704, was married to Joseph Shelton, of Stratford, Conn. Ann, born January 16, 1707, was married to Ebenezer White, of Middletown, Conn. Esther, born August 28, 1709, was married to Thaddeus Shelton, of Stratford, Conn., October 17, 1733.

77 Sarah, born October 25, 1676. Was married to Benjamin Talcott, of Glastenbury, January 5, 1699. She died October 15, 1715, aged 39, nearly. Deacon Benjamin Talcott died November 12, 1727, aged 53.—*Children*,—Sarah, born October 30, 1699, and died October 15, 1715. Benjamin, born June 27, 1702. John, born December 17, 1704. Hannah, born October 16, 1706. Samuel, born February 12, 1708. Elizur, born December 31, 1709. Mehitabel, born July 17, 1713. Abigail, born October 10, 1715, and died October 28, 1715.

78 Elizabeth, born March 30, 1678. Was married to Doct. Joseph Steele, of Kensington Society, Berlin, Conn., February 16, 1715. He died ———, 1750, leaving surviving, his wife and ten children,—five sons and five daughters.

79 David, born November 21, 1681. Settled in Glastenbury. Mr. David Hollister, died December 27, 1753, in the 76th year of his age. His widow, Mrs. Charity Hollister, died January 12, 1786, in the 89th year of her age. *Children*,—Six, named in his will.

80 Ephraim, born March 15, 1684. Settled in Glastenbury. Was married to Elizabeth Greene, daughter of Tobias Greene, of ———, April 1, 1707. He died ———, 1733. She died ———. *Children*,—recorded to them on Glastenbury Records,— Ephraim, born January 1, 1708, and died January 5, 1708. Elizabeth, born February 23, 1710.

81 Charles. born July 29, 1686. Probably died young.

DESCENDANTS IN THE LINE OF MARY GOODRICH, DAUGHTER OF WILLIAM GOODRICH, THE SETTLER.

SECOND GENERATION.

VIII.

MARY GOODRICH was married to Joseph Butler, of Wethersfield, Conn., about 1667.

Mr. Joseph Butler died December 10, 1732, in the 85th year of his age.

His widow, Mrs. Mary Butler, died June 1, 1735.

11

Children,—named in his will.

82 Richard,   born   1667. Settled at Rocky Hill, in Wethersfield.
                                          Married Sarah Goodrich, daughter
                                          of Ephraim Goodrich, of Wethers-
                                          field, December 15, 1725. He died
                                          October 27, 1757, aged —. She died
                                          May 6, 1795, in the 98th year of her
                                          age. *Children,*—Sarah, born Feb.
                                          20, 1727. Joseph, born December
                                          20, 1729. Charles, born July 19,
                                          1732. Sarah married a Grimes, of
                                          Simsbury, Conn.

83 Gershom,   born about   1683. Settled in Middletown, Conn. Mar-
                                          ried Mary Deming, daughter of Jon-
                                          athan Deming, of Wethersfield, 1719.
                                          He died May 21, 1765, aged 81. She
                                          died April 22, 1771, aged 79. *Chil-
                                          dren,*—David, born May 14, 1720.
                                          Anna, born February 7, 1722. Mele,
                                          born March 3, 1724. Gideon, born
                                          May 29, 1727. George, born June
                                          19, 1730. Gershom, born February
                                          24, 1737.

84 Charles,   born about   1686. Settled in Wethersfield, or Middletown.
                                          Was married to Susanna Williams,
                                          daughter of Amos Williams, de-
                                          ceased, of Wethersfield, May 17, 1704.
                                          " He died on the 25th of September,
                                          1711, being in the Queen's service.
                                          Died at Milford, as he was coming
                                          home." *Children,*—Mary, born Feb-
                                          ruary 25, 1706. Bathsheba, born
                                          September 21, 1709. Charles, born
                                          March 11, 1712, "and died on the
                                          last day of April, or the 1st of May,
                                          1713, being about fourteen months
                                          old." [Wethersfield Records.]

85 Benjamin,   born about   1673. Settled in Middletown. Married to
                                          Thankful Sage, daughter of John
                                          Sage, of Middletown, December 5,
                                          1734. She was born February 9,
                                          1717. *Children,*—Mary, born Sep-
                                          tember 7, 1735. Lucia, born Sep-
                                          tember 21, 1736. Comfort, born
                                          January 23, 1738. Eli, born May
                                          26, 1740. Joseph, born August 26,
                                          1742. Martha, born August 21, 1744.
                                          Hannah, born June 26, 1746. Chloe,
                                          born October 2, 1747. Grace, born
                                          January 30, 1749.

86 Joseph,   born about   1675. Settled in Middletown. Married to
                                          Patience Horton, daughter of Benoni
                                          and Mary Horton, of Middletown,
                                          August, 1738. She was born April
                                          15, 1700. After his death, she was
                                          married to a Crossman. Mr. Joseph
                                          Butler died in 1740. *Children,* re-
                                          corded to him on Wethersfield Re-
                                          cords. Son, born March 23, 1739,
                                          died March 25, 1739. Mary, born
                                          September 3, 1740. Haughton D.,
                                          born June 30, 1743.

87 Mary,   born about   1677.

DESCENDANTS IN THE LINE OF ABIGAIL GOODRICH, DAUGHTER OF WILLIAM GOODRICH, THE SETTLER.

SECOND GENERATION.

IX.

ABIGAIL GOODRICH was married to Thomas Fitch, of Wethersfield, Conn., —— —— 1680. [After her death, he was married to Sarah Boardman, daughter of Samuel Boardman, of Wethersfield, by whom he had four children. Thomas Fitch was born in 1652, and was son of Mr. Samuel Fitch, of Hartford, Conn., many years an instructor of youth in that town, and of Susannah his wife, widow of the Worshipful William Whiting, one of the first settlers of Hartford. Mr. Samuel Fitch died in 1659, and she was again married in 1663, to Hon. Alexander Bryan, of Milford, Conn., being his second wife. She died at Middletown, Conn., July 8, 1673, at the house of her son-in-law, Rev. Nathaniel Collins, minister of that town.]

Mrs. Abigail Fitch, died November 7, 1684, aged ——.

Mr. Thomas Fitch died October 17, 1704, aged 52.

Children.

88 Thomas,	born July	20, 1681.	Died in early life.
89 Sibbil,	born November	2, 1684.	Died December 18, 1684.

[For other particulars relating to the Goodrich Family, *see* Appendix GOODRICH Family.]

JOHN GOODRICH,

BROTHER OF WILLIAM GOODRICH.

JOHN GOODRICH, of Wethersfield, Conn., was twice married. 1. To Elizabeth Edwards, daughter of Thomas Edwards, of Wethersfield, 1645. She died in child-bed, July 5, 1670. 2. To Mary Stoddard, widow of John Stoddard, late of Wethersfield, deceased, and daughter of Nathaniel Foote, one of the first settlers of that town, 1674. [After his death, she was married to Lieut. Thomas Tracy, of Norwich, in the same State.] Mr. John Goodrich died in April, 1680. Mrs. Mary Goodrich, alias Stoddard, alias Tracy, died ———.

FIRST GENERATION.

Children,—by his first wife.

I. Elizabeth,	born November 2, 1645.	Married Daniel Rose, of Wethersfield, 1664.
II. John,	born September 8, 1647.	Settled in Wethersfield. Married Mary ———. He died in May, 1676, leaving surviving wife, Mary, and daughter, Mary, born April 23, 1676.
III. Mary,	born December 15, 1650.	Was married about 1677, to Thomas Read, Jun., of Sudbury, Mass. For the names and times of birth of their children, see Sudbury Records.
IV. Joseph,	born January 10, 1653.	Went to Sudbury, Mass., and there died in October, 1680, without children, leaving a will, which is recorded in Middlesex County Probate records, in which he devises his estate to his brothers and sisters.
V. Jonathan,	born	Settled in Wethersfield. Was married to Abigail Crafts, daughter of Moses Crafts, of Wethersfield, December 3, 1691. *Children,*—Jonathan, born February 1, 1692–3. Abigail, born November 28, 1694. Married to Samuel Wright, son of Samuel Wright, of Wethersfield, January 2, 1717–18. Moses, born July 19, 1697. Lucy, born September 9, 1699. Married Daniel Fuller, of Wethersfield, August 7, 1723. Rebecca, born December 24, 1701.
VI. Hannah,	born	Was married to Zechariah Maynard, of Sudbury, Mass., about 1679, and after the death of Mr. Maynard, to Isaac Heath, of Framingham, Mass.

Children,—by her first husband,—
Zechariah, John, Daniel, Joseph,
Moses, Elizabeth, who married
Thomas Walker, of Sudbury, Hannah, who married Nathaniel Harsey,
of Sudbury, Abigail, who married
Jonathan Blodd, of Concord, Mass.,
and Mary, who married Benjamin
Treadway, of Framingham.

Children,—*by his second wife,*—*none.*

WILLIAM GURLEY,

FIRST SETTLERS OF NORTHAMPTON, MASS.

FIRST GENERATION.

WILLIAM GURLEY,* of Northampton, Mass, was married to Hester Ingersoll, daughter of John Ingersoll, of Westfield, Mass., formerly of Hartford, Conn., and Northampton, Mass., 1684. [After his death, she was married to Benoni Jones, of Northampton, January 23, 1689, by whom she had four children, viz: Jonathan, born January 4, 1695, and died young. Benjamin, born 1696, settled in Coventry, Conn. Ebenezer, born November 12, 1698. Jonathan, born March 3, 1703; the two last, together with their father, were slain by the enemy, at Poscummuck, north end of Mount Tom, Northampton, May 13, 1704.]

Mr. William Gurley died by drowning, May 1, 1687.

Mrs. Hester Gurley, alias Jones, was captured by the enemy, at the time her Jones husband and children were slain, and carried to Canada, and there died, after being tormented by the Catholic priests who were trying to convert her.

SECOND GENERATION.

Child of William Gurley and Hester his wife,—one only.

I. Samuel, born May 6, 1686.

DESCENDANTS IN THE LINE OF SAMUEL GURLEY, SON OF WILLIAM GURLEY.

THIRD GENERATION.

I.

SAMUEL GURLEY, of North-Coventry, Conn., afterwards of Mansfield, in the same State, was married to Experience Rust,

---

* William Gurley, the first of the name, was brought into New England from Scotland; as he said,—probably from Edinburgh. He was born in the year 1665, but left no record by which we are able to satisfy ourselves concerning his parents or relations. He was brought up in the family of the Rev. Mr. Solomon Stoddard, of Northampton. He died at the age of 22 years, having been accidentally drowned in Connecticut river, leaving an only child, a son, about one week old. He is reputed to have been truly pious, and a sincere follower of Jesus Christ. *Manuscript relating to the Gurley Family.*

daughter of Nathaniel Rust, of North-Coventry, formerly of North-ampton, Mass., and Mary, his wife, who was Mary Atchison, of Hatfield, Mass., about 1712. She was born in November, 1693. Nathaniel Rust was son of Israel Rust, of Northampton, and Re-becca, his wife, daughter of William Clark, of the same town.

Mr. Samuel Gurley died February 23, 1760, in the 74th year of his age. [Gravestone, Gurley burying-ground, North Mansfield.] " He was distinguished for piety, and was eminently useful in the cause of religion and humanity."

His widow, Mrs. Experience Gurley, died July 10, 1768, in the 74th year of her age. [Gravestone, Gurley burying-ground.]

Children.

2 Esther,	born February	24, 1713.	
3 Jonathan,	born April	2, 1715.	
4 Samuel,	born June	30, 1717.	
5 Lois,	born January	17, 1720.	
6 Eunice,	born June	14, 1722.	Married a Marsh, who settled in Vermont. Have no other reliable information respecting her.
7 Experience,	born January	16, 1725.	
8 Margaret,	born May	4, 1727.	Died April 12, 1737, in her 10th year.
9 Mary, }			Died January 1, 1746, in her 17th year.
10 Daugh- } twins.	born March	7, 1729.	
ter, }			Died soon after birth.
11 Abigail,	born June	30, 1731.	Said to have married a Williams, who settled in Vermont.

FOURTH GENERATION.

2.

ESTHER GURLEY was married to John Storrs, of Mansfield, Conn, January 2, 1735. [After her death, he was married to Mary Chaplin, of Pomfret, Conn., who, after his death, was married to Joseph Denny, of Mansfield, March 14, 1750, by whom he had one child, only, a son, Nathaniel, born in 1751.]

Mrs. Esther Storrs died March 15, 1746, in her 33d year. [Gravestone, South Mansfield burying-ground.]

John Storrs, Esq., died October 6, 1753, aged 51. [Gravestone, North Mansfield burying-ground.]

Children.

12 John,	born December	1, 1735.
13 Son,	born August	2, 1738. Died August 17, 1738.
14 Lydia,	born August	18, 1742.

3.

JONATHAN GURLEY, of Mansfield, Conn., was married to Han-nah Baker, daughter of Joseph Baker, of Tolland, in the same State, August 4, 1737. She was born April 9, 1709.

Deacon Jonathan Gurley, died November 12, 1778, in the 64th year of his age. [Gravestone, Gurley burying-ground, Mansfield.]

His widow, Mrs. Hannah Gurley, died May 16, 1796, in the 88th year of her age. [Gravestone, Gurley burying-ground.]

Children.

15 William,	born June	4, 1738.	
16 Hannah,	born August	9, 1740.	Married Lot Dimock, of Mansfield, afterwards of Coventry, Conn. She died September 7, 1774. He died in 1792.
17 Jacob Baker,	born July	28, 1742.	
18 Jonathan,	born April	10, 1744.	
19 Daniel,	born November	2, 1745.	
20 Ebenezer,	born May	25, 1747.	
21 Esther,	born June	16, 1749.	Married Eliphalet Carpenter, Jun. Dwelt in Coventry. She died in October, 1819, leaving a large family.
22 Titus,	born May	15, 1752.	

4.

SAMUEL GURLEY, of Mansfield, Conn., was thrice married. 1. To Hannah Baker, daughter of Daniel Baker, of Tolland, Conn., June 16, 1742. She died April 19, 1756, in her 39th year. 2. To Hannah Walker, of Union, in the same State, August 31, 1757. She died May 9, 1782, in her 54th year. 3. To Susannah Curtis, widow of Samuel Curtis, deceased, of Mansfield, and daughter of ———— Bosworth, of the same town.

Capt. Samuel Gurley died November 14, 1796, in his 80th year. Mrs. Susannah Gurley, alias Curtis, died February 15, 1810, aged 87.

Children,—by his first wife.

23 Zebulon,	born July	12, 1743.	
24 Sarah,	born August	27, 1744.	Married Deacon Oliver Dimock, of Mansfield, April, 1764. [After her death, Deacon Dimock was married to Mrs. Lucy Dimock, September 17, 1792. She died January 5, 1820, aged 69.] Mrs. Sarah Dimock died July 22, 1790, aged 46, nearly. Deacon Oliver Dimock died February 10, 1823, aged 84.
25 Israel,	born December	20, 1745.	
26 Mary,	born September	19, 1747.	Died March 2, 1812, unmarried. [Gravestone, Gurley burying-ground.]
27 John,	born February	8, 1749.	
28 Phineas,	born March	30, 1751.	
29 Eunice,	born January	1, 1752.	Died December 28, 1776, in her 25th year, unmarried. [Gravestone, Gurley burying-ground.]
30 Samuel,	born June	27, 1754.	Died August 28, 1778, in his 25th year, "he being a member of Yale College." [Gravestone, Gurley burying-ground, Mansfield.]
31 Zenas,	born [no date.]		

Children,—by his second wife.

32 Hannah,	born August,	6, 1758.	Married Nathan Dexter, of Mansfield, June 6, 1785. She died February 16, 1803.
33 Nahum,	born March	23, 1761.	Died October 14, 1776. [Gravestone, Gurley burying-ground.]
34 Lois,	born March	10, 1763.	Married Abraham Oakes, of Whitestown, N. Y., January 31, 1793.

35 Margaret, born [no date.]   Married Timothy White, of Coventry,
                                         Conn., November 11, 1790.

Children,—by his third wife,—none.

5.

LOIS GURLEY was married to Nathaniel Southworth, of Mansfield, son of Nathaniel Southworth, of that town, December 31,
1741.
Mrs. Lois Southworth died November 4, 1754, aged 34.
Mr. Nathaniel Southworth died in June, 1790.

Children.

36 Nathaniel, born November 26, 1742.
37 Samuel,   born November 22, 1744.
38 Lois,   born December 25, 1746.
39 Lydia,   born December 17, 1748.
40 Eunice,   born August   11, 1751.

7.

EXPERIENCE GURLEY was married to Joseph Storrs, Esq., of
Mansfield, Conn., ———— 1743, being his second wife. [His first
wife, Hannah, to whom he was married May 1, 1735, died August
28, 1741. By her he had one child only, a daughter, Hannah, who
was born April 3, 1736.]
Mrs. Experience Storrs died June 9, 1767, in her 43d year.
[Gravestone, North Mansfield burying-ground.]
Joseph Storrs, Esq., died October 5, 1783, in his 74th year.
[Gravestone, North Mansfield burying-ground.]

Children.

41 Eunice,   born November 30, 1744.
42 Mary,   born August   23, 1746.
43 Hannah,   born March   2, 1749.
44 Experience, born March   17, 1751.
45 Joseph,   born March   6, 1753.
46 Cordial,   born
47 William,   born
48 Augustus,   born
49 Royal,   born

FIFTH GENERATION.

15.

WILLIAM GURLEY, of Mansfield, Conn., was thrice married.
1. To Betty Field, daughter of Bennet Field, of the same town,
September 22, 1763. She was born in Lebanon, Conn., August 10,
1747, and died November 16, 1776, aged 39. 2. To Ruby West,
of Tolland, Conn., August 5, 1779. She died October 5, 1781,
in her 33d year. 3. To Sibbil Chapin, of Somers, Conn., May
2, 1782.
Mr. William Gurley died August 16, 1804, aged 66.
His widow, Mrs. Sibbil Gurley, died March 15, 1823, aged 77.

12

Children—by his first wife.

50 William,	born October	24, 1764.	Died July 30, 1768.
51 Bennet,	born January	23, 1767.	
52 William,	born May	24, 1769.	
53 Betty,	born September	10, 1771.	Married Mr. Howland, of Bridgewater, N. Y.
54 Experience,	born April	26, 1774.	Married Mr. Blakeman, of Bridgewater, N. Y.

Child,—by his second wife,—one only.

55 Ichabod,	born April	30, 1780.	Died March 26, 1814. Administration on his estate granted April 27, 1814, to Hannah, his widow.

Children,—by his third wife.

56 Gideon Chapin,	born May	1, 1783.	
57 Jesse,	born May	1, 1785.	
58 Son, (not named,)	born September	4, 1787.	Died September 6, 1787.

17.

JACOB BAKER GURLEY, of Mansfield, Conn., was married to Hannah Brigham, daughter of Uriah Brigham, of Coventry, in the same State, May 19, 1766. She was born April 9, 1746.

Mr. Jacob B. Gurley died of small pox, February 20, 1804, aged 62.

His widow, Mrs. Hannah Gurley, died April 6, 1813, in her 67th year.

Children.

59 Lydia,	born June	6, 1767.	Married Benjamin Pierce, of Brooklyn, Conn., December 24, 1786. She died August 12, 1787.
60 Artemas,	born April	9, 1769.	
61 Jacob Baker,	born August	2, 1771.	
62 Uriah,	born May	30, 1774.	Died October 4, 1775.
63 Ebenezer,	born July	25, 1776.	Lives in Mansfield. Married Sarah Balcom, daughter of Joseph Balcom, of that town.
64 Abigail,	born February	7, 1778.	Married to Elijah Hinckley, of Cambridge, Ver., January 29, 1799.
65 Uriah Brigham,	born November	19, 1780.	Died October, 1783.
66 Mercia,	born March	24, 1782.	Died December, 1783.
67 Lucia,	born November	14, 1784.	Lives in Mansfield, with her sister, Mrs. Turner.
68 Hannah,	born May	5, 1791.	Married Anson Turner, of Mansfield, Conn., April 22, 1814. They have had eight children.

18.

JONATHAN GURLEY, of Mansfield, Conn., was married to Jerusha Bennet, daughter of Joseph Bennet, of that town, May 17, 1764.

Capt. Johnathan Gurley died November 23, 1814, in his 71st year.

His widow, Mrs. Jerusha Gurley, died January 20, 1835, aged 91.

Children.

69 Ephraim,	born February	12, 1765.

Ephraim Gurley died September 2, 1845, aged 80. Bethiah Brooks, his wife, died May 23, 1844, aged 77. Their children were as follows : Clarissa. Ephraim, died February 7, 1829. Olive, died October 19, 1827. Marcia, now Mrs. Dunham. Lucius. Chauncey. Sophia, now Mrs. Winchester. Esther, died April, 1830. Maria, now Mrs. Barrows.

70 Roger,	born September 13, 1766.	
71 Jonathan,	born September 20, 1768.	
72 Anna,	born October	16, 1770.

Married Abner Abbot, of West Stockbridge, Mass., November 24, 1791. She died in September, 1823. Eight children.

73 Jerusha,	born November	18, 1772.

Married Ichabod Griggs, of Tolland, Conn., 1792. Five children.

74 Esther,	born April	29, 1775.

Married Isaac Hall, of Bridgewater, N. Y., January 25, 1798. She died October 25, 1803.

75 Olive,	born August	6, 1777.

Married Levi Goodell, of Mansfield. Seven children.

76 Rebecca,	born April	9, 1780.

Married Capt. Allen Stewart, of Hartford, Conn., April 18, 1797. He died September 12, 1849, aged 73. Six children.

77 Flavel,	born October	25, 1782.
78 Son,	born	Died in infancy.
79 Harriet	born June	10, 1790.

Married Jacob Dunham, of Mansfield, afterwards of Portland.

19.

DANIEL GURLEY, of Mansfield, Conn., was twice married. 1. To Elizabeth Ellis, daughter of ——— Ellis, of Norwich, Conn., March 12, 1769. She died November 2, 1807, aged 61. 2. To Mary Tinney, of Mansfield, January 1, 1811.
Mrs. Mary Gurley died July 16, 1813, aged 55.
Mr. Daniel Gurley died ———.

Children,—by his first wife.

80 Alice,	born June	30, 1771.
81 Daniel,	born April	22, 1773.
82 Rial,	born August	13, 1775.
83 Nahum,	born September 13, 1777.	
84 Child, (not named,)	born August	16, 1787. Died in infancy.
85 Child,	born	1788. Died March 22, 1792.

20.

EBENEZER GURLEY, of Mansfield, Conn., was married to Desire Dimock, daughter of Capt. Timothy Dimock, of the same town.
Rev. Ebenezer Gurley died July 17, 1776, aged 29.
His widow, Mrs. Desire Gurley, died August 1, 1830, aged —.

Child,—one only.

86 Child, (name not ascertained.)   Died in Portland, M.

22.

TITUS GURLEY, of Mansfield, Conn., was married to Anna Dimock, daughter of Capt. Timothy Dimock, of the same town, June 4, 1772.

Mr. Titus Gurley died in October, 1783.

His widow, Mrs. Anna Gurley, died ———.

Children,—none.

23.

ZEBULON GURLEY, of Mansfield, Conn., was twice married. 1. To Sarah Field, daughter of Bennet Field, of the same town, May 22, 1766. She died January 1, 1793, in her 49th year. 2. To Mary ———.

Mr. Zebulon Gurley died January 13, 1800, in his 58th year.

Mrs. Mary Gurley died ———.

Children,—by his first wife.

87 Zebulon,	born June	23, 1767.	
88 Sarah,	born January	11, 1769.	
89 Elizabeth,	born May	1, 1770.	Died August 12, 1793. [Gravestone, Gurley burying-ground.]
90 Hannah,	born December	22, 1771.	
91 Eunice,	born October	25, 1773.	Married Samuel Badcock, January 31, 1793.
92 Israel,	born January	18, 1776.	Married Roxalana Fitch, June 26, 1803.
93 Samuel,	born April	20, 1778.	Married Eunice Dimock, October 17, 1802.
94 Matilda,	born February	27, 1780.	Supposed to have died before her father, as she is not mentioned in his will.
95 Anson,	born May	11, 1782.	
96 Martha, } twins.	born September	8, 1784.	
97 Mary, }			

25.

ISRAEL GURLEY, of Mansfield, Conn, was married to Eunice ———. [After his death, she was married to Elihu Marvin, Esq., of Hebron, Conn.]

Mr. Israel Gurley died in January, 1777, aged 32.

Mrs. Eunice Gurley, alias Marvin, died ———.

Children.

98 Timothy,	born	1772. Settled in Mansfield. Married Eunice ———. He died October 19, 1801, in his 29th year. She died September 18, 1845, aged 75. Polly, their daughter, died November 1, 1846, aged 48.
99 Eunice,		
100 Desire,		

27.

REV. JOHN GURLEY, of Lebanon, Conn., first Pastor of the Congregational Church in Exeter Society in that town, was mar-

ried to Mary Hosford, widow of Doct. Joel Hosford, of Marlborough, Conn., and daughter of Deacon Pelatiah Porter, of Hebron, in the same State. Doct. Hosford died November 15, 1773,
in the 29th year of his age. [After the death of Rev. Mr. Gurley,
she was married to General Absalom Peters, of Lebanon, in the
same State, about 1827. He died in the city of New York, March
29, 1840, in the 86th year of his age. His remains were interred
in the Episcopal church-yard at Hebron, and a monument erected
at his grave, by his son, John R. Peters, Esq., of the city of New
York.]

Rev. John Gurley died February 27, 1812, aged 63, and in the
37th of his ministry. [Gravestone, Exeter burying-ground.]

Mrs. Mary Gurley, alias Hosford, alias Peters, died April 27,
1837, aged 80. [Gravestone, Exeter burying-ground.]

Children.

101 John Ward, born	John Ward Gurley married Grace Stackpole,—had one daughter who married Major Grafton, of Boston, who has a large family. J. W. G. was Attorney-General of Louisiana. Died in 1807.
102 Mary, born	Mary Gurley was married to Rev. Dr. Gillet, of Hallowell, Me. They have a large family.
103 Henry Hos-ford, born	Henry H. Gurley married Eliza Goodwin, of Portland. They had eight children, all living in 1840. He was a member of Congress, and a Judge in Louisiana. He and his wife have been dead some years,—buried at Baton Rouge. Left 7 children.
104 Austin, born	Austin Gurley died at Fayettville, N. C., 1820, of bilious fever.
105 Ralph Randolph, born May 26, 1797.	Ralph R. Gurley married Eliza M. Gurley, daughter of Royal Gurley, of Portland, Me., and resides in Washington City, D. C. Two of six children are living.
106 John Addison, born	John Addison Gurley lived in New York. Is deceased. Has one child.
107 Abby Porter, born	Abby Porter Gurley married Rev. Onamel Hinckley, late Professor in Oakland College, Miss. Died of yellow fever at Natchez, about 1840. Mrs. Hinckley is still living at Washington City, D. C. Had no children.

28.

PHINEAS GURLEY, of Mansfield, Conn., was married to ———
Swift, daughter of ——— Swift, of ———. Mr. Gurley subsequently removed from Mansfield to St. Lawrence, N. Y.

Mr. Phineas Gurley died ———.

His widow, Mrs. ——— Gurley, died ———.

Children.

108 Juliana,
109 Phineas,   Father of Rev. Dr. Phineas D. Gurley,
                                 recently settled at Washington City,
                                 D. C.
110 Susannah,
111 John Clark,
112 Joshua,
113 Lucinda, }
114 Clarinda, }

31.

ZENAS GURLEY, of Mansfield, Conn, was twice married. 1.
To Lavinia Dimock, daughter of ———— Dimock, of the same
town, April 9, 1789. She died December 7, 1791, aged 22. 2.
To Experience Hovey, daughter of Joseph Hovey, of Mansfield.
Mr. Zenas Gurley died ————.
His widow, Mrs. Experience Gurley, died ————.

Child,—by his first wife,—one only.

115 Samuel,   born June   30, 1790.

Children,—by his second wife.

116 Henry,   born   Married, and has children. Dwells in
                             Bridgewater, Ver.
117 Lavinia,   born   Married, and has children. Dwells in
                             Bridgewater, Ver.

SIXTH GENERATION.

56.

ARTEMAS GURLEY, of Mansfield, Conn., was twice married.
1. To Sarah Steele, daughter of John Steele, of Tolland, Conn.,
March 29, 1792. She died January 16, 1804, aged 35. 2. To
Patty Hovey, widow of Elisha Hovey, deceased, of Mansfield,
and daughter of Jesse Shepard, of Plainfield, Conn., March 24,
1805.
Artemas Gurley, Esq., died suddenly, May 18, 1822, in the 53d
year of his age. [Gravestone, Gurley burying-ground.]
His widow, Mrs. Patty Gurley, died at Paluski, N. Y., January
4, 1848, in the 72d year of her age.

Children,—by his first wife.

118 Lovina,   born October   2, 1794. Married ———— Storrs, February 12,
                                        1815.
119 Sarah,   born November 7, 1796.
120 Abigail,   born March   21, 1799.
121 Uriah
    Brigham, born September 27, 1801.

Children,—by his second wife.

122 Artemas
    Shepard, born July   31, 1807. Died February 28, 1808.
123 George,   born April   6, 1809. Married, 1. Sarah Melissa Dimmick,
                                        of Mansfield, April 22, 1835. She
                                        died April 12, 1841, aged 26. 2. So-
                                        phia Dimmick, daughter of Rode-
                                        rick Dimmick, of Mansfield, Octo-
                                        ber, 1841.

124 Charles Ar-
    temas,   born May   8, 1811.
125 Mary,   born June   24, 1813.   Died October 16, 1815.

57.

JACOB BAKER GURLEY, Esq., of New London, Conn., was married to Elizabeth Griswold, daughter of Deacon John Griswold, of Blackhall, Lyme, Conn., March 28, 1802. Both Mr. and Mrs. Gurley are (1854) living.

Children.

126 Charles,   born April   19, 1803.   Died October 1, 1805.
127 Sarah
    Griswold, born November 26, 1804.   Married Joseph Noyes, of Lyme, May
                                  14, 1823. She died March 21, 1835.
                                  He died April 10, 1836. They had 5
                                  children, and a number of grand
                                  children.
128 Mary
    Brainard, born September 11, 1806.   Died May 9, 1849.
129 Charles,   born June   4, 1808.   Died July 4, 1828.
130 Elizabeth,   born May   20, 1810.   Died December 19, 1829.
131 Ursula
    Wolcott,   born May   13, 1812.   Died August 28, 1828.
132 Hannah
    Brigham, born April   10, 1814.   Died February 2, 1831.
133 John Gris-
    wold,   born January   27, 1816.   Died July 1, 1830.
134 Ellen,   born December 25, 1817.   Married Charles Artemas Gurley, son
                                    of Artemas Gurley, Esq., deceased,
                                  of Mansfield, Conn., October 22,
                                  1851.
135 Lydia Ann, born March   31, 1819.   Died November 5, 1820.
136 Ann,   born November 27, 1823.

65.

EPHRAIM GURLEY, of Mansfield, Conn., was married to Bethia Brooks, daughter of ——— Brooks, of ———, March 20, 1788. Mrs. Bethia Gurley died May 23, 1844, aged 77. [Gravestone, North Mansfield burying-ground.] Mr. Ephraim Gurley died September 2, 1845, aged 80. [Gravestone, North Mansfield burying-ground.]

Children.

137 Clarissa,   born
138 Ephraim,   born   Died February 7, 1829, at Troy, N. Y.
139 Olive,   born   Died October 19, 1827.
140 Marcia,   born   Now Mrs. Dunham.
141 Lucius,   born
142 Chauncey, born
143 Sophia,   born   Now Mrs. Winchester.
144 Esther,   born   Died April, 1830.
145 Maria,   born   Now Mrs. Barrows.

66.

ROGER GURLEY, of Mansfield, Conn., was married to Pamela Bicknell, daughter of Moses Bicknell, of the same town, March 22, 1792.

Capt. Roger Gurley died October 27, 1836, aged 70. [Grave-stone, North Mansfield burying-ground.]

His widow, Mrs. Pamela Bicknell, died February 9, 1842, aged 69. [Gravestone, North Mansfield burying-ground.]

Children.

146 Jonathan, born March   1, 1793. Married Phila Allen, daughter of Capt.
                                        Simeon Allen. She died April 11,
                                        1825, and he married Mary P. Dun-
                                        ham, daughter of Seth Dunham, of
                                        Mansfield, October 26, 1825.

147 Pamela,   born July   31, 1794. Married Samuel Storrs Dimock, Feb-
                                        ruary 17, 1716.

148 Josephus, born March   26, 1796. Married, 1. Dorathy Farwell, of Mans-
                                        field, October 2, 1719. She died
                                        March 14, 1823. 2. Cornelia Royce,
                                        March, 1825. He died January 24,
                                        1837. By his first wife, 2 children,
                                        and by his last, 4 or more.

149 Almira,   born October   10, 1797. Married Joseph Woodward, May 6,
                                        1829.

150 Orvilla,   born August   19, 1800. Died July 22, 1822.
151 Sally,   born May   28, 1802. Married Orra Carpenter, September
                                        24, 1838.

152 Harriet,   born August   11, 1804. Married Charles Lyon, September 23,
                                        1829.

153 Julia,   born January   20, 1807. Married, 1. Marcus Cossett, April 25,
                                        1828. He died August 16, 1830. 2.
                                        Lorenzo T. Skinner, of Vernon,
                                        Oneida Co., N. Y.

154 Moses
    Bicknell, born December 13, 1809. Was drowned July 1, 1830.
155 Daughter,
    (not named,) born June 22, 1811. Died in infancy.
156 Louisa,   born October 1, 1812. Died October 28, 1822.
157 Harrison, born January 14, 1814. Residence, Hartford, Conn. Married
                                        Isabella Milakin Hamilton, daughter
                                        of James Hamilton, of Canaan Four
                                        Corners, September 10, 1846.

67.

JONATHAN GURLEY, of Coventry, Conn., was married to Abigail Rose, of the same town, 1790.

Mr. Jonathan Gurley died December 5, 1791, aged 23.

His widow, Mrs. Abigail Gurley, ———.

Child,—one only.

158 Electa,   born   1791, " Died at the age of 20 months."

JOHN HOLLISTER.

JOHN HOLLISTER, one of the first settlers of Wethersfield, Conn., was married to Joanna Treat, daughter of Richard Treat, who, likewise, was one of the first settlers of Wethersfield.

Mr. John Hollister died in April, 1665.

His widow, Mrs. Joanna Hollister, died in October, 1694.

DESCENDANTS OF JOHN HOLLISTER.

FIRST GENERATION.

The children of the above named John Hollister, and of Joanna, his wife.

I. Mary,	born	
II. John,	born	
III. Thomas,	born	
IV. Joseph,	born	Died unmarried, 1673.
V. Lazarus,	born about 1656.	Died unmarried, in September, 1709.
VI. Stephen,	born	
VII. Elizabeth,	born	
VIII. Sarah,	born	

DESCENDANTS IN THE LINE OF MARY HOLLISTER, DAUGHTER OF JOHN HOLLISTER, THE SETTLER.

SECOND GENERATION.

1.

MARY HOLLISTER was married to John Welles, of Stratford, Conn., son of John Welles, of that town, and grandson of Thomas Welles, of Wethersfield, one of the first settlers of that town and Hartford, Conn., and one of the early governors of the colony of Connecticut.

Mr. John Welles died March 24, 1714.

His widow, Mrs. Mary Welles, died ———.

Children.

9 Mary,	born		
10 Thomas,	born		
11 Sarah,	born January	2,	1674.
12 John,	born		1676.
13 Comfort,	born		
14 Joseph,	born June	21,	1679.
15 Elizabeth,	born		
16 Robert,	born September,		1688.

13

DESCENDANTS IN THE LINE OF JOHN HOLLISTER, SON
OF JOHN HOLLISTER, THE SETTLER.

SECOND GENERATION.

2.

JOHN HOLLISTER, of Wethersfield, Conn., was married to Sarah
Goodrich, daughter of Ensign William Goodrich, one of the first
settlers of Wethersfield, November 20, 1667.
Mrs. Sarah Hollister died about 1700.
Mr. John Hollister died November 24, 1711.

Children.

17 John,   born August   9, 1669.
18 Thomas,   born January   14, 1672.
19 Joseph,   born July   8, 1674.
20 Sarah,   born October   25, 1676.
21 Elizabeth, born March   30, 1678.   Died in childhood.
22 David,   born November 21, 1681.
23 Ephraim,   born March   15, 1684.
24 Charles,   born July   29, 1686.
25 Elizabeth, born [no date.]

THIRD GENERATION.

17.

JOHN HOLLISTER, of Glastenbury, Conn., was twice married.
1. To his cousin, Abiah Hollister, daughter of Lieut. Thomas Hollister, of Wethersfield, Conn., 1693. She died August 28, 1719,
aged 47. 2. To Susannah ———.
Mr. John Hollister died December 13, 1741, in the 73d year of
his age.
Mrs. Susannah Hollister died ———.

Children,—by his first wife.

26 Benjamin,   born February   5, 1694.   Married Ruth Hale, daughter of Thomas
                                          Hale, of Glastenbury. He settled on
                                          the Oblong, in Duchess county, N. Y.

27 Jeremiah,   born October   21, 1696.
28 Sarah,   born January   6, 1699.   Married a Judd.
29 Abigail,   born August   11, 1701. Died November 17, 1712.
30 Abraham,   born May   5, 1705.   Supposed to have married Sarah Hub-
                                          bard, daughter of John Hubbard.

31 Prudence,   born March   3, 1707.   Married a Miller.
32 Mehitabel, born February   4, 1709.   Died December, 1728.
33 Martha,   born March   20, 1712. Married John Hubbard, Jr., of Glasten-
                                          bury, July, 1732. He was great-
                                          grandfather of the Hon. David E.
                                          Hubbard, of Glastenbury.

34 Abigail,   born January   26, 1713. Married Benjamin Loveland, of Glas-
                                          tenbury.

35 Elizabeth, born December   5, 1715.   Died February 19, 1737.

Children,—by his second wife.

36 Susannah,   born [no date.]   Married to Benoni House, of Glasten-
                                          bury, May 4, 1741.

18.

THOMAS HOLLISTER, of Glastenbury, Conn., was married to Dorathy Hill, daughter of Joseph Hill, of Glastenbury, 1696.

Mrs. Dorathy Hollister died October 5, 1741, in the 64th year of her age.

Mr. Thomas Hollister died October 12, 1741, in the 70th year of his age.

Children.

37 Josiah,	born June	7, 1696.	Married Martha ʼMiller, daughter of William Miller, of Glastenbury, January 18, 1718. He died January 3, 1749, in the 53d year of his age. She died July, 1777, in the 79th year of her age.
38 Dorathy,	born October	17, 1697.	Married Abram Fox, of Glastenbury, January 3, 1717.
39 Gideon,*	born September	23, 1699.	Settled in Eastbury Society, Glastenbury. Married and had children. He died February 15, 1785, in his 86th year. [Gravestone.] His widow, Mrs. Rachel Hollister, died June 13, 1790, aged 85.
40 Charles,	born July	26, 1701.	He settled in Eastbury Society, Glastenbury. Was married to Prudence Francis, daughter of John Francis, of Wethersfield, April 5, 1729. They had four children. He died February 2, 1753, aged 52.
41 Elizabeth,	born December	17, 1703.	Married William Miller, of Glastenbury, son of William Miller, of the same town, October 14, 1731, by whom she had six children. She was his second wife.
42 Hannah,	born December	26, 1705.	Died October 12, 1712.
43 Thomas,†	born January	13, 1707.	Married to Abigail Talcott, daughter of Deacon Nathaniel Talcott, of Glastenbury, about January 1, 1734. He settled in Eastbury Society, Glastenbury. Died September 17, 1784, in the 76th year of his age. His widow, Mrs. Abigail Hollister, died March 31, 1812, in the 95th year of her age.
44 Ruth,	born October	13, 1710.	Married Nehemiah Smith, of Hartford, Conn.
45 Rachel,	born July	27, 1712.	Married Joshua Talcott, of Bolton, Conn.
46 Hannah,	born February	16, 1714.	Married William House, of Glastenbury.
47 Eunice,	born		Married Thomas Loveland, of Glastenbury.
48 Susannah,	born		Married Benoni House, of Glastenbury.

* Gideon Hollister left a will, which is dated January 31, 1781, and recorded in vol. I.: page 45, of the Records of the Probate Court for the District of East Windsor, in which he names wife Rachel, and children, Gideon, Nathaniel, Israel, Mary Strickland, Rachel Holden, Jemima Brainard, Anna Howe, and Elizabeth Howe.

† Administration on the estate of Thomas Hollister was granted November 1, 1784, by the Probate Court for the District of East Windsor, and on the 20th of April, 1790, the estate of the deceased was ordered to be distributed to Abigail Hollister, widow of deceased, and to Thomas Hollister, Nehemiah Hollister, George Hollister, Aaron Hollister, Abigail, wife of Eleazur Hubbard, Dorathy Hudson, and Ruth, wife of Isaac Hills, children of the deceased.

49 Elisha,   born   1722. Was twice married. 1. To Experi-
                                    ence Robbins, daughter of Richard
                                    Robbins, of Wethersfield. She died
                                    July 7, 1765, aged 37. 2. To Penel-
                                    ope Graves, of Belchertown, Mass.
                                    He died November 12, 1800, in his
                                    78th year. She died in 1801. He
                                    had children by both wives. Pame-
                                    lia Hollister, daughter of Deacon
                                    Elisha Hollister, and Penelope, his
                                    wife, bap. April 26, 1778, was mar-
                                    ried to David E. Hubbard, Esq., of
                                    Eastbury Society, Glastenbury, Oc-
                                    tober 6, 1799.

19.

JOSEPH HOLLISTER, of Glastenbury, Conn., was twice married.
1. To Ann, daughter of ———, of ———, November 27, 1694.
She died October 5, 1712, in the 34th year of her age. 2. To
Sarah ———.
   Mr. Joseph Hollister died July 9, 1746, in the 72d year of his
age.
   Mrs. Sarah Hollister died ———.

Children,—by his first wife.

50 Joseph,   born December 28, 1696. Was married to Mary White, daughter
                                    of Joseph White, of Middletown,
                                    Conn., December 28, 1721. He died
                                    October 8, 1746, in the 50th year of
                                    his age.
51 William,   born July   8, 1699. Died 1733.
52 Timothy,   born [no date.]
53 Mary,   born August   25, 1704. Married Joseph Shelton, of Stratford,
                                    Conn.
54 Ann,   born January 16, 1707. Married Ebenezer White, of Middle-
                                    town, May 27, 1731. He died March
                                    26, 1756. They had eight children.
55 Esther,   born August   28, 1709. Married Thaddeus Shelton, of Strat-
                                    ford, October 17, 1733.

Children,—by his second wife,—none.

20.

SARAH HOLLISTER was married to Benjamin Talcott, of Glas-
tenbury, Conn., January 5, 1699.
   Mrs. Sarah Talcott, died October 15, 1715, aged 39 nearly.
   Deacon Benjamin Talcott died November 12, 1727, aged 53.

Children.

56 Sarah,   born October   30, 1699. Died October 15, 1715.
57 Benjamin,   born June   27, 1702.
58 John,   born December 17, 1704.
59 Hannah,   born October   16, 1706.
60 Samuel,   born February 12, 1708.
61 Elizur,   born December 31, 1709.
62 Mehitabel,   born July   17, 1713.
63 Abigail,   born October   10, 1715. Died October 28, 1715.

22.

DAVID HOLLISTER, of Glastenbury, Conn., was married to Charity ———, daughter of ———, of ———.

Mr. David Hollister died December 27, 1753, in the 76th year of his age.

His widow, Mrs. Charity Hollister, died January 12, 1786, in the 89th year of her age.

Children,—named in his will.

64 Jonathan,	born		
65 Jemima,	born	1712.	Died October 8, 1745, in her 23d year. [Gravestone.]
66 Tryon,	born		
67 Goodrich,	born		
68 Rebecca,	born		Married to Timothy Goslee, of Glastenbury, October 19, 1743.
69 Smith,	born		
70 Goodrich,	born		
71 Hollister,	born		Amos Hollister, son of Lieut. Jonah and Bathsheba, daughter of David Hollister, married April 27, 1749.
72 David,	born		

23.

EPHRAIM HOLLISTER, of Glastenbury, was married to Elizabeth Greene, daughter of Tobias Greene, of ———, April 1, 1707.

Mr. Ephraim Hollister died ———, 1733.

His widow, Mrs. Elizabeth Hollister, died ———.

Children.

73 Ephraim,	born January	1, 1708.	Died January 5, 1708.
74 Elizabeth,	born February	23, 1710.	
75 Ephraim,	born May,	1731.	

25.

ELIZABETH HOLLISTER was married to Doctor Joseph Steele, of Kensington Society, in that part of Farmington, Conn., now called Berlin, February 16, 1715.

Doctor Joseph Steele died 1750, aged 60.

His widow, Mrs. Elizabeth Steele, died ———.

Children.

76 Elizabeth,	born December	16, 1715.	
77 Sarah,	born July	17, 1717.	
78 James,	born May	18, 1719.	Died July 27, 1775, in his 55th year. [Gravestone, Kensington Ancient burying-ground.]
79 Abigail,	born January	5, 1721.	
80 Samuel,	born February	24, 1723.	
81 Anna,	born January	23, 1725.	
82 Ebenezer,	born May	18, 1727.	
83 Jonathan,	born [no date.]		
84 Elizur,	born [no date.]		Married Mary Roods, daughter of William Roods, of Wethersfield, November 17, 1765.
85 Lucy,	born [no date.]		

DESCENDANTS IN THE LINE OF THOMAS HOLLISTER, SON OF JOHN HOLLISTER, THE SETTLER.

THIRD GENERATION.

3.

THOMAS HOLLISTER, of Wethersfield, Conn., was twice married. 1. To Elizabeth Lattimer, daughter of John Lattimer, one of the first settlers of Wethersfield. She was born December 26, 1652, and died ———. 2. To Elizabeth Williams, widow of Amos Williams, deceased, of Wethersfield, about 1690. [Amos Williams died August 20, 1683, leaving surviving him, four children, viz., Amos, born 1670. Samuel, born 1675. Elizabeth, born 1677. Susannah, born 1680.]

Lieut. Thomas Hollister died November 8, 1701, aged —.

Mrs. Elizabeth Hollister, alias Williams, died ———.

Children,—by his first wife.*

86 Thomas,	born	1672.	
87 Jonathan,	born		Married Elizabeth ———. Died in 1712. *Children,*—Jonathan, Jacob, Stephen, born 1708, Elizabeth, and Mary.
88 Joseph,	born	1675.	
89 John,	born		Died in 1711, unmarried.
90 Mary,	born		
91 Sarah,	born		
92 Abiah, (or Abigail,)	born		
93 Stephen,	born September 30, 1681.	Died October 26, 1681.	

Children,—by his second wife,—none.

FOURTH GENERATION.

2.

JONATHAN HOLLISTER, of Stepney Parish, Wethersfield, Conn., was married to Elizabeth Williams, daughter of Amos Williams, deceased, of Wethersfield, September 22, 1698. She was born March 3, 1677.

Mr. Jonathan Hollister died 1714.

His widow, Mrs. Elizabeth Hollister, died ———.

Children.

94 Jonathan,	born		Estate distributed March 27, 1724.
95 Jacob,	born		
96 Stephen,	born	1708.	Guardian appointed November 3, 1724, at which time he was about sixteen years of age.
97 Elizabeth,	born		Married Samuel Goffe, of Wethersfield, Conn.

---

* There is no record of the names and times of birth of the children of Lieut. Thomas Hollister. The list here given is taken from probate proceedings in the settlement of his estate.

98 Mary,   born   Married Jonathan Lattimer, of Sims-
                     bury, Conn., December 5, 1734.

5.

MARY HOLLISTER was married to Walter Harris, of Wethersfield, Conn.

6.

SARAH HOLLISTER was married to John Williams, of Wethersfield, Conn., January 24, 1695.

Children,—on Wethersfield Records.

99 Mary,   born September 19, 1695.
100 Dorathy,   born February 25, 1698.

7.

ABIAH HOLLISTER was married to her cousin, John Hollister,
of Glastenbury, Conn., son of John Hollister, Jr., of that town,
1693.

Mrs. Abiah Hollister died August 28, 1719, aged 47.

Mr. John Hollister died December 13, 1741, in the 73d year of
his age.

Children.

101 Benjamin,   born February   5, 1694.
102 Jeremiah,   born October   21, 1696.
103 Sarah,   born January   6, 1699.
104 Abigail,   born August   11, 1701.   Died November 17, 1712.
105 Abraham,   born May   5, 1705.
106 Prudence,   born March   3, 1707.
107 Mehitabel, born February   4, 1709.   Died December, 1728.
108 Martha,   born March   20, 1712.
109 Abigail,   born January   26, 1713.
110 Elizabeth, born December   5, 1715.   Died February, 19, 1737.

DESCENDANTS IN THE LINE OF STEPHEN HOLLISTER, SON OF JOHN HOLLISTER, THE SETTLER.

THIRD GENERATION.

6.

STEPHEN HOLLISTER, of Wethersfield, Conn., was twice married. 1. To Abigail Treat, daughter of Matthias Treat, of Wethersfield, 1683. She was born in 1659, and died ———. 2. To
Elizabeth Reynolds, widow of Jonathan Reynolds, of Wethersfield,
deceased, and daughter of John Coleman, or Coltman, of the same
town. She was married to Jonathan Reynolds, of Wethersfield,
November 4, 1697.

Capt. Stephen Hollister died at Greenbush, near Albany, of
camp distemper, " about October 2, 1709."

Mrs. Elizabeth Hollister, alias Reynolds, died ———.

Children,—by his first wife.

111 Jerusha, born January   7, 1684. Died September 30, 1710, unmarried.
112 Stephen, born November 12, 1686. Died April 29, 1707.
113 Abigail, born August 16, 1688. Married Ebenezer Seymour, of Farmington, Conn., afterwards of Windsor, in the same state, December 29, 1709.
114 Ann, born March 16, 1690. Married Robert Boothe, of Stratford, Conn., November 27, 1712.
115 Gershom, born April 2, 1692. Settled in Farmington, Conn., where he died in 1750, leaving children,— Abel, who died before his father, childless, Thomas, Stephen, Gideon, and Esther, who married Elisha Boothe.
116 Samuel, born 1694. Settled in Farmington, Conn. John Curtis, Jr., appointed his guardian, April 3, 1710.
117 Eunice, born 1696. Ebenezer Deming, of Wethersfield, appointed her guardian, May 5, 1712.
118 Gideon, born 1698.
119 Daniel, born 1700. Ebenezer Seymour, of Farmington, appointed his guardian, March 1, 1720.
120 Nathaniel, born 1702. At a Probate Court, April 3, 1710, Thomas Welles appointed guardian of Nathaniel, son of the late Capt. Stephen Hollister, aged about 8. Settled in Farmington, Conn., but subsequently removed to New Fairfield, Conn., where we find him in 1744.

Child,—by his second wife, one only.

121 Stephen, born September 12, 1709. November 3, 1724, Samuel Goffe appointed his guardian, and March 1, 1726, Elizabeth Hollister, mother of the minor, appointed in place of Mr. Goffe.

FOURTH GENERATION.

3.

ABIGAIL HOLLISTER was married to Ebenezer Seymour, of Farmington, Conn., afterwards of Windsor, in the same state, December 29, 1709.

4.

ANN HOLLISTER was married to Robert Boothe, of Stratford, Conn., November 27, 1712.

5.

GERSHOM HOLLISTER, of Farmington, Conn., where we first find him in 1715.

Children.

122 Thomas, born May 5, 1726.
123 Stephen, born Angust 6, 1729.
124 Esther, born May 26, 1733.

6.

SAMUEL HOLLISTER, of Farmington, Conn., afterwards of
Sharon, in the same state.

Children.

125 Elisha,	born February	25, 1735.
126 Gershom,	born May	26, 1748.

10.

NATHANIEL HOLLISTER, first of Farmington, Conn., afterwards
of New Fairfield, in the same state, (where we find him in 1744.)

11.

STEPHEN HOLLISTER, first of Wethersfield, Conn., afterwards
of Farmington, in the same state.

DESCENDANTS IN THE LINE OF ELIZABETH HOLLISTER,
DAUGHTER OF JOHN HOLLISTER, THE SETTLER.

THIRD GENERATION.

ELIZABETH HOLLISTER was married to Samuel Welles, of that
part of Wethersfield, Conn., now called Glastenbury, son of Thomas
Welles, one of the first settlers of Hartford, Conn., and Wethersfield, and one of the early governors of the colony of Connecticut,
1659.   [After her death Mr. Welles was married to Hannah Lamberton, daughter of George Lamberton, of New Haven, Conn., who
after the death of Mr. Welles, was married to the " Hon. Lieut.
Col. John Allyn," of Hartford.   She was his second wife.   His first
wife was Mary Smith, daughter of Henry Smith, of Springfield,
Mass., and grand-daughter of Hon. William Pynchon, the principal
founder of that town.   Col. John Allyn died November 6, 1696.
Mrs. Hannah Allyn, alias Welles, died ———.]
Mrs. Elizabeth Welles died ———.
Hon. Samuel Welles died July 15, 1675.

Children.

127 Samuel,	born April	13, 1660.
128 Thomas,	born July	29, 1662.
129 Sarah,	born September	29, 1664.
130 Mary,	born November	23, 1666.
131 Ann,	born	1668.
132 Elizabeth,	born	1670.

14

DESCENDANTS IN THE LINE OF SARAH HOLLISTER,
DAUGHTER OF JOHN HOLLISTER, THE SETTLER.

THIRD GENERATION.

8.

SARAH HOLLISTER was twice married. 1. To Rev. Hope
Atherton, first minister of Hatfield, Mass., son of Major General
Humphrey Atherton, of Dorchester, Mass., 1674. He was born
in 1646, and died June 8, 1677, aged about 31. 2. To Lieut.
Timothy Baker, of Northampton, Mass., about 1679. She was his
second wife. His first wife, to whom he was married January 26,
1673, was Ruth Marsh. She died in 1676.
Mrs. Sarah Baker, alias Atherton, died December 8, 1691.
Lieut. Timothy Baker died August 30, 1729.

Children,—by her first husband.

| 133 Hope, 134 Joseph, | born January | 7, 1675. | Died young. Settled in Deerfield, Mass. Was twice married. 1. To Mary Taylor. She died in 1709. 2. To Mindwell Brown. By his first wife, he had two children, and by his last, six. The family seem to have lived in that part of Deerfield, now called Greenfield, where some of the descendants are living at the present time. |
| 135 Sarah, | born October | 26, 1676. | Was married to John Parsons, of Northampton. Mass., 1696, by whom she had ten children. |

Children,—by her second husband.

136 John,	born February	3, 1680.	Married and settled in Northampton. Had eight children, six sons and two daughters.
137 Thomas,	born May	14, 1682.	Was married to Christine Le Beau, widow of — Le Beau, of Canada, and daughter, by his third wife, of Richard Otis, of Dover, N. H. She was born in March, 1689. On the night of Thursday, the 27th of June, 1689, the dwelling-house of her father was attacked by the Indians, and himself shot as he was rising up in bed, and his son Stephen and daughter Hannah were killed, the latter, then two years old, by dashing her head against the chamber stairs. The wife and infant child of three months, (Christine Otis,) with others, twenty-nine in all, were carried captive to Canada, and sold to the French.
138 Edward,	born November	12, 1685.	Was married, and had several children, all daughters.
139 Prudence,	born May	14, 1687.	Was married to John Alvord.
140 Deliverance,	born November	13, 1689.	Died in 1710, at New Haven.

JOHN HOPKINS.

JOHN HOPKINS, of Hartford, Conn., and one of the first settlers of that town, was married to Jane ————.

After his death, she was married to Nathaniel Ward, of Hadley, Mass.

Mr. John Hopkins died in 1654.

Mrs. Jane Hopkins, alias Ward, died ————.

FIRST GENERATION.

Children of John Hopkins and Jane his wife.

I. Stephen,	born about	1634.
II. Bethia,	born about	1635.

DESCENDANTS IN THE LINE OF STEPHEN HOPKINS, SON OF JOHN HOPKINS, THE SETTLER.

SECOND GENERATION.

I.

STEPHEN HOPKINS, of Hartford, Conn., was married to Dorcas Bronson, daughter of John Bronson, of Farmington, in the same state.

Mr. Stephen Hopkins died October, 1689.

His widow, Mrs. Dorcas Hopkins, died May 13, 1697.

Children.

3 John,	born	
4 Stephen,	born	
5 Ebenezer,	born	Married Mary Butler.
6 Joseph,	born	
7 Dorcas,	born	Married Jonathan Webster.
8 Mary,	born	Married Samuel Sedgwick.

THIRD GENERATION.

3.

JOHN HOPKINS, of Waterbury, Conn., was married to Hannah ————, 1683.

Mrs. Hannah Hopkins died May 30, 1730.

Mr. John Hopkins died November 4, 1732.

Children.

9 Daughter,	born	1684.	Died January 4, 1684.
10 John,	born March	29, 1686.	Died December 5, 1709.
11 Consider,	born March	29, 1687.	

12 Stephen,	born November	19, 1689.	
13 Timothy,	born November	16, 1691.	
14 Samuel,	born December	27, 1693.	Yale College, 1718. Minister of West Springfield, Mass.
15 Mary,	born January	27, 1697.	
16 Hannah, } twins	born April	25, 1699.	
17 Child, }			Died June 13, 1699.
18 Dorcas,	born February	12, 1706.	

4.

STEPHEN HOPKINS, of Hartford, Conn., was twice married. 1. To Sarah Judd, daughter of Thomas Judd, of Waterbury, November 17, 1686. She died May 11, 1693, in her 28th year. 2. To Hannah Strong, daughter of John Strong, Jr., of Windsor, Conn. She was born August 11, 1660.

Mr. Stephen Hopkins died in October, 1702, aged —.

His widow, Mrs. Hannah Hopkins, died November, 1745, aged 86.

Children,—by his first wife.

19 Sarah,	bap. August	21, 1687.	
20 Rachel,	born	1689.	
21 Thomas,	born	1692.	

Children,—by his second wife.

22 Child, (not named,)	born	Died January 16, 1695.
23 Child, (not named,)	born	Died March 16, 1697.
24 Child, (not named,) Twin to last above.	born	Died March 16. 1697.

5.

EBENEZER HOPKINS, of Hartford, Conn., was married to Mary Butler, daughter of Deacon Samuel Butler, of Wethersfield, in the same state, January 21, 1691.

Mr. Ebenezer Hopkins died ———.

His widow, Mrs. Mary Hopkins, died ———.

Children.

25 Ebenezer,	bap. November	19, 1693.	Died in childhood.
26 Jonathan,	bap. June	28, 1696.	
27 Ebenezer,	bap. June	25, 1700.	
28 Mary,	bap. January	30, 1705.	
29 Stephen,	bap. August	8, 1707.	
30 Isaac,	bap. November	28, 1708.	
31 Sarah,	bap. June	25, 1710.	

6.

JOSEPH HOPKINS, of Hartford, Conn., was married to Hannah Peck, daughter of Deacon Paul Peck, of the same town, April 27, 1693. After his death, she was married to John Porter, of ———, December 3, 1713.

Mr. Joseph Hopkins died in 1712.

Mrs. Hannah Hopkins, alias Porter, died ———.

Children.

32 Mary,	bap. March	10, 1700.	
33 Hannah,	bap.	1702.	
34 Dorcas,	bap. March	18, 1704.	Married Timothy Bronson.
35 Ruth,	bap. November	9, 1707.	
36 Joseph,	bap. January	14, 1711.	

FOURTH GENERATION.

12.

STEPHEN HOPKINS, of Waterbury, Conn., was twice married. 1. To Susannah Peck, daughter of John Peck, of Wallingford, Conn., 1717. She died December 2, 1755, aged ——. 2. To Abigail Webster, widow of John Webster, of Farmington, Conn., May 25, 1756.

Mr. Stephen Hopkins died January 4, 1769, aged 79.

Mrs. Abigail Hopkins, alias Webster, died ———.

Children,—by his first wife.

37 John,	born July	20, 1718.	
38 Stephen,	born June	28, 1719.	
39 Anna,	born September	25, 1723.	
40 Susannah,	born November	10, 1725.	
41 Mary,	born June	4, 1728.	Died June 1, 1735.
42 Joseph,	born June	6, 1730.	
43 Jesse,	born February	12, 1733.	Died December 3, 1754.
44 Mary,	born November	26, 1735.	Died September 27, 1748.
45 Lois,	born June	22, 1738.	
46 David,	born October	14, 1741.	Died September 23, 1748.

Children,—by his second wife,—none.

13.

TIMOTHY HOPKINS, of Waterbury, Conn., was married to Mary Judd, daughter of Deacon Thomas Judd, of the same town, June 25, 1719.

Timothy Hopkins, Esq., died February 5, 1749, aged 57.

His widow, Mrs. Mary Hopkins, died ———.

Children.

47 Samuel,	born September 17, 1721.	Yale College, 1741. "The great theologian." Minister of Great Barrington, Mass., and subsequently of Newport, R. I.
48 Timothy,	born September 8, 1723.	
49 Huldah,	born December 22, 1725.	
50 Hannah,	born April 11, 1728.	
51 Sarah,	born May 25, 1730.	
52 James,	born June 26, 1732.	
53 Daniel,	born October 16. 1734.	Yale College, 1758. Pastor of the third Church in Salem, Mass. Died December 14, 1814, in the 81st year of his age. He was a faithful minister.
54 Mary,	born June 27, 1737.	
55 Mark,	born September 18, 1739.	Was a lawyer.

14.

REV. SAMUEL HOPKINS, second Pastor of the First Congregational Church at West-Springfield, Mass., was married to Esther

Edwards, daughter of Rev. Timothy Edwards, first Pastor of the Second Congregational Church, at East-Windsor, Conn., June 28, 1727.

Rev. Mr. Samuel Hopkins died October 5, 1755, in his 62d year. His widow, Mrs. Esther Hopkins, died June 17, 1766, in her 72d year.

Children.

56 Timothy,	bap. June	23, 1728.	
57 Samuel,	bap. October	20, 1729.	Yale College, 1749.
58 Hannah,	bap. January	29, 1731.	
59 Esther,	bap. July	21, 1733.	Died March 23, 1740.

21.

THOMAS HOPKINS, of Hartford, Conn., was married to Mary Beckley, only daughter of Nathaniel Beckley, of Wethersfield, in the same state, March 1, 1717.

Mrs. Mary Hopkins died March 7, 1759, aged 63.
Mr. Thomas Hopkins died June 17, 1764, aged 72.

Children.

60 Abigail,	born March	11, 1718.	Died in early life.
61 Sarah,	born October	28, 1719.	
62 Stephen,	born May	8, 1722.	Died May, 1804, aged 82.
63 Thomas,	born August	29, 1725.	
64 Moses,	born January	1, 1727.	
65 Aaron,	born July	14, 1729.	
66 Elisha,	bap. October	17, 1731.	
67 Benjamin,	bap. May	11, 1734.	
68 Abigail,	bap. August	28, 1737.	

FIFTH GENERATION.

42.

JOSEPH HOPKINS, of Waterbury, Conn., was married to Hepzibah Clark, daughter of Thomas Clark, of Waterbury, November 28, 1754.

Joseph Hopkins, Esq., died March 27, 1801, in the 71st year of his age.

His widow, Mrs. Hepzibah Clark, died July 29, 1800, aged 70.

Children.

69 Lavinia,	born August	27, 1755.	Married Rev. Dr. Benoni Upson, of Kensington Society, Berlin, Conn.
70 Asa,	born September	1, 1757.	Married Miss Payne, of Hartford, Conn., where he settled.
71 Joseph.	born January	9, 1760.	Married Ruth Gilbert, of Bridgeport, Conn. Settled in Waterbury, from whence he removed to Rutland, Jefferson county, N. Y.
72 Daniel,	born April	8, 1762.	Settled in Hartford. Married, 1. Elizabeth Payne, daughter of Hon. Benjamin Payne, of Hartford, and after her death, a Miss Deming, of Berlin.
73 Esther,	born February	5, 1764.	Married Mark Bronson, Esq., of Waterbury.

74 Jesse,   born May   20, 1766.   Was twice married. 1. To Elizabeth
                                            Goodwin, daughter of Nathaniel
                                            Goodwin, of Hartford.
75 Hepzibah,   born March   14, 1768.   Married Ethel Bronson, Esq., of Mid-
                                            dlebury, Conn., brother of Isaac
                                            Bronson, Esq., of New York.
76 Hannah,   born May   31, 1770.   Married Stiles Thompson, Esq., of Mid-
                                            dlebury, Conn.
77 Sally,   born November   17, 1772.   Died at Henderson, Jefferson county.
                                            N. Y., July, 1839, unmarried.

47.

Rev. Samuel Hopkins, first minister of Housatonic, now
Great-Barrington, Mass., afterwards minister of Newport, R. I.,
was twice married. 1. To Joanna Ingersoll, daughter of Joseph
Ingersoll, Esq., of Great-Barrington, January 13, 1748. She died
in Great-Barrington, August 31, 1793, having gone there on a visit
to her children, aged 68. 2. To Elizabeth West, of Boston, Mass.,
residing in Newport, September 14, 1794. She was niece of Rev.
Dr. Stephen West, of Stockbridge, Mass.

Rev. Dr. Samuel Hopkins died December 20, 1803, aged 82.

His widow, Mrs. Elizabeth Hopkins, died at Taunton, Mass..
April 9, 1814, aged 75.

Children,—by his first wife.

78 David,   born
79 Levi,   born
80 Moses,   born
81 Samuel,   born
82 David,   born
83 Betsey,   born
84 Joanna,   born
85 Rhoda,   born

Children,—by his second wife,—none.

55.

Mark Hopkins, of Great-Barrington, Mass., was married to
Electa Sargeant, daughter of Rev. John Sargeant, missionary
among the Indians at Stockbridge, January 31, 1765. She was
born August 31, 1740, and was the first white child born in Stockbridge.

Col. Mark Hopkins died at White Plains, the day after the
battle.

His widow, Mrs. Electa Hopkins, died at Stockbridge, July 11,
1798, aged 58.

Children.

86 Archibald,   born March   23, 1766.   Father of Professor and President Hop-
                                            kins.
87 Henry,   born December   28, 1767.   Died in 1788, unmarried.
88 Sewall,   born July   27, 1769.   Was twice married. 1. To a Miss Nor-
                                            ton, by whom he had one daughter,
                                            Cornelia. 2. To Miss Prudence
                                            Hart; by her his children were, Cath-
                                            arine, Janet, Frances, Mark, Mary,
                                            Anne. Of these Catharine only sur-
                                            vives.

89 John Sar-
   geant,   born August   27, 1771. Was merchant at Stockbridge. Mar-
                                   ried Lucinda Fellows, and her chil-
                                   dren were Electa, Huldah, Lucinda
                                   Jane, William, John, Henry, and
                                   Mary Gross.
90 Louisa,   born July   17, 1774. Married Joseph Woodbridge, Esq., of
                                   Stockbridge, Mass., and her children
                                   were Catharine, Henry, Joseph, and
                                   William.
91 Effingham, born   1776. Died early.

56.

TIMOTHY HOPKINS, of West-Springfield, Mass., was married to
Dinah Miller, of the same town, December 9, 1756.
Mrs. Dinah Hopkins died of consumption, July 1, 1793, aged 62.
Mr. Timothy Hopkins died ———.

Children.

92 Esther,   born January   13, 1758. Married Isaac Newton, of Greenfield,
                                   Mass., March 2, 1779.
93 Joseph,   born July   15, 1759. Died January 30, 1803.
94 Hannah,   born August   25, 1760.
95 Timothy, born April   9, 1762.
96 Augustus, born January   2, 1764.
97 Amanda,   born April   2, 1765. Died August 25, 1767.
98 Malah,   born August   21, 1767. Died February 2, 1790.
99 Mary Ed-
    wards,   born February 12, 1770.
100 Edward,   born May   16, 1771. Died September 18, 1777.
101 John Wor-
    thington, born April   5, 1773.
102 Bela, (a
    lad.)   bap. July   6, 1778, at his father's house. [Pastor's Record.]

57.

REV. SAMUEL HOPKINS, Pastor of the Congregational Church
at Hadley, Mass., was twice married. 1. To Sarah Williams,
widow of Rev. Chester Williams, his predecessor in the ministry at
Hadley, and daughter of Hon. Eleazur Porter, of the same town,
1756. She died February 5, 1774, aged 48. 2. To Margaret
Stoddard, of Chelmsford, Mass., daughter of Rev. Sampson Stoddard, son of Rev. Sampson Stoddard, and grandson of Anthony
Stoddard, of Boston, October, 1776.
Rev. Dr. Samuel Hopkins died March 8, 1811, aged 81.
His widow, Mrs. Margaret Hopkins, died October 3, 1796,
aged 66.

Children,—by his first wife.

103 Samuel,   born October   31, 1756. Yale College, 1777. Was a physician.
                                   Died unmarried, at Martinique, W. I.,
                                   of yellow fever, July 11, 1782.

104 Mabel,   born August   28, 1758.
105 Hannah,   born August   10, 1760.
106 Jerusha, born July   4, 1762.
107 Stephen, born June   1, 1764.
108 Polly,   born March   6, 1766.
109 Lucy,   born February 6, 1768.

Children,—by his second wife,—none.

110 John, born January 17, 1770.
111 Elizabeth, born June 12, 1772.

Children,—by his third wife,—none.

58.

HANNAH HOPKINS was married to John Worthington, Esq., of Springfield, Mass., January 10, 1759. [After her death, Mr. Worthington was married to Mary Stoddard, daughter of Major John Stoddard, of Northampton, Mass., and grand-daughter of Rev. Solomon Stoddard, first minister of that town, December 7, 1768. She died July 12, 1812, in her 80th year. By this marriage, Mr. Worthington had one child only,—a son,—John, born April 22, 1770, and died August 11, 1770.]

Mrs. Hannah Worthington died November 25, 1766, in her 36th year.

Hon. John Worthington, LL. D., died April 25, 1800, in his 81st year.

Children.

112 Mary, born March 7, 1760.
113 Hannah, born June 17, 1761.
114 John, born August 10, 1762. Died August 30, 1763.
115 John, born September 2, 1763. Died November 10, 1765.
116 Frances, born October 29, 1764.
117 Sophia, born December 5, 1765.

63.

THOMAS HOPKINS, of Hartford, Conn., was twice married. 1. To Anna ———, of ———, about 1748. She died May 27, 1759, aged —. 2. To Allice Howard, daughter of Capt. Samuel Howard, deceased, of Hartford, September 13, 1761.

Mrs. Allice Hopkins died April 23, 1778, aged 38.

Capt. Thomas Hopkins died September 28, 1797, in his 73d year.

Children,—by his first wife.

118 Theodore, bap. December 10, 1749. Died April 13, 1803, in his 53d year.
119 Huldah, bap. May 17, 1752. Married a Mr. Austin, of Philadelphia.
120 Charles, bap. May 26, 1754.
121 Anna, bap. January 13, 1756. Married Robert Watts, of Savannah, Georgia, November, 1795.
122 Child, (un-
named,) bap. March 17, 1759. Died in infancy.

Children,—by his second wife.

123 Mary, bap. March 20, 1763. Died June 25, 1763.
124 Mary, bap. August 26, 1764. Married Ashbel Welles, Jr., of Hartford, September, 1794. She was his second wife. His first wife, Britta, died April 1, 1793, aged 31.
125 Jennett, bap. May 11, 1766. Married Peter W. Gallaudet, of Philadelphia, afterwards of Hartford, merchant. He died ———. She died ———. They had several children, among them, Rev. Thomas Hopkins Gallaudet, born December 10, 1787, in Philadelphia. Died at Hartford,

15

September 1, 1851, in the 64th year
of his age.

126 Sarah,   bap. June   4, 1769.
127 Jason,   born   Died at Savannah, Georgia, 1798.
128 Thomas,   born

SIXTH GENERATION.

80.

MOSES HOPKINS, of Great-Barrington, Mass., was married to
Anna Whiting, of ———, May 4, 1775.

Children.

129 Harrietta				
Byron,	born April	5, 1776.	Died January 22, 1813.
130 Appelana				
Franks,	born November	17, 1777.		
131 Mark,	born June	27, 1779.	Died November 27, 1828.
132 Betsey,	born May	6, 1781.	Died December 26, 1812.
133 Nancy,	born May	15, 1783.		
134 Richard,	born February	17, 1785.		
135 Charles				
Whiting,	born February	5, 1787.	Resides in Great-Barrington, Mass.
136 Thomas,	born February	9, 1789.	Died August 1, 1830.
137 Edward,	born May	10, 1791.	Died October 6, 1828.

86.

ARCHIBALD HOPKINS, of Great-Barrington, Mass., was married
to Mary Curtis, October 22, 1800. She was born October, 1772.
Archibald Hopkins, Esq., died ———.
His widow, Mrs. Mary Hopkins, is still living, [October 12,
1854.]

Children.

138 Mark,	born February	4, 1802.	Is President of Williams College.
139 Henry,	born January	18, 1804.	Died at Richmond, Virginia, September 5, 1834.
140 Albert,	born July	14, 1807.	

104.

MABEL HOPKINS was married to Moses Hubbard, of Hadley,
Mass., afterwards of Brookfield, Vermont, October 28, 1779.
Moses Hubbard, Esq., died in May, 1822.
His widow, Mrs. Mabel Hubbard, died at the house of her son,
Roswell Hubbard, Northampton, Mass., April 19, 1829, in her
71st year.

Children.

141 Roswell,	born September	11, 1780.	Resides in Northampton.
142 Moses,	born March	11, 1782.	Resided in Brookfield, Vermont. Died in March, 1825.
143 Mehitabel,	born May	7, 1784.	Married a Mr. Chamberlain, of Brookfield, Vermont. Died in 1828.
144 Cynthia,	born March	31, 1786.	Married a Mr. Waters.
145 Sarah P.,	born February	27, 1788.	Died July 16, 1795.
146 Jerusha,	born March	22, 1790.	Married a Mr. Meachum. They settled in Pennsylvania.

147 Lawrence, born March 14, 1792.
148 John, born November 24, 1793. Was a lawyer in Worcester, Mass.
Died September 19, 1825.
149 Sophia, born November 22, 1795. Married a Mr. Edgerton, of Brookfield,
Vermont.
150 Elmira, born April 19, 1799. Died January 24, 1811.

105.

HANNAH HOPKINS was married to Rev. Samuel Spring, of Newburyport, Mass., November 4, 1779.
Rev. Samuel Spring died March 4, 1819, in his 73d year.
His widow, Mrs. Hannah Spring, died June 11, 1819, aged 59.

Children.

151 Child, born September 4, 1780. Died in infancy.
152 Margaret, born April 26, 1783. Died July 25, 1816.
153 Gardner, born February 24, 1785.
154 Hannah, born September 6, 1788. Died May 16, 1795.
155 Walton, born September 15, 1790. Died May 8, 1809.
156 Samuel, born March 9, 1792.
157 Lewis, born October 20, 1793. Left his native shore, January 15, 1815, and never heard from.
158 Mary, born November 12, 1795. Died August 30, 1796.
159 Pinckney, born July 19, 1798. Yale College, 1819. Died September 9, 1820.
160 Charles, born July 25, 1800.
161 John Hopkins, born September 21, 1802.

106.

JERUSHA HOPKINS was married to Rev. Samuel Austin, of Worcester, Mass., September 14, 1788.
Rev. Dr. Samuel Austin died at Glastenbury, Conn., December 5, 1830, aged 70.
His widow, Mrs. Jerusha Austin, died at Glastenbury, March 28, 1841, aged 79, nearly.

Children,—none.

107.

STEPHEN HOPKINS, of Peacham, Vermont, was twice married.
1. To Nancy Turner, daughter of John Turner, of Hanover, N. H., November 11, 1787. She died January 3, 1803, aged 36. 2. To Susannah Chamberlain, daughter of Deacon Abial Chamberlain, of Peacham, January 16, 1804.
Mr. Stephen Hopkins died January 13, 1827, in his 63d year.
His widow, Mrs. Susannah Peacham, died ———.

Children,—by his first wife.

162 Harriet, born September 19, 1788.
163 Stephen, born September 21, 1790.
164 Samuel P., born February 7, 1793. Settled in Belchertown, Mass.
165 Electa, born May 9, 1795. Married William Holland, of Belchertown, Mass., missionary to the Cherokees. She died at Jackson, Illinois, about 1847.

166 Nancy,   born February   12, 1797.   Married John Hutchins.
167 John Tur-
     ner,   born May   13, 1799.

Child,—by his second wife,—one only.

168 Susannah, born December 24, 1804.   Married J. Carter.

108.

POLLY HOPKINS was married to Benjamin Colt, of Hadley, Mass., afterwards of Brookfield, Vermont, December 15, 1785.
Mrs. Polly Colt died September 14, 1813, aged 47.
Mr. Benjamin Colt died November 16, 1848, aged 86.

Children.

169 Samuel,   born November 23, 1787.   Died September 1, 1789.
170 Polly,   born July   6, 1789.
171 Samuel,   born March   1, 1791.   Died March 3, 1791.
172 Etherlinda, born September 5, 1792.
173 Daniel,   born May   13, 1794.
174 Emily,   born January   1, 1796.
175 Eliza,   born May   4, 1798.
176 Benjamin, born January   8, 1801.
177 Julia,   born

109.

LUCY HOPKINS was married to Rev. William Riddel, of Bristol, Me., September 4, 1797. Rev. Mr. Riddel was afterwards settled in Whitingham, Vermont, and he resided some time in Bernardstown, Mass., and also, in Gill, Mass.
Mrs. Lucy Riddel died at Gill, Mass., December 17, 1813, aged 47.
Rev. William Riddel died at Deerfield, Mass., October 24, 1849, aged 81 years and 9 months.

Children.

178 Lucy,   born July   17, 1798.   Died October 31, 1798.
179 Samuel H., born January   2, 1800.
180 William,   born April   15, 1801.   Died April 24, 1801.
181 Jane,   born June   17, 1802.   Married William Hadley, and resides in Ohio.
182 Selian,   born June   19, 1807.   Married Caleb A. Cooley, of South-Deerfield, Mass., where she died March 2, 1837.
183 Child,   born October 29, 1811.   Died November 4, 1811.

110.

JOHN HOPKINS, of Northampton, Mass., was married to Lydia Thompson, daughter of Thomas Thompson, of Newburyport, in the same state, June 12, 1797.
Mrs. Lydia Thompson Hopkins, wife of John Hopkins, born April 17, 1773, died at Northampton, April 10, 1842, aged 69. [Gravestone, Hadley burying-ground, where her remains were interred.]

Capt. John Hopkins died at Northampton, January 9, 1842, after an illness of five days, aged 72, nearly. His remains were interred at Hadley.

Children.

184 Sarah Ann
    Wait,   born January   20, 1799. Married Rev. Dr. John Wheeler, Presi-
                                            dent of Vermont University, and
                                            died November 2, 1847.
185 Elizabeth,   born May   18, 1802. Died August 1, 1802.
186 Thomas
    Thompson,   born December   13, 1804. Died June 27, 1805.
187 Samuel,   born April   11, 1807. A clergyman. Settled first at Montpe-
                                            lier, Vermont, then at Saco, Maine.
188 Erastus,   born April   7, 1810. A clergyman. Settled for several
                                            years at Troy, N. Y. Now resides
                                            in Northampton, Mass.
189 George,   born September 13, 1812. Died March 16, 1830, while a member
                                            of Yale College.

111.

ELIZABETH HOPKINS was married to Rev. Leonard Worcester, of Peacham, Vermont, November 1, 1793.

Mrs. Elizabeth Worcester died September 4, 1818, aged 46.

Rev. Leonard Worcester died May 28, 1846, aged 79 years and 5 months.

Children.

190 Leonard,   born December   30, 1794. Died July 11, 1795.
191 Elizabeth
    Hopkins,   born June   11, 1796. Died March 30, 1817.
192 Samuel
    Austin,   born January   19, 1798. Missionary of the A. B. C. F. M.,
                                            among the Cherokees.
193 Leonard,   born May   20, 1799. Died in 1835.
194 Hannah S., born March   14, 1801. Died May 2, 1838.
195 Jerusha,   born September   20, 1802. Died March 15, 1803.
196 Jerusha,   born March   3, 1804. Died November 3, 1829.
197 Evarts,   born March   24, 1807. Was a clergyman at Littleton, N. H.
                                            Died October 31, 1836.
198 Isaac Red-
    ington,   born October   30, 1808. A clergyman. Succeeded his brother
                                            at Littleton, N. H. Now a District
                                            Secretary of the American Board for
                                            Massachusetts.
199 Lydia,   born October   2, 1810. Died August 24, 1811.
200 John Hop-
    kins,   born May   28, 1812. A clergyman. First settled at St.
                                            Johnsbury, Vermont, now in Bur-
                                            lington, in the same state.
201 Ezra Car-
    ter,   born July   25, 1814. Died August 21, 1814.
202 Ezra Car-
    ter,   born February   28, 1816. A physician in Thetford, Vermont.
203 Lydia
    Eliza,   born April   27, 1817. Died September 6, 1817.

DESCENDANTS IN THE LINE OF BETHIA HOPKINS, DAUGHTER OF JOHN HOPKINS, THE SETTLER.

SECOND GENERATION.

II.

BETHIA HOPKINS was twice married. 1. To Deacon Samuel Stocking, of Middletown, Conn., May 27, 1652. He died December 30, 1683. 2. To James Steele, of Hartford, in the same state. Mrs. Bethia Stocking, alias Steele, died ————. Mr. James Steele died —— ——.

Children,—by her first husband.

204 Samuel,	born	1656.
205 Bethia,	born	1658. Married Thomas Stowe, of Middletown.
206 John,	born	1660.
207 Lydia,	born	1662.
208 George,	born	1664.
209 Ebenezer,	born	1666.
210 Stephen,	born	1673.
211 Daniel,	born	1677.

Children—by her second husband,—none.

JOHN INGERSOLL.

JOHN INGERSOLL, first of Hartford, Conn.,—then of Northampton, Mass., to which place he removed about 1655, and then of Westfield, Mass., to which place he removed from Northampton, in or about 1665, was thrice married. 1. To Dorathy Lord, daughter of Thomas Lord, one of the first settlers of Hartford, about 1651. She died at Northampton, in January, 1657, aged about 26. 2. To Abigail Bascom, daughter of Thomas Bascom, one of the first settlers of Windsor, Conn., afterwards of Northampton, September 12, 1657. She was born at Windsor, where she was baptized, June 7, 1640. 3. To Mary Hunt, sister of Jonathan Hunt, of Northampton, about 1667. Mary Hunt's mother was Mary Webster, daughter of John Webster, one of the first settlers of Hartford, Conn., and fifth Governor of the Colony of Connecticut. In 1659, Mr. Webster removed from Hartford to Hadley, Mass., and there continued to reside until his death.

Mr. John Ingersoll died at Westfield, September 3, 1684.

His widow, Mrs. Mary Ingersoll, died at Westfield, September 1, 1690.

SECOND GENERATION.

Children of John Ingersoll,—by his first wife.

I. Hannah,	born		1652, probably in Hartford.
II. Dorathy,	born		1654, probably in Hartford.
III. Margery,	born January,		1656, in Northampton.

Children,—by his second wife.

IV. Abigail,	born January	11, 1659, in Northampton.	
V. Sarah,	born October	30, 1660, in Northampton, married —— Barnes.	
VI. Abiah,	born August	24, 1663, in Northampton.	
VII. Hester,	born September	9, 1665, in Westfield.	

Children,—by his third wife.

VIII. Thomas,	born March	28, 1668, in Westfield.	
IX. John,	born October	19, 1669, in Westfield.	
X. Abel,	born November	11, 1671, in Westfield.	Was a single man, and dwelt many years in Northampton.
XI. Ebenezer,	born October	15, 1673, in Westfield.	Died March 4, 1682.
XII. Joseph,	born October	16, 1675, in Westfield.	He was slain at Deerfield, Mass., when that town was destroyed by the French and Indians, February 29, 1704. Unmarried.
XIII. Mary,	born November	17, 1677, in Westfield.	Died August 18, 1690.
XIV. Benjamin,	born November	15, 1679, in Westfield,	Died before 1704.
XV. Jonathan,	born May	10, 1681, in Westfield.	

DESCENDANTS IN THE LINE OF HANNAH INGERSOLL. DAUGHTER OF JOHN INGERSOLL, THE SETTLER.

THIRD GENERATION.

I.

HANNAH INGERSOLL was married to Stephen Kelsey, of Hartford, Conn., November 15, 1672. He was son of William Kelsey, one of the first settlers of Hartford, and was baptized November 7, 1647.

Mr. Stephen Kelsey died November 30, 1710, aged 63.

His widow, Mrs. Hannah Kelsey, died ———.

Children.

16 Hannah,	born	1675.	
17 Stephen,	born September	20, 1677.	
18 John,	born January	20, 1680.	
19 Daniel,	born September	14, 1682.	
20 William,	born February	19, 1685.	
21 James,	born August	21, 1687.	
22 Charles,	born June	15, 1692.	Settled in Hartford. Died July 1, 1777, aged 85.

DESCENDANTS IN THE LINE OF DORATHY INGERSOLL, DAUGHTER OF JOHN INGERSOLL, THE SETTLER.

THIRD GENERATION.

II.

DORATHY INGERSOLL was twice married. 1. To Jacob Phelps, of Westfield, Mass., May 2, 1672. He was son of George Phelps, of Windsor, Conn., afterwards of Westfield, and of Frances his second wife, widow of Thomas Dewey, and was born February 7, 1649. He died October 6, 1689, in the 41st year of his age. 2. To ——— Root.

Mrs. Dorathy Root, alias Phelps, died ———.

Mr. ——— Root died ———.

Children,—by her first husband.

23 Dorathy,	born December	18, 1673.	Died February 2, 1674.
24 Dorathy,	born May	10, 1675.	Married Edward Kibbe, of Enfield, Conn., November 30, 1693.
25 Hannah,	born November	26, 1677.	Married John Kibbe.
26 Israel,	born April	3, 1681.	
27 Benjamin,	born January	8, 1683.	
28 Joseph,	born August	5, 1686.	
29 Jedediah,	born December	7, 1688.	

Children,—by her second husband.   *Supposed,—none.*

DESCENDANTS IN THE LINE OF MARGERY INGERSOLL. DAUGHTER OF JOHN INGERSOLL, THE SETTLER.

THIRD GENERATION.

III.

MARGERY INGERSOLL was twice married. 1. To Jacob Goffe, of Wethersfield, Conn., December 5, 1679. He died October 21, 1697, in the 49th year of his age. 2. To Jonathan Buck, of Wethersfield.

Mr. Jonathan Buck died ————.

Mrs. Margery Buck, alias Goffe, died ————.

Children,—by her first husband.

30 Jacob,	born November	5, 1680.	Died December 14, 1680.
31 Moses,	born March	10, 1682.	Died before 1708, when his father's estate was distributed, as he is not mentioned in the order of distribution.
32 Mabel,	born October	31, 1690.	Married Daniel Andrus, of Wethersfield, October 30, 1707. They had 7 children.
33 Mary,	born November	15, 1693.	Married John Andrus, of Wethersfield, June 26, 1712. He died June 16, 1740. 2 children.
34 Eunice,	born March	27, 1696.	

Children,—by her second husband,—none.

DESCENDANTS IN THE LINE OF ABIGAIL INGERSOLL, DAUGHTER OF JOHN INGERSOLL, THE SETTLER.

THIRD GENERATION.

IV.

ABIGAIL INGERSOLL was twice married. 1. To Thomas Rix, of Wethersfield, Conn. He died May 21, 1690. 2. To Lieut. Joshua Wills, of Windsor, Conn., about 1696. She was his third wife. His first wife died September 12, 1676. His second wife died in November, 1694.

Lieut. Joshua Wills died January 6, 1721, in the 75th year of his age. [Grave stone, East Windsor, old burying ground.]

Mrs. Abigail Rix, alias Wills, died ————.

Child,—by her first husband,—one only.

35 Abigail,	born	Married John Burt, jun., of Springfield, Mass., October, 1710. They had 6 children. She died in child-bed, February 17, 1727, and Mr. Burt was married to Mary Sikes, December 22, 1727.

Children,—by her second husband,—none.

16

DESCENDANTS IN THE LINE OF ABIAH INGERSOLL, DAUGHTER OF JOHN INGERSOLL, THE SETTLER.

THIRD GENERATION.

VI.

ABIAH INGERSOLL was married to Jedediah Strong, jun., of Northampton, Mass., about January 1, 1688. Mr. Strong resided in Northampton until about 1695, when he removed to Lebanon, Conn., and there continued to reside until his death.

Mr. Jedediah Strong died October 12, 1709, aged ———.
His widow, Mrs. Abiah Strong, died November 2, 1732, aged 69.

Children.

36 Azariah,	born October	7, 1689, in Northampton. Died October 30, 1689.
37 Stephen,	born November	24, 1690, in Northampton. Died in Lebanon, February 2, 1785, in the 95th year of his age. His widow, Mrs. Abigail Strong, died October 24, 1788, in her 87th year. [Grave stones, Exeter Society burying ground.]
38 David,	born June	19, 1693, in Northampton. Died May 2, 1712.
39 Supply,	born October	10, 1697, in Lebanon.
40 Jedediah,	born January	15, 1700, in Lebanon.
41 Ezra,	born March	2, 1702, in Lebanon. Married Abigail Caverly, January 12, 1731. 6 children recorded to them.
42 Freedom,	born May	16, 1704, in Lebanon. Married John Buel, of Lebanon, May 19, 1726. 8 children recorded to them.

DESCENDANTS IN THE LINE OF HESTER INGERSOLL, DAUGHTER OF JOHN INGERSOLL, THE SETTLER.

THIRD GENERATION.

VII.

HESTER INGERSOLL was twice married. 1. To William Gurley, of Northampton, Mass., 1684. He died May 1, 1687, drowned. 2. To Benoni Jones, of Northampton, January 23, 1689.

Mr. Benoni Jones was slain at Pascommuck, north end of Mount Tom, Northampton, May 13, 1704.

Mrs. Hester Jones, alias Gurley, was taken May 13, 1704, and carried to Canada, and died there, after being tormented by the Catholic priests, who were trying to convert her.

Child,—by her first husband,—one only.

43 Samuel,	born May	6, 1686. Settled in Coventry, Conn., but subsequently removed to Mansfield, Conn., where he died.

Children,—by her second husband.

44 Jonathan,	born January	4, 1695. Died young.

45 Benjamin,	born	1696.	Settled in Coventry, Conn. Married and had nine children, whose names and times of birth are recorded on Coventry Records.
46 Ebenezer,	born November	12, 1698.	Slain at Pascommuck, Northampton, May 13, 1704.
47 Jonathan,	born March	3, 1703.	Slain at Pascommuck, Northampton, May 13, 1704.

DESCENDANTS IN THE LINE OF THOMAS INGERSOLL, SON OF JOHN INGERSOLL, THE SETTLER.

THIRD GENERATION.

VIII.

Thomas Ingersoll, first of Westfield, Mass., and afterwards of Springfield, in the same state, was thrice married. 1. To Sarah Ashley, daughter of David Ashley, of ———, July 22, 1692. She was born September 10, 1673, and died ———. 2. To Abigail Dickinson, widow of Hezekiah Dickinson, of Springfield, Mass., daughter of Samuel Blakeman, of Stratford, Conn., and grand-daughter of Rev. Adam Blakeman, first minister of that town, January 21, 1708. She died March 30, 1719. 3. To Ruth Child, of Watertown, May, 1720.

Mr. Thomas Ingersoll died November 14, 1732, in the 65th year of his age.

Mrs. Ruth Ingersoll died ———.

Children,—by his first wife.

48 Thomas,	born November	27, 1692.	
49 Moses,	born February	10, 1694.	
50 Miriam,	born June	4, 1697.	
51 David,	born September	30, 1699.	Married Lydia Child, February, 1721.

Children,—by his second wife,—none.

Children,—by his third wife,—none.

DESCENDANTS IN THE LINE OF JOHN INGERSOLL, SON OF JOHN INGERSOLL, THE SETTLER.

THIRD GENERATION.

IX.

John Ingersoll, of Westfield, Mass., was married to Isabel Brown, daughter of ——— Brown, of ———, April 12, 1699.

Mr. John Ingersoll died May 18, 1750, in the 81st year of his age.

His widow, Mrs. Isabel Ingersoll, died January 26, 1772, in the 96th year of her age. [Gravestone, Agawam, West Springfield burying ground.]

Child,—one only, recorded to them.

| 52 Isabel, | born March | 18, 1701. |

DESCENDANTS IN THE LINE OF JONATHAN INGER-SOLL, SON OF JOHN INGERSOLL, THE SETTLER.

THIRD GENERATION.

XV.

JONATHAN INGERSOLL, of Milford, Conn., was married to Sarah ——— of ———.

Mrs. Sarah Ingersoll died February 14, 1748, in the 62d year of her age. [Gravestone.]

Mr. Jonathan Ingersoll died November 28, 1760, in the 80th year of his age. [Gravestone.]

Children.

53 Jonathan,	born	1713.	
54 Sarah,	born June	16, 1716.	Died in childhood.
55 Mary,	born December	14, 1718.	Died in early life.
56 David,	born September	4, 1720.	
57 Jared,	born June	3, 1722.	
58 Sarah,	born		

FOURTH GENERATION.

53.

JONATHAN INGERSOLL, (Yale College, 1736,) minister of Ridgefield, Conn., was married to Dorcas Moss, daughter of Rev. Joseph Moss, minister of Derby, Conn., November 10, 1740.

Rev. Jonathan Ingersoll died October 2, 1778, in the 65th year of his age, and 40th of his ministry.

His widow, Mrs. Dorcas Ingersoll, died September 29, 1811, in the 86th year of her age.

Children.

59 Sarah,	born October	28, 1741.	
60 Dorcas,	born October	15, 1743.	Married ——— Andrus, of that part of Stamford, now called Darien.
61 Jonathan,	born April	16, 1747.	
62 Mary,	born December	20, 1748.	
63 Abigail,	born May	7, 1751.	Married David Olmsted, of Ridgefield.
64 Joseph,	born August	11, 1753.	
65 Hannah,	born April	9, 1756.	Married Josiah Raymond, of Bedford, N. Y., afterwards of Manlius, N. Y.
66 Esther,	born August	10, 1760.	Married Ebenezer Olmsted, of Ridgefield, Conn.
67 Moss,	born June	9, 1763.	First of Ridgefield, Conn., afterwards of Auburn, N. Y. Was married to Ruth Smith. He died at Auburn, N. Y.
68 Anne,	born April	5, 1765.	

56.

DAVID INGERSOLL, of Milford, Conn., was married to Mehitabel Bryan, daughter of Richard Bryan, jun., of Milford, and of Mehitbel, his first wife, daughter of Samuel Clark, of the same town, about March, 1740. She was born August 15, 1721.

Mr. David Ingersoll died February 14, 1742, in the 23d year of his age. [Gravestone.]

His widow, Mrs. Mehitabel Ingersoll, died June 7, 1798, in the 77th year of her age. [Gravestone.]

Child,—one only.

69 David,   born December 11, 1740.

57.

JARED INGERSOLL, of New Haven, Conn., was married to Hannah Whiting, daughter of the Hon. Col. Joseph Whiting, of New Haven, August 1, 1743. She was born February 21, 1712. Col. Whiting was son of Rev. John Whiting, fourth minister of Hartford, Conn., and of Phebe, his wife, daughter of Thomas Gregson, of New Haven, and grandson of the Hon. William Whiting, one of the first settlers of Hartford.

Hon. Jared Ingersoll died at New Haven, August 25, 1781, aged 59.*

His widow, Mrs. Hannah Ingersoll, died ———.

---

* Mr. Ingersoll was graduated at Yale College in 1742; settled at New Haven as a lawyer, and was agent of the colony in England, in 1757; but being appointed distributor of stamps in Connecticut, under the stamp act, he lost his popularity. The people of New Haven compelled him to resign, August 24, 1765. Not deeming this resignation explicit, a large company from the eastern part of Connecticut set out on a journey to New Haven. They met Mr. Ingersoll at Wethersfield, when they compelled him to resign, and cry out three times, Liberty and Property. The next day 500 men escorted him to Hartford. On being appointed admiralty judge for the middle district, about the year 1770, he removed to Philadelphia; but in consequence of the Revolution, he returned to New Haven, where he died. The following account of this affair is taken from the Connecticut Courant, of September 23, 1765, published at Hartford.

" Last Wednesday afternoon a large company of able bodied men came to town, (on horseback,) from the eastern part of this government, and informed those who were willing to join them, that they were on their way to New Haven to demand the stamp officer of the colony to resign his office; that a number of their associates had gone on the lower roads, and that they had all agreed to rendevous at Branford the next day, (Thursday,) and that they should tarry in town that night: they then dispersed to different parts of the town for lodging. In the evening, advice was received that Mr. Ingersoll was on the road to this place,—that he would be in town next day, and that he intended to apply to the assembly for their protection; and it being conjectured that he might come to town in the night, to shun the mob, (who he heard were on their way to pay him a visit,) it was agreed that a watch should patrol the streets all night, to prevent his coming in unnoticed, but they made no discoveries. On Thursday morning, the whole body (including a considerable number from this town,) set off on the intended expedition, and in about an hour, met Mr. Ingersoll at the lower end of Wethersfield, and let him know their business. He at first refused to comply; but it was insisted upon that he should resign his office of stamp master, so disagreeable to his countrymen. After many proposals, he delivered the resignation mentioned below, which he read himself in the hearing of the whole company. He was then desired to pronounce the words, Liberty and Property, three times, which he having done, the whole body gave three cheers. Mr. Ingersoll then went to a tavern, and dined with several of the company. After dinner, the company told Mr. Ingersoll, as he was bound to Hartford, they would escort him there, which they did to the number of five hundred persons, on horseback. After they arrived in town, Mr. Ingersoll again read his resignation in public, when three huzzas were given, and the whole company immediately dispersed, without making the least disturbance.

" The following is a copy of Mr. Ingersoll's resignation :

" WETHERSFIELD, September 19, 1765.

" I do hereby promise that I never will receive any stampt papers which may arrive from Europe, in consequence of any act passed in the Parliament of Great Britain, nor officiate in any manner as stamp master, or distributor of stamps within the colony of Connecticut, directly or indirectly. And I do hereby notify all the inhabitants of his majesty's colony of Connecticut, (notwithstanding the said office or trust has been committed to me,) not to apply to me ever hereafter for any stamped papers, hereby declaring that I do decline said office, and execute these presents of my own free will and accord, without any equivocation, or mental reservation. In witness whereof, I have hereunto set my hand.

" J. INGERSOLL."

Children.

70 James,	born April	21, 1748.
71 Jared,	born October	24, 1749.

58.

SARAH INGERSOLL was married to John Whiting, of New Haven, Conn., brother of the wife of her brother, Jared Ingersoll, November 7, 1751. [After her death, Mr. Whiting was married to Sarah Trowbridge, daughter of Lieut. Stephen Trowbridge, of New Haven, May 24, 1770. She died in April, 1795.]

Mrs. Sarah Ingersoll Whiting died July 24, 1769.

Mr. John Whiting died ———.

Children.

72 John,	born December	25, 1753.
73 Jonathan,	born April	12, 1756.
74 Sarah,	born January	21, 1758.
75 William,	born October	15, 1760.
76 Samuel,	born September	9, 1762.
77 Hannah,	born August	5, 1765.

FIFTH GENERATION.

59.

SARAH INGERSOLL was married to Seth Lee, of Farmington, Conn., son of Deacon Jared Lee, of Southington, Conn., September 3, 1767. Yale College, 1759. Was a physician.

Mrs. Sarah Lee died July 15, 1770, aged 28.

Doct. Seth Lee died ———.

Child,--one only.

78 Sarah Inger- soll,	born February	26, 1769.

61.

JONATHAN INGERSOLL, of New Haven, Conn., was married to Grace Isaacs, daughter of Ralph Isaacs, Esq., of Branford, Conn., April 1, 1786.

Hon. Jonathan Ingersoll died January 12, 1823, in the 76th year of his age.

His widow, Mrs. Grace Ingersoll, died ———.

Children.

79 Grace,	born February	20, 1787.
80 Ralph,	born February	8, 1789.
81 Mary,	born March	27, 1791.
82 William Isaacs,	born May	25, 1793.

62.

MARY INGERSOLL was married to Joseph Hooker, of Farmington, Conn., and after 1792, of Litchfield, Herkimer county, N. Y.. 1771. He was born March 30, 1749.

Children.

83 Jared Inger-			
soll,	born March,	1772.	Dwelt in Sangerfield, Oneida county, N. Y. Married, and had eight children.
84 Mary,	born August	24, 1774.	Married Rev. John Eastman, September 30, 1799, by whom she had four children.
85 Jonathan,	born November	12, 1778.	Lives in Acadia, Wyoming county, N. Y. Married, and has six children.
86 Lewis,	born October	26, 1781.	Lived on his father's place, and had three children.
87 Elias,	born November	12, 1784.	Died in 1802.
88 Joseph,	born October	26, 1786.	Physician in the army of 1812. Married a daughter of Doct. Caleb Sampson, and died at Oswego, N. Y., in 1829. Left two children.

68.

ANNE INGERSOLL was married to Joshua King. Esq., of Ridgefield, Conn.

Mrs. Anne King died December 30, 1838, in the 74th year of her age.

Joshua King, Esq., died August 13, 1839, in the 81st year of his age.

Children.

89 Catharine,	born September	15, 1785.	Married William Hawley, of ———, December 24, 1806.
90 Frances,	born November	14, 1787.	Married Rev. William Neill, February 25, 1811, died October 13, 1832.
91 Sophia,	born March	11, 1790.	Married William McHarg, of Albany, N. Y., April 16, 1810, died March 24, 1838.
92 John Fran-			
cis,	born June	30, 1792.	Died November 28, 1838.
93 Rufus How-			
ard,	born November	30, 1794.	Married Amelia Laverty, September 15, 1824.
94 Ann Maria,	born March	10, 1797.	Married Elisha W. Skinner, of Albany, N. Y., November 27, 1816.
95 Charles			
Clark,	born July	1, 1799.	Died at Ridgefield, Conn., January 1, 1854.
96 Joshua In-			
gersoll,	born August	11, 1801.	
97 Mary Ann,	born August	19, 1803.	Died November 20, 1828.
98 Grace,	born April	16, 1809.	

69.

DAVID INGERSOLL, of Milford, Conn., was married to Clement Treat, daughter of Lieut. Joseph Treat, of the same town, March 9, 1768.

David Ingersoll, Esq., died June 10, 1774, in the 34th year of his age.*

---

* In Memory of David Ingersoll, Esq. His piety was early and unaffected : His benevolence, pure and universal. As a civil officer,—a minister of God, for good. In friendship, endearing and faithful. A pattern of conjugal and parental affection. In prospect of a better state, he departed this life July 10, 1774, in the 34th year of his age. All on earth is shadow : all beyond is substance. The reverse is folly's creed. How solid all where change shall be no more.   [Grave stone, Milford burying ground.]

His widow, Mrs. Clement Ingersoll, died May 18, 1817, in the 74th year of her age.

Children.

99 Mehitabel, born October   25, 1768.
100 David Bry-
    ant,   born August   16, 1771.
101 Jonathan, born October   24, 1773.

71.

JARED INGERSOLL, Yale College, 1766, LL. D., Judge of the District Court of Pennsylvania, attained a high rank as a lawyer in Philadelphia. He was also a member of Congress and of the convention which formed the constitution of the United States. The office of Attorney General of Pennsylvania he resigned in 1816. At the time of his death he was judge. In 1812 he was the federal candidate for the office of Vice-President of the United States. He died October 31, 1822, aged 73. He was the father of Charles J. Ingersoll and of Joseph R. Ingersoll of Philadelphia.

LEWIS JONES.

LEWIS JONES, of Watertown, Mass., and one of the first set-tlers of that town, was married to Ann ———.
Mrs. Ann Jones died May 1, 1680, aged 78.*
Mr. Lewis Jones died April 11, 1684.†

FIRST GENERATION.

Children of Lewis Jones and of Ann Jones, his wife.

I Lydia,	born	
II Josiah,	born	1640.
III Shubael,	born October	14, 1651.

---

*Here lyeth the Body of Ann Jones, aged 78 years, dyed the 1 of May, 1680.—Upon yᵉ death of that pious Matron : She lived a pious, holy, godly life,—being now escaped free from hate and strife." [Grave stone, Watertown Ancient burying ground.]

† IN the Name of God, Amen. I, Lewis Jones, in Watertown, in New-England, being at this present of perfect understanding and memory, though weak in body,—committing my soul into the hands of Almighty Good, and my body to [decent burial, in hope of a resurrection unto eternal life through the merits and power of Jesus Christ my most gracious Saviour and Redeemer ; do thus dispose of that estate which God hath graciously given unto me : Considering the weak and helpless condition of my dear wife Ann Jones and of my son Shubael Jones, my will and pleasure is, that the whole of my estate, (after the discharge of my debts and my burial,) be improved for their supply, the benefit of it, and also, the principal, if they stand in need thereof. And further, my will and pleasure is, that when the Lord shall please to remove either of them by death, that then that which remaineth shall be wholly entitled to the use of the other so long as either of them shall live ; and if the Lord shall so dispose that anything remaineth after their death, that then what remaineth be divided, two parts to my daughter Lydia Whitney, if she be then living, and one to my son Josiah ; but if Lydia be dead, that then what remaineth be divided equally to my son Josiah, or such of his children as shall be living, and the children of my daughter Lydia that shall be then living. And of this my last will, I do constitute my son Josiah Jones, my sole Executor, and do earnestly desire my loving friend and brother John Stone to be overseer to assist my son in the managing of the estate so as may be best for the comfort of my poor wife and child aforesaid. And in confirmation hereof, I have set hereunto my hand and seal.

Simeon Stone.   The mark ꓓ & seal of
John Stone.   Lewis Jones.
                              this 7th of the 11th, 1678. [January 7, 1678.]

A Codicil annexed to the above will, 19. 2. 1682. [April 19, 1682.] The wife of the Testator being then deceased. As a further addition to my last will and testament, I do nominate and appoint my assured friends Simon Stone and John Stone, of Watertown, to be guardians unto my son Shubael Jones, to whose wisdom and prudence and wisdom, I do commit and send the government of my said son, and the disposal of all that estate as well real and personal to my said son bequeathed : and I do hereby authorize and empower said guardians or the longest liver of them, to make sale of any part of my house and land, as there shall appear to them needful, for the relief of my said son Shubael Jones.

                                                            his mark.
                                                      Lewis ꓓ Jones.

Middlesex County Land Records, Book 9, page 168, December 29, 1684. By deed of this date, Josiah Jones, executor of the last will and testament of his father, Lewis Jones, late of Watertown, deceased, John Stone, overseer to said will, and Simon Stone and John Stone, guardians to Shubael Jones, as appeareth in the last will of the father of the said Josiah, for valuable consideration sell and convey to Sargeant John Coolidge, of said town of Watertown, a convenient dwelling house, an orchard, and by estimation, ten acres of land, (being estate of said deceased,) bounded south with the county road, west with Deacon Dwight, north with Joseph Mason, and east with a highway.

17

DESCENDANTS IN THE LINE OF LYDIA JONES, DAUGHTER OF LEWIS JONES, THE SETTLER.

SECOND GENERATION.

I.

LYDIA JONES was married to Jonathan Whitney, of Watertown, Mass., October 30, 1656.

Children.

4 Lydia,	born July	3, 1657.
5 Jonathan,	born October	20, 1658.
6 Anna,	born April	28, 1660.
7 John,	born June	27, 1662.
8 Josiah,	born May	19, 1664.
9 Ellen,	born October	12,‡1666.
10 James,	born November	25, 1668.
11 Isaac,	born January	12, 1670.
12 Joseph,	born March	10, 1672.
13 Abigail,	born August	18, 1675.
14 Elenor,	born November	23, 1677.
15 Benjamin,	born January	6, 1679.

DESCENDANTS IN THE LINE OF JOSIAH JONES, SON OF LEWIS JONES THE SETTLER.

SECOND GENERATION.

II.

JOSIAH JONES, of Watertown, Mass., was married to Lydia Treadway, daughter of Nathaniel Treadway, of Watertown, and of Sufferanna Treadway, his wife, "y° 2. 8 mo: 1667." [October 2, 1667.]

Mr. Josiah Jones died October 3, 1714, aged 74.

His widow, Mrs. Lydia Jones, died September 16, 1743, in the 94th year of her age.

Children.

16 Lydia,	born September	25,.1668.
17 Josiah,	born October	20, 1670.
18 Mary,	born December	10, 1672.
19 Nathaniel,	born December	31, 1674.
20 Samuel,	born July	9, 1677.
21 Sarah,	born February	6, 1681.
22 Ann,	born June	28, 1684.
23 John,	born March	19, 1686.
24 James,	born [no date.]	
25 Isaac,	born [no date.]	
26 Daughter,	born [no date.]	

THIRD GENERATION.

17.

JOSIAH JONES, of Watertown, Mass., was married to Abigail Barnes, daughter of ——— Barnes, of Marlborough, in the same state, about 1692.

Mr. Josiah Jones died ———.
His widow, Mrs. Abigail Jones, died November 4, 1749.

Children.

27 Daniel,   born February   2, 1693.
28 Abigail,   born September 14, 1694.
29 Josiah,   born October   24, 1701.
30 William,   born January   4, 1707.
31 Elisha,   born November 20, 1710.

FOURTH GENERATION.

27.

DANIEL JONES, of Colchester, Conn., was married to Mary Worthington, daughter of William Worthington, Esq., of the same town, October 13, 1720. [After his death, she was married to Capt. Benjamin Lathrop, of Norwich, Conn., June 15, 1741. She was his second wife.]

Mr. Daniel Jones died June 18, 1740, in his 48th year.

Mrs. Mary Jones, alias Lathrop, died at Norwich, August 4, 1770, in her 69th year.

Children.

32 Mary,   born May   26, 1724. Died June 13, 1729.
33 Amasa,   born October   2, 1726.
34 Mary,   born June   13, 1729. Died unmarried.
35 Abigail,   born May   1, 1732.
36 Ann,·   bap. October   5, 1735. Married to Nun Clark, of Lyme, Conn., April 20, 1758.
37 Elizabeth, bap. September 24, 1738. Married Nathaniel Clark, of Colchester, Conn., October 25, 1757.

28.

ABIGAIL JONES was married to Col. Ephraim Williams, of Newton, Mass., afterwards of Stockbridge, in the same state, May 21, 1719. She was his second wife. [The first wife of Col. Williams, was Elizabeth Jackson, daughter of Abraham Jackson, of Newton, by whom he had two children,—Ephraim, (Col.,) born February 23, 1715,—killed in the French war, September 8, 1755,—gave all his estate for the founding of Williams College. Thomas, (Doct.,) born February 24, 1718.]

Col. Ephraim Williams died at Deerfield, Mass., in August, 1754, aged 63.

His widow, Mrs. Abigail Williams, died at Stockbridge, December 4, 1684, aged 90.

Children.

38 Abigail,   born April   20, 1721. Was twice married. 1. To Rev. Mr. John Sargeant, missionary among the Indians at Stockbridge, August 16, 1739. He died July 27, 1749, aged 39.* 2. To Hon. Gen. Joseph

---

* The following lines, (says Miss Electa F. Jones, in her History of Stockbridge,) inscribed upon the stone which covers the grave of Rev. Mr. Sargeant, were composed by one of the Indians whom he was instructing:

Dwight, of Great Barrington, Mass.,
formerly of Brookfield, in the same
state, about 1752. He died June 9
1769, aged 62. Mrs. Abigail Dwight,
alias Sargeant, died February 15,
1791, aged 69. *Children,*—by her
first husband,—*Electa Sargeant,* born
1740, (the first white child born in
Stockbridge,) married to Col. Mark
Hopkins, of Great Barrington, Mass.,
by whom she had three children,
Louisa, the wife of Joseph Woodbridge, Esq., of Stockbridge, Archibald, father of President and Professor Hopkins, and John, a merchant
in Stockbridge. Col. Hopkins died
at White Plains, October 26, 1776, a
day or two previous to the battle
fought there, aged 37. He was brother of Rev. Samuel Hopkins, the the-
ologian. His widow, Mrs. Electa
Hopkins, died at Stockbridge, July
11, 1798, aged 58. *Erastus Sargeant,*
born 1742, settled at Stockbridge,
was a distinguished physician, dea
con in the church, married Elizabeth
Partridge, of Hatfield. He died November 14, 1814, aged 72. *John Sargeant,* born 1747, preacher to the
Stockbridge (N. Y.) Indians, married
Mary Codner, of Boston, Mass. Rev.
John Sargeant died at New Stockbridge, N. Y., September 8, 1824,
aged 77. *Children,*—by her second
husband,—*Pamela Dwight,* born
1753, married to Hon. Theodore
Sedgwick, of Stockbridge, Mass.,
being his second wife. She died
September 20, 1807, aged 54. Hon.
Theodore Sedgwick died January 24,
1813, aged 66. Their children, The-
odore, Harry, Robert and Charles,
lawyers, and Eliza, Frances and
Catharine M., authoress. *Henry W.
Dwight,* married Abigail Welles,
daughter of Ashbel Welles, of West-
Hartford, Conn., June 8, 1796. He
died September 15, 1804, aged 50.
She died May 31, 1840, aged 77.
They were the parents of Hon. Col.
H. W. Dwight, Rev. Edwin W.
Dwight, and Rev. Louis Dwight,
Secretary of the Prison Discipline
Society.

39 Josiah,   born   1723. Married Miss Sargeant, of New Jersey.
He was wounded at Lake George,
at the time his half-brother, Col.
Ephraim Williams, Jun., was killed,
but died at Stockbridge, May 6, 1759,
aged 37.

"Where is that pleasing form? I ask: thou can'st not show:
He's not within, false stone there's nought but death below.
And where's that pious soul, that thinking, conscious mind?
Wilt thou pretend, vain cypher, that's with thee enshrin'd?
Alas, my friends, not here with thee that I can find;
Here's not a Sargeant's body, or a Sargeant's mind.
I'll seek him hence, for all's alike deception here,
I'll go to Heaven, and I shall find my Sargeant there."

40 Judith,	born	1729.	Married Rev. Ezra Thayer, of Ware, Mass., September 17, 1761. He died February 12, 1775. She died at Stockbridge, April 5, 1801, aged 72.
41 Elizabeth,	born November 28, 1731.		Married Rev. Dr. Stephen West, of Stockbridge. She died September 15, 1804, aged 73. He died May 13, 1819, aged 83. They had no children.
42 Elijah,	born November 15, 1733.		Known as Col. Elijah Williams. Married Sophia Partridge, of Hatfield, Mass. He died June 19, 1815, aged 82. She died October 25, 1830, aged 84.

29.

JOSIAH JONES, first of Watertown, Mass., afterwards of Stockbridge, in the same state, was twice married. 1. To Anna Brown, daughter of Deacon Benjamin Brown, of Watertown, December 24, 1724. She was born March 2, 1704, and died May 15, 1747, aged 43. 2. To Sarah Whittlesey, of Stockbridge, formerly of Litchfield, South Farms, Conn., widow.

Mr. Josiah Jones died March 22, 1769, aged 68.

Mrs. Sarah Jones, alias Whittlesey, died in 1799, aged 96.

Children,—by his first wife.

43 Josiah,	born October	24, 1725.	
44 Micah,	born October	4, 1728.	
45 Anna,	born February	4, 1731.	Married Oliver Warner, of Alford, Mass.
46 Keziah,	born April	6, 1733.	Married a Mr. Kellogg, of Egremont, Mass.
47 Elijah,	born January	3, 1735.	Died in childhood.
48 Abigail,	born November	17, 1738.	Married Josiah Warren.
49 Elijah,	born	1741.	Married Rhoda Stoddard, of Litchfield, South Farms.

Children,—by his second wife,—none.

30.

WILLIAM JONES, of Lunenburg, Mass., was married to ———.
Mr. William Jones died ———.
His widow died ———.

Children.

50 William,	born
51 Enos,	born
52 Josiah,	born
53 Samuel,	born
54 Sarah,	born
55 Abigail,	born
56 Hannah,	born
57 Silence,	born

31.

ELISHA JONES, of Weston, Mass., was married to Mary Allen, daughter of Deacon Nathaniel Allen, of the same town.

Elisha Jones, Esq., died at Boston, Mass., February 15, 1775, aged 64.

His widow, Mrs. Mary Allen Jones, died ———.

Children.

58 Nathan,	born	
59 Child, (not		
named,)	born	Died in infancy.
60 Elisha,	born	
61 Israel,	born	
62 Daniel,	born	
63 Elias,	born	
64 Josiah,	born	
65 Silas,	born	
66 Mary,	born	
67 Ephraim,	born	
68 Simeon,	born	
69 Stephen,	born	
70 Jonas,	born	
71 Philemore,	born	
72 Charles,	born	

FIFTH GENERATION.

33.

AMASA JONES, of Colchester, Conn., was twice married. 1. To Elizabeth Chamberlain, daughter of William Chamberlain, of the same town, July 12, 1749. She died September 23, 1753. 2. To Hope Lord, daughter of Epaphrus Lord, Esq., of Colchester, August 27, 1754. She was born at Middletown, Conn., November 22, 1736.

Mr. Amasa Jones died at Hartford. Conn., February 24, 1785, aged 57.

His widow, Mrs. Hope Jones, died at Hartford, December 11, 1798, aged 63.

Children,—by his first wife.

73 Rhoda,　　born October　　5, 1750. Married Aaron Kellogg, of Colchester, July 3, 1766, and after his death, Major Bulkeley.

74 Daniel,　　born May　　27, 1752. Died October 27, 1753.

Children,—by his second wife.

75 Daniel,　　born August　　28, 1755. Settled in Hartford. Was a merchant. Was twice married. 1. To Olive Tinker, daughter of Sylvanus Tinker, Esq., of East-Haddam, Conn., March 11, 1781. She died February 7, 1788, aged 27. 2. To Rhoda Mather, daughter of Dr. Charles Mather, of Hartford, October 7, 1798. Mr. Daniel Jones died February 1, 1802, aged 46.* His widow, Mrs. Rhoda Jones, died November 26, 1847, aged 81, nearly. *Children,—* by his first wife,—Nancy, married Henry King, of Westfield, Mass., merchant, September 30, 1804. Eliza-

---

* " Died February, 1802, Major Daniel Jones, of this city, merchant, aged 46. Mr. Jones has through life been esteemed a man of strict integrity, fair and honorable in his dealings, and of very amiable deportment, and will be long remembered with affection by his numerous friends and acquaintance. His funeral was attended by a numerous concourse of people. The Governor's Horse Guards, of which he was lately the commander, with the officers now in commission, and those who had formerly belonged to it, walked in the procession. We have seldom seen our citizens express more sincere regret on any similar occasion."

beth, married Noble Day, Esq., of New Preston, Conn., April, 1805. Olivia, married Rev. Dr. Jeremiah Day, of New Haven, Conn., President of Yale College, September 24, 1811. *Children,*—by his second wife, Daniel, born about 1800, merchant. Henry, born about 1802, clergyman.

76 Amasa, born July 27, 1757. Settled at Hartford, Conn., in the mercantile line. Married Cynthia Jones, daughter of Israel Jones, of Adams, Mass. Mr. Amasa Jones died 1808, aged —. They had eight children, four of whom died in infancy.

77 Samuel
Phillips, born September 23, 1759. Dwelt some time in Orangeburg, N. C.

78 Hope, bap. November 1, 1761. Married Horace Seymour, of Lansingburg, N. Y., afterwards of the city of New York, merchant.

79 Epaphrus, bap. February 19, 1764. Lived many years at New Albany, Indiana, and there died.

80 Richard L., bap. June 14, 1767. Settled in Hartford. Was a merchant. Married Hannah Hooper.

81 Abigail
Warren, bap. April 23, 1769. Married Charles Selden, of Troy, N. Y., merchant. He was father of Hon. Dudley Selden.

82 George. Married a Miss Bogardus, of Catskill, N. Y.

83 William. Settled in East-Hartford, Conn. Married Eunice Buckland, daughter of Aaron Buckland, Esq., of the same town.

84 Mary. Died, unmarried.

85 Hannah. Married Josiah Sherman, of Albany, N. Y., merchant.

43.

JOSIAH JONES, of Stockbridge, Mass., was married to Mabel Woodbridge, daughter of Joseph Woodbridge, of the same town, and grand-daughter of Rev. John Woodbridge, Pastor of the Congregational Church at West-Springfield, Mass., November 9, 1757. Capt. Josiah Jones died April 2, 1795, aged 69. His widow, Mrs. Mabel Jones, died March 5, 1808, aged —.

Children.

86 Solomon, born January 26, 1754. Twice married. 1. To Olive Bristol, about 1783, and after her death, to Elizabeth Hinsdale. He died in Owego, N. Y., about 1835.

87 Stephen
Woodbridge, born February 4, 1761. Married Margery Sparks, October 13, 1786, and died in Owego, N. Y.

88 Clarissa, born January 12, 1763. Married Enos Boughton. Died in Victor, N. Y., April 19, 1821.

89 Elizabeth, born May 22, 1765. Married Joel Bristol, Esq., October 13, 1786. Died in Clinton, N. Y.

90 Josiah, born September 9, 1767. Married Fidelia West, daughter of Nathaniel West, of Tolland, Conn., and of Lucretia, his wife, daughter of Russell Woodbridge, of East-Hartford, Conn., son of Rev. Samuel Woodbridge, first minister of that

town, January 6, 1797. She was adopted by Rev. Dr. West, of Stockbridge. Deacon Josiah Jones died February 10, 1834, aged 64. His widow, Mrs. Lucretia West, still survives. They had nine children,—among them, Electa Fidelia Jones, a well-read antiquarian and genealogist, and Cornelia, wife of Wolcott Marsh Spencer, of Springfield, Ohio.

91 Horatio, born December 30, 1769. Settled in Stockbridge. Married Elizabeth Brown, of that town, October 22, 1800. Died April 26, 1813. He was a physician.

92 Anna, born August, 1772. Married Roswell Lombard, October 4, 1789. Died at Coxsackie, N. Y., September 21, 1803.

93 William, born April 1, 1775. Married Clarissa Brown, of Stockbridge, December 18, 1805. Died in Victor, N. Y., April 25, 1825. He was a physician.

94 Mary, born January 31, 1778. Died at Stockbridge, Mass., July 19, 1830.

WILLIAM JUDSON.

WILLIAM JUDSON, first of Concord, Mass., then of Stratford, Conn., afterwards of New-Haven, Conn., was twice married. 1. In England, to Grace ———. She died in New-Haven, Conn., September 29, 1659. 2. To Elizabeth Wilmot, of New-Haven, widow, February 8, 1660, at New-Haven, "by Mr. Gilbert."
Mr. William Judson died in New-Haven, Conn., July 29, 1662.
His widow, Mrs. Elizabeth Judson, alias Wilmot, died ———.

SECOND GENERATION.

Children of William and Grace Judson,—all born in England.

1 Joseph,	born	1619.
2 Jeremiah,	born	1621.
3 Joshua,	born	

DESCENDANTS IN THE LINE OF JOSEPH JUDSON, SON OF WILLIAM JUDSON, THE SETTLER.

THIRD GENERATION.

1.

JOSEPH JUDSON, of Stratford, Conn., was married to Sarah Porter, daughter of John Porter, of Windsor, in the same state, October 24, 1644.
Mr. Joseph Judson died October 8, 1690, aged 71.
His widow, Mrs. Sarah Judson, died March 16, 1696, aged 70.

Children.

4 Sarah,	born March	2, 1645.	Married Edmund Howell, of Southampton, Long Island, November 1, 1664.
5 John,	born December	10, 1647.	
6 James,	born April	24, 1650.	
7 Grace,	born February	19, 1651.	Married Samuel Prudden, son of Rev. Peter Prudden, of Milford, December 30, 1669.
8 Joseph,	born March	10, 1654.	Died February 1, 1678, unmarried.
9 Hannah,	born December	31, 1657.	
10 Esther,	born August	20, 1660.	Married Benjamin Curtis, of Stratford, Conn.
11 Joshua, ⎫ (twins)	born October	27, 1664.	Not mentioned in his father's will: probably died young.
12 Ruth, ⎭	born October	27, 1664.	
13 Phebe,	born October	29, 1666,	and died November 1, 1676.
14 Abigail,	born September	15, 1669.	Married Josiah Curtiss, of Stratford, Conn., and died November 21, 1697.

18

5.

JOHN JUDSON, first of Stratford, Conn., afterwards of Woodbury, in the same state, was thrice married. 1. To Elizabeth (or, Eliza) Chapman, daughter of ———— Chapman, of Stamford, Conn., March 12, 1673. She died ————. 2. To Hann'ah ————. She died July 23, 1698. 3. To Mary Orton, of Farmington, in the same state, July 5, 1699.

Mr. John Judson died January 12, 1709, aged 62.

Children.

15 John,	born March	12, 1676, in Stratford.	
16 Joshua,	born July	23, 1678, in Stratford.	
17 Joseph,	born October	24, 1679, in Stratford.	Married Mary Walker, daughter of Deacon Zechariah Walker. He died March 22, 1758.
18 Chapman,	bap. December,	1681.	Died May 8, 1700.
19 Jonathan,	bap. December,	1682.	Died in infancy.
20 Jonathan,	bap. December,	1684.	
21 Martha,	bap. December,	1686.	Married Hon. William Preston, June, 1705.
22 Eliphalet,	bap. February,	1689.	
23 Ephraim,	bap. September,	1694.	
24 Isaac,	bap. June	3, 1700.	
25 Daniel,	bap. February	6, 1702.	
26 Mary,	bap. April	11, 1704.	Married a Curtis.
27 Jeremiah.			

FOURTH GENERATION.

6.

JAMES JUDSON, of Stratford, Conn., was twice married. 1. To Rebecca Welles, daughter of Thomas Welles, Esq., of Hartford, in the same state, and grand-daughter of Thomas Welles, one of the early Governors of the colony of Connecticut, August 18, 1680. She was born in 1655, and died November 3, 1717, aged 62. 2. To Ann Steele, widow of James Steele, late of Wethersfield, Conn., deceased, November 20, 1718.

Capt. James Judson died February 25, 1721, aged 71, nearly.

His widow, Mrs. Ann Judson, alias Steele, died in Wethersfield, 1739.

Children,—by his first wife.

28 Hannah,	born May	30, 1681.	Married James Lewis, of Stratford, Conn.
29 Sarah,	born February	16, 1683.	Married Rev. Nathaniel Chauncey, Pastor of the Congregational Church in Durham, Conn., son of Rev. Nathaniel Chauncey, minister first at Windsor, Conn., and then at Hatfield, Mass., and nephew of Israel Chauncey, Pastor of the Congregational Church in Stratford.
30 Rebecca,	born February	25, 1685, and died February 26, 1698.	
31 Joseph,	born January	10, 1687.	Married Hannah Hawley, of Stratford, Conn.
32 James,	born April	31, 1689.	Married Martha Lewis, of Stratford.
33 Phebe,	born October	2, 1691.	Married Joseph Lewis, of Stratford, Conn.
34 David,	born August	7, 1693.	

Children,—by his second wife,—none.

9.

HANNAH JUDSON was married to Samuel Wadsworth, of Farmington, Conn., June 12, 1689.

Lieut. Samuel Wadsworth died ———.

His widow, Mrs. Hannah Wadsworth, died August 22, 1732.

Children.

35 Hannah,   bap. February 11, 1694.
36 Sarah,   bap. October   20, 1695.
37 Samuel.

12.

RUTH JUDSON was married to Samuel Welles, of Hartford, Conn., son of "the Honoured Mr. Thomas Welles," of the same town.

Capt. Samuel Welles died October 3, 1733, in the 73d year of his age.

His widow, Mrs. Ruth Welles, died May 2, 1744, in the 80th year of her age.

Children.

38 Hannah.
39 Samuel.
40 Ruth.
41 Sarah.
42 Rebecca.

FIFTH GENERATION.

17.

JOSEPH JUDSON, of Woodbury, Conn., was married to Mary Walker, daughter of Deacon Zechariah Walker, of Woodbury, and grand-daughter of Rev. Zechariah Walker, of Woodbury, Conn.

Mr. Joseph Judson died March 22, 1758, aged 78.

His widow, Mrs. Mary Judson, died ———.

Children.

43 Joseph,   born November 25, 1708. Died August 20, 1712.
44 Chapman, born December 31, 1710. Died August 26, 1712.
45 Mary,   born April   19, 1713.
46 Joseph,   bap. February 12, 1715.
47 Chapman, born January 11, 1717.
48 Susanna, born May   13, 1719. Died in early life.
49 Elizabeth, born March   4, 1721. Married Seth Preston. She died August 16, 1814, aged 93. They had a number of children,—among them Elizabeth, who married Josiah Beers, January 1, 1778, by whom she had 5 children, among them Seth P. Beers, born July 1, 1781,—and now residing in Litchfield, Conn.

50 David,   born March   2, 1723.
51 Nathan,   born February, 1725.
52 Samuel,   bap. November 9, 1727.
53 Susanna, bap. October 11, 1730.

54 Joshua,   bap. December 14, 1732. Married twice. 1. To Ann Walker,
                  and after her death, 2. To Deborah
                  Leavenworth, who, after his death,
                  was married to Capt. James Judson,
                  of Woodbury. Children of Joshua
                  Judson,—Joshua, Mary, Deborah
                  Ann. Deborah Ann married Phine-
                  as Smith, Esq., of Woodbury, and
                  they were the parents of Hon. Tru-
                  man Smith, of Litchfield, Conn.

20.

JONATHAN JUDSON, of Woodbury, Conn., was married to Mary
Mitchell, daughter of Deacon Matthew Mitchell, August 22, 1711.
Mr. Jonathan Judson died May 16, 1727.
His widow, Mrs. Mary Judson, died February 9, 1743, aged
about 56.

Children.

55 Elnathan,	born May	8, 1712.
56 Abigail,	born October	30, 1714.
57 Elijah,	born December	15, 1716.
58 Martha,	born October,	1718.
59 Elisha,	born July	12, 1721.
60 Peter,	born August,	1723.
61 Jerusha,	born November,	1726.
62 Jonathan,	born	1728.

34.

DAVID JUDSON, of Stratford, Conn., was married to Phebe
Stiles, born 1696, daughter of Ephraim Stiles and Batsheba, his
wife, of Stratford, Conn., October 29, 1713.
Mr. David Judson died May 5, 1761, in the 68th year of his
age.
His widow, Mrs. Phebe Judson, died May 20, 1765, in the 79th
year of her age.

Children.

63 David,   born September 26, 1715. Married Mary Judson, daughter of
                  Joshua Judson, of Stratford, 1743.
                  He was Rev. David Judson, first
                  Pastor of the Congregational Church
                  in Newtown, Conn. Rev. David
                  Judson died September 24, 1776,
                  aged 61 years wanting 2 days.
64 Phebe,   born February 19, 1718. Married Matthew Curtis, of Stratford,
                  son of Capt. Joseph Curtis of that
                  town, 1737. They afterwards remo-
                  ved from Stratford to Newtown.
                  She died September 18, 1758, aged 40.
65 Abel,   born January   31, 1721, and died in childhood.
66 Abel,   born February 12, 1722. Married Sarah Burton, daughter of
                  Judson Burton, of Stratford, 1744,
                  and after her decease, Mehitabel
                  Tousey, of Newtown, 1750. He died
                  July 17, 1775, aged 53.
67 Agur,   born March   23, 1725. Married Hannah Curtis, daughter of
                  Eliphalet Curtis, of ——, 1746.
                  He died July 5, 1790, aged 65.

68 Ruth,	born April	26, 1726.	Married Benjamin Stiles, of Woodbury, Conn., son of Francis Stiles, of that place, 1747.
69 Daniel,	born April	26, 1728.	
70 Sarah,	born October	17, 1730.	Married Stephen Curtis, son of Abram Curtis, ———, 1750.
71 Abner,	born June	9, 1733.	Married Hannah Curtis, daughter of Capt. Stiles Curtis, of Stratford, Conn., 1756.
72 Betty,	born February	12, 1737.	Married William Pixley, son of Peter Pixley, of ———, 1756.

SIXTH GENERATION.

55.

ELNATHAN JUDSON, of Woodbury, Conn., was married to Rebecca Minor, daughter of Ephraim Minor, of Woodbury, about 1735.

Mrs. Rebecca Judson died ———.

Capt. Elnathan Judson died December 14, 1796, aged 84.

Children.

73 Ephraim,	born December	5, 1737.	Yale College, 1763. Minister of the second church at Norwich, Conn.; then minister of Taunton, Mass., and in May, 1789, settled at Sheffield, Mass. Died February 23, 1813, aged 76.
74 Thaddeus,	bap. October	14, 1739.	
75 Mary,	bap. October	18, 1741.	
76 Noah,	bap. July	15, 1744.	
77 Elisha,	bap. July	20, 1746.	Died in infancy.
78 Elisha,	bap. November	8, 1747.	
79 Adoniram,	born July	15, 1750.	

69.

DANIEL JUDSON, of Stratford, Conn., was twice married. 1. To Sarah Curtis, born May 17, 1731, daughter of Capt. Stiles Curtis, of the same town, January 1, 1752. She died May 30, 1808, aged 77. 2. To Mercy Burritt, of Stratford, February 20, 1809.

Mr. Daniel Judson died November 14, 1813, in the 86th year of his age.

His widow, Mrs. Mary Judson, died ———.

Children.

80 Stiles,	born November	18, 1752.	Married Naomi Lewis, daughter of George Lewis, of Stratford, Conn., July 17, 1777.
81 Silas,	born August	31, 1754.	Married Mary Whiting, daughter of Col. Samuel Whiting, of Stratford, Conn., May 12, 1777. He died December, 1808, aged 54.
82 Phebe,	born October	16, 1756.	Married William Brooks, of Stratford, son of John Brooks, Esq., of that town, January 7, 1778.
83 Rebecca,	born November	15, 1758.	Married Rev. Abraham Fowler, of Salem Society, of Waterbury, Conn.,

		September 7, 1793. Rev. Abraham Fowler died November 10, 1815, aged 70.
84 Charity,	born December 19, 1760.	Married Elisha Hawley, of Ridgefield, Conn., December 31, 1786.
85 Daniel,	born November 4, 1763.	Father of David P. Judson. Died October, 1847, aged 84.
86 Sarah,	born March 23, 1766.	Married John Booth, of Stratford, Conn., son of John Booth, December 6, 1802.

SEVENTH GENERATION.

79.

REV. ADONIRAM JUDSON was married to Abigail Brown, of Tiverton, R. I., about 1784.

Rev. Adoniram Judson died at Scituate, Mass.,

Children.

| 87 Adoniram,* born | | 1787. Brown University, 1817. Studied theology at Andover. Died April 12, 1850, aged 63. The celebrated missionary. |

88 Elnathan.
89 Mary.
90 Abigail.

85.

DANIEL JUDSON was married to Sarah Plant, daughter of Solomon Plant, of Stratford, Conn., September 10, 1799.

Mr. Daniel Judson died October 4, 1847, in the 84th year of his age.

Mrs. Judson is still living.

Children.

| 91 Sarah
Amanda, born August 11, | | 1779. Married Rev. David L. Ogden, Pastor of the Congregational Church, in Southington, Conn., January 14, 1824. |

---

* From New-York Express, of Monday, June 5, 1854.

The late Mrs. Emily Judson, (whose death, at Hamilton, in this State, was announced by telegraph, yesterday,) was about 40 years of age. Her maiden name was Emily Chubbuck. Her native place was Eaton, in Madison county, New York. She first became known to the public as a writer for periodicals, and under the assumed name of "Fanny Forester," she acquired great reputation as a writer of refined taste. Her success as a writer induced Miss Chubbuck to appear, under her literary cognomen of "Fanny Forester," as the author of "Alderbrook," and other volumes, in the school of light literature, all inculcating moral lessons, and tending to increase her reputation as a female writer of great delicacy and elegance of style. In June, 1846, Miss Chubbuck astonished her many admirers by an entire change in her career and pursuits, in announcing her resolution to devote herself to a missionary life, and of course leaving her native country with but doubtful prospects of a future return to her relatives and friends. At that time she became the third wife of the Rev. Adoniram Judson, D. D., Baptist missionary to Burmah, in Asia, and on the 11th of July she embarked with her husband and other missionaries, in the ship Fanueil Hall, from Boston for India. The missionary labors of Dr. Judson in Burmah, or eastern India, extended over a period of about thirty-nine years, terminating with his death in September, 1850. While in Burmah his views respecting baptism underwent a change, in consequence of which he left the Congregationalists in 1814, and joined the Baptist church. Soon after the death of her husband, Mrs. Judson returned to the United States, and for the last two years had been in somewhat feeble health.

92 Daniel,	born November	30, 1801, and died September 17, 1815.
93 Catharine		
Plant,	born February	7, 1805. Married Horace Holden, Esq., of the
		city of New York, December 25,
		1833.
94 Mary Re-		
becca,	born April	10, 1807. Married Capt. John W. Sterling, of
		Bridgeport, Conn., January 18, 1832.
95 David Plant,	born April	16, 1809.
96 Julia Maria,	born January	11, 1811. Married Rev. John H. Hunter, of Fair-
		field, Conn., September 10, 1829.
97 William,	born June	9, 1813.
98 Daniel,	born October	6, 1816, and died December 6, 1823.

DESCENDANTS IN THE LINE OF JEREMIAH JUDSON, SON OF WILLIAM JUDSON, THE SETTLER.

THIRD GENERATION.

2.

JEREMIAH JUDSON, of Stratford, Conn., was twice married. 1. To Sarah Foote, daughter of Nathaniel Foote, of Wethersfield, Conn., and one of the first settlers of that town, 1652. She died 1673, aged about 41. 2. To Catharine Fairchild, widow of Thomas Fairchild, late of Stratford, deceased, November 8, 1675. Her maiden name was Catharine Cragg. She was married to Mr. Fairchild, in London, about the close of the year 1662, and was his second wife. Mr. Fairchild died December 14, 1670. At or about the time of his second marriage, viz., on the 22d of December, 1662, Mr. Fairchild executed a bond "to John Winthrop, of Hartford," (who was then in London,) "for Mrs. Elizabeth Whiting, of the city of London,"—with condition, that so soon as he, the said Fairchild, should arrive at Stratford, he would invest his wife with a good title to sundry parcels of real estate, situated in that town. This Mrs. Elizabeth Whiting may have been the wife of William Whiting, of London, merchant, son of William Whiting, one of the first settlers of Hartford, Conn.

Mr. Jeremiah Judson died of Palsy, after a protracted illness, May 15, 1701, in the 79th year of his age.

His widow, Mrs. Catharine Judson, alias Fairchild, died May, 1706.

Children,—by his first wife.

99 Isaac,	born March	10, 1653.
100 Mary,	born December	31, 1655.
101 Elizabeth,	born February	24, 1658.
102 Sarah,	born April	7, 1662.
103 Mercy,	born June	1, 1665.
104 Jeremiah,	born March	1, 1671. Married Mary Wells, daughter of John
		Wells, of Stratford, Conn., April 24,
		1695.

FOURTH GENERATION.

99.

ISAAC JUDSON, of Stratford, Conn., married Mary ———.

Children.

105 Elizabeth, born October   10, 1681.
106 Mary,   Married John Wells, of Stratford, Dec.
                               15, 1698.

DESCENDANTS IN THE LINE OF JOSHUA JUDSON, SON OF WILLIAM JUDSON, THE SETTLER.

THIRD GENERATION.

3.

JOSHUA JUDSON, of Stratford, Conn., was married to Ann ———.
After his death his widow was married to John Hurd, senior, of
Stratford, November 24, (December 10,) 1662.
Mr. Joshua Judson died ———, 1661, aged ———.
Mrs. Ann Judson, alias Hurd, died ———.

Children.

107 Joshua,   born December   3, 1658.
108 Samuel,   born August   27, 1660.
109 Ann,   Married Arthur Perry.

JOHN KENT.

JOHN KENT,* of Suffield, Conn., was twice married. 1. To Abigail Dudley, daughter of ——— Dudley, May 9, 1686.† She died October 26, aged ——. 2. To Abigail Winchel. John Kent, Esq., died April 11, 1721, aged ——. Mrs. Abigail Kent, alias Winchell, died March 21, 1767, aged ——.

Children,—by his first wife.

1 Mary,	born January 26, 1686–7.	Died March 9, 1687–8.
2 John,	born January 26, 1687–8.	
3 Abigail,	born September 28, 1690.	
4 Deborah,	born August 22, 1693.	
5 Dudley,	born October 23, 1695.	
6 Mary,	born October 29, 1697.	Died February 8, 1697–8.
7 Samuel,	born December 14, 1698.	
8 Abner,	born June 7, 1701.	
9 Elisha,	born July 9, 1704.	

Children,—by his second wife.

10 Joseph,	born Febr'ry 26, 1709–10.	
11 Noah,	born April 28, 1714.	
12 Experience,	born March 4, 1717.	

2.

JOHN KENT, of Suffield, Conn., was twice married. 1. To Mary Smith. She died May 27, 1729, aged ——. 2. To Hannah Marsh, of Hadley, Mass., December 1, 1732. John Kent, Esq., died June 24, 1737, aged 49.

---

* John Kent (who was married May 9, 1686,) was probably born about 1660 or 1665. He died in 1721. Mr. Judd, in his letter of February 14, 1853, says,—" In the settlement of the estate of John Kent, a reference is made to the will of *John Kent*, his father. We may therefore assume that his father's name was *John*, but his place of residence is not given."

N. B. I think Mr. Judd is mistaken in his above statement, for being at Northampton August 26, 1853, I examined the proceedings in the county clerk's office on the settlement of the estate of John Kent, (Book 4, page 101,) in which, among an account of debts due *from* the estate of John Kent, late of Suffield, deceased, I found the following entry, (it being no doubt, the same entry on which Mr. Judd, from hasty inspection, founded his opinion,) viz.: " Due to John Kent, for a yoke of oxen and a horse given to him in his grandfather's will, to which will, his father, John Kent, deceased, was executor." *This entry is, I think, an index to the name of the father of John Kent, whose estate is here under settlement.*

† William Dudley, of Saybrook, Conn., was married to Mary Roe, November 4, 1661, by whom he had children, born in Saybrook, viz.

Mary,	born September 6, 1662.	
William,	born August 8, 1665.	
Abigail,	born May 24, 1667.	Supposed by me to have been the first wife of John Kent. Died July 26, 1670.
Joseph,	born March 3, 1668–9.	
Deborah,	born November 11, 1670.	
Samuel,	born November 4, 1672.	
Joseph,	born September 14, 1674.	
Sarah,	born January 3, 1676.	
Elizabeth,	born May 4, 1678–9.	

William Dudley died about 1700.

19

Children,—by his first wife.

13 Moses, born September 25, 1710. Supposed to have married Joannah Huxley, of Suffield, May 12, 1731.
14 Mary, born January 12, 1715–16.
15 John, born March 25, 1719–20. Married Elizabeth Spencer, as is supposed, July 5, 1739.
16 Mercy, } born December 28, 1722.
17 Thankful, } twins.
18 Cephas, born April 13, 1725. Married to Hannah Spencer, May 20, 1747.
19 Aaron, born May 19, 1727. Died June 27, 1727.

Child,—by his second wife,—one only.

20 Hannah, born August 11, 1735. Died December 4, 1735.

3.

ABIGAIL KENT was married to Samuel Copeley, of Suffield, Conn., February 4, 1713–14.

Children.

21 Samuel, born January 16, 1715–16.
22 Daniel, born July 23, 1718.
23 Mary, born October 19, 1720.
24 Abigail, born April 26, 1723.
25 Elisha, born August 26, 1728.

4.

DEBORAH KENT was married to Shadrach Hathaway, of Suffield, Conn., April 25, 1717.

Mr. Shadrach Hathaway died 1721, aged —.

His widow, Mrs. Deborah Hathaway.

Children.

26 Shadrach, born Febr'ry 11, 1717–18.
27 Simeon, born June 25, 1719.

5.

DUDLEY KENT, of Suffield, Conn., was married to Ruth Ruggles, daughter of Rev. Benjamin Ruggles, and of Mercy, his wife, daughter of Rev. John Woodbridge, pastor of the First Church in Hartford, August 30, 1723. She was born January 29, 1703–4.

Mrs. Ruth Kent died August 29, 1752, in the 49th year of her age.

Dudley Kent, Esq., died October 27, 1766, aged 71.

Children.

28 Maria, born June 1, 1724–5.
29 Paul, born September 15, 1727.
30 Ruth, born December 28, 1729.
31 Dudley, born October 2, 1732.
32 Oliver, born November 23, 1734.
33 Catharine, born November 15, 1736.
34 Deborah, born April 23, 1739.
35 Sibbel, born June 11, 1741.
36 Lucy, born June 11, 1743.
37 John, born February 12, 1745–6.

7.

SAMUEL KENT, of Suffield, Conn., was thrice married. 1. To Abia Dwight, daughter of Nathaniel Dwight, of Northampton, Mass., February 28, 1722. She died February 23, 1748, aged 45. 2. To Tamer Durby, widow of ———— Durby, of Springfield, Mass. She died July 18, 1756, in the 47th year of her age. 3. To Hannah Hooker, widow of Thomas Hooker, of Hartford, Conn. Samuel Kent, Esq., died October 28, 1772, in the 74th year of his age.

Mrs. Hannah Kent, alias Hooker, died ————.

Children,—by his first wife.

38 Elijah,	born January 6, 1722-3.	Married twice. 1. To Rachel Kellogg, daughter of Joseph Kellogg, February 27, 1745. She died July 17, 1747. 2. To Jemima Kellogg, October 26, 1748, daughter of Martin Kellogg, of Newington, Conn.
39 Lucy,	born September 27, 1724.	Married Ensign Jonathan Kellogg, of Suffield, January 13, 1741.
40 Abiah,	born August 10, 1727.	Married to John Leavitt, Esq., of Suffield, June 20, 1745. She died June 12, 1782, in her 55th year. He died April 5, 1798, in his 74th year. They had a large family of children.
41 Phillis,	born July 29, 1729.	
42 Anna,	born October 2, 1730.	
43 Elihu,	born June 1, 1733.	Was thrice married. 1. To Rebecca Kellogg, daughter of Joseph Kellogg, and of Rachel, his wife, daughter of Rev. Ebenezer Devotion, February 10, 1757. She was born at Fort Dummer, April 8, 1729. She died August 27, 1761. 2. To Susanna Lyman, November 9, 1763. She died February 1, 1770. 3. To Sibbil Dwight, February 2, 1774. Major Elihu Kent died February 12, 1814, in his 81st year. His widow, Mrs. Sibbil Kent, died July 9, 1822, aged 76.
44 Mehitabel,	born January 6, 1734-5.	

Children,—by his second wife,—none.

Children,—by his third wife,—none.

8.

ABNER KENT, of Suffield, Conn., was married to Abigail Rowe, daughter of ———— Rowe, of Suffield, January 5, 1726-7.

Child.

45 Seth,   born September 6, 1727, in Suffield.

9.

ELISHA KENT died at Philippi, N. Y., July 17, 1776.*

---

* The following obituary is taken from the Connecticut Courant, July, 1776:
" Died on the 17th of July, 1776, after a short confinement, the Rev. Elisha Kent, of Philippi, New York government, in the 72d year of his age, and 42d of his ministry. He

10.

JOSEPH KENT, of Suffield, Conn., was twice married. 1. To
Hannah Gillet, daughter of Samuel Gillet, of Suffield, February
26, 1728. She was born June 19, 1709. She died November 2,
1746, aged 37. 2. To Elizabeth Palmer, daughter of Timothy
Palmer, of Suffield, March 7, 1748. She was born August 8,
1718.

Children.

46 Abigail,	born May	10, 1730.	
47 Chloe,	born February	7, 1732.	Married to Ebenezer King, of Suffield, December 11, 1751.
48 Joseph,	born March	14, 1734.	
49 Hannah,	born September	4, 1736.	Supposed to have married Ephraim Gleason, about 1757.
50 Seth,	bap. March	19, 1738.	
51 Experience,	bap. March	9, 1741.	

11.

NOAH KENT, of Suffield, Conn., was married to Deliverance
Granger, daughter of Samuel Granger, of the same town, October
3, 1734. She was born August 8, 1713.

Mr. Noah Kent died May 25, 1755, aged 41.

His widow, Mrs. Deliverance Kent, died ———.

Children.

52 Phebe,	born November	12, 1735.	Married Medad Pomeroy.
53 Noah,	born August	27, 1737.	
54 Gideon,	born July	26, 1739.	
55 Elizabeth,	born October	3, 1745.	
56 Dan,	born December	3, 1747.	Died September 20, 1750.
57 Abel,	born September	20, 1753.	
58 Deborah,	born September	20, 1748.	
59 Mary,	born November	14, 1750.	
60 Nathaniel,	born November	22, 1751.	
61 Deliver'nce,	born December	1, 1755.	

12.

EXPERIENCE KENT was married to Aaron Hitchcock, of Suffield,
Conn., September 18, 1739.

Mrs. Experience Hitchcock died December 19, 1795, in her
78th year.

---

was endued by the great author of all good gifts, with a sprightly genius, a quickness of
invention and readiness of thought ; was of a cheerful, sociable, compassionate, hospitable
disposition,—furnished with a rich treasure of knowledge, both human and divine, which
being sanctified by divine grace, rendered him very useful in life. As a Christian, he ex-
celled in the cardinal grace of humility : was ever inclined to think low of his attainments
and performances : he was enriched with many ministerial gifts and qualifications ; with
an uncommon faculty to prevent and heal difficulties ; was much improved and greatly
serviceable in 'councils : but 'tis well known, to all his judicious acquaintance, that he ex-
celled more especially as to pulpit talents. His composition was truly good,—his matter
sound and instructive,—his manner of address, solemn and serious :—he delivered with a
pathos becoming the importance of the subject ;—he was a faithful, painful, profitable,
searching preacher, and as such was exceeded by but few ; and to human appearance, it
pleased God to improve him as an instrument of gathering in many lost souls to Christ.
He quitted mortality with a Christian fortitude and serenity, and with good reason we conclude he is gone to receive the rewards of a faithful servant of Christ. He left a second wife
a disconsolate widow, and seven children. His bereaved widow is sister to the late Hon.
Governor Fitch.''

Capt. Aaron Hitchcock died September 25, 1808, aged 93.

Children.

62 Aaron,   born August   9, 1740. Died September 25, 1740. [Gravestone.]

63 Experience, born January 28, 1741-2.
64 Ruth,   born February 2, 1749-50.
65 Lucinda,   born August   16, 1754.
66 Apollus,   born March   8, 1759.
67 Lucinda
   Patten,   born November 10, 1789.

RICHARD MATHER.

FIRST GENERATION.

RICHARD MATHER, of Dorchester, Mass., one of the first settlers of that town, and third minister of the same, was twice married. 1. To Catharine Hoult, or Holt, daughter of Edmund Hoult, September 29, 1624, in England. She died in 1665. 2. To Sarah Cotton, widow of Rev. John Cotton, second minister of the First Church in Boston, August 26, 1656. Her maiden name was Sarah Rossiter.

Rev. Richard Mather died April 22, 1669, aged 73.

Mrs. Sarah Mather, alias Cotton, died May 27, 1676, aged 75.

SECOND GENERATION.

Children of Rev. Richard Mather,—by his first wife.

I. Samuel,	born May	13, 1626, in England.	
II. Timothy,	born	1628, in England.	
III. Nathaniel,	born March	20, 1630, in England.	
IV. Joseph,	born	[no date,] in England.	Died young.
V. Eleazur,	born May	16, 1637, in Dorchester.	
VI. Increase,	born June	21, 1639, in Dorchester.	

DESCENDANTS IN THE LINE OF SAMUEL MATHER, SON OF THE REV. RICHARD MATHER.

THIRD GENERATION.

I.

SAMUEL MATHER was graduated at Harvard College, in 1643; admitted freeman of Massachusetts, 1648,—went to England, from thence to Scotland, and finally settled as a minister, in Dublin. Married the sister of Sir John Stevens, of Dublin.*

Rev. Samuel Mather died in Dublin, October 29, 1671, aged 45.

Children,—four or five, all died young, except one,—a daughter.†

---

* Farmar, and Genealogical Register, for January, 1852.

† Genealogical Register, for January, 1852.

DESCENDANTS IN THE LINE OF TIMOTHY MATHER, SON OF THE REV. RICHARD MATHER.

THIRD GENERATION.

II.

TIMOTHY MATHER, of Dorchester, Mass., was twice married.
1. To ——— Atherton, daughter of Major-General Humphrey
Atherton, of the same town, about 1650. She died ———. "To
Elizabeth Weeks, daughter of Ammiel Weeks, of Dorchester,
March 20, 1679. She was born October 18, 1657."
Timothy Mather, Esq., died January 14, 1684, aged about 56,
by a fall from a scaffold in a barn.
Mrs. Elizabeth Mather died February 19, 1710.

Children,—by his first wife.

7 Samuel,	born July,	1651.	
8 Richard,	bap. November	2, 1653.	
9 Nathaniel,	born September	2, 1658.	
10 Joseph,	born May	25, 1661.	Married Sarah Clapp, of Dorchester, June 2, 1689, and died in 1691. One child.
11 Atherton,	bap. October	4, 1663.	
12 Katharine,	bap.		Died, unmarried, in 1694.

Children,—by his second wife,--none.

FOURTH GENERATION.

7.

REV. SAMUEL MATHER, of Windsor, Conn., third minister of the
First Congregational Church in that town, was married to Hannah
Treat, daughter of Hon. Robert Treat, of Milford, Conn., Lieut.
Governor, afterwards Governor of the colony of Connecticut. He
was son of Richard Treat, one of the first settlers of Wethersfield,
Conn.
Mrs. Hannah Mather died March 8, 1708, aged 47.
Rev. Samuel Mather died March 18, 1728, aged 77.

Children.

13 Samuel,	born	1677.	
14 Azariah,	born August	29, 1685.	Died in Saybrook.
15 Nathaniel,	born August	8, 1716.	

8.

RICHARD MATHER, of Dorchester, until about 1690, and after
that time, of Lyme, Conn., was married to Elizabeth Wise, of Dorchester, July 1, 1680.
Mr. Richard Mather died ———.
His widow, Mrs. Elizabeth Mather, died ———.

Children.

16 Timothy, born March 20, 1681. Died July 25, 1755. [Grave-stone, Lyme burying-ground.]

17 Elizabeth,   born November 20, 1682.
18 Samuel,   born January   3, 1684. Died July 17, 1725. [Grave-stone,
                                            Lyme burying-ground.]
19 Joseph,   born January   29, 1686. Died September 30, 1749. [Grave-
                                            stone, Lyme burying-ground.]

11.

ATHERTON MATHER, first of Windsor, Conn., afterwards of
Suffield, then under the jurisdiction of Massachusetts, now under
that of Connecticut, was twice married. 1. To Rebecca Stoughton,
daughter of Thomas Stoughton, of Windsor, one of the first settlers
of that town, and of Mary, his wife, daughter of the Hon. William
Wadsworth, one of the first settlers of Hartford, Conn., September
20, 1694. She was born June 19, 1673, and died in 1704. 2.
To Mary ———, about 1706.

Ensign Atherton Mather died November 9, 1734, at Suffield,
aged about 71.

His widow, Mrs. Mary Mather, survived her husband, and
died ———.

Children,—by his first wife.

20 William,   born March   2, 1698, in Windsor. Married Silence Buttolph,
                                           November 7, 1721. He died in 1747.
21 Jerusha,   born July   18, 1700, in Windsor. Married Samuel Smith, of
                                           Suffield.

Children,—by his second wife.

22 Joshua,   born November 26, 1706, in Windsor.
23 Richard,   born March   31, 1708, in Windsor. Married Lois Burbank,
                                           daughter of John Burbank, of Suf-
                                           field, March 24, 1734. She was born
                                           January 15, 1715.
24 Mary,   born March   9, 1711, in Windsor.
25 Thomas,   born April   5, 1713, in Suffield.
26 Eliakim,   born July   10, 1715, in Suffield.
27 Catharine, born January   5, 1718, in Suffield. Died January 20, 1733.

FIFTH GENERATION.

18.

SAMUEL MATHER, of Lyme, Conn., was married to Deborah
Champion, daughter of ——— Champion, of Lyme, January 1,
1712.

Mr. Samuel Mather died July 17, 1725.

His widow, Mrs. Deborah Mather, died ———.

Children.

28 Richard,   born December 22, 1712.
29 Mary,   born November 14, 1715.
30 Deborah,   born January   15, 1718. Married Benjamin Marvin, November
                                           11, 1742.
31 Lucy,   born December 28, 1720. Married Nathaniel Peck, May 24, 1744.
32 Mehitabel, born December 28, 1723. Died September 17, 1741, unmarried.

SIXTH GENERATION.

28.

RICHARD MATHER, of Lyme, Conn., was married to Deborah Ely, daughter of ――― Ely, of Lyme, May 18, 1742.

Children.

33 Mehitabel,	born March	7, 1743. Married Samuel Holden Parsons, Esq. He was a brigadier-general in the army of the Revolution. Drowned in Ohio, in December, 1789. Father of Enoch Parsons, deceased, of Hartford, Conn.
34 Samuel,	born February	22, 1745. Married Lois Griswold, daughter of Thomas Griswold, of Lyme, and grand-daughter of Gov. Matthew Griswold. She died November 17, 1804.
35 William,	born September	15, 1746. Died September 24, 1746.
36 William,	born November	21, 1747. Married Rhoda Marvin, of Lyme, May 1, 1768. Removed to Massachusetts.
37 Elias,	born January	1, 1750.
38 Deborah,	born October	3, 1752. Married Capt. Ezra Lee, died June 5, 1816.
39 Ezra,	born February	25, 1755. Died June 4, 1755.
40 Ezra,	born April	27, 1756. Died November 10, 1758.
41 Sylvester,	born September	1, 1758. Married Elizabeth Wait, daughter of Richard Wait, of Lyme. He died in 1811.
42 Polly,	born March	31, 1760. Married William Champlin, of Lyme, January 13, 1780.
43 Lucia,	born March	13, 1763.
44 Richard,	born July	4, 1765. Married Eunice Caulkins, daughter of Doct. Caulkins.

SEVENTH GENERATION.

37.

ELIAS MATHER, of Lyme, Conn., was married to Lucinda Lee, daughter of Abner Lee, of the same town, October 17, 1771.

Capt. Elias Mather died August 30, 1788, aged 38. He was an officer in the Revolutionary army, and during his service, participated in several of the most important engagements.

His widow, Mrs. Lucinda Mather, died in January, 1813, aged 61.

Children.

45 Andrew,	born September	26, 1772. Married Mary Wetmore, daughter of Ichabod Wetmore, of Middletown, Conn., July 7, 1810. Father of Hon. John P. C. Mather, late Secretary of State in Connecticut.
46 Clarissa,	born August	10, 1774. Married Benjamin Griffin, of Ohio.
47 Elias,	born June	25, 1776. Dead. Was a merchant, doing business in Albany, N. Y.
48 William Lee,	born August	1, 1779. Died in London, England, in 1802.
49 Sylvester,	born February	8, 1782. Living in Ohio, unmarried.
50 Nathaniel Greene,	born November	25, 1784. Died April 4, 1785.
51 Charles,	born June	17, 1787. Died in 1813, unmarried.

20

DESCENDANTS IN THE LINE OF NATHANIEL MATHER, SON OF THE REV. RICHARD MATHER.

THIRD GENERATION.

III.

NATHANIEL MATHER was graduated at Harvard College, in 1647,—went to England, and was presented to a living at Barnestaple, by Oliver Cromwell, in 1656, from which he was ejected after the restoration. Succeeded his brother in Dublin. He died in London, July 26, 1697, aged 67, having preached forty-seven years in England, Ireland and Holland. See Allen's Biographical Dictionary. Farmar.

Have no knowledge of descendants in his line.

DESCENDANTS IN THE LINE OF ELEAZUR MATHER, SON OF THE REV. RICHARD MATHER.

THIRD GENERATION.

V.

REV. ELEAZUR MATHER, minister of Northampton, Mass., was married to Esther Warham, daughter of Rev. John Warham, first minister of Windsor, Conn. [After his death, she was married to Rev. Solomon Stoddard, successor to Rev. Mr. Warham, in the ministry at Northampton.]

Rev. Eleazur Mather died July 24, 1669, aged 32.

Mrs. Esther Mather, alias Stoddard, died February 10, 1736, in her 92d year.

Children.

52 Warham,	born September 7, 1666.	
53 Eliakim,	born September 22, 1668.	
54 Eunice,	born August 2, 1664.	Married Rev. John Williams, minister of Hatfield, Mass. Was captured by the Indians.

DESCENDANTS IN THE LINE OF INCREASE MATHER, SON OF THE REV. RICHARD MATHER.

THIRD GENERATION.

VI.

REV. INCREASE MATHER, of Boston, Minister of the North Church in that town, and President of Harvard University, was twice married. 1. To Maria Cotton, daughter of Rev. John Cotton, Colleague Pastor with Rev. John Wilson, first minister of Boston, March 16, 1662. She died April 4, 1714. 2. To Anna Cotton, widow of Rev. John Cotton, of Hampton, N. H., grandson of Rev. John Cotton. She was Anna Lake, daughter of Capt. Thomas Lake.

Rev. Increase Mather died at Boston, August 23, 1723, aged 84.
Mrs. Anna Mather, alias Cotton, died at Brookline, November 27, 1737, aged 74.

Children,—by his first wife.

55 Cotton,	born February	12, 1663.	
56 Maria,	born March	16, 1665.	Married Bartholomew Green, and after his death, Richard Fifield, November 6, 1713. She died November 24, 1746.
57 Elizabeth,	born July	6, 1666.	Married William Greenough, July, 1696, and after his death, Josiah Byles, October 6, 1703.
58 Nathaniel,	born July	6, 1669.	Died October 17, 1688, at Salem, Mass.
59 Sarah,	born November	9, 1671.	Married Rev. Nehemiah Walter. of Roxbury, Mass. She died November 24, 1746. He died September 17, 1750.
60 Samuel,	born August	28, 1674.	Settled in England.
61 Abigail,	born April	13, 1677.	Married Newcomb Blake, and after his death, Rev. John White, of Gloucester, Mass.
62 Hannah,	born May	30, 1680.	Married John Oliver, January 28, 1697. She died December 2, 1706.
63 Catharine,	born September	14, 1682.	Died June 11, 1683.
64 Jerusha,	born April	16, 1684.	Married Peter Oliver, March 8, 1710. She died December 20, 1710.

FOURTH GENERATION.

55.

REV. COTTON MATHER, of Boston, Minister of the North Church in that town, was thrice married. 1. To Abigail Phillips, daughter of Col. John Phillips, of Charlestown, Mass., May 4, 1686. She was born June 19, 1670, and died November 28, 1702. 2. To Elizabeth Hubbard, widow, daughter of Doct. John Clarke, August 18, 1703. She died November 8, 1713. 3. To Lydia George, widow of John George, of Boston, and daughter of Rev. Samuel Lee, July 5, 1715.

Rev. Dr. Cotton Mather died February 13, 1728, aged 65.*

---

* Suffolk county probate records, vol. xxvi., page 187.
At a court July 22, 1728. Administration on the estate of the Rev. Dr. Cotton Mather, late of Boston, deceased, granted to Nathaniel Goodwin, of Boston, shopkeeper.
Same vol. and date, page 189, is a record of " An Inventory of the Estate of Rev. Dr. Cotton Mather, taken by John Barnard, John Goldthwait, Graffton Faveryear, the estate being shown to them by Mrs. Lydia Mather, the widow of the deceased, and the children of the deceased."
Amount of inventory, (among the articles of which are 147 ounces silver plate, at 16s. 6d. the ounce, £121 5s. 6d., and 500 acres of land in the county of Hampshire; at cost, £36,) £271 10s. 10d.
Vol. xxviii., page 10. To all people to whom these presents shall come. Madam Lydia Mather, of Boston, within the county of Suffolk, and province of the Massachusetts Bay, in New-England, relict widow of the Rev. Dr. Cotton Mather, late of Boston aforesaid, clerk, deceased, and Mr. Samuel Mather, aforesaid, gentleman. only surviving son of said Cotton Mather, send greeting :—Know ye, that we the said Lydia Mather and Samuel Mather, as well for and in consideration of the sum of thirty pounds to us in hand at and before the ensealing and delivery of these presents, well and truly paid by Mrs. Hannah Mather, of Boston, aforesaid, spinster, only surviving daughter of the said Cotton Mather, as for divers other causes and considerations us thereunto especially moving, we the said Lydia Mather and Samuel Mather, have granted, bargained, sold, remised, released, quit-claimed, conveyed and confirmed, and by these presents do grant, bargain, &c., unto the said Hannah Mather, all our and each of our right, estate, title, interest, share, part, portion, proportions, dividend, dower, thirds, claims and demands whatsoever of, in and unto

Mrs. Lydia Mather, alias George, died January 22, 1734.

Children—by his first wife.

65 Katharine,	born		" Understood Latin and read Hebrew fluently." Died December, 1716, unmarried.
66 Abigail,	born August	22, 1687.	Died before 1693.
67 Joseph,	born March	28, 1693.	Died April 1, 1693.
68 Abigail,	born June	14, 1694.	Married Daniel Willard. Died September 26, 1721.
69 Hannah,	born	1697.	Was living unmarried in 1728.
70 Increase,	born July,	1699.	Lost at sea before 1728.
71 Samuel,	born	1700.	Died before 1728.

Children,—by his second wife.

72 Elizabeth,	born July	13, 1704.	Married Edward Cooper, July 30, 1724, died August 7, 1726. No children.
73 Samuel,	born October	30, 1706.	Was a minister in Boston, ordained in the same church in which his father was settled. He died June 27, 1785.
74 Nathaniel,	born May	16, 1707.	Died November 24, 1709.
75 Jerusha,	born April,	1711.	Died November, 1713.
76 Eleazur, } 77 Martha, }	born	1713.	Died November, same year.

Children,—by his third wife,—none.

---

all the goods, chattels and personal estate of the said Cotton Mather which belonged and appeared to him at the time of his decease, as the same are particularly named and expressed in an inventory of the same exhibited into the probate office for the county of Suffolk, on the 5th day of August, 1728, to have and to hold, &c.

Dated April 24, 1730.

Vol. xxviii. page 22. Court, May 28, 1730. Suffolk, *ss.* By the Hon. Josiah Willard, Esq., Judge of Probate. Whereas, it appears to me by the inventory and account presented by Nathaniel Goodwin, administrator to the estate of the Reverend Doctor Cotton Mather, late of Boston, clerk, deceased, that there is clear personal estate, amounts to two hundred and forty and five pounds, five shillings and two pence, after administration charges and payments by him made are deducted, one-third part thereof, being eighty-one pounds fifteen shillings and three pence, belongs by law to Lydia Mather, wife of said Cotton Mather, he dying intestate,—two single shares or fourth parts of the remaining two-thirds, being eighty-one pounds eleven shillings and two pence, appertains and belongs to Samuel Mather, clerk, only surviving son of the said deceased, and the rest of his children, viz., Abigail Willard, deceased, wife of Daniel Willard, also deceased, their children, as legal representatives, and Hannah Mather, spinster, are by law entitled to a single share of their said father's estate, amounting to forty pounds, fifteen shillings and ten pence half penny, to each of them.

I do therefore hereby order the said administrator to pay the said widow and children, or their respective guardians, their parts and shares of their said father's estate, accordingly,— they bearing their proportion of all such debts as shall hereafter appear due and owing from his estate.

Given under my hand and seal of the said court of probate the 25th of May, 1730.

Exam'd p^r John Boydell, Reg.   JOSIAH WILLARD.

MICHAEL METCALF.*

MICHAEL METCALF,† one of the first settlers of Dedham, Mass., was twice married. 1. To Sarah ——, October 13, 1616, in England. She died November 30, 1644, at Dedham, aged 51. 2. To Mary Pidge, of Roxbury, widow, August 13, 1645.

Mr. Michael Metcalf died December 27, 1664, aged 78.

Mrs. Mary Metcalf, alias Pidge, died ——.

FIRST GENERATION.

Children of Michael Metcalf, by his first wife, Sarah Metcalf,—all born in England.

I. Michael,	born November	13, 1617.	Died young, in England.
II. Mary,	born February	14, 1618.	Married Henry Wilson, November 24, 1642.
III. Michael,	born August	29, 1620.	
IV. John,	born September	5, 1622.	Settled in Medfield. Married Mary Chickering, daughter of Francis Chickering, of Dedham, March 22, 1647, died November 27, 1675.

* See Genealogical Register, April, 1852.

† Michael Metcalf, the emigrant ancestor of this family, was born in Tatterford, county of Norfolk, England, 1586. His wife Sarah was born in the adjoining town of Wearham, June 17, 1593, where they were married. October 13, 1616. Their seven oldest children were born in St. Benedict's, Norwich, and four, afterwards, at St. Edmondsbury. "I was persecuted," he writes, "in the land of my father's sepulchres, for not bowing at the name of Jesus, and observing other ceremonies in religion, forced upon me, at the instance of Bishop Wren, of Norwich, and his chancellor Dr. Corbet, whose violent measures troubled me in the Bishop's Court, and returned me into the High Commissioners' Court. Suffering many times for the cause of religion, I was forced, for the sake of the liberty of my conscience, to flee from my wife and children, to go into New-England ; taking ship for the voyage at London, the 17th of Sept 1636 ; being by tempests tossed up and down the seas till the Christmas following, then veering about to Plymouth in Old England, in which time I met with many sore afflictions.

"Leaving the ship, I went down to Yarmouth, in Norfolk county, whence I shipped myself and family, to come to New-England; sailed 15th April, 1637, and arrived three days before midsummer, with my wife, nine children and a servant." The name of this servant appears to have been Thomas Comherbach, aged 16. [Manuscript of Hon. James Savage.]

The above extracts we take from a copy of his letter, written in Plymouth, Eng., Jan. 13, 1636, on his voyage hither ; directed, "To all the true professors of Christ's Gospel within the city of Norwich." In the postscript, he remarks, "my enemies conspired against me to take my life, and, sometimes, to avoid their hands, my wife did hide me in the roof of the house, covering me over with straw."

History informs us, that one of the charges brought against Bishop Wren, by a Committee of Parliament, was, that during the term of two years and four months, while he held the See of Norwich, "3000 of his Majesty's subjects, many of whom use trades, spinning, weaving, knitting, making cloth, stuff, stockings, and other manufactures of wool, some of them setting a hundred poor people at work," "transported themselves into Holland," and "other parts beyond the seas" in consequence of his "superstition and tyranny." [See appendix to Dr. Lamson's Hist. Discourses.]

Michael Metcalf was admitted a townsman at Dedham, July 14, 1637 ; joined the church in 1639, and was selectman in 1641. His name stands first on the Committee chosen to "contrive the fabricke of a meeting house."

V. Sarah,   born September 10, 1624. Married Robert Onion, of Dedham.
VI. Elizabeth,born October   4, 1626. Married Thomas Bancroft, of Reading,
                                            September 15, 1648.
VII. Martha, born March   -27, 1628. Married 1. William Brignall. 2. Chris-
                                            topher Smith, August 2, 1654. 3.
                                            ——— Stow.
VIII. Thomas, born December 27, 1629. Married 1. Sarah Paige, September 12,
                                            1655 or '6. 2. Anne Paine, Decem-
                                            ber 2, 1679. He was deacon at Ded-
                                            ham, died November 16, 1702.
IX. Ann,   born March   1, 1631. Died young, in England.
X. Joan,   born March   24, 1632. Married Samuel Walker, of Rehoboth.
XI. Rebeka,   born April   5, 1635. Married John Mackintosh, of Dedham,
                                            April 5, 1659.

Children of Michael Metcalf, by his second wife,—none.

DESCENDANTS IN THE LINE OF MICHAEL METCALF, SON OF MICHAEL METCALF, THE SETTLER.

THIRD GENERATION.

III.

MICHAEL METCALF, of Dedham, Mass., was married to Mary Fairbanks, daughter of John Fairbanks, senior, April 2, 1644.
Mr. Michael Metcalf died December 24, 1654, aged 34.
His widow, Mrs. Mary Metcalf, died ———.

Children.

12 Michael,   born January 21, 1645. Married Elizabeth Kingsbury, daugh-
                                            ter of John Kingsbury, September
                                            17, 1672. He died September 1,
                                            1693. She died October 24, 1732.
13 Mary,   born August   15, 1646. Married John Ware, December 10, 1668.
14 Sarah,   born December 7, 1648. Married Robert Ware, of Wrentham,
                                            June 4, 1677.
15 Jonathan,   born September 21, 1650.
16 Eleazur,   born March   20, 1653. Was Deacon at Wrentham. Married
                                            April 9, 1684.

FOURTH GENERATION.

15.

JONATHAN METCALF, of Dedham, Mass., was married to Hannah Kenric, daughter of John Kenric, April 10, 1674.
Mr. Jonathan Metcalf died May 27, 1727, in his 77th year.
His widow, Mrs. Hannah Metcalf, died December 23, 1731.

Children.

17 Jonathan,   born March   16, 1676.
18 John, (Esq.) born March   20, 1678. Died October 6, 1749. Married 1.
                                            Mehitabel Savels, of Braintree, April
                                            29, 1701, by whom he had 6 children.
                                            She died March 30, 1712, aged 29.
                                            2. Bethia Savels, cousin of his first
                                            wife, February 12, 1713, by whom
                                            he had 2 children. She died May
                                            22, 1717, aged 35. 3. Grace Williams,
                                            daughter of Stephen Williams, of
                                            Roxbury, October 25, 1718. By her
                                            he had 9 children. She died Novem-
                                            ber 11, 1749, aged 61.

19 Ebenezer,	born February	14, 1680.	
20 Joseph,	born April	11, 1682.	Harvard University, 1703. Was minister in Falmouth, Mass. Married Abiel Adams, youngest daughter of Rev. William Adams, of Dedham. He died in 1723. His widow married Rev. Isaac Chauncey, second minister of Hadley, Mass.
21 Timothy,	born November	18, 1684.	Died July 3, 1695.
22 Eleazur,	born February	14, 1687.	Married Hannah Ware, September 6, 1711.
23 Hannah,	born April	10, 1689.	Married James Richards, of Dedham.
24 Nathaniel,	born April 17 or 22, 1691.		Married Mary Gay, February 13 or 17, 1713.
25 Mehitabel,	born [no date.]		Married John Huntington.
26 Mary,	born [no date.]		Married, 1. John Pratt. 2. Ichabod Warner, of Windham, Conn.

FIFTH GENERATION.

17.

JONATHAN METCALF, of Lebanon, Conn., was married to Hannah Avery, January 15, 1701.

Jonathan Metcalf, Esq., died March 30, 1739, in his 63d year.[*]

His widow, Mrs. Hannah Metcalf, died ———.

Children.

27 Hannah,	born January	17, 1702.	Married Samuel Huntington, of Lebanon.
28 Jonathan,	born August	10, 1704.	Married, and had 9 sons and 1 daughter.
29 Mehitabel,	born July	26, 1706.	Married John Huntington, of Lebanon.
30 William,	born August	17, 1708.	
31 Mary,	born April	17, 1711.	Married Rev. Peter Pratt, of Sharon, July 6, 1741.
32 Job,	born November	23, 1712.	Died March 24, 1715.
33 Abigail,	born September	7, 1714.	Died March 25, 1716.

19.

EBENEZER METCALF, of Lebanon, Conn., was married to Hannah Abel.

Mr. Ebenezer Metcalf died November 15, 1755, in his 76th year.

His widow, Mrs. Hannah Metcalf, died ———.

Children.

34 Ebenezer,	born	
35 Benjamin,	born	
36 Timothy,	born	
37 Joseph,	born July	8, 1711.
38 Lucy,	born December	25, 1713.
39 Anna,	born March	18, 1716.
40 Jabez,	born November	30, 1718.

NOTE. The Genealogical Notes of Michael Metcalf, from the first generation to the fourth, both inclusive, were gathered and compiled by Dr. Luther Metcalf Harris, Jamaica Plain, Roxbury, Mass., and form part of a communication on the subject, made by him to the editor of the New England Historical and Genealogical Register, and published in the April number, 1852, of that work.

* Here lies the body of Mr. Jonathan Metcalf, a virtuous, Christian, and generous merchant and benefactor of the Church and first Society in Lebanon, who having been long and solicitiousley trading for the Pearl of Great Price, exchanged this life in the hope of a better and more enduring substance, March 30, 1738–9, in the 63d year of his age. [Grave-Stone Lebanon burying ground.]

SIXTH GENERATION.

30.

WILLIAM METCALF, of Lebanon, Conn., was married to Abigail Edwards, daughter of Rev. Timothy Edwards, Pastor of the Congregational Church at East Windsor, Conn., October 25, 1737. Mrs. Abigail Metcalf died September 24, 1764, in her 57th year.* William Metcalf, Esq., died June 15, 1773, in his 65th year.†

Children.

41 Abigail,	born April	2, 1739.	
42 William,	born June	14, 1742.	Died July 5, 1750.
43 Eliphalet,	born July	10, 1744.	Died in May, 1745.
44 Lucy,	born May	25, 1746.	
45 Eliphalet,	born November	25, 1747.	

SEVENTH GENERATION.

41.

ABIGAIL METCALF was married to Moses Bliss, Esq., of Springfield, Mass., July 20, 1763.

Mrs. Abigail Bliss died August 29, 1800, in her 62d year.

Hon. Moses Bliss died July 4, 1814, in his 79th year.

Children.

46 George,	born December 13, 1764.	Settled in Springfield. Was thrice married. 1. To Hannah Clark, daughter of Doct. John Clark, of Lebanon, Conn., May 22, 1789. She died September 19, 1795, aged 32, 2. To Mary Lathrop, daughter of John Lathrop, of New Haven, Conn., May 29, 1799. She died May 1, 1833, aged 36. 3. To Abigail Rowland, daughter of Rev. David Sherman Rowland, of Windsor, Conn., November 15, 1804. Hon. George Bliss, LL. D., died March 8, 1830, aged 65. His widow, Mrs. Abigail Bliss, died January 21, 1832, aged 58. Children, by his first wife, 4,—by his second wife, none,—and by his third wife, 4.
47 Lucy,	born June 19, 1766.	Married Doct. Hezekiah Clark, of Lebanon., Conn., afterwards of Pompey, N. Y., June 2, 1785. He died at Pompey, March 4, 1826, aged 68. She died January 19, 1850, at Syracuse, N. Y., January 19, 1850, aged 83.
48 Abigail,	born November 20, 1768.	Married William Ely, Esq., of Springfield, Mass., 1803. Hon. William

---

* Here lies the body of Mrs. Abigail Metcalf, wife of William Metcalf, Esq. Pious, virtuous, faithful in life, and by faith in Jesus pass'd through Death with resignation to the will of God, and cheerful hope of blessedness in him, September 24, 1764, in the 57th year of her age. [Grave-stone, Lebanon burying ground.]

† Here lies the body of William Metcalf, Esq., who was many years a judicious, faithful magistrate, a serious professor of religion, who, after long and patient enduring extreme pain, departed this life in hope of a better, June 15, 1773, in the 65th year of his age Grave-stone, Lebanon burying ground.]

49 William
Metcalf, born October 23, 1770.
50 Frances B , born May 10, 1772.

51 Moses, born July 10, 1774.

52 Edmund, born November 10, 1775.
53 Emily, born August 26, 1780.
54 Harriet, born March 23, 1782.

Ely died October 9, 1817, in the 53d year of his age.ᐧ His widow, Mrs. Abigail Ely, died October 7, 1827, aged 59. They had no children.

Married Rev. Henry A. Rowland, Pastor of the Congregational Church, Windsor, Conn., April 18, 1700. She was his second wife. His first wife, Elizabeth W., died August 12, 1796, aged 23. He died November 28, 1835, aged 72. She died January 18, 1833, in her 61st year. They had 8 children.

Settled in Springfield, married Mary Wolcott, daughter of ——— Wolcott, of Saybrook, Conn., 1804. Moses Bliss, Esq., died September 11, 1849, aged 75. His widow, Mrs. Mary Bliss, died ———. They had 10 children: among them Mary, born May 8, 1810, and Caroline, born September 17, 1817, were married to William B. Bristol, Esq., of New-Haven, Conn., the former in 1836, and after her death, which occurred February 12, 1849,—the latter November, 1850.

Died young.
Died May 5, 1797.
Married Daniel Bontecew, of Springfield, 1816. Two children are found recorded to them.

44.

LUCY METCALF was married to John Huntington, of East-Haddam, Conn., May 25, 1746.

Mrs. Lucy Huntington died April 13, 1818, aged 72, nearly.

Mr. John Huntington died March 5, 1830, aged 93.

Children.

55 Frances, born January 21, 1770.
56 Lucy, born January 25, 1772.
57 John, born March 25, 1773.
58 Abigail, born November 21, 1776.
59 Israel, born June 2, 1780.
60 Eunice, born October 31, 1784.
61 William, born [no date.]

45.

ELIPHALET METCALF, of Lebanon, Conn., was married to Mary West, daughter of Joshua West, of the same town, December 21, 1775. She was born January 2, 1754.

Eliphalet Metcalf, Esq., died March 15, 1834, aged 86.

His widow. Mrs. Mary Metcalf, died March 12. 1835, in her 82d year.

Children.

62 William, born December 10, 1776. Married Margaret Van Tuyl, of Nor-

21

63 John,	born May	24, 1779.	thumberland, N. Y., March, 1808. He died July 25, 1825, aged 48. Lives in Northumberland, N. Y.
64 Mary,	born February	11, 1781.	Died September 4, 1783.
65 Abigail,	born June	18, 1783.	Married Ariel Burchard, of Bozrah, Conn., March 31, 1808. She died August 12, 1811.
66 Eliphalet,	born May	29, 1785.	Married Mary Jones, daughter of Isaac Jones, of Monson, Mass., formerly of Lebanon, March 20, 1817.
67 Mary,	born August	28, 1787.	Married Benjamin S. Van Tuyl, of the city of New York, March 20, 1817.
68 Lucy,	born October	20, 1789.	Died December 3, 1809.
69 Elizabeth,	born February	16, 1792.	Resides in Lebanon.
70 Timothy Edwards,	born September	10, 1795.	Residence,—Lebanon,—on the Metcalf Farm.
71 Emily,	born September	2, 1798.	Resides in Lebanon.

JOSEPH MYGATT.

FIRST GENERATION.

JOSEPH MYGATT, one of the first settlers of Hartford, was married to Ann ———.

Deacon Joseph Mygatt died December 7, 1680, age unknown.
His widow, Mrs. Ann Mygatt, died in 1686.

SECOND GENERATION.

Children.

1 Jacob,	born	1633.
2 Mary,	born	1637.

THIRD GENERATION.

1.

JACOB MYGATT was married to Sarah Whiting, daughter of William Whiting, late of Hartford, merchant, deceased, about the year 1655.

Mr. Jacob Mygatt died ———.

His wife survived him, and was married to John King, of Northampton, Mass. She died about 1704.

Children.

3 Joseph,	born
4 Sarah,	born

2.

MARY MYGATT was married to John Deming, jun., of Wethersfield, September 20, 1657.

Mr. John Deming died ———.

His widow, Mrs. Mary Deming, died ———.

Children.

5 John,	born September	9, 1658.
6 Joseph,	born June	1, 1661.
7 Jonathan,	born February	12, 1663.
8 Mary,	born July	1, 1666.
9 Samuel,	born August	25, 1668.
10 Jacob,	born August	26, 1670.
11 Sarah,	born January	17, 1672.

FOURTH GENERATION.

3.

JOSEPH MYGATT was married to Sarah Webster, daughter of Lieut. Robert Webster, of Hartford, November 5, 1677.   He died in 1698.

Children.

12 Joseph,	born October	23, 1678.	
13 Susanna,	born October	3, 1680.	
14 Mary,	born December	4, 1682.	
15 Jacob,	born December	9, 1684.	Died January 29, 1685.
16 Jacob,	born November	9, 1686.	
17 Thomas,	born September	11, 1688.	
18 Sarah,	born March	9, 1691.	
19 Zebulon,	born November	3, 1693.	Rachel, wife of Zebulon Mygatt, born 1701, died May 14, 1721, aged 20. [Tombstone, Suffield burying-ground.]
20 Dorothy,	born January	26, 1696.	

4.

SARAH MYGATT was married to John Webster, of Hartford. He died 1696.   His widow was married to Benjamin Graham, of Hartford, November 20, 1698.

Children,—by her first husband.

21 John.	
22 Ebenezer.	
23 Jacob.	
24 Daniel.	
25 Sarah.	Married a Talcott.
26 Ann.	Married Thomas Olmsted, Jr.
27 Abigail.	Married a Merrill.

Children,—by her second husband.

28 Elisha,	born Feb.	24, 1699–1700.
29 Isaac,	born July	2, 1702.

NOTE.   Jacob Mygatt, son of Zebulon Mygatt, and of Dorathy, his wife, born (May or July 17,) 1721.   [Hartford Records.]

JOHN NOTT.

FIRST GENERATION.

JOHN NOTT, of Wethersfield, Conn., and one of the first settlers of that town, was married to Ann ———.
Sargeant John Nott died January 25, 1682, aged —.
His widow, Mrs. Ann Nott, died ———.

SECOND GENERATION.

Children of John Nott, and of Ann, his wife.

I. Elizabeth, born [no date.]
II. Hannah, born June 10, 1649.
III. John, born January 10, 1651.

DESCENDANTS IN THE LINE OF ELIZABETH NOTT, DAUGHTER OF JOHN NOTT, THE SETTLER.

THIRD GENERATION.

I.

ELIZABETH NOTT was married to Robert Reeve, of Hartford, Conn., and one of the first settlers of that town, about 1662.
Mr. Robert Reeve died in February, 1681.
His widow, Mrs. Elizabeth Reeve, died ———.

Children.

4 Sarah, born December 25, 1663. Married Asa Merrills.
5 Mary, born July 31, 1665.
6 Elizabeth, born December, 1668. Married Samuel Webster, of Hartford. He died February 1, 1744. She died in 1747. They had no children.
7 Hannah, born October, 1670. Married a Stratton, of Long Island.
8 Nathaniel, born October, 1672. Believed to have died before 1693. See book 5, p. 122, Hartford Records.
9 Robert, } twins born April, 1675. Married Elizabeth, and *perhaps* after her death, Sarah Adkins.
10 Ann, } Died March 10, 1690.
11 Abraham, born September, 1677. Settled at East-Hampton, on Long-Island.
12 Mehitabel, born March, 1680. Married John Peck, of Hartford, November 11, 1707.

DESCENDANTS IN THE LINE OF HANNAH NOTT, DAUGHTER OF JOHN NOTT, THE SETTLER.

THIRD GENERATION.

II.

HANNAH NOTT was married to John Hale, of Wethersfield, Conn., May 8, 1668. He was son of Samuel Hale, of Wethersfield, and was born February 21, 1647.

Children.

13 John,	born February	7, 1669.
14 Samuel,	born April	3, 1671.
15 Hannah,	born June	1, 1673.
16 Thomas,	born September,	1675.

DESCENDANTS IN THE LINE OF JOHN NOTT, SON OF JOHN NOTT, THE SETTLER.

THIRD GENERATION.

III.

JOHN NOTT, of Wethersfield, Conn., was married to Patience Miller, daughter of William Miller, March 28, 1683.

Sargeant John Nott died May 21, 1710, in his 62d year.

His widow, Mrs. Patience Nott, is supposed to have died in Saybrook, Conn., after 1745, at an advanced age.

Children.

17 John,	born November	23, 1683.	Dwelt in Fairfield in 1739.
18 Jonathan,	born June	4, 1685.	Married Sarah Dix, daughter of Samuel Dix, of Wethersfield, April 3, 1707. She died June 30, 1757. He died March 30, 1773.
19 William,	born November	19, 1686.	Married Elizabeth Hall, daughter of John and Rebina Hall, of Wethersfield, February 2, 1710. She was born February 25, 1691, and died May 3, 1733. After her death he was married to ———. He died November 24, 1737.
20 Thomas,	born October	1, 1688.	
21 Nathaniel,	born April	18, 1691.	Married Hannah Gilbert of Wethersfield.
22 Gershom,	born March	19, 1693.	Married Sarah Waterhouse, of Wethersfield, September 17, 1721. He died September 17, 1772. She died March 1, 1779. 5 children.
23 Thankful,	born January	6, 1695.	Married William Blinn, of Wethersfield.
24 Abraham,	born January	29, 1697.	
25 Ann,	born July	29, 1699.	Married Thomas Harris, of Wethersfield, December 28, 1729.

FOURTH GENERATION.

24.

ABRAHAM NOTT, of Saybrook, Conn., first Pastor of the Second Congrégational Church in that town, (now Essex Society,) was married to Phebe Tapping.* After his death she was married, in June, 1758, to Lieut. John Pratt, of Saybrook.

Rev. Abraham Nott died January 24, 1756, in his 61st year.

Mrs. Phebe Nott, alias Pratt, died ———.

Children.

26 Abraham,	born about	1724.	
27 Keturah,	born about	1726.	
28 Stephen,	born July	24, 1728.	
29 Temperance,	born February,	1731.	Died October 8, 1731, aged 8 months.
30 Josiah,	born	1732.	
31 Epaphrus,	born [no date.]		

FIFTH GENERATION.

26.

ABRAHAM. NOTT, of Saybrook, Conn., was twice married. 1. To Abigail, daughter of ——— Selden, September 22, 1748. She died October 20, 1750, aged 21. 2. To Abigail Parker, daughter of Abner Parker, of Saybrook. She was born October 12, 1730. After his death she was married to Stephen Clark, of Essex Society, Saybrook.

Mr. Abraham Nott died in 1756.

Mrs. Abigail Nott, alias Clark, died ———.

Child,—by his first wife,—one only.

32 Child, (not named,)	born	Died in infancy.

Children,—by his second wife.

33 Selden,	born [no date.]
34 Abigail,	born [no date.]

27.

KETURAH NOTT was twice married. 1. To Capt. Abner Parker, jun., of Saybrook, Conn. He died in 1756, in his 32d year. To Doct. Joseph Bishop, of Saybrook. After her death Doct. Bishop was married to widow Pelton.

Mrs. Keturah Bishop, alias Parker, died ———.

Doct. Joseph Bishop died ———.

Children,—by her first husband.

35 Child, (not named,)	born [no date.]		Died in infancy.
39 Child, (not named,)	born [no date.]		Died in infancy.
37 Lovisa,	born about	1750.	Died May 19, 1763, in her 13th year.

28.

STEPHEN NOTT, first of Middletown, Conn., then of Saybrook, Conn., then of East-Haddam, Conn., and afterwards of Ashford, in the same state, was twice married. 1. To Deborah Selden, daughter of Samuel Selden, of Lyme, Conn., December 15, 1749.

---

* Supposed daughter of John Tapping, of Southampton, L. I., who died 1747, leaving a daughter Phebe.

She died at Ashford, October 24, 1788, aged 55. To Abigail
Bradford, widow, November 1, 1789.

Mr. Stephen Nott died at Franklin, Conn., January 29, 1790,
in his 62d year.

Mrs Abigail Nott, alias Bradford, died ————.

Children,—by his first wife.

38 Temperance,born October	7, 1752, at Middletown. Died at Saybrook, August 25, 1759, in her 7th year.
39 Samuel, born January	23, 1754, at Saybrook. Yale College, 1780. Minister of Franklin, Conn.* He died at 2 o'clock, P. M., Wednesday, May 26, 1852, at the parsonage house, Franklin,—in the 99th year of his age.
40 Phebe, born March	11, 1756, at Saybrook. Died at Colesville, N. Y., August 25, 1829.
41 Temperance,born March	10, 1760, at Saybrook. Married a Mr. Spalding, and died at Orwell, Ver., about September, 1807.
42 Charlotte, born August	17, 1762, at Saybrook. Married a Mr. Chester. Died at East-Granville, Mass., April 10, 1844.
43 Lovice, born February,	1764, at East-Haddam, Conn. Married a Mr. Moore, of Granby, Conn., where she died, August 19, 1796, leaving 6 children.
44 Rhoda, born December	1, 1768, at East-Haddam. Married Benjamin Walker, of Ashford, Conn. She died December 1, 1790. They had 2 children,—both daughters.
45 Deborah, born March	20, 1770, at East-Haddam.
46 Eliphalet, born June	25, 1773, at Ashford.

30.

JOSIAH NOTT, of Saybrook, Conn., was married to Zerviah
Clark, daughter of ———— Clark, of the same town, November 17,
1757.

Deacon Josiah Nott died December 17, 1814, in his 82d year.

His widow, Mrs. Zerviah Nott, died December 1, 1816, in her
88th year.

Children.

47 Sarah, born July	26, 1758.
48 Keturah, born December	26, 1759. Died April 8, 1794.
49 Jos'ah.†	
50 Rebecca, born April	28, 1763. Died March 16, 1837.
51 Zerviah, born February	17, 1766.
52 Abraham, born February	5, 1768.
53 Clark, born October	14, 1770. Was Deacon in the church,—town clerk of Saybrook, many years, and father of the wife of the present clerk of that town, Selden M. Pratt, Esq.

* " The 98th anniversary of Rev. Dr. Nott's birth was observed by a numerous company
of Parishioners and friends, at his house in Franklin, Ct., on the 23d of January, 1852.
There were 150 persons present, whose overflowing baskets of rich provisions, &c., showed
the abiding esteem in which the people hold their venerated pastor. The aged divine.
trembling under the blasts of 98 winters, leaning on the arm of his grand-daughter, stood
at the end of the long table groaning under the weight of tempting eatables tastefully
arranged, and invoked the blessing of God in appropriate terms. He also led in prayer near
the close of the pleasant and cheerful interview. The entertainment finally wound up
with singing. The Doctor's bodily health is still good, though now the oldest pastor in the
Union."

† Sally," wife of Josiah Nott died August 10, 1819, aged 50. [Grave-stone, Pettipaug.]
Probably wife of this Josiah.

31.

EPAPHRUS NOTT, first of Saybrook, Conn., then of Wallingford, in the same state, and afterwards of the state of Maryland, was married to Isabel Parker, daughter of Abner Parker, of Saybrook, June 17, 1759. She was born July 17, 1734.

Mr. Epaphrus Nott died ———.

His widow, Mrs. Isabel Nott, died ———.

Children.

54 Polly,	born April	28, 1760, in Saybrook.
55 Lovisa,	born October	28, 1761, in Wallingford.
56 Hannah,	born October	22, 1763, in Wallingford.
57 Abraham,	born August	29, 1765, in Wallingford.
58 Lucy,	born June	20, 1767, in Wallingford.
59 Isabel,	born [no date.]	

22

JOHN PORTER.

JOHN PORTER, one of the first settlers of Windsor, Conn., was married in England to Rose ———.

"Mr. John Porter died and was buried April 22, 1648." [Windsor Records.]

"His widow, Mrs. Rose Porter, was buried May 12, 1648." [Windsor Records.]

FIRST GENERATION.

Children of John Porter and Rose his wife.

I. John,	born		
II. James,	born		Was a merchant in London and agent of the colony of Connecticut—See Trumbull, Vol. I., p. 406.
III. Sarah,	born	1626.	Married to Joseph Judson, of Milford, Conn., Oct. 24, 1644. He died Oct. 8, 1690, aged 71. She died March 16, 1696, aged 70.
IV. Samuel,	born		
V. Rebecca,	born		
VI. Rose,	born		
VII. Mary,	born		
VIII. Anna,	born		
IX. Joseph,	born		
X. Nathaniel,	born July	19, 1640.	
XI. Hannah,	born September	4, 1642.	

SECOND GENERATION.

IV.

SAMUEL PORTER, of Hadley, Mass., was married to Hannah Stanley, daughter of Thomas Stanley, one of the first settlers of Hartford, Conn., and Hadley, Mass., about 1659.

Mr. Samuel Porter died September 6, 1689, aged ———.

His widow, Mrs. Hannah Porter, died December 18, 1708.

Children.

12 Samuel,	born April	6, 1660.	
13 Child,	born April	26, 1662.	Died the same day.
14 Thomas,	born April	17. 1663.	
15 Hezekiah,	born January	7, 1665.	
16 John,	born December	12, 1666.	Married Mary Butler, April 3, 1690.
17 Mehitabel,	born September	15, 1673.	Married Deacon Nathaniel Goodwin, of Hartford.
18 Experience,	born August	5, 1676.	
19 Ichabod,	born June	17, 1678.	

THIRD GENERATION.

12.

SAMUEL PORTER, jun., of Hadley, Mass., was married to Joanna Cook, daughter of Aaron Cooke, of the same town, February 22, 1684. She was born July 10, 1667.

Samuel Porter, Esq., died July 29, 1722, aged 62.

His widow, Mrs. Joanna Porter, died ———.

Children.

20 Samuel,	born May	25, 1685.	Married Ann Colton, daughter of Thomas Colton, third son of George Colton, one of the first settlers of Springfield, Mass., and of Elizabeth his first wife, daughter of ——— Griswold, of Lyme, Conn. 7 children.
21 Joanna,	born December	24, 1686.	
22 Aaron,	born July	19, 1688.	
23 Moses,	born June	28, 1690.	
24 Sarah,	born December	12, 1692.	Married Josiah Goodrich, of Wethersfield, Conn., but subsequently of Tolland, Conn., December 5, 1711. She died in July, 1726. After her death he was again married. He died in 1731, at Tolland.
25 Mehitabel,	born September	12, 1694.	
26 Miriam,	born April	3, 1696.	Died October 15, 1703.
27 Eleazur,	born February	25, 1698.	
28 Hannah,	born July	2, 1699.	Died August 12, 1699.
29 Nathaniel,	born July	12, 1700.	Died November, 1700.
30 Ruth,	born November	10, 1701.	Married Rev. Stephen Steele, of Tolland, Conn., May 2, 1720.
31 Mary,	born November	4, 1703.	
32 Daughter,	born October	20, 1705.	Died same day.
33 Son,	born December	5, 1706.	Died same day.

FOURTH GENERATION.

27.

ELEAZUR PORTER was married to Sarah Pitkin, sister of Col. John Pitkin, and daughter of ——— Pitkin, of East Hartford, Conn., about 1721.

Hon. Eleazur Porter died November 6, 1757, aged 60.

His widow, Mrs. Sarah Pitkin Porter, died June 6, 1784, aged 82. Born 1702.

Children.

34 Jerusha,	born February	24, 1722.	Died August 5, 1726.
35 Eleazur,	born October	28, 1723.	Died August 6, 1726.
36 Sarah,	born April	18, 1726.	Died February 5, 1774.
37 Eleazur,	born June	27, 1728.	Was Hon. Eleazur.
38 Jerusha,	born August	11, 1730.	
39 Elizabeth,	born November	11, 1732.	Died September 14, 1755.
40 Mary,	born May	2, 1736.	Died September 4, 1736.
41 William,	born April	13, 1738.	Died November 28, 1738.
42 Mehitabel,	born December	3, 1739.	Died November 7, 1755.
43 Elisha,	born January	29, 1741.	
44 William,	born April	13, 1746.	Died October 5, 1755.
45 Mary,	born September	16, 1748.	Died June 24, 1782.

FIFTH GENERATION.

37.

ELEAZUR PORTER, Esq., of Hadley, Mass., was twice married. 1. To Anna Pitkin, daughter of Col. John Pitkin, of East Hartford, Conn., about 1754. She died November 7, 1758, in her 24th year. 2. To Susanna Edwards, daughter of Rev. Jonathan Edwards, Minister of Northampton, Mass., afterwards President of the College in New Jersey, September 17, 1761. Hon. Eleazur Porter died May 27, 1797, aged 69. His widow, Mrs. Susannah Porter, died May 2, 1803, in her 63d year.

Children,—by his first wife.

46 Elizabeth,	born August 29, 1755.	Died October 14, 1755.
47 Anne,	born September 25, 1756.	Married Selah Norton, of East Hartford. He died October 20, 1821, aged 78. She died in East Hartford, February 20, 1850, aged 93.
48 Elizabeth,	born October 17, 1758.	

Children,—by his second wife.

49 Eleazur,	born June 14, 1762.
50 William P.,	born December 9, 1763.
51 Jonathan Edwards,	born May 17, 1766.
52 Moses,	born September 19, 1768.
53 John,	born July 27, 1772.
54 Pierpont,	born June 12, 1775.

SIXTH GENERATION.

49.

ELEAZUR PORTER, of Hadley, Mass., was married to Sarah Keyes, daughter of David Keyes, of Weston, Mass., January 5, 1783.

Mrs. Sarah Porter died March 26, 1838, aged 76.

Eleazur Porter, Esq., died May 2, 1849, aged 87, nearly.

Children.

55 David K.,	born February 25, 1784.	
56 Susan,	born December 20, 1786.	Died January 11, 1830
57 Edwin,	born June 12, 1790	
58 Henry,	born September 1, 1792.	Died October 3, 1826.
59 Maria,	born July 2, 1797.	
60 Eleazur,	born August 15, 1799.	
61 Horace,	born July 11, 1803.	Died January 21, 1834.

50.

WILLIAM PORTER was twice married. 1. To Lois Eastman, daughter of Deacon John Eastman, of Hadley, December 9, 1788. She died December 12, 1792, aged 29. To Charlotte Williams, daughter of Hon. William Williams, of Dalton, Mass., June 10, 1794.

Mrs. Charlotte Porter died November 13, 1842, aged 72.

Doct. William Porter died November 6, 1847, aged 84, nearly.

Children,—by his first wife.

62 Daughter, born October 14, 1789. Died in infancy.
63 John, born October 24, 1790.

Children,—by his second wife.

64 Eleazur
　Williams, born May 29, 1795. Died February 29, 1797.
65 Caroline
　Williams, born May 19, 1797.
66 Mary Ed-
　wards, born December 11, 1799. Died May 13, 1803.
67 Lois East-
　man, born February 8, 1801.
68 James Bay-
　ard, born February 10, 1803.
69 Jeremiah, born December 27, 1805.
70 Charles, born May 12, 1807. Died September 1, 1807.
71 Charles, born July 28, 1808. Died July 30, 1808.

51.

JONATHAN EDWARDS PORTER, of Hadley, Mass., was married to Fidelia Dwight, daughter of Timothy Dwight, Esq., of Northampton, Mass., January 16, 1793.

Mr. Jonathan Edwards Porter died March 24, 1821, aged 55.

His widow, Mrs. Fidelia Porter, died July 27, 1847, aged 80.

Children.

72 Julia, born April 16, 1794. Died December 18, 1830.
73 Timothy
　Dwight, born June 4, 1797.
74 Theodore
　Woolsey, born July 15, 1799.

52.

MOSES PORTER, of Hadley, Mass., was married to Amy Colt, daughter of Benjamin Colt,* of the same town, August 30, 1791.

Mrs. Amy Porter died February 14, 1843, aged 71.

Moses Porter, Esq., died May 22, 1854, aged 85.†

---

* Lieut. Benjamin Colt, [of Hadley?] died August 30, 1781, aged 43. He was the father of Christopher Colt, of Hartford, Conn.

† " Died in Hadley, on the night of May 22d, Moses Porter, Esq., 85 years, 8 months and 4 days. A few words in memory of this father in Israel, will gratify many of your readers. He was a grandson of the elder President Edwards, and the oldest of his descendants, at the time of his death, it is believed. He had lived all his life, and died, in the house in which he was born. In youth he gave his heart to Jesus, and through his long and active life, love to God and men, governed his actions. Sound in judgment, prompt and energetic in action, kind and generous in his feelings, and influenced by Christian principle, in his dealings with his fellows, he naturally secured the confidence, and received the honors of his fellow-citizens, in those days, when to hold an office was an honor. He often represented his native town in the Legislature, was a member of the Constitutional Convention of 1820, and held various commissions of honor and usefulness, both civil and military.

" In him the widow and the fatherless, always found a friend and safe counsellor ; and he administered upon more estates, than ever any other man, in the County of Hampshire,— a fact equally honorable to his business ability, his uprightness, and his kindness of heart.

" To the poor his hand was ever open, and to the sick his frequent visits and prayers were ever welcome. He was a happy, cheerful, consistent Christian,—constant and faithful in his public duties, and exhibiting the appropriate fruits in his daily life. His conversation naturally and fitly turned to religious topics, upon which he seemed to speak out of the abundance of his heart. Hundreds who have partaken of his abounding hospitalities, so kindly and gracefully proffered, will recollect how, as they listened to his words, and perceived to what an extent his views of all subjects were modified by their relations to God

Children.

75 Benjamin Colt,	born June	8, 1792.	Died June 3, 1793.
76 Elizabeth,	born January	2, 1794.	
77 Benjamin,	born October	5, 1795.	
78 Sophia,	born November	7, 1797.	Died April 3, 1841.
79 Moses,	born October	13, 1799.	
80 Amy,	born September	20, 1801.	Died October 29, 1832.
81 Susanna Edwards,	born January	18, 1804.	Died November 20, 1805.
82 Eleazur,	born January	20, 1806.	
83 Susanna,	born January	30, 1808.	Died January 27, 1849.
84 Lucretia Colt,	born May	15, 1810.	
85 Delia Dwight,	born July	7, 1812.	Died August 17, 1813.
86 Jonathan Edwards,	born April	6, 1815.	
87 Emily,	born May	25, 1817.	

54.

PIERPONT PORTER was married to Hannah Wiggin, daughter of ——— Wiggin, of Suffield, Conn., November 27, 1797.

Mr. Pierpont Porter died January 15, 1805, aged 69.

His widow, Mrs. Hannah Porter, died August 30, 1836, aged 69.

Children.

88 Jerusha,	born July	22, 1798.	Died January 15, 1805.
89 Lucretia,	born November	23, 1799.	
90 Frederick,	born December	31, 1801.	
91 Leicester W.,	born January	7, 1805.	

and his providence,—and especially as they joined in those precious family devotions, when he commended to his Father in heaven, with such touching simplicity and earnestness of faith, not only his own loved ones, but themselves and theirs,—the conviction came over them that he, while enjoying in rare abundance the blessings of this life, was truly seeking a better country, even an heavenly.

" Well does the writer remember with what power, in his youth, a day's sojourn under the roof of this aged servant of Christ testified to the power of religion, and commended it to his acceptance. Would that such a savor of Christ was found in every Christian life.

" His end, for which he had long waited in calm and joyful hope, was peaceful and fitting. After leading in family devotions and preparing his house for night, as usual, he was suddenly called away, and departed in his ordinary attire to meet the God with whom he had so long walked on earth. Precious is the *life* and precious the death, of those who love the Lord." [Newspaper.]

ROBERT SEDGWICK.

FIRST GENERATION.

GENERAL ROBERT SEDGWICK, of Charlestown, Mass., and one of the first or early settlers of that town, was married in England, to ————. [After his death, she was married to Rev. Thomas Allen, Pastor of the Congregational Church in Norwich, England, formerly teacher of the Church in Charlestown from about 1639, to 1651, when he returned to England, by whom she had no children. She was his second wife. He died September 21, 1673, aged 65.*]

Gen. Robert Sedgwick died at Jamaica, W. I., May 24, 1656.†

---

* History of Charlestown, by Richard Frothingham, jun., Esq.

† Robert Sedgwick was one of the most distinguished men of his time. The family is supposed to have sprung from the northern counties of England. Johnson furnishes the earliest notice of Mr. Sedgwick, writing that he " was nursed up in London's artillery garden," and " was stout and active in all feats of war." He was admitted an inhabitant of this town June 3, 1636; a freeman in 1637, and this year chosen representative, and several times afterwards. He was also selectman, and often engaged in town business. He was probably, a merchant, and on occasion of selling his goods too high, was admonished, (1639,) by the Court, to take heed of oppression. He was the captain (1636) of the first " trained band " of this town, the first major (1644) of the Middlesex regiment, and elected major general May 26, 1652. In 1641, 1645, and 1648, he commanded the Ancient and Honorable Artillery Company, and in 1641, the Castle. In 1645, he had a commission to take care of the fortifications of the town, and to keep it and the harbor " from all hostile and mutinous attempts or insurrections." He was, among other duties, directed to have always in readiness " a barrel of powder for every six pieces of ordnance, with twelve shot and five pound of match, if any ships in the harbor shall quarrel and shoot one another; whereby the people, or houses may be endangered."

Previous to July 1, 1654, General Sedgwick had visited England, and engaged in the service of Cromwell, as commander of a contemplated expedition against the Dutch at New York. In a letter to the Protector, of this date, Sedgwick informed him of his arrival here, and of his proceedings; namely, that in fourteen days he had victualled his ships, and in six more was ready with nine hundred foot and a company of horse, to act against the enemy, when, June 1, news of peace arrived; and that commissioners, at a meeting in Charlestown, June 17, had determined to employ the force against the French forts in Nova Scotia. Sedgwick sailed, July 4, 1654, from Boston, with a fleet, consisting of the Augustine, Church, Hope, and a Ketch; arrived at St. John's, a strong fort, on the 14th; captured it on the 17th, then took Port Royal and another French fort, and sailed for Piscataqua.

Though the General Court questioned General Sedgwick's authority for doing this, yet such vigorous action was so acceptable to Cromwell, that the next year he was appointed to an important service in the West Indies. Jamaica had been captured; and General Sedgwick was sent, with a fleet under his orders, with reinforcements for the army under General Venables. He sailed from Plymouth July 11, 1655; and arrived at Barbadoes, August 27, when he learned that Venables had met with a repulse, losing four hundred men. A few extracts from Sedgwick's letters show the state of his feelings. Writing to Cromwell, September 1, 1655, he says :—

" I must confess, I cannot bring my own spirit to stand and consider what I may understand of the mind and will of God, and what he speaks in so loud a voice as this. I must conclude this, that God is righteous in his proceedings, to curb and bring low the pride of the sons of men."

The same letter concludes in the following manner :—

" I am resolved to attend my business with as much wisdom and vigor as God shall assist me with, I thank God, my heart in some measure beareth me witness, that it is the glory

Mrs. Johanna Sedgwick, alias Allen, died ————.*

SECOND GENERATION.

Children of Gen. Robert Sedgwick.

I. Samuel,	bap.		1639.
II. Hannah,	bap.		1641.
III. William,	bap.	[no date.]	
IV. Robert,	bap.	[no date.]	
V. Sarah,	bap.	[no date.]	

of God, that I intended in this employment, and I hope he will yet own us. Our condition, I am confident, is often remembered by you in your approaches to Heaven, and I hope will yet be. Religion and God was pretended, and I question not intended, and I know must now be attended, if we prosper. Let your highness be pleased to pardon my boldness and prolixity. I thank God my prayers are for you, and that the God of wisdom and grace may yet own you in your so many weighty affairs, that you may be a blessing to your generation, and serviceable to Christ, and to his people.

"Sir, I am willing to be, and wish I were,
"Your Lordship's humble Servant,
"ROBERT SEDGWICK."

General Sedgwick's letters, [in Thurloe's State Papers,] long, able and interesting, present a vivid view of the difficulties he had to encounter. "The truth is " he writes the Protector, November 5, 1655, "God is angry, and the plague is begun, and we have none to stand in the gap." "Sir, you cannot conceive us so sad as we are, broken and scattered, God rending us in twain, a senseless hearted people, not affected with his dealings towards us." There was the evil of a divided command. A council for managing the affairs of the island was formed, of which Sedgwick, appointed commissioner by Cromwell, was one, and General Fortesque was president. The latter soon fell a victim to the climate. At this time General Sedgwick made two requests to the Protector:—

"One is, if God spare me life, that your highness would be pleased to permit me to come to England. But I am not very solicitous in that, sometimes thinking that another place will be my portion, before I may hear again from your highness.

"The other petition is : I left behind me a dear and religious wife, who through grace hath much of the fear and knowledge of God in her. I have also five children, to me dear and precious. I would only by this, that your highness would cast one thought towards them ; that whatever hazard or hardship I may go through, yet my relations may not be forgotten. I only expect, what your highness was pleased to promise me, that she may not be troubled in obtaining it in such seasons, as may tend to her comfort."

Gen. Sedgwick renews the latter request,—in relation to his pay,—to Cromwell's secretary, Thurloe, in letters dated November 7, and November 12, 1665; remarking, "the truth is, my heart and spirit are in a confusion, and (I) think it may sometimes finish my few days I have here to be." His presentiment proved true. So far from granting his request to return, the Protector sent him a commission to command the army. "He never enjoyed himself," writes one of his officers, "after he received his commission," "but as was apparent to all men, from that time lost much of freedom and cheerfulness." He died May 24, 1656.

Charlestown has cause to remember the public spirit of General Sedgwick. He took a warm interest in its welfare; and either as selectman, representative, or a member of an important committee, was constantly in its service. He was an enterprising merchant, as we find him building wharves on the shore east of the old ferry-ways, carrying on a brewing establishment, building the old Tide Mills, and interested in the Iron Works at Lynn. He was zealous in disciplining his company,—freely spending time and money, Johnson says, for this purpose. The train band manifested their feelings towards him by the grant, somewhat irregularly, of a piece of land, which the town "to gratify the major," confirmed. His residence was in the market place, now the square, near the site of the Bunker Hill Bank.

Robert Sedgwick was a representative of the liberal Puritans of early New-England. Religion was in all his thoughts, and yet he openly opposed the prevailing intolerance. His regard for education is seen in his gifts to the College. He was "a very brave, zealous and pious man," "beloved and esteemed by all." Aylesbury, June 25, 1656, in Thurloe, Vol. IV., p. 604. "He was truly a religious man, and of the most innocent conversation I ever accompanied." [History of Charlestown, by Richard Frothingham, jun., Esq.]

* Middlesex County Land Records, Vol. IV., page 230, May 20, 1657. By deed of this date, "Johanna Sedgwick, of the Parish of Stepney, in the County of Middlesex, the widow and relict of Major General Robert Sedgwick, late of Jamaica, in the parts beyond the seas, deceased," for the consideration of twelve pounds ten shillings, sells and conveys to Francis Norton, of Charlestown, "a right of commonage in Charlestown, for five cows." The deed is witnessed by Henry Moss, notary public, Jno. Leveritt, Jere. Jenoway and Peter Tilley, Boston,—and to the same is appended the following attestation :

"Boston, May 28, 1672. Massachusetts Colony. John Leveritt, Esq., deputy governor, being sworn, do say and attest that he was present and saw Joanna Sedgwick sign, seal and deliver this within instrument of conveyance, to the grantee, Francis Norton, of Charlestown, and that he subscribed his name as a witness thereto."
Underneath is endorsed,—Deed entered for Record, 1672.

DESCENDANTS IN THE LINE OF SAMUEL SEDGWICK, SON OF GEN. ROBERT SEDGWICK.

THIRD GENERATION.

I.

SAMUEL SEDGWICK, of London, England, was married to Elizabeth ———.

I do not find that he had or had not children : but have collected the following particulars relating to him.

Mr. Samuel Sedgwick was in the city of London, in 1657, as appears by the subscription of his name, as a witness to the will of Jonathan Wade, of Ipswich, Mass., which purports to have been executed in that city, on the 17th of June, 1657, and was proved before and approved by a Court of Probate held at Boston, July 8, 1686, and is recorded on Suffolk County Probate Records, Vol. XI., p. 40. Next after said Record is an entry of the following deposition :

" The deposition of Elizabeth Sedgwick, aged 33 years, or thereabouts. This deponent testifieth and saith, that for the space of six years, wherein she was wife to Mr. Samuel Sedgwick, late of London, deceased, she well knew his hand writing, and was perfectly acquainted therewith, and that she hath well viewed and considered the subscription of the said Sedgwick's name as a witness, and that she verily believes the same to have been done by himself, and no other. Taken upon oath, December 1, 1683, before Peter Bulckley, assistant.

Vol. III., page 332, of Middlesex County Land Records, is recorded an Indenture in writing, purporting to have been executed in the city of London, on the 20th of May, 1667, by Samuel Sedgwick, in which he describes himself as " citizen and cloathworker, of London, sonne & heire of Robert Sedgwick, late of Charlestowne in New-England, in the parts beyond the Seas, Esq[r] deceased," and by which he conveys to " Francis Willoughby, of Charlestowne, in New-England, aforesaid, Esq[r] " his the said Samuel Sedgwick's house and land in Charlestown, and some other real estate, in, or in the vicinity of Charlestown.

DESCENDANTS IN THE LINE OF WILLIAM SEDGWICK, SON OF GEN. ROBERT SEDGWICK.

THIRD GENERATION.

III.

WILLIAM SEDGWICK, of Hartford, Conn., was married to Elizabeth Stone, daughter of Rev. Samuel Stone, second minister of Hartford, Conn. She was divorced from him, by the Court of

23

Assistants upon her own application, and subsequently married to John Roberts, of Hartford, afterwards of ——— , New-Jersey.*
Mr. William Sedgwick died ———.
Mrs. Elizabeth Sedgwick, alias Roberts, died ———.

Child,—one only.

6 Samuel,   born   1667.

FOURTH GENERATION.

6.

SAMUEL SEDGWICK, of Hartford, Conn., was married to Mary Hopkins, daughter of Stephen Hopkins, of Hartford, and granddaughter of John Hopkins, one of the first settlers of that town, 1689.

Capt. Samuel Sedgwick died March 24, 1735, in his 69th year. [Grave-stone, West-Hartford burying-ground.]

His widow, Mrs. Mary Sedgwick, died September 4, 1743, aged 73. [Grave-stone, West-Hartford burying-ground.]

Children.

7 Samuel,	born August	22, 1690.	
8 Jonathan,	born March	29, 1693.	
9 Ebenezer,	born February	25, 1695.	
10 Joseph,	born May	16, 1697.	
11 Stephen,	born March	17, 1701.	
12 Abigail,	born February	23, 1703.	
13 Mary,	born July	1, 1705.	
14 William,	born June	29, 1707.	
15 Elizabeth,	born December	10, 1708.	
16 Thankful,	born November	3, 1710.	Not named in the distribution of her father's estate, which is dated July 14, 1735: she is, therefore, supposed to have deceased prior to that time. A Thankful Sedgwick, probably this one, died July 20, 1720.
17 Mercy,	born January	18, 1713.	
18 Benjamin,	born November	7, 1716.	

FIFTH GENERATION.

7.

SAMUEL SEDGWICK, of Hartford, Conn., was married to Ruth Peck, daughter of Paul Peck, of the same town, February 1, 1711. [After his death, she was married to Samuel Culver of Wallingford, Conn., January 3, 1728, by the Rev. Mr. Cotton, of Hartford, West Society. She was his second wife. His first

---

* Court of Assistants, October 1, 1674. "Elizabeth Sedgwick is divorced from her husband, upon her own application, provided he doth not return by the first day of January next."

It is said by Hinman, that "Mr. Sedgwick spent much of his time in passing to and from the West Indies, in the neglect of his family. His wife became dissatisfied with his absence and negligence, and petitioned the Court of Assistants for a bill of divorce."

Middlesex County Land Records, Vol. III., page 383, September 7, 1668. By deed of this date, "William Sedgwicke, of Hartford, in Connecticut Colony, in New-England, gentleman, the second sonne of Major Robert Sedgwicke, sometime of Charlestowne, in the County of Middlesex, in the Massachusetts Colony, in New-England aforesaid,"—sells and conveys to Francis Willoughby, of said Charlestown, all his the said William Sedgwick's right and interest in and to the estate of his said father, Major Sedgwick, in Charlestown.

wife, whose Christian name, likewise, was Ruth, died January 18, 1727. By his second wife Mr. Culver had two children,—Samuel, born September 25, 1728, and Ann, born October 3, 1732, as appears by entries on Wallingford Town Records.]
Mr. Samuel Sedgwick died December 25, 1724, aged 34.
Mrs. Ruth Sedgwick, alias Culver, died ———.

Children.

19 Ruth,	born January	22, 1712.	Married Caleb' Merriman, of Wallingford, August 31, 1732. Mrs. Ruth Merriman died before her husband. " Caleb Merriman, Esq., deacon of the consociated Church of Christ,.in Wallingford, died of the small pox, June 2, 1770." *Children,*—recorded to them on Wallingford Records,— Sarah, born May 25, 1733. George, born 1736, and died April 24, 1757. Elizabeth, born November 24, 1739. Ruth, born November 1, 1741.
20 Mary,			Married Isaac Brocket, of Wallingford, June 16, 1731. After her death, he was married to Elizabeth Culver, of Wallingford, February 25, 1737, who, after his death, was married to Daniel Frisbie, May 4, 1748. Mrs. Mary Brocket died January 19, 1734. Mr. Isaac Brocket died October 18, 1746. I find one child only, recorded to them, viz., Rachel Brocket, born May 23, 1732.
	twins born January	7, 1714.	
21 Jerusha,			Married Samuel Tyler, of Wallingford, February 4, 1734. *Children* recorded to them on Wallingford Records,—Lauthrop, born June 22, 1734. Samuel, born December 14, 1735, and died March 13, 1823. Daniel, born March 17, 1738. Moses, born March 5, 1740, and died January 15, 1743. Jerusha, born July 23, 1743, and died May 3, 1744. Moses, born February 12, 1747.
22 Samuel,	born January	18, 1717.	Died January 8, 1725.
23 Daniel,	born July	24, 1719.	Supposed to have died young, as no trace of him can be found.
24 Thankful,	born April	21, 1721.	Married Jehiel Preston, of Wallingford, October 21, 1741. I find but one child recorded to them on Wallingford Records, viz., Hannah, born July 5, 1748.

8.

JONATHAN SEDGWICK, of Hartford, Conn., was twice married. 1. To Isabella Stebbins, of ———, March 7, 1716–7. She died ———, aged —. 2. To Anna Brace, widow of Lieut. Henry Brace, late of Hartford, deceased, and daughter of ———, of the same town.
Mrs. Anna Sedgwick, alias Brace, died July 13, 1764, aged 77.
Mr. Jonathan Sedgwick died August 16, 1771, aged 78.

Children,—by his first wife.

25 William, born December 21, 1717. Married Elizabeth Brace, daughter of Henry Brace, of Hartford, May 8, 1740. She died July 4, 1759, aged 41. He died in 1771. *Children,—* Elizabeth, bap. July 5, 1741. Abigail, bap. February 13, 1743. Isabel, bap. October 26, 1746. Rhoda. Jonathan, bap. November 6, 1748. Lucy, bap. November 18, 1750.* Mercy, bap. June 10, 1753. Nancy, (or Mary,) bap , 1756. Son, not bap. April 1, 1758, and died in infancy. Child, not named, born July 4, 1759, and died in infancy.

26 Jonathan, born April 15, 1721.
27 Mehitabel, born March 18, 1723–4. Died in early life.
28 Isabel, } twin. Married Thomas Lee, of Farmington, Conn.

9.

EBENEZER SEDGWICK, of Hartford, Conn., was married to Prudence Merrills, daughter of Deacon Abraham Merrills, of the same town, June 30, 1720. She was born December 22, 1700. After the death of Mr. Sedgwick, she was married to Col. David Whitney, of Canaan, Conn., July 28, 1767.

Mr. Ebenezer Sedgwick died December 2, 1759, aged 63.

Mrs. Prudence Sedgwick, alias Whitney, died at Hartford, February 1, 1793, aged 92. She fell into the fire.

Children.

29 Abraham, born April 27, 1721. Married Abi Brace, daughter of Henry Brace, of Hartford, Conn., September 19, 1745. *Children,—*Jonathan, born February, 1746, in West-Hartford, and scalded to death, May 27, 1748. Thankful, bap. March 29, 1748. Ebenezer, bap. April 1, 1750. Abi, bap. June 7, 1752. Wealthana, bap. January 19, 1754. Linda and Sina, twins, bap. April 7, 1757. Abraham, bap. April 29, 1759. All the baptized children were baptized in Wintonbury, by the Pastor of the church there.

30 Abigail, born December 2, 1722. Married Elisha Seymour, of Hartford, son of John Seymour of the same town, July 5, 1743. He died June 19, 1790, aged 68. *Children,—*Elisha, bap. January 27, 1744. Abigail, bap. January 19, 1746, and married Enos Kellogg, of Sheffield, Mass., June 11, 1765. Thankful, bap. January 17, 1748. Enos. Prudence, bap. March 1, 1752.

---

*Seth, son of Robert Collins, and Lucy, daughter of William Sedgwick, married August 25, 1768. Lucy, their daughter, baptized June 20, 1782, was married to Rev. Joab Brace, pastor of the Congregational Church in Newington Society, Wethersfield, Conn., January 21, 1805.

Cynthia, April 9, 1758. Abner, August 19, 1759. Eli, bap. January 3, 1762. Levi, bap. March 18, 1764. Ebenezer.

31 Prudence,	born September 14, 1724.	Married Amos Kellogg.
32 Mary,	born April 29, 1726.	Married John Ensign, jun., of Hartford, Conn., afterwards of Salisbury, Conn., June 6, 1746. She died February 19, 1805, in the 79th year of her age. *Children*,—John, bap. January 18, 1747. Molly, bap. July 7, 1751. She was the grandmother of Chief Justice Church, as says Hinman.
33 Thankful,	born April 7, 1728.	Supposed to have died before her father, as she is not mentioned in his will.
34 Elizabeth,	born June 17, 1731.	Married Elisha Ensign, of Hartford, July 18, 1754.
35 Ebenezer,	born March 14, 1734–5.	Died in November, 1759. There is some appearance that he married and raised a family of children.

10.

JOSEPH SEDGWICK, first of Hartford, Conn., then of Tyringham, Berkshire County, Mass., was married to Ruth Smith, daughter of Joseph Smith, of Farmington, in the same state, January 24, 1722–3.

Mr. Joseph Sedgwick died ———.
Mrs. Ruth Sedgwick died ———.

Children.

36 Samuel,	born April 11, 1725.	
37 Experience,	born March 12, 1726–7.	
38 Esther,	born January 1, 1728–9.	
39 Son, (not named,)	born February 5, 1730–1.	And died in infancy, (February 5, 1731.
40 Ruth,	born March 20, 1731–2.	
41 Naomi,	born July 19, 1735.	
42 Joseph,	born July 22, 1739.	Supposed to have died December, 1776, in the army.

11.

STEPHEN SEDGWICK, of Farmington, Conn., was twice married. 1. To Mary Harris, widow of Joseph Harris, late of Litchfield, Conn., deceased,* December 16, 1725. She died November 2, 1760, in the 61st year of her age. 2. To Elizabeth Porter.

---

* The settlement of the town of Litchfield, the Indian name of which was Bantam, was commenced in the year 1720. During the frequent wars between England and France, the Canadians and Indians often harassed our borders ; and Litchfield, being a frontier town, was exposed to their ravages.

"In the month of August, 1721, Mr. Joseph Harris (one of the first settlers of Litchfield, from Middletown) a respectable inhabitant, was at work in the fields alone, and being attacked by a party of Indians, attempted to make his escape. The Indians pursued him ; and finding that they could not overtake him, they shot him dead and scalped him. As Mr. Harris did not return, the inhabitants were alarmed, and some search was made for him ; but the darkness of the night checked their exertions. The next morning they found his body, and gave it a decent burial. Mr. Harris was killed near the north end of the Plain where the road turns to Milton, a little east of a school-house now standing ; and for a long time after, this Plain was called Harris' Plain." The place of his interment remained unmarked for more than a century, but rested in the memory of the older inhabitants.

Mr. Stephen Sedgwick died August 13, 1768, of malignant fever, aged 67.

Mrs. Elizabeth Sedgwick died August 13, 1780, aged 78.*

Children.

43 Ann,	born September 16, 1726.		Married Hezekiah Orton, of Farmington, afterwards of Litchfield, Conn.
44 Mary,	{ born March { bap. March	1, 1729. 2, 1729.	Married Daniel Hooker, of ——. She died April 7, 1791, aged 62. He died September 12, 1802, aged 72. Children.
45 Stephen,	{ born June { bap. July	3, 1731. 4, 1731.	
46 Dorcas,	{ born December 24, 1734. { bap. December 29, 1734.		Married John Martin, of Litchfield, Conn., March 20, 1760.
47 Hannah,	{ born December 16, 1736. { bap. December 19, 1736.		Died, unmarried, February 28, 1811, in the 75th year of her age. [Tombstone.]
48 Huldah,	bap. July	5, 1741.	Married Ebenezer Bibbins, of Salisbury, Conn., June 1, 1769.

12.

ABIGAIL SEDGWICK was married to Benjamin Kellogg, of Farmington, Conn., son of Samuel Kellogg, of Hartford, in the same State, November 9, 1721. He was born in January, 1701.

Children.

49 Margaret,	bap. February	17, 1723.
50 Benjamin,	bap. October	11, 1724.
51 John,	bap. September	4, 1726.

13.

MARY SEDGWICK was married to Jacob Kellogg, of Hartford, Conn., February, 1723. [After her death, he was married in 1760, to Ruth Judd, widow of William Judd, deceased, of Farmington, and daughter of John Lee, of Farmington. William Judd was the father of William Judd, Esq., of Farmington, famous in the political history of Connecticut, who died November 13, 1804, aged 63.]

Mrs. Mary Kellogg died August 12, 1759, of fever, cancer, &c., aged 60.

Lieut. Jacob Kellogg died July 31, 1763, of complicated fever, diabetes, &c., aged 70.

Children.

52 Timothy,	born November	25, 1723.	
53 Elizabeth,	born August	8, 1727.	Married Joseph Hinsdale.
54 Lydia,	born July	22, 1729.	Married Timothy Seymour, of Hartford, December 1, 1748.
55 Jacob,	bap. July	11, 1731.	

He was buried in the west burial ground, near the village of Litchfield. In 1830, a suitable monument, with an appropriate inscription, was erected at his grave by voluntary contribution."

* July 5, 1761, admitted to Church by letter from 1st Church in Farmington.
[Morris' Statistical Account of Litchfield. Woodruff's History of the Town of Litchfield.]

56	Azariah,	bap. [date not entered.]	
57	Ozias,	bap. September 4, 1735.	Died of consumption, June 1, 1759.
58	George,	bap. July 10, 1737.	Married Sarah Clark, of Hartford. He died August 24, 1808, aged 71.
59	Hannah,	bap. May 13, 1739.	Married Caleb Croswell, of Hartford, February 26, 1767. He died October 1, 1806, aged 73. She died April 9, 1829, aged 90, nearly. They had six sons and two daughters,— two of whom, only, are now living, viz., Rev. Dr. Croswell, Rector of Trinity Church, New-Haven, Conn., and Archibald Croswell, of Gilboa, N. Y.

14.

WILLIAM SEDGWICK, of Hartford, Conn., was married to Mirriam Hopkins, widow of Elias Hopkins, of Hartford, deceased, and daughter of Capt. Daniel Webster, of Hartford, May 14, 1761.* Elias Hopkins was son of Consider Hopkins, of Hartford, and was born in 1726. [After the death of Mr. Sedgwick, she was married to John Marsh, of New-Hartford, Conn., November 27, 1777. She was his third wife. He died November 10, 1805, aged 78. His first wife, to whom he was married February 2, 1758, was Lucina Seymour. She died May 14, 1762. He was married June 17, 1763, to Sarah Nash, daughter of Moses Nash, of Wintonbury. She died July 17, 1775, aged 37. By her Hopkins husband, who is said to have died in Egremont, Mass., she had children, Elias, born 1752, Mirriam, born 1755, and Freelove, born 1757.]

Mr. William Sedgwick died 1771, aged 64.

Mrs. Mirriam Sedgwick, alias Hopkins, alias Marsh, died September 17, 1819, aged 90, nearly.

---

* Capt. Daniel Webster was great-grand-son of John Webster, one of the first settlers of Hartford, Conn., and one of the early Governors of the Colony of Connecticut,—and after 1659, of Hadley, Mass., (where he died,) in the line of his son Robert Webster, and grandfather of the late Noah Webster, LL. D.

Capt. Daniel Webster aforesaid was twice married. 1. To Mirriam Kellogg, widow of Abraham Kellogg, and daughter of Noah Cooke, of Northampton, Mass., and of Sarah his wife, who, as appears to me, was daughter of Joseph Nash, one of the early settlers of Hartford, about 1719. She was born September 30, 1690. Abram Kellogg died soon after his marriage to Miss Cooke, leaving no issue. Noah Cooke was born June 14, 1657, and was son of Capt. Aaron Cooke, who came from England to Dorchester, Mass., in 1630, and removed to Windsor, Conn., in 1635 or 1636; to Northampton about 1660. After that he lived some years in Westfield, Mass., but returned to Northampton, where he died September 5, 1690, aged 80. Capt. Cooke married first, a daughter of Thomas Ford, of Windsor, and subsequently a daughter of Nicholas Denslow, and after her death, Elizabeth Nash, and after her death, Rebecca Smith, widow of Lieut. Philip Smith, of Hadley, Mass., deceased, and daughter of Nathaniel Foote, one of the first settlers of Wethersfield, Conn. Lieut. Smith died in 1684. Mather, in his Magnalia, says he was "murdered with an hideous witchcraft." The Denslow woman was the mother of Noah Cooke. The family name of the second wife of Capt. Daniel Webster, is unknown. Her Christian name was Hannah; she survived him, and died October 17, 1776. Daniel Webster died in 1765. His children, whose names and times of birth follow, were by his first wife.

Daniel,	born February	16, 1720.	
Noah,	born March	25, 1722.	He was the father of Noah Webster, Esq., who was born October 16, 1758.
Zephaniah,	born June	1, 1724.	
Abraham,	born January	17, 1727.	
Mirriam,	born October	21, 1729.	
Daniel,	born September	4, 1731.	
Elihu,	born November	1, 1733.	Died unmarried.

Children.

60 William,	bap. June	6, 1762.	
61 Timothy,	bap. December	18, 1763.	Died October 2, 1833, aged 70 nearly.
62 Isabel,	bap. October	20, 1765.	
63 Sarah,	bap. December	6, 1767.	
64 Miles,	bap. February	3, 1771.	Died March 3, 1774.

15.

ELIZABETH SEDGWICK was married to Thomas Orton, jun., of Farmington, Conn., afterwards of Cornwall, Conn., June 18, 1730. [After her death, he was married to Hepzibah Buel, and subsequently removed from Farmington.] Mrs. Elizabeth Orton died May 16, 1738, aged ——. [Farmington Records, 1738.]
Mr. Thomas Orton died ———.

Children.

65 Roger,	born March	11, 1731.	Died September 20, 1731.
66 Elizabeth,	born November	8, 1732.	
67 Esther, (?)	born		Died April 1, 1738.
68 Anna,	born May	8, 1736.	
69 Esther,	born May	12, 1738.	

17.

MERCY SEDGWICK was twice married. 1. To Caleb Merrill, of Hartford, Conn., son of John Merrills, of the same town, August 2, 1733. He was born July 14, 1707, and died September 24, 1735, aged 28. 2. To Ebenezer Mix, of Hartford, ———. [After her decease, viz., in 1754, Mr. Mix was married to Anna Goodwin, daughter of Isaac Goodwin, of Hartford, by whom he had three children, John, born April 13, 1755, Samuel, born in 1760, and Elisha, bap. July 1, 1764. Mrs. Anna Mix died September 9, 1814, aged 93.]
Mr. Ebenezer Mix died August 3, 1766, aged 50.
Mrs. Mercy Mix, alias Merrill, died June 16, 1745, in the 32d year of her age.

Children,—by her first husband.

70 Abijah,	born May	2, 1734.
71 Mercy,	born April	10, 1736, (posthumous.)

Children,—by her second husband.

72 Elizabeth,	born January	1, 1738. Married to William Judd, Esq., of Farmington, Conn., December 8, 1765. He died November 13, 1804, aged 63. She died September 23, 1806, aged 68.
73 Mary,	born May	8, 1743.

18.

BENJAMIN SEDGWICK, of Hartford, Conn., until about 1748, and after that year, of Cornwall, Conn., was married to Ann Thompson, daughter of John Thompson, of Wallingford, Conn. Her father, John Thompson, died at Cornwall, November 22, 1765, aged 77. After his death, she was married to Timothy

Judd, Esq., of Westbury Society, Waterbury, Conn., now Watertown, August 8, 1764. She was his third wife. After her death, Mr. Judd was married to Mary Foote, widow of Samuel Foote, deceased, of Watertown, June 6, 1780,—being his fourth wife. She died in October, 1788, and Mr. Judd afterwards married a fifth wife. Timothy Judd, Esq., died January 23, 1796, aged 82. For over 20 sessions, he was a representative from Waterbury in the General Court of Connecticut. He was brother of the Rev. Jonathan Judd, Pastor of the church at Southampton, Mass., the grandfather of Sylvester Judd, Esq., of Northampton, Mass.

Deacon Benjamin Sedgwick died of apoplexy, February 7, 1757, aged 41.*

Mrs. Ann Sedgwick, alias Judd, died ———.

Children.

74 Sarah,	bap. March	25, 1739.	Married Rev. Hezekiah Gold, of Cornwall, Conn., November 23, 1758. She died August 28, 1766, in her 28th year. Rev. Hezekiah Gold died June, 1790, aged 59. *Children,*—Thomas, born November 23, 1759. Hezekiah, born May 7, 1761. Died April 6, 1766. Benjamin, born June 25, 1762. Thomas Ruggles, born November 4, 1764. Hezekiah, born August 1, 1766.
75 John,	bap. March	7, 1742.†	
76 Benjamin,	bap. March	11, 1744.	
77 Theodore,	bap. May,	1746.	Yale College, 1765. Was one of the great and good men of his time. His civil and political history is too well known, to need repetition in this place. He was thrice married. 1. To Eliza Mason, and after her death, 2. To Pamela Dwight, daughter of Gen. Joseph Dwight, of Great-Barrington, Mass., and of Abigail his second wife, widow of Rev. John Sargeant, senior, missionary to the Indians, at Stockbridge, and daughter of Ephraim Williams, sometime of Stockbridge, and of Abigail his second wife, daughter of Josiah Jones, jun., of Watertown, Mass. She died September 20, 1807, aged 54. 3. To Penelope Russell, of Boston. Hon. Theodore Sedgwick, LL. D., died January 24, 1813, aged 66. *Children,*—by his first wife,—none. By his second wife,—Theodore, Henry, Robert and Charles Sedg-

---

* The epitaph of Deacon Sedgwick is expressive of the manner of his death :

" In an instant he is call'd
Eternity to view;
No time to regulate his house,
Or bid his friends adieu."

† "Died in Simsbury, Conn., May 18, 1854, at the residence of her niece, Miss Sarah Mather, Sally Sedgwick, widow of the late Gen. John Sedgwick, of Cornwall, Conn., aged 96." [Conn. Courant, May 20, 1854.]

Mrs Sedgwick was Sally Lewis, of Farmington, sister of the wife of William Mather, Esq., late of Simsbury, deceased, and was the second wife of Gen. Sedgwick, by whom she had no children.

wick, all lawyers, and eminent in
their profession. Eliza, who married Doct. Pomeroy, of Northampton,
Mass., afterwards of Stockbridge.
Pamelia, who married Elkanah Watson, Esq., of Albany. Frances P.,
who married Ebenezer Watson, of
New-York, April 9, 1801, and Catharine M., extensively known and
appreciated as a fine writer. *Children*,—by his third wife,—none.

78 Mary Ann, born July   27, 1749. Married Rev. Job Swift, D. D., some-
time minister of Bennington, Ver.,
[November 6, 1769.] He was born
in Sandwich, Mass., in 1743, and
died at Enosburgh, N. Y., October
20, 1804, aged 61. His widow, Mrs.
Mary Ann Swift, died at Addison,
Ver., February 6, 1826. They were
the parents of Hon. Benjamin Swift,
U. S. Senator from Vermont, and
Hon. Samuel Swift, many years
Secretary of the State of Vermont.

79 Lorain,   born [no date.] Married Jacob Parsons, of Richmond,
Mass.

SIXTH GENERATION.

75.

JOHN SEDGWICK, of Cornwall, Conn., was twice married. 1.
To Abigail Andrews, daughter of Capt. Stephen Andrews, of Wal-
lingford, Conn., about 1763. She died April, 1811, aged 66. 2.
To Sarah Lewis, widow of ——— Lewis, of Farmington, Conn.

Gen. John Sedgwick died August 28, 1820, in the 79th year
of his age.

Mrs. Sarah Sedgwick, alias Lewis, died in Simsbury, May 18,
1854, aged 96.

Children,—by his first wife.

80 John An- drews,	born March	8, 1764.	
81 Sarah,	born December	27, 1765.	Died unmarried.
82 Henry,	born September	13, 1767.	
83 Roderick,	born March	8, 1770.	Died at the age of 13 years.
84 Parnel,	born October	4, 1771.	
85 Anne,	born April	6, 1775.	Died, unmarried.
86 Elizabeth,	born October	9, 1777.	Died January 4, 1778.
87 Pamela,	born December	21, 1778.	
88 Benjamin,	born January	26, 1781.	
89 Stephen,	} twins.		
90 Eliza- beth,	} born March	1, 1783.	Died, unmarried.
91 Roderick,	born January	26, 1785.	Resides in the city of New York and is a lawyer.

Children,—by his second wife,—none.

SEVENTH GENERATION.

80.

JOHN A. SEDGWICK married and had children,—

92 Charles F.,	born	A lawyer in Sharon.
93 Albert,	born	Commissioner of the School Fund.

| 94 Mary Ann, | born | Married a Mr. Noyes. |
| 95 Amanda, | born | Married a Mr. Bridgman. |

88.

BENJAMIN SEDGWICK, of Cornwall, Conn., was married to Olive, daughter of Philo Collins, of Goshen, Conn., and of Olive his wife, daughter of Ebenezer Foote, of Watertown, Conn., afterwards of Cornwall, Ver., July 9, 1809. Mr. Collins was son of Cyprian Collins, of Goshen, and grandson of Rev. Timothy Collins, first minister of Litchfield, Conn.

Children.

96 Philo Collins,	born July	18, 1810.	Married and resides in Harrisburg, Penn., and is clerk of the Supreme Court of Pennsylvania.
97 John,	born September 13, 1813.		Is a Major in the Army of the U. S.
98 Olive Collins,	born January	15, 1817.	Married and resides in Kent, Conn.
99 Emily,	born November	6, 1819.	Resides at home.
100 Eliza,	born November	7, 1824.	Died February 15, 1831.

DESCENDANTS IN THE LINE OF ROBERT SEDGWICK, SON OF GEN. ROBERT SEDGWICK.

THIRD GENERATION.

IV.

ROBERT SEDGWICK, of Boston, Mass., was married to Sarah ———.

Mr. Robert Sedgwick died [in a foreign land, probably.]* His widow, Mrs. Sarah Sedgwick, ———.

Child,—one only is recorded to them on Boston Records.

101 Sarah,   born December 19, 1667.

DESCENDANTS IN THE LINE OF SARAH SEDGWICK, DAUGHTER OF GEN. ROBERT SEDGWICK.

THIRD GENERATION.

V.

SARAH SEDGWICK was married to John Leverett, Esq., afterwards Deputy Governor, and "Governo' of y' Matthachusetts Colony in N–E," about 1644. She was his second wife. His first wife was Hannah Hudson, daughter of Ralph and Mary Hudson, of Boston. She died about 1643 or 1644. By her he had 3 children, viz., Hudson, born May 3, 1640, (his son John,

---

* On Suffolk County Probate Records, Vol. IX., page 68, is recorded,—"Inventory of goods left in the hands of Mrs. Sarah Sedgwick, widow, by Mr. Robert Sedgwick, deceased, when he left her. Inventory approved by the Court, April 26, 1683, and all the goods therein named granted to the widow, for the use of herself and children."

born August 25, 1662, was eighth President of Harvard College ;)
John, born June 1, 1641 ; Hannah, born April 16, 1643.
Hon. John Leverett died March 16, 1679, aged about 63.*
His widow, Mrs. Sarah Leverett, died January 2, 1705, aged
74.†

Children.

102 John,	born March	17, 1646.	Died young.
103 Sarah,	born July	12, 1648.	Died young.
104 Sarah,	born August	2, 1649.	Died young.
105 Elizabeth,	born April	26, 1651.	Married Doct. Elisha Cooke. She died July 21, 1715. He died October 31, 1715, aged 78. He was a man of note. They had a family of children.
106 Ann,	born November	23, 1652.	Married John Hubbard, son of Rev. William Hubbard, of Ipswich, Mass., by his second wife Mary Rogers. He died at Boston, January 8, 1710, aged 61. She died in 1717.
107 Sarah,	born	1654.	Died young.
108 Mary,	born February	12, 1656.	Married Paul Dudley, the youngest son of Governor Thomas Dudley, by his second wife Catharine, about 1676. After his death, which occurred at Boston, December 1, 1681, she was married to Col. Penn Townsend, being his second wife. She died in 1699. Col. Townsend died August 21, 1727. She had 2 children, both by her first husband.
109 Hannah,	born after 1657, and probably in 1662, or 1663.‡		Married Thomas Davis, of Boston, an innholder. He was son of William Davis, and of Huldah, his first wife, daughter of Rev. Zechariah Symnes, minister of Charlestown, Mass. She died in July, 1707. She is supposed to have had a previous husband, named Allen.
110 Rebecca,	born December	5, 1664.	Married James Lloyd, November 3, 1691. He came from Somerset, England, about 1670, and resided in Boston, where he died in July, 1693. She died about 1739, leaving a will in which she names an only child, Mrs. Rebecca Oliver, wife of James Oliver, of Boston.

---

* His Epitaph. " To yᵉ Sacred Memory of N. E's Heroe, Mars his Generall, Virtues standard-bearer, & Learning's glory, yᵗ faithfully pious, and piously faithfull subject to yᵣ Great Majesty of Heaven & Earth, yᵗ Experienced Souldier in yᵉ Church Militant, lately Listed in yᵉ Invincible Triûphant Army of yᵉ Lord of Hosts, yᵉ deservedly Worshipfull Jnᵘ Leverett, Esqʳ yᵉ Just, Prudent, and Impartiall Governoᵗ of yᵉ Mattachusetts Colony In N-E, who surrendered to yᵉ all Conquering Command of Death, March. 16. Anno Dom: 1678-9, et Ætatis suæ 63." He was buried on the 25th of the same month, with great pomp and ceremony.

† She was buried on the 8th of January, 1705. Cotton Mather, who preached her funeral sermon, in his peculiar manner, said,—"Fitly enough might she have been styled, as diverse Holy, and Famous Women in the Scripture were,—a Daughter of Asher; THE SEDGWICK was an *Asher*, that is to say, *An Happy Man* that was the *Father* of such a Daughter." " Unto the *seventy-fifth* year of her *Age* did she continue serving of her LORD and waiting for him, when she died of a palsy."

‡ "1665. In the beginning of Decembʳ Cap. Jnᵒ Leveret set sayle for London, in a little friggot built at new france, and there taken by the English with the forts."
" 1661. 19. 5. The Charls arrived frõ Londõ with 80 passengers, & J. Leveret one."
[Hull's Diary.]

111 John, born August 20, 1668. Died young.
112 Sarah, born June 30, 1670. Died young.
113 Sarah, born June 15, 1673. Married Col. Nathaniel Byfield, April 17, 1718. He was son of Rev. Richard Byfield, pastor of the Parish of Long Ditton, in Surrey, and held several high civil offices. After her death, he was again married. He died in Boston, June 6, 1733, in his 80th year.

REV. HENRY SMITH.

FIRST GENERATION.

REV. HENRY SMITH, first settled minister of Wethersfield, Conn., is supposed, from the tenor of his will, to have been twice married. Of his first wife nothing is known ; of his second wife, her Christian name only, which was Dorathy. After his death, she was married to Mr. John Russell, of Wethersfield, father of Rev. John Russell, jun., successor of her first husband, in the ministry at Wethersfield, and afterwards first minister of Hadley, Mass. She was his second wife. Mr. John Russell died May 8, 1680, aged 83.*

Rev. Henry Smith died in 1648.

Mrs. Dorathy Smith, alias Russell, died at Hadley, in 1694.

SECOND GENERATION.

Children of Rev. Henry Smith,—by his first wife.†

I. Peregrine, born	Died, unmarried, before his father.
II. Daughter, born	Name unknown. Married, and had children before her father's death. Nothing more known of her.
III. Daughter, born	Name unknown. Married, and had children before her father's death. Nothing more known relating to her.

Children,—by his second wife.

IV. Dorathy,	born	1636.
V. Samuel,	born January	27, 1639.
VI. Joanna,	born December	25, 1641.
VII. Noah,	born February	25, 1644.
VIII. Elizabeth,	born August	25, 1648.

---

* Mr. John Russell removed from Wethersfield to Hadley, with his son Rev. John Russell and his other children, in 1659.

† The births of the four youngest children of Rev. Mr. Smith are recorded in Wethersfield Records. In his will Mr. Smith mentions son Peregrine, deceased, and two married daughters, who had children : these daughters must, of course, have been older than those recorded. By the will of Mrs. Smith, alias Russell, there was a daughter Dorathy ; she was older than those born in Wethersfield, and younger than the two elder daughters. Thus there is proof that there had been at least eight children. From these premises, it may confidently be inferred, that the two married daughters were by a first and different wife, and that Dorathy was by a second wife. As Noah and Elizabeth are not mentioned in the will of their mother, it is to be concluded they died young.

DESCENDANTS IN THE LINE OF DORATHY SMITH, DAUGHTER OF THE REV. HENRY SMITH.

THIRD GENERATION.

IV.

DORATHY SMITH was married four times. 1. To John Blakeman, of Stratford, Conn., son of Rev. Adam Blakeman, first minister of that town, about 1653. He died in 1662.* 2. To Francis Hall, of Stratford, October 31, 1665. She was his second wife. He died in 1689.† 3. To Mark Sension, of Norwalk, Conn. She was his second wife. He died in 1693, "aged about 59 years."‡ 4. To Deacon Isaac Moore, of Farmington, Conn., formerly of Norwalk, whom she survived. She was likewise his second wife.

Deacon Isaac Moore died ――――.

Mrs. Dorathy Moore, alias Sension, alias Hall, alias Blakeman, died in 1706, at Farmington.

Children,—by her first husband.

9 John,	born	Settled in Fairfield, Conn. Married Mary Curtis, daughter of widow Hannah Curtis, of Stratford. They had 1 child only.
10 Ebenezer,	born	Settled in Stratford. Was married to Patience Willcoxson, daughter of John Willcoxson, of Stratford, by his second wife, October 4, 1681, and after her death, to Abigail Curtis, daughter of widow Hannah Curtis, of Stratford, November 3, 1692. By his first wife he had 4 children, and by his second, 5.
11 Joseph,	born	Was twice married. To Hannah Hall, of Stratford, July 14, 1674, and after her death to Esther Wheeler, of Stratford, Conn., January 29, 1705.? By his first wife he had 5 children.

Children,—by her other husbands,—none by either of them.

---

* Mr. John Blakeman left a will which is dated January 19, 1662, in which he says, " Son Joseph, if he conducts himself dutifully towards his mother, he shall have 10 pounds more than the rest."

† Mr. Francis Hall left a will, which is dated May 6, 1686, and was presented to court July 9, 1689. His wife, Dorathy Hall, executrix. In this Instrument, Testator gives " to my loving wife, my written books that are legible : all that are written in correctness she may dispose of as she pleases. As for all my other books, my will is, that my wife, my son Samuel, and my daughter Mary, shall divide an distribute among themselves and to my other daughters, as they see cause,—all of them to have benefit by ' Looking unto Jesus,' which is the title of one of my books,—a Looking unto Jesus, by Mr. Huaradbeny."

‡ Mr. Mark Sension left a will, containing no date, but Inventory presented, and Court action thereon, November 7, 1693. An Indenture, signed by Mark Sension and Dorathy Hall, is recorded, by which in case of death, each abandons claim to the Survivor's property. This is dated January 21, 1692.

DESCENDANTS IN THE LINE OF SAMUEL SMITH, SON OF THE REV. HENRY SMITH.

THIRD GENERATION.

V.

SAMUEL SMITH, of Northampton, Mass., from 1666 to about 1680,—then of Hadley, in the same State, was married to Mary Ensign, daughter of James Ensign, of Hartford, Conn., one of the first settlers of that town, about 1662.

Mr. Samuel Smith died at Hadley, September 10, 1703, in his 65th year.

His widow, Mrs. Mary Smith, died ———.

Children.

12 Samuel,	born	before his father went to Northampton.
13 Sarah,	born	before her father went to Northampton. Married John Lawrence, October 16, 1684.
14 Dorathy,	bap.	1667, at Northampton. Married William Rooker, May 30, 1687.
15 Ebenezer,	bap.	1668, at Northampton.
16 Ichabod,	born January	24, 1670, at Northampton.
17 Mary,	born January	18, 1673, at Northampton. Married James Barnes, 1696.
18 James,	born June	12, 1675, at Northampton.
19 Preserved,	born August,	1677, at Northampton.

FOURTH GENERATION.

12.

SAMUEL SMITH, of Northampton, Mass., until about 1716, and after that time, of Suffield, Conn., was married to Joanna McLathlin, November 18, 1685, at Hadley, Mass.*

Deacon Samuel Smith died at Suffield, September 1, 1723, aged about 70.

His widow, Mrs. Joanna Smith, died ———.

Children.

20 Mary,	born April	18, 1688.	Married John Kent, of Suffield, son of John Kent, of that town, 1709. Died May 27, 1729. This marriage may not be right; Kent's wife may have been another Smith's daughter.
21 Samuel,	born March	13, 1690.	
22 Thankful,	born May	13, 1692.	Married Jedediah Winchell, 1710.
23 Mindwell,	born February	28, 1694.	Died in childhood.
24 Noah,	born May	12, 1698.	Admitted to Suffield Church, July 5, 1719. Mary his wife admitted November 29, 1724.
25 Experience,	born November	9, 1700.	Admitted to Suffield Church, October 31, 1718.
26 Ebenezer,	born December	6, 1702.	
27 Mindwell,	born March	5, 1705.	Died March 17, 1705.
28 Mercy,	born July	5, 1706.	

* Himself and wife admitted to the Church in Suffield, October 31, 1718, by letter from Northampton Church.

SMITH FAMILY. 193

15.

EBENEZER SMITH, of Hadley, Mass., until about 1698, and after that time, of Suffield, Conn., was married to Sarah Huxley, daughter of Thomas Huxley, of Suffield, about 1693. After his death, she was married to Martin Kellogg, of Suffield, October 5, 1732.

Mr. Ebenezer Smith died September 15, 1728, aged about 60.
Mrs. Sarah Smith, alias Kellogg, died ———.

Children.

29 Sarah,	born September	17, 1694, at Northampton.
30 Dorathy,	born December	21, 1696, at Hadley.
31 Ebenezer,	born April	12, 1699, at Suffield. Admitted to Suffield Church, May 28, 1721.
32 Nathaniel,	born March	3, 1702, at Suffield. Admitted to Suffield Church, February 27, 1725.
33 Joanna,	born June	8, 1703, at Suffield.
34 Jonathan,	born August	1, 1705, at Suffield.
35 Dorcas,	born November	19, 1707, at Suffield.
36 Mary,	born March	26, 1710, at Suffield. Died August 26, 1711.
37 Mary,	born July	24, 1713, at Suffield. Died April 10, 1716.

16.

ICHABOD SMITH, of Hadley, Mass., until about 1699, and after that time of Suffield, Conn., was married to Mary Huxley, daughter of Thomas Huxley, of Suffield, about 1692.

Children.

38 Child, (un- named,)	born February	1, 1693, at Hadley. Died February 13, 1694.
39 Mary,	born May	20, 1696, at Hadley.
40 Hannah,	born January	21, 1698, at Hadley.
41 Samuel,	born November	5, 1700, at Suffield.
42 Ichabod,	born January	1, 1708, at Suffield.
43 James,	born March	15, 1711, at Suffield.
44 Joseph,	born January	1, 1717, at Suffield.

18.

JAMES SMITH, of Hadley, Mass., until about 1706, and after that time of East Haddam, Conn., was married to Elizabeth Smith, daughter of Chileab Smith, of Hadley, October 26, 1698.

Children.

45 Elizabeth,	born July	26, 1699, at Hadley.
46 James,	born December	30, 1700, at Hadley.
47 Noah,	born August	24, 1702, at Hadley.
48 Samuel,	born April	28, 1704, at Hadley.
49 Chileab,	born February	11, 1706, at East-Haddam.
50 Hannah,	born July	3, 1708, at East-Haddam.
51 Ebenezer,	born February	26, 1710, at East-Haddam.
52 Mindwell,	born April	22, 1714, at East-Haddam.

19.

PRESERVED SMITH, of Hadley, Mass., was married to Mary Smith, daughter of Chileab Smith, of the same town, December 15, 1697. She was born August 16, 1681. After his death, she was married to Peter Montague, of Hadley, April 22, 1721.

25

Mr. Preserved Smith died in 1713, aged about 36.
Mrs. Mary Smith, alias Montague, died after 1746.

Children.*

53 Mary,	born January	3, 1699.	Died in 1714.	
54 Preserved,	born November	9, 1700.	Died in 1727.	Had 2 children.
55 Ebenezer,	born February	4, 1702.		
56 Samuel,	born October	1, 1705.		
57 Chileab,	born May	21, 1708.		
58 James,	born September	23, 1710.		
59 Moses,	born October	30, 1712.	Died in 1726.	

FIFTH GENERATION.

41.

SAMUEL SMITH, of Suffield, Conn., son of Ichabod Smith, of Suffield, was married to Jerusha Mather, daughter of Atherton Mather, of the same town, November 8, 1725. She was born July 18, 1700, at Windsor, Conn., where Mr. Mather then dwelt.

Mr. Samuel Smith died at Suffield, August 25, 1767, in the 67th year of his age.

His widow, Mrs. Jerusha Smith, died at Sharon, Conn., at the house of her son, the Rev. Cotton Mather Smith, minister of that town, November 5, 1789, in the 90th year of her age.

Children.

60 Elizabeth,	born November	10, 1726.
61 Dan,	born October	25, 1728.
62 Cotton Math-er,	born October	15, 1730.
63 Simeon,	born August	6, 1733.
64 Paul,	born September	15, 1736.

42.

ICHABOD SMITH, Jun., of Suffield, Conn., was married to Elizabeth Stedman, January 1, 1731.

Mr. Ichabod Smith died February 26, 1749, aged —.

His widow, Mrs. Elizabeth Smith, died February 8, 1803, aged 96.

Children.

65 Phineas,	born June	9, 1732.	Died November 21, 1742.
66 Elizabeth,	born February	28, 1735.	
67 Ruth,	born November	14, 1736.	
68 Ichabod,	born November	26, 1738.	
69 Asahel,	born November	26, 1739.	
70 Jerusha,	born August	13, 1742.	
71 Anne,	born November	26, 1744.	
72 Phineas,	born October	28, 1746.	

SIXTH GENERATION.

60.

ELIZABETH SMITH was married to Graves Loomis, of Suffield, Conn., May 10, 1749.

---

* Some of Mr. Smith's children became Baptists, and two were Baptist preachers, or exhorters.

Graves Loomis, Esq., died January 18, 1790, in the 63rd year of his age.

His widow Mrs. Elizabeth Loomis, October 1, 1803, aged 77.

Children.

73 Belinda,	born April	7, 1750.	Died August 10, 1751.
74 Anna,	born May	31, 1751.	Died July 2, 1751.
75 Belinda,	born June	24, 1752.	
76 Elizabeth,	born September	16, 1760.	
77 Luther,	born June	24, 1754.	He was father of Hon. Luther Loomis.
78 Anne,	born July	22, 1756.	Died October 24, 1789.
79 Nathaniel,	born July	8, 1758.	Died November 27, 1794.
80 Elizabeth,	born July	8, 1762.	
81 Keziah,	born August	18, 1764.	Died October 8, 1777.
82 Graves,	born December	25, 1766.	Died September 24, 1777.
83 Jerusha,	born August	14, 1770.	

61.

DAN SMITH, of Suffield, Conn., was married to Keziah Devotion, daughter of the Rev. Ebenezer Devotion, pastor of the Congregational Church at Suffield, and of Sarah his third wife, who was Sarah Hobart, April 2, 1752.

Mrs. Keziah Smith died March 17, 1761, in her 28th year.

Mr. Dan Smith died January 23, 1762, aged 33, leaving a will; Cotton Mather Smith, of Sharon, and Paul Smith, of Suffield, Executors.

Children.

84 Lucy,	born February	24, 1754.
85 Phineas,	born January	5, 1755.*
86 Apollus,	born December	5, 1756.
87 Dan,	born January	28, 1759.*

62.

REV. COTTON MATHER SMITH, of Sharon, Conn., ordained Pastor of the church in that town, August 28, 1755, was married to Temperance Gale, widow of Doct. Moses Gale, of Goshen. Orange County, N. Y., May 31, 1758. She was Temperance Worthington, daughter of Rev. William Worthington, Pastor of the church in that part of Saybrook, Conn., now known by the name of Westbrook, and was born April 8, 1732.

Mrs. Temperance Smith, alias Gale, died at Albany, N. Y., at the house of her son-in-law, Hon. Jacob Radcliff, one of the Justices of the Supreme Court of that State, on her return from Saratoga, June 26, 1800, aged 68.

Rev. Cotton Mather Smith died November 27, 1806, aged 75.

Children.

| 88 Elizabeth, | born June | 29, 1759. | Married Doct. Lemuel Wheeler, of Red Hook, N. Y. Died January, 1788. |
| 89 Juliana, | born February | 12, 1761. | Married Hon. Jacob Radcliff, of Albany, one of the Justices of the Supreme Court of Judicature of that State. Died June 25, 1823. |

* 1760, October 4, Phineas and Dan Smith, sons of Dan and Keziah Smith, offered for baptism by their grandmother, widow Jerusha Smith, who, on November 3, 1771, was dismissed by Suffield Church to Church in Sharon. [Suffield Church Records.]

90 Thomas
    Mather,   born January   21, 1763.   Died April 18, 1782.
91 John Cotton, born February   12, 1765.
92 Lucretia,   born January   20, 1767.   Died 1773.
93 Mary,   born February   16, 1769.   Married Rev. Daniel Smith, of Stam-
                                                ford, Conn. Died January 10, 1801.

64.

PAUL SMITH, first of Suffield, Conn., and afterwards of Sharon, in the same State, was married to Jerusha Smith, daughter of Ichabod Smith, of that town, and of Elizabeth his wife, who was Elizabeth Stedman, October 30, 1760.   She was born August 13, 1742.

Mrs. Jerusha Smith died February, 1814, in the 72nd year of her age.

Children,—two only recorded on Suffield Records.

94 Anna,   born April   1, 1762, in Suffield.
95 Paul,   born October 28, 1763, in Suffield.

DESCENDANTS IN THE LINE OF JOANNA SMITH, DAUGHTER OF THE REV. HENRY SMITH.

THIRD GENERATION.

VI.

JOANNA SMITH was married to Philip Russell, of Hadley, Mass., son of John Russell, of Hadley, and brother of Rev. John Russell, first minister of that town, February 4, 1664. [After her death, he was married to Elizabeth Terry, daughter of Stephen Terry, of Hadley, January 10, 1665, and after *her* death,* to Mary Church, of Hadley, December 25, 1679.]

Mrs. Joanna Russell died December 28, 1664, aged 23.

Mr. Philip Russell died May 19, 1693.

Child,—one only.

96 Joanna,   born October   31, 1664. "Died December, 1664, and was buried
                                         with its mother, December 29, 1664."
                                         [Hadley Records.]

---

* Mrs. Elizabeth Russell, wife of Philip Russell, and her son Stephen Russell, were slain by the Indians, September 19, 1677. [Hadley Records.]

JARED SPENCER.

Sargeant JARED SPENCER, first of "The New Town," Cambridge, Mass., then of Lynn, Mass., and afterwards, one of the first settlers of Haddam, Conn., was married to Hannah ——.
Mrs. Hannah Spencer died ——.
Ensign Jared Spencer died in 1685.*

SECOND GENERATION.

Children of Jared Spencer.

I. John, born
II. Hannah, born
III. Allice, born
IV. Mehita-
    bel, born
V. Thomas, born
VI. Samuel, born
VII. William, born
VIII. Nathan-
    iel, born
IX. Rebecca, born
X. Ruth, born
XI. Timothy, born

DESCENDANTS IN THE LINE OF JOHN SPENCER, SON OF JARED SPENCER, THE SETTLER.

THIRD GENERATION.

I.

John Spencer, of Haddam, Conn., was married to Rebecca Howard, daughter of Robert Howard, about 1665. She was born August 17, 1648.
Mr. John Spencer died August 3, 1682, aged ——.
His widow, Mrs. Rebecca Spencer, died ——.

Children.

12 Rebecca,	born March,	1666.	Was married to John Ackley, of Haddam, May 23, 1699, at Hartford, Conn.
13 Jared,	born January,	1669.	
14 Benjamin,	born March,	1671.	
15 Lydia,	born	1673.	Married John Ventrous, of Haddam.
16 Grace,	born February,	1677.	

---

* At a meeting of the Council at Hartford, September 14, 1675. Present,—William Leete. Esq., Deputy Governor; Major John Talcott, Mr. Henry Wolcott, Capt. John Allyn, Major Robert Treat, Capt. Benjamin Newberry, Mr. John Wadsworth.
" The inhabitants of Haddam having presented Jarrad Spencer, for an Ensigne for their Trayn Band, affirming him to be legally chosen, the Councill doe accordingly commissionate him to be their Ensigne and to commande them according to lawe; and Wm. Ventrus is confirmed to be their Sarj^t. This to stand till the Gen^ll Court order otherwise."

FOURTH GENERATION.
13.

JARED SPENCER, of Haddam, Conn., was married to Deborah Birge, daughter of Daniel Birge, of Windsor, Conn., November 12, 1692. She was born November 26, 1671.

Mrs. Deborah Spencer died ———.

Sargeant Jared Spencer died November 24, 1744, aged 74.

Children.

17 John,	born October	17, 1692.	Died in infancy.
18 John,	born March	28, 1694.	Died April 26, 1735, aged 41.
19 Deborah,	born December	5, 1697.	
20 Jared,	born August	12, 1699.	
21 Benjamin,	born April	21, 1702.	
22 Lydia,	born August	20, 1705.	

DESCENDANTS IN THE LINE OF HANNAH SPENCER, DAUGHTER OF JARED SPENCER, THE SETTLER.

THIRD GENERATION.
II.

HANNAH SPENCER was married to Daniel Brainard, of Haddam, Conn., and one of the first settlers of that town, about 1665.

Mrs. Hannah Brainard died ———.

Deacon Daniel Brainard died April 1, 1715, aged 74.

Children.

23 Daniel, born 1666. Settled in East-Haddam. Married Susannah Ventrus, daughter of Moses Ventrus, of Haddam, 1688. Deacon Daniel Brainard died February 28, 1743, in his 77th year. His widow, Mrs. Susannah Brainard, died January 26, 1754, in the 86th year of her age.

24 Hannah, born 1667. Married Thomas Gates, of East-Haddam, Conn., 1693. He died April 20, 1734, in his 70th year. She died September 7, 1750, in her 83d year.

25 James, born 1669. Settled in Haddam. Was twice married. 1. To Deborah ———, April 1, 1696, by whom he had 8 children. She dying July 22, 1709, he married Sarah ———, May 23, 1711, by whom he had 6 children. Deacon James Brainard died February 10, 1742, aged 73.

26 Joshua, born 1672. Settled in East Haddam. Married, 1. Mary Olmsted, and after her death, which occurred December 5, 1704, 2. Mehitabel Dudley, July 12, 1710. Capt. Joshua Brainard died May 13, 1755, in his 84th year. They had 10 children,—all by his second wife.

27 William, born 1674. Settled on Haddam Neck. Father of Rev. Chiliab Brainard, first ordained Minister of Eastbury Parish in Glastenbury, Conn. He married Abigail Fiske, daughter of Rev. Phineas

28 Caleb,   born   1676.

29 Hezekiah, born   1681.

30 Elijah,   born   1686.

Fiske, second minister of Haddam,
Conn. Rev. Chiliab Brainard died
January 1, 1739.   After his death
she was married to Rev. Noah Merrick, minister of Wilbraham, Mass.,
one of the ancestors of Hon. George
Merrick, of Glastenbury.   She died
in 1807, aged 89.
Settled in Haddam.   Married Elizabeth
———, May 1, 1701.   He died August 11, 1742, in his 66th year.
Settled in Haddam.   Married Dorathy
Mason, widow of Daniel Mason,
deceased, of Lebanon, Conn., and
daughter of Rev. Jeremiah Hobart,
minister of Haddam, whose wife was
a daughter of the "Rev. Timothy
Whiting, minister of the gospel, first
at Boston, in Lincolnshire, Eng., and
afterwards, in Lynn, Mass.," October
1, 1707.   Worshipful Hezekiah Brainard died at Hartford, during a session
of the Assembly, May 24, 1727, aged
46.   His grave is in the old burying
ground in that place.   Mrs. Dorathy
Brainard, alias Mason, died March
11, 1732, in her 53d year.   They had
9 children,—among them,—Nehemiah, their 3d child, born February 20,
1712, and died November 9, 1742,
was the second ordained minister of
Eastbury Parish, in Glastenbury,
Conn.   His wife was Elizabeth Fiske,
daughter of Rev. Phineas Fiske,
minister of Haddam.   She died December 4, 1793, aged 73.   Martha,
their 5th child, born September 1,
1716, was married to Joseph Spencer,
(afterwards a major general in the
army of the Revolution,) son of
Isaac Spencer, of East-Haddam,
August 2, 1738,—David their 6th
child, born April 20, 1718, and died
at Northampton, Mass., October 10,
1747, was "an eminent preacher, and
a faithful and laborious missionary
to the Stockbridge, Delaware and
Susquehannah Tribes of Indians."
Died April 20, 1748, aged about 62.
On his inventory it is said he died
April 20, 1740.

DESCENDANTS IN THE LINE OF ALLICE SPENCER DAUGHTER OF JARED SPENCER, THE SETTLER.

THIRD GENERATION.

III.

ALLICE SPENCER was twice married. 1. To Thomas Brooks,
of Haddam, Conn., 1662.   He died October 18, 1668.   2. To
Thomas Shaylor, of Haddam, 1673.

Mrs. Allice Shaylor, alias Brooks, died ———.

Mr. Thomas Shaylor died about 1692. He sailed for the West Indies, in 1692, and was lost at sea.

Children,—by her first husband.

31 Sarah,	born December,	1662.	
32 Thomas,	born June,	1664.	Was a Deacon of the church at Haddam.
33 Mary,	born June,	1666.	
34 Allice,	born December,	1668.	(Posthumous.)

Children,—by her second husband.

35 Thomas,	born about	1674.	Married Catharine ———, October 22, 1696, by whom he had 10 children.
36 Abel,	born		Was twice married. By his first wife, 3 children, and by his last. 6.
37 Timothy,	born		Was twice married. 6 children are recorded to him, 2 by his first wife, and 4 by his last.
38 Anna,	born		Married John Clark, of Hartford, Conn.

DESCENDANTS IN THE LINE OF MEHITABEL SPENCER, DAUGHTER OF JARED SPENCER, THE SETTLER.

THIRD GENERATION.

IV.

MEHITABEL SPENCER was married to Daniel Cone, of Haddam, Conn., one of the first settlers of that town.*

Mrs. Mehitabel Cone died ———.

Daniel Cone, Esq., died October 24, 1706, in the 80th year of his age.

Children.

39 Daniel,	born	1665.	Settled in East-Haddam. Married Mary Gates, February 14, 1693. Deacon Daniel Cone died June 16, 1725, in his 60th year.
40 Jared,	born	1674.	Settled in East-Haddam. Died May 12, 1742, in her 68th year. 9 children are recorded to them on East-Haddam Town Records.
41 Stephen,	born		Settled in East-Haddam.
42 Caleb,	born	1679.	Settled in Haddam. Capt. Caleb Cone died September 25, 1742, in his 63d year.

DESCENDANTS IN THE LINE OF THOMAS SPENCER, SON OF JARED SPENCER, THE SETTLER.

THIRD GENERATION.

V.

THOMAS SPENCER, first of Haddam, Conn., afterwards of Westbrook Society, in Saybrook, Conn., was married to a Bates of Haddam.

He died before 1703.

---

* Ancestor of William R. Cone, Esq., of the firm of Hungerford & Cone, of this City, attorneys.

Children.

43 Jared,   born October   8, 1673, in Haddam.
44 Thomas,   born
45 Caleb,   born

DESCENDANTS IN THE LINE OF SAMUEL SPENCER, SON OF JARED SPENCER, THE SETTLER.

THIRD GENERATION.

VI.

SAMUEL SPENCER, of Millington Society, East-Haddam, Conn., was twice married. 1. To Hannah Blachford, [or Blachfield,] widow of Peter Blachford,* deceased, of Haddam, formerly of New-London, Conn., alias Hannah Hungerford, widow of Thomas Hungerford,† deceased, of New-London, Conn., and daughter of Isaac Willey, of New-London, 1673. She died about 1681. 2. To Mirriam Willey, widow of John Willey, deceased, of Haddam, formerly of New-London, and daughter of Miles Moore, of that town, 1689. Mr. John Willey died May 2, 1688.
Mr. Samuel Spencer died August 7, 1705.
His widow, Mrs. Mirriam Spencer, alias Willey, died ———.

Children,—by his first wife.

46 Grace,   born July   27, 1674.
47 John,   born September 17, 1676.
48 Isaac,   born January   8, 1678.
49 Hannah,   born   1680.

Children,—by his second wife,—none.

---

* Peter Blachfield died at Haddam, September 1, 1671, aged 46. The children of Peter and Hannah Blachford were Joanna, born 1667, at New-London. Peter, born 1669, at New-London, settled in Salem, West-Jersey, Mary, born 1671, at Haddam.

East-Haddam Records, Book 1, p. 40. Feb. 7, 1703–4. By deed of this date, Peter Blachfield, now living in Salem, West-Jersey, only son and heir of Peter Blachfield, late of Haddam, dec., from love and good affection that I have and bear to my two brothers-in-law, John Spencer and Isaac Spencer, living in Haddam, east side, conveys to said John and Isaac, certain lands in Haddam, that did belong to his father, Peter Blachfield, late of said Haddam, deceased.

Old Haddam Records, Book 2, p. 184. January 4, 1718. By deed of this date, John Spencer, of Haddam, east side, conveys to his brother Isaac Spencer, land laid out, or to be laid out on the right of the estate of Peter Blachford, and warrants against the claim of our sister, *Hannah Ross, (or Rose,) whose maiden name was Hannah Hungerford.*

Old Haddam Records, Book 2, p. 197. April, 1719. By deed of this date, Hannah Ross, (or Rose,) of the plantation of the Narragansetts, in Rhode-Island, conveys land in Haddam, to John Spencer, of Haddam, that did belong to her brother, Peter Blachford, dec.

Old Haddam Records, Book 2, page 224. May 1, 1727. By writing of this date, Isaac Spencer gives notice that he has taken possession of a lot of land in Haddam, that was laid out on the right of his brother, Peter Blachford, deceased.

† Thomas Hungerford was twice married. 1. To ——— ———. 2. To Hannah Willey, daughter of Isaac Willey, of New-London, about 1658. After the death of Mr. Hungerford, she was married to ——— Blachfield, (or Blachford,) of New-London. but who removed to Haddam in 1669. Thomas Hungerford died at New-London in 1663. His children were Thomas, born about 1648; Sarah, born about 1654, married Lewis Hughes, of Lyme; and by his second wife, Hannah, born May 1, 1659, married Mr. Ross, (Rose,) of Rhode-Island.

Hartford County Court and Probate Records, Book 3, page 6. Court July 9, 1663. The Inventory of Thomas Hungerford, of New London, was exhibited into Court, and John Willey and Peter Blachford are appointed by this Court to husband the state, and pay debts that appear to be due from the state, and take care of the children, until the Court see cause to come to a distribution of the state.

Same Book, page 15. Court, May 10, 1664. This Court accepts the account of the payment of debts to the creditors of Thomas Hungerford, and do order that the estate be thus divided:

To the relict the whole estate, she paying these portions, viz., To Thomas Hungerford, 7 pounds: to Sarah Hungerford, 4 pounds, and to Hannah Hungerford, 4 pounds,—the son to be paid at 21, and the daughters at 18.

FOURTH GENERATION.

46.

GRACE SPENCER was married to John Day, of Hartford, Conn., but after about 1701, of Colchester, Conn., January, 21, 1696. [After her death, Mr. Day was married to Mary Hale, daughter of Samuel Hale, jun., of Glastenbury, Conn., and of Mary his wife, daughter of Samuel Wells, of that town, about 1716. She died November 2, 1749, aged 74.]
Mrs. Grace Day died May 12, 1714, in her 40th year.
Mr. John Day died November 4, 1752, aged 75.

Children,—by his first wife.

50 Lydia,	born April	11, 1698, at Hartford. Married Joseph Fuller, of Kent, Conn.
51 Mary,	born August	14, 1699, at Hartford. Married Jonathan Northam, of Colchester, December 20, 1722.
52 John,	born June	6, 1701, at Hartford. Married Sarah Loomis, of Colchester, August 20, 1725.
53 Joseph,	born September	27, 1702, at Colchester. Married Esther Hungerford, April 1, 1729.
54 Benjamin,	born February	7, 1704, at Colchester. Married Margaret Foote, daughter of Ephraim Foote, of Colchester, March 6, 1729.
55 Editha,	born September	10, 1705, at Colchester. Married David Bigelow, of Colchester, December 11, 1729.
56 Daniel,	born March	9, 1709, at Colchester. Died in 1712.
57 David,	born July	18, 1710, at Colchester. Married Hannah Kellogg, of Colchester.
58 Abraham,	born March	17, 1712, at Colchester. Married Irene Foote, daughter of Ephraim Foote, of Colchester, November 20, 1740.
59 Isaac,	born May	17, 1713, at Colchester. Married Ann Foote, daughter of Nathaniel Foote, jun., of Colchester, July 3, 1740.
60 Daniel,	born	Died unmarried, about 1746.

47.

JOHN SPENCER, of East-Haddam, Conn., was married to Elizabeth ———.
Mrs. Elizabeth Spencer died June 15, 1725.
Mr. John Spencer died ———.

Children.

61 Hannah,	born April	8, 1705.
62 Elizabeth,	born March	15, 1707.
63 John,	born January	24, 1709.
64 Peter,	born [no date.]	
65 Sarah,	born March	6, 1714.
66 Dorathy,	born February	14, 1716.
67 Ebenezer,	born February	2, 1721.

48.

ISAAC SPENCER, of East-Haddam, Conn., was married to Mary Selden, October 2, 1707.

Children.

68 Samuel,	born July	16, 1708.
69 Mary,	born June	24, 1710.

70 Rebecca,	born August	1, 1712.	
71 Joseph,	born October	3, 1714.	Was a major-general, &c.
72 Esther,	born December	16, 1716.	
73 Jared,	born November	5, 1718.	
74 Elihu,	born February	12, 1721.	Was Rev. Dr. Elihu Spencer, of the New Jersey College.
75 Isaac,	born May	3, 1723.	
76 Mehitabel,	born March	29, 1725.	
77 Anna,	born November	29, 1729.	
78 Israel,	born February	30, 1732.	

DESCENDANTS IN THE LINE OF WILLIAM SPENCER, SON OF JARED SPENCER, THE SETTLER.

THIRD GENERATION.

VII.

WILLIAM SPENCER, of East-Haddam, Conn., was married to Sarah Ackley, daughter of Nicholas Ackley, of Haddam, one of the first settlers of that town.

Children.

79 Joseph,	born
80 Elizabeth,	born
81 James,	born
82 Micajah,	born
83 Margaret,	born
84 Hezekiah,	born
85 William,	born
86 Jonathan,	born
87 Ichabod,	born

DESCENDANTS IN THE LINE OF NATHANIEL SPENCER, SON OF JARED SPENCER, THE SETTLER.

THIRD GENERATION.

VIII.

NATHANIEL SPENCER, of Haddam, Conn., was twice married.
1. To Lydia Smith, daughter of Thomas Smith, of Haddam, 1681.
2. To Hannah ———.
Mr. Nathaniel Spencer died before 1722.
Mrs. Hannah Spencer died February 20, 1742.

Children,—by his first wife.

88 Lydia,	born August	10, 1682.	
89 Nathaniel,	born July	15, 1684.	
90 Elizabeth,	born January	18, 1686.	
91 John,	born March	30, 1688.	
92 Mary,	born June	9, 1692.	Married Samuel Belden, of Wethersfield, Conn., April 10, 1712.
93 Daniel,*	born August	20, 1694.	
94 Susanna,	born November	8, 1696.	
95 Dorathy,	born March	8, 1699.	
96 Phineas,	born March	20, 1701.	

Children,—by his second wife,—none.

---

* By Hartford Probate Records, Book 12, p. 16, Court, 1734, it appears that a Daniel Spencer, of Haddam, married Abigail Clark, daughter of Daniel Clark, of Haddam.

DESCENDANTS IN THE LINE OF REBECCA SPENCER, DAUGHTER OF JARED SPENCER, THE SETTLER.

THIRD GENERATION.

IX.

REBECCA SPENCER was twice married. I. To John Kenard, of Haddam, Conn., about 1682. He died in 1689. 2. To John Tanner, of Lyme, Conn., afterwards of East-Haddam, Conn. Mrs. Rebecca Tanner, alias Kenard, died before 1706. Mr. John Tanner died ———.

Children,—by her first husband.

97 John,	born	1683.	Died at East Haddam, in 1710.
98 Elizabeth,	born April	28, 1688.	Married John Smith, of East Haddam, August 28, 1707. They had 10 children.

Children,—by her second husband,—none discovered.

DESCENDANTS IN THE LINE OF RUTH SPENCER, DAUGHTER OF JARED SPENCER, THE SETTLER.

THIRD GENERATION.

X.

RUTH SPENCER was married to Joseph Clark, of Haddam, Conn., son of William Clark, of that town.

Children,—from deeds on Haddam Records and his will.

99 William, born
100 Joseph, born
101 Daniel, born
102 John, born
103 Catharine, born
104 Hannah, born

DESCENDANTS IN THE LINE OF TIMOTHY SPENCER, SON OF JARED SPENCER, THE SETTLER.

THIRD GENERATION.

XI.

TIMOTHY SPENCER, of Haddam, Conn., was married to ———. Mr. Timothy Spencer died in 1704. His widow, Mrs. —— Spencer, died about 1704.

Children.

105 Timothy,	born		Married in 1702, and had 9 children. He died March 29, 1732.
106 Sarah,	born		Married Joseph Chapman, of Saybrook, Conn.
107 Hannah,	born		Married Azariah Dickinson.
108 Deborah,	born		Married John Hungerford, of East-Haddam, Conn., August 23, 1695.
109 Jonathan,	born	1692.	Died unmarried, and his estate divided among his brothers and sisters, November 10, 1715.
110 Ruth,	born	1689.	Married Henry Williams, of East-Haddam, Conn.

THOMAS SPENCER.

Sergeant THOMAS SPENCER, one of the first settlers of Hartford, Conn., was twice married. 1. To ———. 2. To Sarah Bearding, daughter of Nathaniel Bearding, also one of the first settlers of Hartford, September 11, 1645.

Mrs. Sarah Spencer died ———.

Sergeant Thomas Spencer died September 11, 1687, aged ———.

FIRST GENERATION.

Children,—by his first wife.

I. Obadiah, born
II. Thomas, born
III. Samuel, born

Children,—by his second wife.

IV. Jared, born
V. Sarah, born   Married Thomas Huxley.
VI. Elizabeth, bap. March   26, 1648.   Married Samuel Andrews, of Hartford.
VII. Hannah, born April   25, 1653.
VIII. Mary, born May   20, 1655.
IX. Martha, born May   19, 1657.   Married a Benton.

DESCENDANTS IN THE LINE OF OBADIAH SPENCER, SON OF THOMAS SPENCER, THE SETTLER.

SECOND GENERATION.

I.

Obadiah Spencer, of Hartford, Conn., was married to Mary Disborough, daughter of Nicholas Disborough,* one of the first settlers of Hartford.

" * In the year 1683, the house of Nicholas Disborough, at Hartford, was very strangely molested by stones, by pieces of earth, by cobs of *Indian* corn, and such other things, from an *invisible hand*, thrown at him, sometimes thro' the door, sometimes thro' the window, sometimes down the chimney, and sometimes from the floor of the room, (tho' very close,) over his head ; and sometimes he met with them in the shop, the yard, the barn, and in the field.

" There was no violence in the motion of the things thus thrown by the *invisible hand ;* and tho' others besides the man, happen'd sometimes to be hit, they were never hurt by them ; only the *man* himself once had pain given to his arm, and once blood fetch'd from his leg, by these *annoyances*, and a fire in an unknown way kindled, *consum'd* no little part of his estate.

" This trouble began upon a controversie between Disborough and another person, about a chest of cloaths which the *man* apprehended to be unrighteously detained by *Desborough ;* and it endured for divers months : but upon the restoring of the cloaths thus detain'd, the trouble ceas'd.

" At *Brightling*, in *Sussex*, in England, there happened a tragedy not unlike to this in the year 1659. 'Tis recorded by *Clark*, in the second volume of his *Examples*." [Mather's Magnalia, Book VII., Vol. II., page 393, Hartford edition.]

Mrs. Mary Spencer died ———.
Mr. Obadiah Spencer died 1712.

Children,—named in his will.

10 Obadiah,	born	1666.	Married Ruth ———. Died August 22, 1741. 6 children.
11 Thomas,	born	1668.	Married and had children.
12 Samuel,	born		Married Deborah Beckley, daughter of John Beckley, of Wethersfield. 4 children.
13 Ebenezer,*	born		Married Mary Boothe, February 28, 1699. 5 children.
14 John,	born		Married Mary Smith, daughter of Joseph Smith, October 4, 1693. Probably, but not certain.
15 Disborough,†born			Married Abigail Elmer, March 27, 1701. She died February 17, 1725, aged 46.
16 Mary,	born		Married a King.

DESCENDANTS IN THE LINE OF THOMAS SPENCER, SON OF THOMAS SPENCER, THE SETTLER.

SECOND GENERATION.

II.

THOMAS SPENCER, of Suffield, Conn., was married to Esther Andrews, daughter of William Andrews, of Hartford, Conn.
Mr. Thomas Spencer died ———.
His widow, Mrs. Esther Spencer, died March 6, 1698.

Children.

17 Abigail,	born		Died October 4, 1680.
18 Thomas,	born		
19 Samuel,	born		Married Elizabeth Mascraft, of Roxbury, Mass., March 18, 1700, at Roxbury.
20 William,	born		Died in 1745.
21 Anna,	born June	6, 1680.	
22 Elizabeth,	born		Married John Taylor, 1686.
23 Esther,	born		Married William Pierce, 1688.

THIRD GENERATION.

19.

SAMUEL SPENCER, of Suffield, Conn., was married to Elizabeth Mascraft, daughter of ——— Mascraft, of Roxbury, Mass., March 18, 1700, at Roxbury.
Mr. Samuel Spencer died November 23, 1743, aged —.
His widow, Mrs. Elizabeth Spencer, died ———.

---

* At a Court, January 29, 1706. This Court do choose order and appoint Ebenezer Spencer, of Hartford, to be master and keeper of her Majesty's Gaol, in the Town of Hartford.

† At a Court, September 7, 1706. Disborough Spencer, of Hartford, and Henry Merry, of Lyme, were complained of before this Court, by Joseph Gilbert, Grand Juryman, for that, on the 2d day of this instant September, they having a quarrel between themselves, did contrary to peace of our Sovereign Lady the Queen and the laws of this Colony, challenge each other to decide their quarrel with swords; and for that purpose, at the common Landing Place in Hartford, did take swords into their hands to fight.

Children.

24 Thomas,	born January	13, 1702.	
25 Daniel,	born November	22, 170–.	Married Elizabeth Stiles, of Suffield, December 22, 1726. He died December 1, 1772. She died January 28, 1803, aged 98. 6 children.

FOURTH GENERATION.

24.

THOMAS SPENCER, of Suffield, Conn., was married to Mary Trumbull, daughter of John Trumbull, 1st, of Suffield, December 15, 1720. She was born December 2, 1701.

Lieut. Thomas Spencer died February 4, 1754, aged 52.

His widow, Mrs. Mary Spencer, died 1755. Her estate was distributed July 1, 1755.

Children.

26 Elizabeth,	born August	3, 1721.	
27 Thomas,	born January	28, 1723.	Died February 28, 1723.
28 Mercy,	born May	1, 1724.	Married Simeon Harmon, March 18, 1745.
29 Hannah,	born July	11, 1728.	
30 Mary,	born April	14, 1730.	Died June 4, 1732.
31 Mary,	bap.	1733.	
32 Thomas,	born October .	31, 1736.	
33 Eliphalet,	born September	5, 1738.	
34 Hezekiah,	born December	16, 1740.	Married Olive Nott, March 4, 1762. She died February 2, 1771. 2. Deborah Eaton, about January 11, 1772. He died August 3, 1797. She died February 21, 1811. 5 children by 1st wife. 7 by 2nd.

FIFTH GENERATION.

33.

ELIPHALET SPENCER, of Suffield, Conn., was twice married. 1. To Elizabeth Smith, daughter of Ichabod Smith, jun., of Suffield, March 2, 1757. She was born February 28, 1735, and died January 28, 1764, aged 28. 2. To Mary Granger, of Suffield, January 24, 1765.

Mrs. Mary Spencer died July 1, 1813, aged 76.

Mr. Eliphalet Spencer died January 22, 1820, in the 82d year of his age.

Children,—by his first wife.

35 Eliphalet,	born January	1, 1758.	
36 Phineas,	born August	2, 1759.	
37 Ichabod,	born February	1, 1762.	Died when about 18 or 20 years of age.
38 Elizabeth,	born January	8, 1764.	

Children,—by his second wife.

39 Anna,	born August	29, 1765.
40 Mary,	born March	25, 1767.
41 Cynthia,	born August	31, 1768.
42 Mary,	born September	25, 1770.
43 Margaret,	born March	24, 1773.

SIXTH GENERATION.

35.

ELIPHALET SPENCER, first of Suffield, Conn., then of Great-Barrington, Mass., and then of Lenox, Madison County, N. Y., was married to —— ——.

Mr. Eliphalet Spencer died in Lenox, or in the adjoining town, Sullivan, 1815, aged 55.

Children.

44 Gen. Ichabod S. Spencer,	of Canisteo, N. Y.
45 Rev. Eliphalet Moncrief Spencer,	of Chenango County, N. Y.
46 Doct. Thomas M. Spencer,	of Geneva College, N. Y.
47 Hon. Joshua A. Spencer,	of Utica, N. Y.

36.

PHINEAS SPENCER, first of Suffield, Conn., and then of Rupert, Bennington County, Ver., was married to Olive Sheldon, daughter of Gershom Sheldon, of Suffield.

Mr. Phineas Sheldon died at Rupert, Ver., in 1815, aged —.

Mrs. Olive Spencer died ———.

Children.

48 Gershom S. Spencer, born	Of West Windham, Penn.
49 Hon. Phineas Spencer, born	Died in Lodi, N. Y., 1839.
50 Rev. Ichabod S. Spencer, born	Of Brooklyn, N. Y.
51 Solon Spencer, born	Of Lodi, Cattaraugus Co., N. Y.

DESCENDANTS IN THE LINE OF JARED SPENCER, SON OF THOMAS SPENCER, THE SETTLER.

SECOND GENERATION.

IV.

JARED SPENCER, of Hartford, Conn., was married to Hannah Pratt, daughter of John Pratt, of Hartford, December 22, 1680.

Mrs. Hannah Spencer died October 22, 1692.

Mr. Jared Spencer died in 1712.

Children.

52 Hannah,	born October	12, 1681.	
53 Jared,	born January	15, 1682.	
54 Nathaniel,	born February	2, 1684.	Died in childhood.
55 John,	born October	25, 1686.	
56 Sarah,			
57 Elizabeth, } twins.	born February	16, 1688.	
58 Nathaniel,	born December	21, 1690.	
59 Mary,	born September	8, 1692.	

THIRD GENERATION.

53.

JARED SPENCER, first of Hartford, Conn., afterwards of New-Hartford, in the same State, was married to Sarah Day, daughter of John Day, of Hartford, June 10, 1708. She was born September 19, 1683.

Mr. Jared Spencer died at New-Hartford, in 1754, aged 72.

His widow, Mrs. Sarah Spencer, died September, 1767, aged 84.

Children.

60 Hannah,	bap. February	2, 1709.	
61 John,	bap. [no date.]		Married Mary Hubbard, of Middletown.
62 Susanna,	bap. [no date.]		
63 Elizabeth,	bap. April	22, 1716.	
64 Nathaniel Bearding,	bap. May	10, 1724.	

FOURTH GENERATION.

64.

NATHANIEL BEARDING SPENCER, of New-Hartford, Conn., was married to Theodocia Bunce, of Hartford, about 1747.

Mr. Nathaniel B. Spencer died July 26, 1773, aged 49.

His widow, Mrs. Theodocia Spencer, died July 27, 1803, in her 80th year.

Children.

65 Nathaniel,	born April	10, 1748.	
66 Asahel,	born July	19, 1749.	Died in August, 1749.
67 Asahel,	born May	25, 1750.	
68 Isaac,	born November	29, 1751.	Died January 5, 1779. Anna, his widow, died January 21, 1779.
69 Anna,	born June	18, 1753.	
70 James,	born March	10, 1755.	Died July 23, 1802.
71 Lucretia,	born April	30, 1757.	
72 Huldah,	born April	3, 1759.	
73 Asa,	born January	9, 1761.	
74 Jared,	born January	7, 1763.	
75 Theodocia,	born October	31, 1764.	Died January 31, 1765.
76 Josiah,	born December	5, 1766.	Died December 3, 1775.
77 Theodocia,	born March	23, 1768.	

FIFTH GENERATION.

65.

NATHANIEL SPENCER, of New-Hartford, Conn., was married to Lois Steele.

Mr. Nathaniel Spencer died ———.

Children.

78 Amelia,	born		Married Arnold Humphrey.
79 Louis,	born		Married Olive Case.
80 Nathaniel,	born August	1, 1776.	
81 Lydia,	born		Married Reuben Loomis.
82 Elizur,	born		
83 Josiah,	born February	25, 1781.	
84 Enon,	born		
85 Amanda,	born		
86 Milton,	born		

27

SIXTH GENERATION.

83.

JOSIAH SPENCER, first of New-Hartford, Conn., now of Springfield, Ohio, was married to Marian Marsh, daughter of Gen. Isaac Marsh, of New Hartford, January 3, 1803.

Mrs. Marian Marsh died June 4, 1841, aged about 57.

Mr. Josiah Marsh (at this date, July 18, 1854) lives at Springfield, Ohio.

Children.

87 Wolcott Marsh,	born February 16, 1804.	Was married to Cornelia Jones, daughter of Deacon Josiah Jones, of Stockbridge, Mass., and sister of the late Electa Fidelia Jones, deceased, of Stockbridge. They have seven children, and reside in Springfield, Ohio.
88 Richard Smith,	born January 23, 1806.	
89 Josiah Franklin,	born May 6, 1808.	
90 Isaac Whiting,	born January 26, 1813.	
91 Charles,	born October 31, 1816.	
92 Mariana,	born September 7, 1822.	

DESCENDANTS IN THE LINE OF SARAH SPENCER, DAUGHTER OF THOMAS SPENCER, THE SETTLER.

V.

SARAH SPENCER was married to Thomas Huxley, of Suffield, Conn.

Mrs. Sarah Huxley died October 24, 1712.

Mr. Thomas Huxley died July 21, 1721.

REV. SAMUEL STONE.

FIRST GENERATION.

REV. SAMUEL STONE, one of the first settlers of Hartford, Conn., and second Pastor of the First Church in that town, appears to have been twice married. 1. To ———— ————. 2. To Elizabeth Allen.* His wife survived him and was married to George Gardiner of Salem, Mass., merchant. [Mr. Gardiner appears to have been of Hartford in 1673.]

Mr. Samuel Stone, the Reverend Teacher of the Church of Christ at Hartford, died July 20, 1663.†

---

* On Boston 1st Church Records, p. 25, date of July 1641. "Letters of commendation were granted to John Winthrop the younger, going to England, the like for our bro. Mr William Hibbins also going to England.

"Mrs Elizabeth Stone, lately called Mrs Eliza Allen, but now the wife of Mr Samuel Stone the teacher of the church of Hartford, in Conn., was granted letters of recommendation thither."

Turning back to 24 March, 1638-9, I find the admissions were Mr^s Elizabeth Allen, Mr^. Penelope Pelham and Elizabeth Story. Whether Elizabeth Allen were maiden or widow is not known to me, but my opinion is that not being called wife of any or widow, she was a young woman, for she lived to 1681. [Judge Savage.]

† The last Will and Testement of the Reverend Mr Sam^ll Stone, late teacher of the church of X^t at Hartford, who deceased July 20th, 1663.

Inasmuch as all men on earth are mortall, and the time of dying, wth the mañer thereof is only foreknowne and predetermined by the Majestie on high, and that it is a duty incumbent on all so farr forth to have their house set in order, as considerately to determine and dispose of all there outward estate, consisting in Heredetaments, Lands, Chattells, Goods of what kind soever, wth all and either there appurtenances, to severall persons, that Righteousness and peace wth love might be mayntained for the future, and whereas at this present: That I Samuel Stone, of Hartford, vpon Coñecticut; am by a gracious visitation, and warneing from the Lord invited and called to hasten this present duty and seruice for ends premised, Being through the gentle and tender dealeing of the Lord in full and perfect memorie, make and appoint this as my last Will and Testament as followes,

Imp: It is my will that Mrs Elizabeth Stone my loving wife shall be my true and sole executrix of this my last Will and Testament. and that w^hout any intanglem^t or snare : the legacies given to herself being firstly possessed, all and every of them as they follow, and the after legacies to be made good out of ye remayneing estate if sufficient, otherwise a distribution according to that proportion, yet if there happen any overpluss to be wholly and solely at the dispose of my sayd wife. Allso I give unto my sayd wife (dureing the terme of her life) half my houseing and lands w^thin the liberties of Hartford and to have the free dispose of the value of the sayd halfe of my lands at the time of her death, by legacy or otherwise. Allso farther it is my will and I doe freely give unto my wife all the houshold stuff that I had wth her when I marryd her. to be at her full and free dispose as shee shall see cause, other gifts which are more casuall appeare in the legacies following,

Itt: Also as my last will and Testament and in token of my fatherly loue and care, I doe freely giue and bequeath unto my son Samuel Stone at the time of my decease the other halfe of my houseing and lands w^thin the liberties of Hartford afoarsayd, and the other halfe of the houseing at the time of the death of my sayd wife, freely w^thout any valuable consideration to be in any wise required, as allso the other halfe of ye Land, but upon a valuable consideration as before premised in the Legacy given to my deare and louing wife. Allso farther I doe freely giue unto my sayd sonne all my Bookes excepting such as are otherwise disposed of in this my sayd last Will and Testament; But, provided my sonne Samuell departe this life before he is marryed, that then the whole of this my present legacy remayneing shall returne to and be wholly at ye disspose of my sayd louing wife.

Mrs. Elizabeth Stone, alias Gardiner, died at Hartford, in 1681.

SECOND GENERATION.

Children of Record.

I. Joseph,   bap. October   18, 1670.
II. Lydia,   bap. Feb.   22, 1647–8.   Probably died young.
III. Son,   bap. April   29, 1649.
IV. Abigail, bap. September   9, 1650.

Named in his will.

V. Samuel, born
VI. Eliza-
    beth, born   Married, 1. Samuel Sedgwick, and
                          then, John Roberts, and removed to
                          New Jersey.
VII. Rebecca, born   Married a Nash, of New Haven.
VIII. Mary,   born   Married Joseph Fitch.
IX. Sarah,   born   Married Thomas Butler, of Hartford.

Itt: Allso unto my daughter Elizabeth, I doe giue and order to be payd the full suñe of one hundred pounds in household goods chattells and other countrey pay, what my louing wife can best part w⟨th⟩all, or in two or three acres of Land at price currant before the sayd Land be diuided betwixt my louing wife and sonne as afoarsayd, and this sayd legacy to be performed and made good w⟨th⟩in two years after the marriage of my sayd daughter Elizabeth, provided that if my sayd daughter shall match or dispose of herself in marriage either w⟨th⟩out or crosse to the minde of her dear mother my louing wife afoarsayd, and the mind and consent of my louing ouerseers hereinafter mentioned, then this my last will concerning her to stand voyd, and she gladly to accept of such a summe and quantity of portion as her sayd mother shall freely dispose to her or : And in case my sayd Daughter shall dye and depart this world before shee receiue her sayd portion, the whole thereof shall fully returne and belong vnto my sayd wife, at her dispose.

Itt: Allso (as a token of my fatherly loue and respect) I doe giue unto my three daughters Rebeccah, Mary and Sarah, forty shillings, each of them to be payd them by my dear wife in houshold stuffe, as it shall be prized in Inventory. And farther whereas the Honoured Court of this Colony were pleased to giue or grante a farme unto me, acknowledging there fauoure therein and requesting them to assigne the same unto my sonn and deare wife in some conuenient place, where they may receiue benefitt by it, to whom I do freely give the same indifferently both for the present benefitt and future disspose :

And farther itt is my desire that such of my manuscripts as shall be judged fitt for to be printed, my Reverend Friend, M⟨r⟩ John Higginson pastor of the church of X⟨t⟩ at Salem may haue the peruseall of them, and fit them for the press, especially my catechisme.

And that my louing wife may have some direct refuge for aduise and helpfullness in all cases of difficulty in and about all or any of the premises my great desire is that my Bretheren and friends M⟨r⟩ Mathew Allyn, Broth. W⟨m⟩ Wadsworth M⟨r⟩ John Allyn and my sonn Joseph Fitch would affoarde their best assistance, whome of this my last will and testament I doe constitute as my most desired overseers, nothing doubting of their readiness herein, and unto whome w⟨th⟩ my loveing wife I doe leave the disposal of. my sonne Samuel and daughter Elizabeth to be aduised and counselled in the feare of the Lord. Subscribed by me
                                               SAMUEL STONE.

In the presence and witnesse of
    Bray Rosseter.

An Inventory of the goods and chattells of M⟨r⟩ Sam⟨ll⟩ Stone the late Reverend teacher of the Church of Christ at Hartford, who departed this life July the 20⟨th⟩ 1663.

	ll	s	dd
Imprimis. In his purss and apparell	18	13	00
In the Hall. In a table joynt stooles and chairs	01	04	00
In a Trammell Andirons Tongs and Bellowes	01	05	06
In a cubboard	00	09	00
In a feather bed, Pillowes Bowlsters, rug, Blanckets, curtains, straw bed	09	15	00
In one flock bed, Boulster, rug, Blanket, a great bedstead a Trucle b.	03	10	00
In y⟨e⟩ Parlor. In a table forme, carpett, joynt stooles, chayres	03	16	00
In a chest of drawers, a green cupboard, cloth, Glass case	02	18	00
In a payer of Scales, weights, hower glass, andirons	00	13	00
In two glass cases, Hamer, gimlet, cushion	00	12	06
In y⟨e⟩ Closet. In plate in seuerall peices	06	16	00
In a flagon, pinte pot, spoones, cutting knife	00	17	00
In a lanthoren, Line, Trenchers, six saucers	00	15	00
In a halfe Bushell, glass case	00	05	06
In Bees wax and Honey and earthen ware	01	04	00
In a Baskett, wooden ware, Butter, candles, china ware	01	16	00

DESCENDANTS IN THE LINE OF SAMUEL STONE, SON OF THE REV. SAMUEL STONE.

THIRD GENERATION.

V.

SAMUEL STONE, of Hartford, Conn., never was married. He was educated for the ministry, and preached some time at Simsbury, Conn., and afterwards at Wethersfield, Conn.

Rev. Samuel Stone died in Hartford, October, 1693. The manner of his death is narrated in the following words:

October 8, 1693, at 9 o'clock in the evening, Mr. Stone came from Henry Howard's house, and falling down the bank of the Riverlett, some small distance eastward beyound the rayles of the bridge, that crosses the sayd riverlett on the south side of the sd River, received severall wounds upon his head which was the occasion of his death.

In the kitchen. In Pewter 40.ᵇ and pewter Bason, candlesticks	04	11	00
In three Brasse candlesticks, three chamber potts,	01	01	00
In five porrengers, small Brasse candlesticks,	00	07	00
In tin ware, earthen ware, three brass skilletts,	01	03	06
In Iron Potts, Pot Hooks, In wooden ware,	02	00	00
In pailes, siues, Tubbs, meal Trough, Baskett	01	03	00
In a Table, Jack Spitts, Gridiron, frying pan	01	14	00
In a Morter pestle, Trammells a piece of Jron, Tonges	00	17	00
In a Brass Copper, Kettles, cheespresse, Bake pan	06	03	00
In a churne, cupboard, a Barrell of Beif Tallow	03	01	00
In two Tubbs	00	05	00
In the Celler. In Cheese, Cyder, Aples, Table, Wooden ware	04	19	00
In the Parloʳ Chamber. In a liuery Cub-board, Andiorns, Bedsted. 2 chests	03	05	00
In cushions, curtaines & valions, Boulsters and Pillowes, Brushes, blancketts	07	18	00
In Goods, Broadcloth searge	07	14	00
In earthen ware, Two sadles, Napkins, Table Cloath	03	04	00
In Napkins, sheets, pillow Beers, Cupboard Cloath	13	10	00
In Napkins, Table Cloath, pillow beers, Towels, sheets & glasses, a wheel, & reale a press, Napkins	09	19	00
In the Kitchen Chamber. In a bedsteed, pillowes, rugg, forme	01	00	00
In yᵉ Hall Chamber. In a Table, bedsteed, cutlash	01	00	00
In a Bed, boulster pillow curtaines & valliance	04	05	00
In a Rugg, Blanketts, sheets	05	14	00
	139	03	00
In the study. In Tables, chayres, chest	001	01	00
In Andiorns, Tonges, firepan	000	10	00
In Bookes &c	127	00	00
In the Garrett In Cask, Bedsteedes, Indian Corne	002	12	00
In a Tronkle Bedsted & Bed	003	00	00
In pease & wheat & caske	001	18	00
In Mault	001	07	00
In Woole	001	00	00
In Cattle	029	10	00
In sheep & swine	010	00	00
In House & Home lott	100	00	00
In Meadow 20 Acres	129	00	00
In fower seuerall wood lotts	010	00	00
In two hiues of Bees	001	00	00
More Hay	006	00	00
Suṁe totall is	£563	01	00

apprized Nouember 1663

p nos JOHN ALLYN
WILL: WADSWORTH.

DESCENDANTS IN THE LINE OF ELIZABETH STONE, DAUGHTER OF REV. SAMUEL STONE.

THIRD GENERATION.

VI.

ELIZABETH STONE was twice married. 1. To William Sedgwick, of Hartford, Conn., about 1669. Upon her own application to the Court of Assistants, she was divorced from him in 1674. 2. To John Roberts, of Hartford, afterwards of New Jersey.

Child,—by her first husband,—one only.

Samuel,   born   1670.

Children,—by her second husband,—one or more; have not their names.

SAMUEL STORRS.

SAMUEL STORRS, the emigrant, was son of Samuel Storrs, and came from Sutton, Nottingham County, England; he was twice married, 1, at Barnstable, Mass., December 6, 1666, to Mary Huckins, daughter of Thomas Huckins; she was born March 29, 1646, and died September 24, 1683; 2, to Esther Egard, December 14, 1685.

Mr. Samuel Storrs died at Mansfield, Conn., April 30, 1719.

His widow, Mrs. Esther Storrs, died April 13, 1730, in the 89th year of her age.

FIRST GENERATION.

Children by his first wife.

I. Mary,	born December	31, 1667.
II. Sarah,	born June	26, 1670.
III. Hannah,	born March	28, 1672.
IV. Elizabeth,	born May	31, 1675.
V. Samuel,	born May	17, 1677.
VI. Lydia,	born June,	1679.

Children by his second wife.

VII. Thomas,	born October	27, 1686.
VIII. Esther,	born October,	1688.
IX. Cordial,	born October	14, 1692.

DESCENDANTS IN THE LINE OF SAMUEL STORRS, SON OF SAMUEL STORRS, THE EMIGRANT.

SECOND GENERATION.

V.

SAMUEL STORRS, of Mansfield, was married to Martha————.
He died August 9, 1727.

Children

10 Samuel,	born August	22, 1701.
11 John,	born October	7, 1702.
12 Martha,	born February,	1703-4.
13 Huckins,	born December	10, 1705.
14 Elizabeth,	born August,	1708.
15 Mary,	born May,	1710.
16 Joseph,	born March	8, 1711-12.

THIRD GENERATION.

10.

SAMUEL STORRS, of Mansfield, was married to Mary Warner, daughter of Andrew Warner, May 5, 1726.

Children.

17 Deborah,	born March	13, 1726–7.	Died April 3, 1727.
18 Martha,	born April	28, 1728.	
19 Samuel,	born March	6, 1729–30.	
20 Deborah,	born April	20, 1733.	
21 Andrew,	born December	20, 1735.	
22 Richard,	born October	1, 1746.	

11.

JOHN STORRS, of Mansfield, was married to Esther Gurley, daughter of Samuel Gurley, of Mansfield, January 2, 1735. She died March 15, 1746, in her 33d year. After her death he again married.

John Storrs died October 6, 1753, aged 51.

Children of John Storrs.

23 John,	born	1735.	
24 Son,	born August	2, 1738.	Died August 17, 1738.
25 Lydia,	born August	18, 1742.	
26 Nathaniel,	born	1751.	

13.

HUCKINS STORRS, of Mansfield, married Eunice Porter, daughter of Deacon Experience Porter, of Mansfield, November 12, 1731.

Children.

27 Huckins,	born November	6, 1732.	
28 Experience,	born September,	18, 1734.	
29 Eunice,	born August	16, 1736.	Died March 21, 1738.
30 Eleazur,	born November	24, 1738.	
31 Aaron,	born May	5, 1741.	
32 Eunice,	born May	2, 1743.	
33 Joseph,	born December	26, 1745.	
34 Abigail,	born April	21, 1748.	
35 Mary,	born May	7, 1750.	
36 Benjamin,	born May	21, 1752.	
37 John,	born September	20, 1755.	
38 Samuel,	born July	28, 1758.	

16.

JOSEPH STORRS, of Mansfield, was twice married. 1. To Hannah Porter, May, 1735. She died August 28, 1741. 2. To Experience Gurley, daughter of Samuel Gurley, of Coventry, Conn., 1743.

Mrs. Experience Storrs died June 9, 1767, in her 43d year.

Joseph Storrs died October 5, 1783, in his 72d year. They had nine children, among whom were

Sons of Joseph Storrs.

39 Joseph,   born
40 Cordial,   born
41 William,   born
42 Augustus,   born
43 Royal,   born

FOURTH GENERATION.

23.

REV. JOHN STORRS* was twice married.   1. To Eunice Howe.
2. To ———.

Sons of John Storrs.

44 Richard Sal-
    ter,   born   1763.
45 John,   born
46 Joshua,   born
47 Luther,   born

FIFTH GENERATION.

44.

RICHARD SALTER STORRS, of ———, was married to ———
Sons of Richard Salter Storrs.

48 Richard Sal-
    ter,   born
49 David,   born
50 Jonathan,   born
51 Charles,   born
52 Eleazur,   born

DESCENDANTS IN THE LINE OF THOMAS STORRS, SON OF SAMUEL STORRS, THE SETTLER.

SECOND GENERATION.

VII.

THOMAS STORRS, of Mansfield, was married to Mehitabel ———, March 14, 1708.

Thomas Storrs, Esq., died April, 1755, in the 69th year of his age.

Mehitabel Storrs died March 10, 1776.

---

* Rev. John Storrs, was ordained August 15, 1763, sixth pastor of the Presbyterian church at Southold, L. I. He left the Island near the commencement of the Revolutionary War, and was absent from his charge from August, 1776, to June, 1782. He was dismissed April 13, 1787. [Rev. Mr. Prime's History of Long island.] "After his dismission, Rev. Mr. Storrs came back to Mansfield, and preached for a time to a congregation in North Windham, as a supply." [Rev. A. S. Atwood, of South Mansfield.] Rev. John Storrs was twice married. 1. To Eunice Howe, widow of Dr. Howe, of Mansfield and daughter of Col. Shubael Conant, of Mansfield, by whom he had a son Richard Salter Storrs, who was settled in the ministry at Long Meadow, Mass. His son, bearing the same name, is Pastor of the church in Braintree, Mass., and his son bearing the same name, is settled over a church in Brooklyn, N. Y. [Zalmon Storrs, Esq., of Mansfield.]

Children of Thomas Storrs.

53 Mehitabel, born March 30, 1709.
54 Rebecca, born August 29, 1710.
55 Zeruiah, born August 27, 1712. Married Seth Paddock, October 10, 1735.
56 Cornelius, born December 30, 1714. Died May 9, 1760.
57 Thomas, born January 16, 1716-17.
58 Prince, born March 12, 1718-19.
59 Josiah, born March 25, 1721.
60 Judah, born September 26, 1723, the fifth day of the week, in the night at seven o'clock.
61 Lemuel, born March 13, 1725-6, on the Lord's day morning, about sunrise.
62 Amariah, born June 11, 1728, about 11 o'clock at night a Tuesday.
63 Anna, born January 18, 1731-2, on Tuesday morning the fourth hour.

THIRD GENERATION.

56.

CORNELIUS STORRS (son of Capt. Thomas) married Martha Porter, daughter of Deacon Experience Porter, of Mansfield, September 4, 1738.

Children.

64 Cornelius, born September 5, 1739.
65 Martha, born October 13, 1741.
66 Constant, born March 20, 1744. Died July 19, 1745.
67 Mehetibel, born June 12, 1745.
68 Nathaniel, born June 21, 1747.
69 Elijah, born March 25, 1750.
70 Constant, born February 11, 1752.
71 Hannah, born April 7, 1754.

57.

THOMAS STORRS, of Mansfield, was married to Eunice Paddock, daughter of Mr. Robert Paddock, of Mansfield, Eebruary 27, 1742-3.
She died May 2, 1795.
He died May 14, 1802.

Children.

72 Zeruiah, born January 6, 1743-4.
73 Martha, born August 21, 1745. Died July 10, 1750.
74 Dan, born February 7, 1748.
75 Eunice, born May 28, 1750.
76 Martha, born June 1, 1752.
77 Thomas, born August 25, 1754, Died at Princeton, N. J., September, 1776.
78 Seth, born January 24, 1756.
79 Zalmon, born August 30, 1758. Died in New Jersey, September 20, 1776.
80 Heman, born September 27, 1761.

58.

PRINCE STORRS married Deliverance Paddock, daughter of Seth Paddock, late of Mansfield, November 30, 1749.

Children.

81 Anne,   born July   28, 1751, on the Sabbath day in the afternoon.
82 Prince,   born September,   9, 1753.
83 Deliverance, born November,   19, 1755.
84 Royce,   born June   7, 1758.
85 Roxilana,   born July   8, 1760.
86 Chipman,   born March   21, 1763.

59.

JOSIAH STORRS married Mary Sargeant, daughter of Mr. Jonathan Sargeant, November 9, 1743. She died July 3, 1794. He died August 9, 1796.

Children.

87 Ebenezer, born August   26, 1744.
88 Mary,   born August   11, 1750. Died October 25, 1754.
89 Josiah,   born April   5, 1754. Died November 6, 1754.
90 Josiah,   born November   3, 1755.
91 Nathan,   born August   5, 1758. Died August 30, 1764.
92 Jonathan, born October   16, 1760.
93 Molly,   born June   18, 1764.

60.

JUDAH STORRS married Lucy Cleaveland, daughter of Henry Cleaveland, December 3, 1744. He died May 29, 1791.

Children.

94 Asael,   born May   3, 1745.
95 Lucy,   born May   3, 1747. Died September 11, 1751.
96 Olive,   born May   15, 1749.
97 Justus,   born April   26, 1751. Died October 25, 1754.
98 Henry,   born September 14, 1753.
99 Justus,   born October   11, 1755.
100 William
    Fitch,   born July   3, 1757.
101 Lucy,   born October   26, 1759.
102 Bezaleel, born August   6, 1761.
103 Frederick, born May   2, 1764.

61.

LEMUEL STORRS was married to Hannah Gillett, June 11, 1749. She died June 29, 1759, aged 29.

Children.

103½ Hannah, born June   10, 1750. Died September 30, 1750.
104 Aaron,   born August   2, 1751.
105 Lemuel,   born April   26, 1753.
105½ Hannah, born March   1755.
106 Roger,   bap. January   8, 1758.

FOURTH GENERATION.

74.

DAN STORRS, of Mansfield, was twice married. 1. To Ruth Conant, daughter of Col. Shubael Conant, of Mansfield, and of Eunice his wife, daughter of Rev. Eleazur Williams, minister of South Mansfield, January 5, 1774. She died April 18, 1792. 2. To Mary Southworth, daughter of Constant Southworth, Esq., October 28, 1793.

Children,—by his first wife.

107 Origin,	born October,	11, 1774.	
108 Zalmon,	born December	18, 1779.	Zalmon Storrs, Esq., Yale College, 1801. Married 1. April 26, 1804, Cynthia Stowell, daughter of Josiah Stowell, of Mansfield. She died April 17, 1833. 2. Clarissa Stowell. Residence South Mansfield, Conn.
109 Juba,	born March	9, 1782.	
110 Sophronia,	born March	2, 1784.	
111 Selima,	born June	29, 1786.	Married Ozias Seymour, father of Judge Origen Storrs Seymour.
112 Lucius,	born June	23, 1789.	
113 Egbert,	born February	7, 1792.	Died May 7, 1792.

Children,—by his second wife.

114 Egbert,	born January	18, 1795.	Died February 25, 1796.
115 Maria,	born July	9, 1800.	
116 Delia,	born July	1, 1806.	Married Rev. Thomas T. Waterman.

105.

LEMUEL STORRS, of Colchester, was married to Betsey, daughter of Col. Henry Champion, October 5, 1783. She was born September 11, 1762.

Lemuel Storrs, Esq., died November 29, 1816.

Mrs. Betsey Storrs, alias Champion, died June 21, 1845.

Children of Lemuel Storrs.

117 Eliza,	born July	26, 1784.	Married Hon. Joseph Trumbull, late Governor of Connecticut, December 1, 1824. One child Eliza Storrs, born October 10, 1826', married Lucius F. Robinson, Esq., of Hartford, Conn., Attorney at Law.
118 Henry Randolph,	born September	3, 1787.	Died August 30, 1838. Children, Henry Samuel, born July 1, 1811, died 1852. Fortune Kingsley, born 1813, died December 12, 1853. Eliza, born 1814, died 1837. William Champion, born 1816. Peyton Randolph, born 1818, died June 13, 1855.
119 Lemuel Gustavus,	born February	22, 1792.	One son, Lemuel Gustavus, born February, 6, 1813, died March 31, 1830.
120 William Lucius,	born March	25, 1795.	Judge of the Supreme Court of Errors. Residence Hartford, Conn.

DESCENDANTS IN THE LINE OF CORDIAL STORRS, SON OF SAMUEL STORRS, THE SETTLER.

SECOND GENERATION.

IX.

CORDIAL STORRS, of Mansfield, was twice married. 1. To Hannah, daughter of Thomas Wood, of Rowley, Mass., deceased September 15, 1724. She died March 18, 1764. 2. To Mrs. Catharine Bicknell, widow of Capt. Zechr. Bicknell, of Ashford, October 10. 1765.

Children.

121 Jabez,	born July	26, 1725.	Died November 10, 1826.
122 Cordial,	born January	3, 1728.	
123 Hannah,	born April	15, 1732.	
124 Mehetibel,	born April	15, 1737.	

SAMUEL TERRY.

SAMUEL TERRY, of Springfield, Mass., (where he appears first, about 1654,) was twice married. 1. To Ann Lobdell, daughter of ———— Lobdell, of ————, 1660. She died ————. 2. To Sarah Scott, 1690. Mr. Terry removed to Enfield about 1700, probably after that year.

Mrs. Sarah Terry died ————.
Mr. Samuel Terry died in 1731.

FIRST GENERATION.
Children of Samuel Terry and Ann his wife.

I. Samuel,	born	1661.	
II. Ephraim,	born	1663.	Died in childhood.
III. Thomas,	born	1665.	
IV. Mary,	born	1667.	
V. Rebecca,	born	1669.	Died in infancy.
VI. Ephraim,	born	1672.	
VII. Rebecca,	born	1673.	
VIII. Elizabeth,	born	1675.	Died young.
IX. Anna,	born		

Children of Samuel Terry and Sarah his wife,—none.

SECOND GENERATION.

I.

SAMUEL TERRY, of Enfield, Conn., was twice married. 1. To Hannah Morgan, daughter of Miles Morgan, of Springfield, 1682, being the first marriage in the settlement. She was born 1656, and died January 7, 1698. 2. To Martha Credan, daughter of ———— Credan, of ————.

Mr. Samuel Terry died in 1730.
Mrs. Martha Terry died May 29, 1743.

Children,—by his first wife.

10 Samuel,	born	1690.	Went to the State of New-York.
11 Ebenezer,	born	1696.	Died 1780. Had 3 children—all sons. Ebenezer, born 1722, died 1817, aged 94. Selah, born 1732, died 1803. Christopher Healms, born 1736, died 1770. Each of the three sons left children.
12 Hannah,	born		Married William Bement, 1706. Four sons.
13 Rebecca,	born		Married John Pasco, 1713.

14 Benjamin,   born October   13, 1698. Married Hannah Pease, daughter of
                                           James Pease, of Enfield, 1721. Had
                                           6 sons and three daughters.

Children,—by his second wife.

15 Ephraim,   born October   24, 1701.
16 Jacob,   born February   20, 1704. Married Mary Pease, daughter of
                                           James Pease, of Enfield, 1730. Had
                                           5 sons and 2 daughters. He died 1779.
17 Martha,   born February   18, 1707. Died in March, 1706.
18 Jonathan,   born November   17, 1707. Married Sarah Pease, daughter of James
                                           Pease, of Enfield, 1738. Had 2 sons
                                           and 2 daughters. He died 1793.
19 Isaac,   born   1713. Died 1783. Married and left children.

THIRD GENERATION.

15.

EPHRAIM TERRY, of Enfield, Conn., was married to Ann Collins, daughter of Rev. Nathaniel Collins, minister of Enfield, and Alice his wife, daughter of Rev. William Adams, minister of Dedham, Mass., September 13, 1723. She was born December 2, 1702.

She died ———.

Ephraim Terry, Esq., died 1783, aged —.

Children.

20 Samuel,   born   1725. Settled in Enfield. Died 1798, leaving
                                        a family.
21 Ephraim,   born   1728. Settled in Enfield. Died in 1807, left
                                        a family.
22 Nathaniel,   born October 3, 1730. Settled in Enfield. Died in 1792, left
                                        a family; father of the late General
                                        Nathaniel Terry, of Hartford.
23 Elijah,   born   1736. Settled in Enfield. Died ——; left a
                                        family.
24 Eliphalet,   born   1742.

FOURTH GENERATION.

24.

ELIPHALET TERRY, of Enfield, Conn., married Mary Hall, December 3, 1765.

Eliphalet Terry died November 2, 1812, aged 70.

Mrs. Mary Terry, alias Hall, died January 10, 1833.

Children.

25 Esther,   born January   5, 1767. Married William Kibbe, June 17, 1792.
                                          Died March, 1850.
26 Simeon,   born October   17, 1768. Died September 19, 1781, unmarried.
27 Mary,   born November 27, 1770. Died December 26, 1854, unmarried.
28 Mabel,   born February 19, 1773. Married 1. William Barton, January
                                          15, 1797. 2. Rev. —— Johns.
29 Eliphalet,   born December 25, 1776. Married 1. Sally Watson, June 18, 1811.
                                          2. Lydia Coit, June 5, 1817. Died
                                          July 8, 1849.
30 Lucy,   born March   12, 1779. Died September 11, 1797, unmarried.
31 Seth,   born January   12, 1781. Married 1. Ann Grew. 2. Hannah
                                          Shepard. Residence Hartford.
32 Abigail,   born January   17, 1783. Married Ephraim Potter, May 12, 1812.
33 Roderick,   born March   2, 1788. Married 1. Harriet, daughter of Rev.
                                          John Taylor. 2. Lucy, daughter of
                                          Dwight Ripley. Died February 9,
                                          1849.

STEPHEN TERRY,

ONE OF THE

FIRST SETTLERS OF WINDSOR, CONN.

STEPHEN TERRY, one of the first settlers of Windsor, Conn., afterwards of Hadley, Mass., was married in Dorchester, Mass., to ———, about 1635.

The wife of Stephen Terry was buried June 5, 1647. [Windsor Records.]

FIRST GENERATION.

Children of Stephen Terry and wife.

I. Mary, born December 31, 1635, in Dorchester.
II. John, born March 6, 1637, in Windsor.
III. Elizabeth, born January 4, 1641, in Windsor. Married Philip Russell, of Hadley, January 10, 1665. She and her son Stephen were slain by the Indians in September, 1677.
IV. Abigail, born September 21, 1646, in Windsor.

SECOND GENERATION.

2.

JOHN TERRY, of Simsbury, Conn., was married to Elizabeth Wadsworth, daughter of William Wadsworth, of Hartford, in the same State, November 27, 1662.

He died ———.

She died March 12, 1715.

Children.

5 Elizabeth, born December 16, 1664.
6 Stephen, born October 6, 1666.
7 Sarah, born November 16, 1668.
8 John, born March 22, 1670.
9 Rebecca, born January 7, 1672. Died in childhood.
10 Mary, born July 19, 1673.
11 Solomon, born March 29, 1675.
12 Rebecca, born February 27, 1677. Died in childhood.

MATTHIAS TREAT,

ONE OF THE

FIRST SETTLERS OF WETHERSFIELD, CONN.

FIRST GENERATION.

MATTHIAS TREAT, one of the first settlers of Wethersfield, Conn., was married to Mary Smith, daughter of Richard Smith, also one of the first settlers of Wethersfield, 1648. [After his death, she was married to Anthony Wright, of Wethersfield.]
Mr. Matthias Treat died in 1662.
Mrs. Mary Treat, alias Wright, died ———.

SECOND GENERATION.

The Children of the above named Matthias and Mary Treat.

I. Henry,	born	1649.	
II. Susanna,	born	1651.	
III. Richard,	born	1655.	
IV. Elizabeth,	born	1657.	
V. Abigail,	born	1659.	Married Capt. Stephen Hollister, of Wethersfield.
VI. Dorcas,	born	1661.	

DESCENDANTS IN THE LINE OF HENRY TREAT, SON OF MATTHIAS TREAT THE SETTLER.

THIRD GENERATION.

I.

HENRY TREAT, of Hartford, Conn., was married to Sarah Andrews, daughter of Edward Andrews of the same town, about 1673.
Mr. Henry Treat died in 1681.
His widow, Mrs. Sarah Treat, died ———.

Children.

7 Sarah,	born	about 1674.
8 Matthias,	born	about 1676.

FOURTH GENERATION.

8.

MATTHIAS TREAT, of Hartford, Conn., was married to Hannah

(supposed to be Hannah Warren,) daughter of ———, of ———, about 1700.

Mr. Matthias Treat died 1726. Inventory executed October 26, 1726.

Mrs. Hannah Treat died ———.

Children.

9 Matthias, born about 1705.
10 Henry, bap. May 4, 1707.

FIFTH GENERATION.

9.

MATTHIAS TREAT, of Hartford, married Dorothy Bidwell, daughter of Daniel Bidwell, of Hartford, (about 1730.)

He died ———.

She died in December, 1797, aged about 85.

Children.

11 Mary,	born	Married a Raymond.
12 Matthias,	born	Married Tryphena Risley, daughter of John Risley. She died April 5, 1822, aged 61. He died June 15, 1827, aged 76.
13 Theodore,	born	Married Mary Williams, daughter of Timothy Williams.
14 Esther,	born	Married a Bunce, and after his death a Hinsdale.
15 Roswell,	born	Married Anna Ensign, daughter of Moses Ensign.

10.

HENRY TREAT married Abigail Gilman, daughter of Richard Gilman, about 1731.

He died October 12, 1794, aged about 87.

Mrs. Abigail Treat died ———.

Children.

16 Ruth,	born		
17 Henry,	born		Married Eunice ———.
18 Stephen,	bap.	1736.	Married Jane ———. She died July 30, 1814, aged 79. He died November 21, 1817, aged 83.
19 Richard,	bap.	1749.	
20 Elizabeth,	bap.	1751.	
21 Sybil,	born	1754.	Married John [Joshua?] Buckland.
22 Anna,	born		Married.
23 George,	born	1756.	Married.
24 John,	born August	12, 1745.	(Father of Selah T.; went to Hartland.)

SIXTH GENERATION.

24.

JOHN TREAT was twice married. 1. To Rachel Burr, August 10, 1775. She was born July 15, 1756, and died July 28, 1787. 2. To Mrs. Abigail Hutchins Andrus, daughter of Benjamin

29

Hutchins, of· East-Hartford, December 6, 1787. She was born
April 10, 1757.

Mr. John Treat died August 26, 1832, aged 87 years, 14 days.

Mrs. Abigail Treat died May 9, 1844.

Children—by his first wife.

25 Rachel,	born December	13, 1776.	Died May 5, 1778.
26 Selah,	born July	15, 1778.	
27 John,	born March	11, 1780.	Died February 17, 1782.
28 John,	born June	4, 1782.	Died February 18, 1786.
29 Rachel,	born November	23, 1784.	Died November 5, 1795.
30 Sinai,	born December	14, 1786.	Died June 28, 1832.

Children,—by his second wife.

31 Clara,	born September	6, 1788.
32 Chester,	born July	16, 1790.
33 Howell,	born June	28, 1793.
34 Lester		
Hutchins,	born June	2, 1798.

SEVENTH GENERATION.

26.

SELAH TREAT was married to Anna Williams, April 21, 1803.
She was born May 17, 1776, and died March 18, 1854.

Children.

35 Selah Burr,	born February	19, 1804.
36 Clarissa		
Ann,	born July	22, 1807.

RICHARD TREAT.

RICHARD TREAT,* one of the first settlers of Wethersfield, Conn., was married in England to Joan ———.
Hon. Richard Treat died in 1669.†
His widow, Mrs. Joan Treat, died ———.

---

*"Anthony Elcock. This may Certify whom it may concern, that Anthony Elcock, master of the vessel called 'The Beginning,' being bound for New-Haven, but miscarrying in the matter, doth protest against the seas as being the cause. RICHARD TREATE."
"WETHERSFIELD, May 30, 1664."

†"The last will and testament of Richard Treat, senior late of Wethersfield, dec. is as followeth:

"Imprimis, I being weak and infirm of body, but of sound understanding, and of competent memory, do resign my soul to the Lord, hoping to be justified and saved by the merits of Christ, and my body to be buried.

"Item. I give and bequeath to my loving wife Alis Treat, after my decease, all the lands of what kind soever, I stand possessed of within the bounds of Wethersfield, and five acres of land lying in the dry swamp which I have improved and prepared for use lying next my son James, his land.

"Item, one piece of meadow lying in the great meadow, commonly called by the name of Send Home.

"Item, the one half or eight acres next home of that piece of meadow commonly called Fillbarn.

"Item, the home lot by the plaine lane site.

"Item, the dwelling house that I formerly lived in with convenient yard room, and that end of the barn on the side the threshing floor, next the dwelling house, with the one half of that lot belonging to the said dwelling house, lying next his son Richard's house and lot, except my wife and son James shall agree otherwise.

"Item, all my pasture land fenced in beyond my daughter Hollister's lott.

"Item, the use of two of my best cows which she shall choose, which if they shall continue and stand longer than my loving wife liveth, they shall be my eldest son Richard Treats.

"Item, I give to my loving wife the standing bed, bedding, bedsted, with all the furniture thereto belonging, with the use of so much of the household goods during her life time as she shall judge needful for her comfort, of what sort soever.

"I give and bequeath to *my eldest son Richard Treat*, the full possession and confirmation of the farm of Nayog, with all the respective privileges thereto belonging, with three of my youngest heifers.

"Item, I give to my *second son, Robert Treat*, [born 1621,] ten pounds. [He settled in Milford. He married Jane Tapp, of Milford. She died April 8, 1703. He married again. Gov. Treat died July 12, 1710, in his 89th year, born 1621.]

"Item, I give *to my youngest son, James Treat*, [born 1634,] besides the lands already made over to him, my mill and grinding stone, fann, timber, chains, steelyards, and my little bible ———. [James Treat died February 12, 1708–9. Caption to his Inventory.]

"Item, I give to my *son-in-law, Matthew Campfield*, 20£ for that which is remaining of his portion. [He settled in Norwalk, and afterwards removed to Newark, N. J.]

"Item, I give to *my daughter Hollister*, 40 shillings.

"Item, to *my daughter Johnson*, 10 shillings.

"Item, My debts being paid, I give to my *loving sons John Demon [Deming] and Robert Webster*, equally, all the rest of my goods and chattels whatsoever, except Mr. Perkins book, which I give to my son John Demon, and my great bible to my *daughter Honour Demon*. And that money in my cousin Samuel Welles, his hand, unto *my cousin David Deming, son of John Demon senior*, and my desire is that

"My son-in-law, *John Demon, Robert Webster and Richard Treat* would be my overseers for their mutuall helpfullness to my louing wife and endeavoure to see the accomplishment this my last will and testament, and for the ratifycation hereof I have this thirteenth day of February, 1668, set to my hand and seale.

RICHARD TREAT, } L. S."
Senior, }

SECOND GENERATION.

Children of Richard Treat and Joan Treat, his wife.

I. Richard, born
II. Robert, born   1622.
III. James, born   1634.
IV. Sarah, born
V. Joanna, born
VI. Daugh-
    ter, born   Married ——— Johnson.
VII. Susan-
    nah, born
VIII. Honour, born

DESCENDANTS IN THE LINE OF RICHARD TREAT, SON OF RICHARD TREAT, THE SETTLER.

THIRD GENERATION.

I.

RICHARD TREAT, of Wethersfield, Conn., was married to Sarah Coleman, daughter of Thomas Coleman, one of the first settlers of Wethersfield,—afterwards of Hatfield, Mass., about 1661.

Richard Treat, Esq., died ———.

His widow, Mrs. Sarah Treat, died August 23, 1734, at Wethersfield Rocky Hill, at the house of her son-in-law, Capt. Ephraim Goodrich.

Children.

9 Richard, born February 14, 1662.
10 Sarah, born June 8, 1664.
11 Mary, born October 8, 1666.
12 Thomas, born December 12, 1668.

FOURTH GENERATION.

10.

SARAH TREAT was married to Ephraim Goodrich, of Wethersfield, Conn., May 20, 1684. She was his first wife. [His second wife, to whom he was married December 25, 1712, and by whom he had two children, was Jerusha Welles, widow of Capt. Thomas Welles, deceased, of Wethersfield, and daughter of Capt. James Treat, of the same town.]

Mrs. Sarah Goodrich died January 26, 1712, in her 48th year.

Capt. Ephraim Goodrich died February 27, 1739, aged 76.

Children.

13 Richard, born February 27, 1685.
14 Sarah, born 1698.
15 Ephraim, born
16 William, born 1701.
17 David, born 1705.
18 Thomas, born
19 Gideon, born

11.

MARY TREAT was married to Thomas Chester, of Wethersfield, Conn., December 10, 1684.

Thomas Chester died December 4, 1712, in his 53d year.
His widow, Mrs. Mary Chester, died January 1, 1748, aged 81.

Children.

20 Eunice,	born November 22, 1685.	
21 Samuel,	born September 29, 1696.	Died March 17, 1710.
22 John,	born December 17, 1699.	Died December 14, 1700.
23 Mary,	born January 6, 1706.	

12.

THOMAS TREAT, of Glastenbury, Conn., was married to Dorothy Bulckley, daughter of Rev. Gershom Bulckley, of Glastenbury, formerly of Wethersfield, Conn., July 5, 1693.
Thomas Treat, Esq., died February 17, 1713, aged 44.
His widow, Mrs. Dorothy Treat, died in 1757.

Children.

24 Richard,	born May	14, 1694.	Supposed to have married Susanna Woodbridge, daughter of the Rev. Timothy Woodbridge, of Hartford, August 7, 1728.
25 Charles,	born February	28, 1696.	
26 Thomas,	born May	3, 1699.	
27 Isaac,	born August	15, 1701.	Died August 21, 1764, aged 63. Rebecca, his wife, died August 19, 1688, aged 83.
28 Dorathy,	} twins born August	25, 1704.	
29 Doretheus,			
30 Sarah,	born January	21, 1707.	
31 Mary,	born January	9, 1710.	Married Joseph Stephens, of Glastenbury, son of Rev. Timothy Stephens, of that town, January 1, 1733. She was his first wife. She died February 12, 1735. After her death, he was married to Jerusha Stow, daughter of Thomas Stow, of Middletown, Conn., October 14, 1736.

DESCENDANTS IN THE LINE OF ROBERT TREAT, SON OF RICHARD TREAT, THE SETTLER.

THIRD GENERATION.

II.

ROBERT TREAT, Esq., of Milford, Conn., was twice married. 1. To Jane Tapp, only daughter of Edmund Tapp, Esq., one of the first settlers of Milford. She died April 8, 1703. 2. To Elizabeth Bryan, widow of —— Bryan, of Milford, and daughter of ——, October 22, 1705.
Mrs. Elizabeth Treat, alias Bryan, died January 10, 1706, aged —.
Hon. Robert Treat died July 12, 1710, in his 89th year [Monument, Milford burying ground.]

DESCENDANTS IN THE LINE OF JAMES TREAT, SON OF RICHARD TREAT, THE SETTLER.

THIRD GENERATION.

III.

JAMES TREAT, of Wethersfield, Conn., was married to Rebecca Lattimer, daughter of John Lattimer, one of the first settlers of Wethersfield, January 26, 1665. She was born October 6, 1646. Lieut. James Treat died February 12, 1709, aged 74. His widow, Mrs. Rebecca Treat, died ———.

Children.

32 James,	born April	1, 1666.	
33 Jemima,	born March	15, 1668.	
34 Samuel,	born	1669.	Died March 5, 1732, aged 63. [Gravestone Wethersfield burying ground.]
35 Salmon,	born	1672, perhaps.	
36 Richard,	born	1675, perhaps.	
37 Jerusha,	born	1678, perhaps.	
38 Joseph,	born	1680.	
39 Rebecca,	born	1686.	Married Ebenezer Deming, Jr., of Wethersfield, December 27, 1704. She died December 26, 1753, in her 68th year.
40 Mabel,	born		

FOURTH GENERATION.

32.

JAMES TREAT, of Wethersfield, Conn., was twice married. 1. To Prudence Chester, daughter of John Chester of the same town, December 17, 1691. She died May 23, 1727, in her 61st year. 2. To Hannah Boardman, widow of Daniel Boardman, of Wethersfield, and daughter of Samuel Wright, of the same town.

James Treat, Esq., died February 18, 1742, in his 76th year.

Mrs. Hannah Treat, alias Boardman, died February 25, 1746.

Children,—by his first wife.

41 Abigail,	born December	6, 1692.	Married David Boardman, of Wethersfield, December 6, 1717.
42 Charles,	born January	29, 1695.	Died October 4, ———.
43 Prudence,	born April	13, 1697.	
44 Eunice,	born January	26, 1699.	Married David Buck, son of David Buck, all of Wethersfield, December 19, 1723.
45 James,	born September	22, 1701.	Married Mary Crane, daughter of Abraham Crane, of Wethersfield, August 11, 1731.
46 Oliver,	born May	31, 1705.	
47 Jerusha,	born March	14, 1707.	Married Wait Welles, of Wethersfield.

33.

JEMIMA TREAT was married to Stephen Chester, jun., of Wethersfield, Conn., December 17, 1691.

Mr. Stephen Chester, jun., died February 9, 1698, in his 38th year.

His widow, Mrs. Jemima Chester, died May 25, 1727, aged 59.

Children.

48 Dorathy,	born September	5, 1692.
49 Sarah,	born March	5, 1694.
50 Mercy,	born October	26, 1696.
51 Stephen John,	born February	14, 1698. (Posthumous.)

35.

Rev. Salmon Treat was married to Dorothy Noyes, daughter of Rev. James, Pastor of the Congregational Church at Stonington, Conn., April 28, 1698. [Rev. Mr. Treat, Harvard College, 1694, Yale, 1702, was ordained Pastor of the Congregational Church at Preston, November 16, 1698, and resigned his ministerial charge in March, 1744.]

He died in 1746.

She died ———.

Children.

52 Anna,	born August	26, 1699.
53 James,	born November	29, 1700.
54 Dorathy,	born February	9, 1702.
55 Jerusha,	born November	21, 1784.
56 Prudence,	born November	23, 1706.
57 Sarah,	born September	19, 1708.
58 Rebecca,	born June	29, 1710.

36.

Richard Treat, of Wethersfield, Conn., was married to Catharine Bulckley, daughter of the Rev. Gershom Bulckley, of Glastenbury, Conn., formerly of Wethersfield, November 23, 1704.

Mrs. Catharine Treat died ———.

Richard Treat, Esq., died May 7, 1713.

Child,—one only.

| 59 Catharine, | born August | 26, 1706. | Married Samuel Deming, of Wethersfield, June 16, 1726. |

37.

Jerusha Treat was twice married. 1. To Capt. Thomas Welles, of Wethersfield, Conn., May 17, 1705. He died December 7, 1711, in his 50th year. 2. To Capt. Ephraim Goodrich, of Wethersfield, December 25, 1712, being his second wife.

Capt. Ephraim Goodrich died February 27, 1739, aged 76.

Mrs. Jerusha Goodrich, alias Welles, died January 15, 1754, in the 76th year of her age.

Children,—by her first husband.

60 William,	born January	12, 1706.
61 Wait,	born January	4, 1708.
62 John,	born February	10, 1710.
63 Ichabod,	born April	26, 1712. (Posthumous.)

Children,—by her second husband.

64 Oliver,   born September 14, 1714.
65 Gurdon,   born December 29, 1717.

38.

JOSEPH TREAT, of Wethersfield, Conn., was married to Mary Robbins, daughter of Capt. Joshua Robbins, of Wethersfield, July 16, 1713.

Lieut. Joseph Treat died September 15, 1756, in his 76th year. His widow, Mrs. Mary Treat, died September 17, 1760, in her 68th year.

Children,—recorded to them on Wethersfield Records.

66 Mary,   born March   17, 1715.
67 Elisha,   born April   3, 1720.
68 John,   born August   23, 1733.

DESCENDANTS IN THE LINE OF SARAH TREAT, DAUGHTER OF RICHARD TREAT, THE SETTLER.

THIRD GENERATION.

IV.

SARAH TREAT was married to Matthew Campfield, first of New-Haven, Conn., then of Norwalk, in the same State, and afterwards of Newark, N. J., and one of the first settlers of that town, about 1644.

Hon. Matthew Campfield died in 1673.

His widow, Mrs. Sarah Campfield, died ———.

Children.

70 Samuel,   bap. October   19, 1645, at New-Haven.
71 Sarah,   born May   24, 1647, at New-Haven.
72 Ebenezer, born   1649, at New-Haven.
73 Matthew,   born May   9, 1650, at New-Haven.
74 Hannah,   born June   21, 1651, at New-Haven.
75 Rachel,   born July   29, 1652, at New-Haven. Supposed to have died before her father, as she is not mentioned in her father's will, which is dated May 19, 1673.

76 Jonathan, born
77 Mary,   born

DESCENDANTS IN THE LINE OF JOANNA TREAT, DAUGHTER OF RICHARD TREAT, THE SETTLER.

THIRD GENERATION.

V.

JOANNA TREAT was married to John Hollister, of Wethersfield, Conn., and one of the first settlers of that town.

Mr. John Hollister died in April, 1665, aged —.

His widow, Mrs. Joanna Hollister, died in October. 1694, aged —.

Children.

78 Mary,   born
79 John,   born
80 Thomas,   born
81 Joseph,   born
82 Lazarus,   born
83 Stephen,   born
84 Elizabeth, born
85 Sarah,   born

DESCENDANTS IN THE LINE OF SUSANNAH TREAT, DAUGHTER OF RICHARD TREAT, THE SETTLER.

THIRD GENERATION.

VII.

SUSANNAH TREAT was married about 1652, to Robert Webster, of Middletown, Conn., until about 1660, then and after, of Hartford, Conn. Mr. Webster was son of John Webster, one of the first settlers of Hartford, and Hadley, Mass.

Robert Webster, Esq., died in 1676.

His widow, Mrs. Susannah Webster, died in 1705.

Children.

86 John,	born November 10, 1653,	at Middletown.
87 Sarah,	born June 30, 1655,	at Middletown.
88 Jonathan,	born January 9, 1657,	at Middletown.
89 Susannah,	born October 26, 1658,	at Middletown.
90 Samuel,	born [no date,]	at Hartford, probably.
91 Robert,	born [no date,]	at Hartford, probably.
92 Joseph,	born [no date,]	at Hartford, probably.
93 William,	born [no date,]	at Hartford, probably.
94 Mary,	born [no date,]	at Hartford, probably.
95 Elizabeth,	born [no date,]	at Hartford, probably.

DESCENDANTS IN THE LINE OF HONOUR TREAT, DAUGHTER OF RICHARD TREAT, THE SETTLER.

THIRD GENERATION.

VIII.

HONOUR TREAT was married to John Deming, of Wethersfield, Conn., and one of the first settlers of that town, about 1637.

Mrs. Honour Deming died ———.

Hon. John Deming died in 1705.

Children.

96 John,   born September 9, 1638. Settled in Wethersfield. Married Mary Mygatt, daughter of Jacob Mygatt, of Hartford, Conn., September 20, 1657. He died January 23, 1712. She died ———. *Children,*—John, born September 9, 1658. Married Mary Graves, daughter of the Widow Graves, of Wethersfield, June 5, 1684. He died November 25, 1729. Joseph, born June 1, 1661. Jona-

than, born February 12, 1663. Mary, born July 1, 1666. Samuel, born August 25, 1668. Jacob, born August 26, 1670. Sarah, born January 17, 1672. Hezekiah, born [no date.]

97 Jonathan, born   1639. Settled in Wethersfield. Was twice married. 1. To Sarah ———, daughter of ———, November 21, 1660. She died June 2, 1668. 2. To Elizabeth Gilbert, daughter of Josiah Gilbert, of Wethersfield, 1673. " Mr. Jonathan Deming died on the 8th of January, 1699–1700, of a very sudden death, being aged about, as he computed, 61 years." [Wethersfield Records.] His widow, Mrs. Elizabeth Deming, died September 4, 1714. *Children,—by his first wife.* Jonathan, born November 27, 1661. Sarah, born August 12, 1663. Mary, born July 11, 1665. Married Joseph Smith, of Wethersfield, November 26, 1685. Comfort, born June 5, 1668. Married 1. Nathaniel Beckley, of Wethersfield, May 18, 1693. He died October 30, 1697. 2. To Thomas Morton, of Wethersfield, May 8, 1698. He died May 1, 1740. *Children,—by his second wife.* Elizabeth, born June 12, 1674. Married Richard Beckley, of Wethersfield, November 23, 1699. Eloisa, born February 16, 1676. Thomas, born November 27, 1679. Married Mary Williams, daughter of Thomas Williams, of Wethersfield, June 2, 1698. Charles, born June 10, 1681. Married Anna Wickham, daughter of Thomas Wickham, of Wethersfield, September 5, 1706. Benjamin, born July 20, 1684. Jacob, born December 20, 1689. Married Dinah ———. Settled in Farmington, Conn. She died October 3, 1751. *Children* recorded in Farmington,—Jacob, born December 13, 1713. Anna, born July 4, 1716. Lucia, born March 18, 1718. Moses, born Sept. 8, 1720. Mary, born October 24, 1692. Married Gershom Bulckley, of Middletown, 1719. Ann, born October 1, 1695. Married Nathaniel Wright, of Wethersfield, March 12, 1712. After his death, she was married to a Church.

98 Samuel, born   1646. Settled in Wethersfield. Married Sarah Kirby, daughter of John Kirby, of Middletown, Conn., March 29, 1694. " Mr. Samuel Deming died April 6, 1709, of his age about 63 years, or in his 63 year near out." [Wethersfield Records.] *Children,—John, born December 7, 1694. David, born December 29, 1696. Samuel, born June 12, 1699. Married Catharine Treat, daughter of Richard Treat, of Wethersfield, June 16,

99 David,   born [no date.]

100 Ebenezer, born [no date.]

101 Daughter, born
102 Daughter, born
103 Mary,   born [no date.]

104 Daughter, born
105 Sarah,   born [no date.]

1726. Honor, born December 16,
1701. Married Hezekiah Goodrich,
of Wethersfield, October 16, 1729.
William, born May 10, 1705. Married Prudence Churchill, daughter
of Josiah Churchill, of Wethersfield.
Settled in Wethersfield, but removed
to Cambridge, Mass., and was there
dwelling in 1697. Married Mary
———, daughter of ———, of ———,
July 16, 1678. *Children*,—David,
born July 20, 1681, at Wethersfield.
Samuel, born August 9 1683, at
Wethersfield. Honor, born May 9,
1685, at Wethersfield. Mehitabel,
born [no date.]
Settled in Wethersfield. Married
Sarah ———, daughter of ———,
of ———, July 16, 1677. He died
May 2, 1705. *Children*,—Ebenezer,
born May 5, 1678. Married Rebecca
Treat, daughter of James Treat, of
Wethersfield. She died December
26, 1753, in her 68th year. John,
born July 25, 1679. He died May 1,
1761, in his 82d year. His grave is
in Newington Society burying
ground. He was a deacon. Sarah,
born January 9, 1681. Married Joseph Talcott, of Wethersfield, April
1, 1701. Deacon Joseph Talcott
died November 3, 1732, aged —.
His widow, Mrs. Sarah Talcott, died
March 19, 1755, aged 74. Ephraim,
born [no date.] Josiah, born [no
date.] Prudence, born [no date.]
Married Thomas Wright, jun., of
Wethersfield, October 4, 1705.
Married a Morgan.
Married a Beckley.
Married John Hurlbut,* of Middle
town, Conn. He was son of Thomas
and Sarah Hurlbut, of Wethersfield,
and was born March 8, 1642. Sargeant John Hurlbut died August 30,
1690, aged 48. His wife survived
him. *Children*,—John, born December 8, 1671. Married Rebecca Warner, daughter of Lieut. Andrew
Warner, of Middletown. Thomas,
born October 20, 1674. Sarah, born
November 5, 1676. Mary, born November 17, 1678. Died in infancy.
Mary, born February 17, 1680.
Ebenezer, born January 17, 1682.
Margaret, born February, 1685. David, born August 11, 1688. Mehitabel, (posthumous,) born November
23, 1690.
Married a Wright.
Married Samuel Moody,† of Hartford,
Conn., until 1659, then and after

---

* Thomas Hurlbut, the father of John Hurlbut, was a soldier in the Pequot war.
† Mr. Samuel Moody is supposed to have had a first wife Hannah.

wards of Hadley, Mass. He was
son of John Moody, one of the first
settlers of Hartford. Mr. Samuel
Moody died September 22, 1689.
Children,—Sarah, born about 1659.
Married John Kellogg, of ———,
December 23, 1680, and died September 10, 1689, leaving four children. John, born July 24, 1661.
Settled in Hartford. Hannah, born
March 5, 1663. Died January 6,
1713, unmarried. Samuel, born November 28, 1670. Settled in Hadley.
Mary, born [no date.] Married 1.
Alexander Panton, or Panthern,
June 30, 1689, and after his death,
2. James Mun, of Springfield, Mass.,
in 1698. Ebenezer, born October
23, 1675. Lived in Hadley and
South-Hadley, Mass. Sarah, beloved wife of Samuel Moody, senior,
died September 29, 1717. [Hadley
Records.]

ANDREW WARD,

FIRST SETTLERS OF WETHERSFIELD, CONN.

FIRST GENERATION.

ANDREW WARD, first of Wethersfield, Conn., and one of the first settlers of that town; then of Stamford, Conn., and one of the first settlers of that town; then of Hempstead, L. I., and afterwards of Fairfield, Conn., was married to Hester ———.

Andrew Ward, Esq., died at Fairfield, in 1659.

His widow, Mrs. Hester Ward, died in the beginning of the year 1667.

SECOND GENERATION.

Children of Andrew Ward and Hester Ward, his wife.

I.	Edmund,	born	Married Mary ———.
II.	William,	born	
III.	Mary,	born	
IV.	Andrew,	born	
V.	Samuel,	born	
VI.	Abigail,	born	
VII.	Anna,	born	
VIII.	John,	born	Married ——— Nichols.
IX.	Sarah,	born	

DESCENDANTS IN THE LINE OF MARY WARD, DAUGHTER OF ANDREW WARD, THE SETTLER.

THIRD GENERATION.

III.

MARY WARD was married to Jehu Burr, of Fairfield, Conn., son of Jehu Burr, one of the first settlers of Springfield, Mass., and Fairfield. After her death he was married to ———.

Mrs. Mary Burr died ———.

Mr. Jehu Burr died ———.

Children.

10 Daniel,	born		Yale College 1738. Was father of President Aaron Burr.
11 Peter,	born	1686.	Harvard College 1690. Peter Burr died December 25, 1742, aged 56 years, 9 months.
12 Samuel,	born		
13 Esther,	born		

14 Elizabeth,   born
15 Sarah,   born
16 Joanna,   born
17 Abigail,   born

DESCENDANTS IN THE LINE OF ANDREW WARD, SON OF ANDREW WARD, THE SETTLER.

THIRD GENERATION.

IV.

ANDREW WARD, of Killingworth, Conn., was married to Tryal Meigs, daughter of John Meigs, of Guilford, in the same state, son of Vincent Meigs, of Guilford.

Andrew Ward, Esq., died about 1691.

His widow, Mrs. Tryal Ward, died ———.

Children.

18 Andrew,   born   1669.
19 John,   born March   16, 1671. Died childless.
20 Abigail,   born September 15, 1672. Married Samuel Norton, of Guilford, Conn., January 25, 1692–3.
21 Sarah,   born November 15, 1674.
22 Peter,   born October 14, 1676. Married Mary Joy, daughter of Jacob Joy, of Killingworth, Conn., March 30, 1693. 6 children.
23 William,   born October 18, 1678. Died in Wallingford, Conn., December 14, 1769; ancestor of Col. James Ward of Hartford, Conn.
24 Samuel,   born September 24, 1680. Died April 30, 1681.
25 Esther,   born May   2, 1684. Died June 17, 1684.
26 Mary,   born [no date.]
27 Anna,   born [no date.]

FOURTH GENERATION.

18.

ANDREW WARD, of Killingworth, Conn., was married to Deborah Joy, daughter of Jacob Joy, of Killingworth, and Elizabeth his wife, daughter of William Wellman, of the same town, November 19, 1691.

Mrs. Deborah Ward died ———.

Capt. Andrew Ward died at noon, August, 1756, aged 86.

Children.

28 Damaris,   born January   27, 1693. Married Benjamin Watrous, of Saybrook, Conn., about 1720.
29 Andrew,   born April   22, 1695.
30 Deborah,   born January   17, 1698. Married a Mr. Peck. He was drowned in Quinniapack river, in coming from ordination at East Haven, Conn. Had one child only, a daughter.
31 John,   born August   11, 1700. Married Sarah Smith.
32 Jehiel,   born November 16, 1702. Died at sea February 15, 1740; his mother would never taste sea food afterwards.
33 Samuel,   born June   3, 1704. Married Lucy Rogers, of New London. Died at Philadelphia, September 9, 1745. He was arrested and confined in prison for debt and died before his

34 Edmund, born September 23, 1706. Married Mehetabel Robinson. Died at
35 Doretheus, born January 4, 1708. Guilford, November, 1779.
36 Diana, born February 11, 1710. Married Joshua Pendleton, who was half brother of Lucy Rogers.

family could obtain information and relieve him. In a letter which he wrote them he requested them to read the 88th Psalm of David in Tate and Brady's version, as descriptive of his situation.

FIFTH GENERATION.

29.

ANDREW WARD, of Guilford, Conn., was married to Elizabeth Fowler, daughter of Abraham Fowler, and Mary Hubbard, daughter of George Hubbard, of the same town, September 1, 1716.

Capt. Andrew Ward died July 14, 1779, in the 85th year of his age.

His widow, Mrs. Elizabeth Ward, died ———.

Children.

37 Andrew, born November 3, 1722. Died September 7, 1723.
38 Elizabeth, born November 19, 1725. Married Timothy Norton, of Guilford, January 1, 1748.
39 Andrew, born November 19, 1727.
40 Abigail, born April 22, 1731. Married Wyllys Eliot.
41 Jacob, } twins. born January 23, 1736. Died February 5, 1735.
42 Mary, } born January 23, 1736. Supposed to have died before her father, as she is not mentioned in the distribution of his estate.

36.

DIANA WARD was twice married. 1. To Lieut. Daniel Hubbard, of Guilford, Conn., October 13, 1730. He died September 28, 1751, aged 54. 2. To Capt. Nathaniel Johnson, of Guilford, about 1754. She was his second wife. He was brother of Samuel Johnson, D. D., first President of Kings, now Columbia College.

Mrs. Diana Hubbard, alias Johnson, died March 20, 1787.

Capt. Nathaniel Johnson died in 1793.

Children.

43 Daniel, born July 25, 1731.
44 Diana, born January 14, 1733. Married her cousin, Andrew Ward, of Guilford, September 7, 1750.
45 Levi, born February 10, 1736.
46 Bela, born August 27, 1739. Yale College, 1758—D. D. Died 1812, aged 73. Was Rector of Trinity Church, New-Haven, Conn.
47 Thankful, born April 8, 1742. Married January 14, 1761, Capt. Asher Fairchild, who was the son of Samuel Fairchild and born August 16, 1734. Their children were Lavinia, born October 7, 1761; married Abner Stone and died February 15, 1837. Nancy, born August 3, 1763; married Dr. Redfield. Rebecca, born May 16, 1768, died September 5, 1769. Harriott, born July 5, 1770; married July 7, 1798, Jeremy Hoadly, Esq.,

and died at Hartford, September 22, 1849. Grace, born February 26, 1775; married Reuben Eliot, son of Wyllys Eliot and Abigail Ward his wife. Hubbard, born October 22, 1776, died September 14, 1800. Charlotte, born December 20, 1778, died December, 1782. Ward, born March 27, 1783. Rebecca, born March 17, 1787, died March 9, 1811. Capt. Asher Fairchild was lost at sea, August, 1795. His widow, Mrs. Thankful Fairchild, died at Guilford, January 17, 1809.

SIXTH GENERATION.

39.

ANDREW WARD, of Guilford, Conn., was married to Diana Hubbard, daughter of Lieut. Daniel Hubbard, of that town, September 7, 1750.

General Andrew Ward died January 29, 1799, aged 71.

His widow, Mrs. Diana Ward, died ———.

Children.

48 Roxana,	born January	7, 1751.	
49 Diana,	born September 24, 1752.		Married Abraham Crittenton, jun., of Guilford, November 17, 1774.
50 Deborah,	born	1756.	Died December 31, 1780, in her 25th year.
51 Mary,	born October	5, 1764.	Died in 1783.
52 Andrew,	born March	23, 1767.	Died in infancy.
53 Andrew,	born		Supposed to have been his son.

SEVENTH GENERATION.

48.

ROXANA WARD was married to Eli Foote, of Guilford, Conn., descendant of Nathaniel Foote, one of the first settlers of Wethersfield, Conn., October 11, 1772.

Mr. Eli Foote died in North Carolina, September 8, 1792, aged 45, nearly.

His widow, Mrs. Roxana Foote, died at Guilford, Conn., October 31, 1840, aged 90.

Children.

54 Harriet,	born July	28, 1773.	Died, single, April 19, 1842.
55 Roxana,	born September 10, 1775.		Married Rev. Dr. Lyman Beecher, September 19, 1799. After her death, he was again married. She died September 26, 1818, aged 43. *Children,*—Catharine Esther. William Henry, Pastor of the Presbyterian Church in Euclid, O. Edward, Pastor of a Congregational Church in Boston, Mass. Mary, wife of Hon. Thomas C. Perkins, of Hartford, Conn. Harriet, died in infancy. George, died in 1843, and at the time of his death, was Pastor of the Presbyterian Church in Chilicothe, O. Harriet Elizabeth, wife of Professor

Calvin E. Stowe, of Andover, Mass.
Henry Ward, Pastor of the Plymouth
Church, in Brooklyn, N. Y. Charles,
Pastor of the Second Presbyterian
Church, Fort-Wayne, Ind.

56 Andrew
  Ward,   born November 9, 1776. Died September 29, 1794.
57 William
  Henry,   born September 8, 1778. Died October 7, 1794.
58 Martha,   born September 23, 1781. Died September 23, 1793.
59 John Par-
  sons,   born June   26, 1783. Settled in Cincinnati, O. Married Jane
        Warner, of the city of New-York,
        September 26, 1811. Has several
        children.

60 Mary Ward, born August 7, 1785. Married James Hubbard, of the island
        of Jamaica, W. I., died September
        1, 1813.
61 Samuel
  Edmond, born October 29, 1787. Settled in Cincinnati, O. Married
        Elizabeth B. Eliot, of Guilford, Sep-
        tember 9, 1827. Has several children.
62 George
  Augustus, born December 9, 1789. Settled in Guilford, Conn. Married
        Eliza Spencer, of that town; has a
        number of children.

31

JOHN WEBSTER,

FIRST SETTLERS OF HARTFORD, CONN.

FIRST GENERATION.

JOHN WEBSTER, one of the first settlers of Hartford, Conn., aud Hadley, Mass., and fifth Governor of the Colony of Connecticut, was married (in England, probably) to Agnes ——— Hon. John Webster died at Hadley, Mass., April 5, 1661. His widow, Mrs. Agnes Webster, died ———

SECOND GENERATION.

Children of John Webster and Agnes his wife,—named in his will.

I.	Matthew,	born
II.	William,	born
III.	Thomas,	born
IV.	Robert.	born
V.	Anne,	born
VI.	Elizabeth,	born
VII.	Mary,	born

DESCENDANTS IN THE LINE OF MATTHEW WEBSTER, SON OF JOHN WEBSTER, THE SETTLER.

THIRD GENERATION.

I.

MATTHEW WEBSTER, of Farmington, Conn., was married to ———.

Mr. Matthew Webster died July 16, 1655.
His widow, Mrs. ——— Webster, died ———.

Children.*

8	John,	born
9	Daughter, (name unknown.)	born

When young, dwelt with Joseph Easton, of Hartford.

---

* Our knowledge of the children of Matthew Webster, is derived from a deed from him to his father, dated in 1660, and recorded in "Book of Deeds" in the office of Secretary of State, page 43. whereby "I the said Matthew, bind over my land in Farmington, in Matthew Woodruff's hands, for the maintenance of my son John, for the whole time of the life of said John. My daughter, who is with Joseph Easton, of Hartford, to have six pounds a year from the rent of the land, for a year or two longer : and this I do bind over to my father Mr. John Webster, to dispose of for the good of my son, after his, my said father's, decease."

DESCENDANTS IN THE LINE OF WILLIAM WEBSTER, SON OF JOHN WEBSTER, THE SETTLER.

THIRD GENERATION.

II.

WILLIAM WEBSTER, of Hadley, Mass., was married to Mary Reeve, daughter of —— Reeve, of ——, February 17, 1670. Mr. William Webster is supposed to have died about 1688. His widow, Mrs. Mary Webster, died in 1696.*

Children,—none.

DESCENDANTS IN THE LINE OF THOMAS WEBSTER, SON OF JOHN WEBSTER, THE SETTLER.

THIRD GENERATION.

III.

THOMAS WEBSTER, of Northampton, Mass., was married to Abigail Alexander, daughter of —— Alexander, of the same town, June 16, 1663.†

Mr. Thomas Webster died at Northfield, Mass., in 1686.

His widow, Mrs. Abigail Webster, survived her husband, but died before March, 1690.

Children.

10 Abigail,	born January	9, 1668, at Northampton.	Died in infancy.
11 Abigail,	born January	10, 1669, at Northampton.	
12 George,	born November	7, 1670, at Northampton.	
13 John,	born February	26, 1673, at Northampton.	
14 Elizabeth,	born November	26, 1676, at Hadley, Mass.	
15 Thankful,	born January	12, 1679, at Hadley, Mass.	Married John Bascom, 1700.
16 Mary,	born May	25, 1681, at Hadley, Mass.	

---

* Mrs. Webster was a reputed witch, and as such, she was tried in Boston, and acquitted. She died in peace.

At a County Court held at Northampton, in and for the county of Hampshire, Mass., March 31, 1685,—" Sam¹¹ Partrigg was allowed pay'nt for drawing out Coppys of Tests to be sent to yᵉ Bay in Goodwife Webster's case wᵘⁱⁿ [wherein] she was accused with familiaritee with yᵉ devell."

† Mr. Thomas Webster settled in Northampton, Mass. In or about the year 1674, he removed to Northfield, but was soon driven away by the Indians, and went to Hadley, Mass. He, however, returned to Northfield, and there resided during the remainder of his life. He probably lost all his estate in Northfield, when attacked by the enemy in 1675, but at the time of his death, he left a good estate there in land ; Northfield being broken up again in 1690, remained desolate over twenty years thereafter, and its lands became valueless. Mr. Webster's children were brought up among the Alexander and other relatives.

Hampshire County Court Records, Book I, p. 127. At a County Court, holden at Northampton, in and for said County, March 28, 1670, " Thomas Webster, and Edward Scott, presented at the last Court at Springfield, for defaming [?] the Sabbath, by travelling to Westfield fromward Windsor late in the night before the Sabbath, and warned here to appear ; and they were both admonished of their offence, and ordered to pay each of them, two and sixpence to the Recorder, as his fees, and so were dismissed."

DESCENDANTS IN THE LINE OF ROBERT WEBSTER, SON OF JOHN WEBSTER, THE SETTLER.

THIRD GENERATION.

IV.

ROBERT WEBSTER, first of Middletown, Conn., and afterwards of Hartford, Conn., was married to Susannah Treat, daughter of Richard Treat, Esq., of Wethersfield, in the same State, and one of the first settlers of that town, about 1652.*
Robert Webster, Esq., died in 1676.
His widow, Mrs. Susannah Webster, died in 1705.

Children.

17 John,	born November	10, 1653,	at Middletown.
18 Sarah,	born June	30, 1655,	at Middletown.
19 Jonathan,	born January	9, 1657,	at Middletown.
20 Susannah,	born October	26, 1658,	at Middletown.
21 Samuel,	born [no date.]		at Hartford, probably.
22 Robert,	born [no date.]		at Hartford, probably.
23 Joseph,	born [no date.]		at Hartford, probably.
24 William,	born [no date.]		at Hartford, probably.
25 Mary,	born [no date.]		at Hartford, probably. Married to Thomas King, of Hartford. She died September 27, 1706. He died December 26, 1711.
26 Elizabeth,	born [no date.]		at Hartford, probably.

FOURTH GENERATION.

17.

JOHN WEBSTER, of Hartford, Conn., was married to Sarah Mygatt, daughter of Jacob Mygatt, of Hartford, and of Sarah his wife, daughter of Hon. William Whiting, one of the first settlers of Hartford, and of Susannah his wife. Jacob Mygatt was son of Deacon Joseph Mygatt, who, likewise, was one of the first settlers of Hartford. [After the death of Mr. Webster, his widow was married to Lieut. Benjamin Graham, of Hartford, being his second wife, November 28, 1698. He died in 1725.]
Mr. John Webster died December 6, 1695, aged 42.
Mrs. Sarah Webster, alias Graham, died ——————

Children.

27 John,	born		Married Abiel Steele in 1712, settled in Southington, and died in 1753.
28 Ebenezer,	born	1689.	
29 Jacob,	born		Married Elizabeth Nichols, and died in 1728.
30 Daniel,	bap. October	1, 1693.	
31 Sarah,	born		
32 Ann,	born		
33 Abigail,	born		Married Jacob Merrill in 1710.

* Robert Webster, settled at Middletown, Conn., and at the organization of the town in 1651, or 1652, was chosen Recorder. He continued at Middletown, until about 1660, when he removed to Hartford.

18.

SARAH WEBSTER was twice married. 1. To Joseph Mygatt, of Hartford, Conn., son of Jacob Mygatt, of Hartford, and grandson of Deacon Joseph Mygatt, one of the first settlers of the town, November 15, 1677. He died in March, 1698. 2. To Bevil Waters, of Hartford, being his second wife, December 13, 1722. Mr. Bevil Waters died February 14, 1729, aged 97.

Mrs. Sarah Mygatt, alias Waters, died in February, 1744, aged 89, nearly.

Children,—by her first husband.

34 Joseph,	born October	27, 1678.	
35 Susannah,	born October	1, 1680.	
36 Mary,	born December	4, 1682.	
37 Jacob,	born December	9, 1684.	Died January 29, 1685.
38 Jacob,	born November	9, 1686.	Died November, 1687.
39 Thomas,	born September	11, 1688.	
40 Sarah,	born March	9, 1691.	Married Thomas King, of Hartford, November 6, 1712. They had 8 children.
41 Zebulon,	born November	6, 1693.	
42 Dorathy,	born January	26, 1696.	Married Jonathan Steele, of Hartford, May 6, 1715.

Children,—by her second husband,—none.

19.

JONATHAN WEBSTER, of Hartford, Conn., was twice married. 1. To Dorcas Hopkins, daughter of Stephen Hopkins, of Hartford, and grand-daughter of John Hopkins, one of the first settlers of the town, May 11, 1681. She died in 1694. 2. To Mary Judd, supposed daughter of Thomas Judd, of Farmington, January 2, 1696.

Mr. Jonathan Webster died in 1735, aged 78.

His widow, Mrs. Mary Webster, died ———.

Children,—by his first wife.

43 Jonathan,	born March	18, 1682.	Married Esther Judd, and settled in Glastenbury, Conn. 8 children are recorded to him on Glastenbury Records.
44 Susannah,	born April	25, 1686.	
45 Mary,	born September	29, 1688.	
46 Mehitabel,	born March	8, 1691.	Married to David Bidwell, of Hartford, July 8, 1714.
47 Stephen,	born January	1, 1693.	Married Mary Burnham, of Hartford, June 6, 1717, who after his death, married Ebenezer Merrill, of Hartford, April 9, 1730. He, Stephen Webster, died in 1724.

Child,—by his second wife,—one only.

48 Benjamin,	born August	9, 1698.	Settled in Litchfield.

20.

SUSANNAH WEBSTER was married to John Grave, of Hartford, Conn., about 1680. [After her death, he was married to Hannah

Davis, daughter of Philip Davis, of Hartford, in 1690, by whom he had six children, two of which, only, viz., John, born March 3, 1695, and settled in Guilford, and Sarah, born September 25, 1698, seem to have survived infancy.]

Mrs. Susannah Grave died in 1688, aged 30.

Mr. John Grave died in August, 1702, aged —.

Children.

| 49 Mehitabel, | born | Married James Henderson, of Hartford, Conn., January 1, 1701. |
| 50 Elizabeth, | born | Married Ebenezer Dudley, of East-Guilford, Conn. He died in 1751, leaving surviving his wife Elizabeth, and 7 children. |

21.

SAMUEL WEBSTER, of Hartford, Conn., was married to Elizabeth Reeve, daughter of Robert Reeve, of the same town. She was born December 14, 1668.

Samuel Webster, Esq., died February 1, 1744, aged —. He was honored with the appointment of High Sheriff of Hartford County, September 7, 1708, which office he resigned August 1, 1721, and recommended Col. William Whiting, of Hartford, as his successor, on whom the office was bestowed.

His widow, Mrs. Elizabeth Webster, died in 1747, aged 79.

Children,—none.

22.

ROBERT WEBSTER, of Hartford, Conn., was thrice married. 1. To Hannah Beckley, daughter of John Beckley, of Wethersfield, Conn., September 10, 1689. She died ———. 2. To Sarah Colefax, widow of Jonathan Colefax, deceased, of Wethersfield, and daughter of Joseph Edwards of the same town, after 1712. She died February 15, 1725, aged 53. 3. To Susannah Baker, daughter of John Baker, of Hartford, and grand-daughter of John Basey, one of the first settlers of the same town, July 30, 1731.

Mr. Robert Webster died in February, 1744.

His widow, Mrs. Susannah Webster, died in December, 1746.

Children,—by his first wife.

51 Robert,	born October	1689.	
52 Abraham,	born September	1, 1693.	
53 Hannah,	born November	7, 1695.	
54 Matthew,	born April	17, 1698.	Died February 2, 1707.
55 Joseph,	born March	7, 1700.	
56 Caleb,	born February	22, 1703.	
57 Mary,	born December	5, 1704.	Died in early life.
58 Abigail,	born January	22, 1711.	

Children,—by his second and third wives,—none.

23.

JOSEPH WEBSTER, of Hartford, Conn., was twice married. 1.

To Mary Judd, daughter of Benjamin Judd,* of Farmington, Conn., February 23, 1696. She died ———. 2. To Hannah Baker, widow of Basey Baker, deceased, of Middletown, Conn., formerly of Hartford, May 11, 1726. She was daughter of Nathaniel Willett, of Hartford.

Mr. Joseph Webster died in May, 1750.

Mr. Hannah Webster, alias Baker, died ———

Children,—by his first wife.

59 Mary,   born May   31, 1697. Married Isaac Kellogg, of Hartford, Dec. 26, 1717.
60 Elizabeth, born March   6, 1700. Married Joseph Waters, of Hartford.

Children,—by his second wife,—none.

24.

WILLIAM WEBSTER, of Hartford, Conn., was married to Sarah Nichols, daughter of Cyprian Nichols, of the same town, November 20, 1700. [After his death, she was married May 13, 1725, to Samuel Catlin, of Hartford, being his second wife. His first wife, to whom he was married January 5, 1702, was Elizabeth Norton, of Farmington, Conn. She died August 4, 1724.]

Ensign William Webster died in June, 1722.

Mrs. Sarah Webster, alias Catlin, died ———.

Children.

61 Cyprian,   born September 3, 1701. Married Elizabeth Seymour, 1729. He removed to Harwinton.
62 Moses,   born   1702. Died in infancy.
63 William,   born September 3, 1703. Settled in Wintonbury.
64 Moses,   born September 26, 1706. Married Mary Brace in 1733.
65 Susannah, born April   18, 1710.
66 Sarah,   born   1712.
67 Samuel,   born   1714.
68 Timothy,   bap. May   29, 1720. Died in early life.

26.

ELIZABETH WEBSTER was married to John Seymour, jun., of Hartford, Conn., December 19, 1693.

Mr. John Seymour died May 17, 1748, aged 82, nearly.

His widow, Mrs. Elizabeth Seymour, died May 15, 1754.

Children.

69 John,   born December 25, 1694.
70 Timothy,   born June   27, 1696.
71 Daniel,   born October   20, 1698.
72 Jonathan, born March   16, 1703.
73 Nathaniel, born November 17, 1704.
74 Susanna,   born April   13, 1706. Married ——— Pomroy.
75 Margaret, born January   30, 1708. Married ——— Catlin.
76 Zebulon,   born May   14, 1709.
77 Moses,   born February 17, 1711.
78 Richard,   born [no date.]

---

* Benjamin Judd had a daughter Mary born in 1675, and she is supposed to have become the wife of Joseph Webster, as her sister Esther born in 1686,—on the 7th of March, 1702, made choice of Joseph Webster to be her guardian.

FIFTH GENERATION.

28.

EBENEZER WEBSTER, of Hartford, Conn., was married to Hannah Webster, daughter of Robert Webster, 2d, of Hartford. She was born November 7, 1695.

Mrs. Hannah Webster died November 11, 1775, aged 80.

Mr. Ebenezer Webster died February 12, 1776, aged 86.

Children.

79 Matthew,	born February	14, 1720.	
80 Hannah,	born		Married Elijah Mills, of Windsor, Conn.
81 Medad,	born	1723.	Married Elizabeth Holton, daughter of Joseph Holton, of Hartford, November 10, 1748. Capt. Medad Webster died April 9, 1793, aged 70.
82 Mary,	born	1727.	Married —— Ensign, of Hartford. She died February 19, 1805, aged 78.
83 Thankful,	born	1728.	Died, unmarried, December 22, 1784, aged 56.
84 Ebenezer,	born	1731.	He died March 25, 1804, aged 72.
85 Sarah,	born		Married —— Clark.
86 Rebecca,	born		Married Samuel Turner, of Hartford.

30.

DANIEL WEBSTER, of Hartford, Conn., was twice married. 1. To Mirriam Kellogg, widow of Abraham Kellogg, deceased,* of Hartford, and daughter of Noah Cooke,† of Northampton, Mass., and of Sarah his wife, daughter of Joseph Nash, one of the early settlers of Hartford, about 1719. She was born September 30, 1690, and died ——. 2. To Hannah Bird, widow of Jonathan Bird, deceased, of Farmington.

Capt. Daniel Webster died December 21, 1765, aged 72.

Mrs. Hannah Webster died October 17, 1776, aged —.

Children,—by his first wife.

87 Daniel,	born February	16, 1720.	Died young.
88 Noah,	born March	25, 1722.	
89 Zephaniah,	born June	1, 1724.	
90 Abraham,	born January	17, 1727.	
91 Mirriam,	born October	21, 1729.	Married 1. William Sedgwick. 2. —— Marsh, of New Hartford.
92 Daniel,	born September	4, 1731.	
93 Elihu,	born November	1, 1733.	Died young and unmarried.

Children,—by his second wife,—none.

SIXTH GENERATION.

79.

MATTHEW WEBSTER, first of Hartford, Conn., afterwards of Schaghticoke, Rensselaer County, N. Y., was married to Mabel Pratt, daughter of William Pratt, of Hartford, 1747.

---

* Abraham Kellogg died soon after his marriage to Mirriam Kellogg, having no issue.

† Noah Cooke was born June 14, 1657, and was son, by his first wife, of Capt. Aaron Cooke, of Dorchester, Mass., in 1630,—one of the first settlers of Windsor, Conn., in 1635 or 1636, of Northampton, Mass., about 1660, afterwards of Westfield, Mass., where he resided a few years, and then of Northampton, where he died September 5, 1690, aged 80.

Mrs. Mabel Webster died ———.

Mr. Matthew Webster died February 9, 1807, aged 86 years, 11 months, and 25 days.

Children.

94 Samuel,   born
95 Mabel,   born   1749. Died December, 1776, aged 27.
96 Hannah,   born
97 Acsah,   born
98 Benjamin, born
99 Charles, ⎱ ⅁born
100 George, ⎰ ᴢborn

87.

NOAH WEBSTER, of Hartford, Conn., was married to Mercy Steele, daughter of Eliphalet Steele of the same town, January 12, 1749.

Mrs. Mercy Webster died October 5, 1794, aged 67.

Noah Webster, Esq., died November 9, 1813, in his 92d year.

Children.

101 Mercy,	born November 8, 1749.	Married John Kellogg Belden, and died August 11, 1820.
102 Abraham,	born September 17, 1751.	Married 1. —— Merrill, of New-Hartford. 2. Dorothy Seymour. 3. Eunice Childs, of Deerfield. He died in Sullivan, N. Y., August 4, 1831.
103 Jerusha,	born January 22, 1756.	Married Joel Lord, of Salisbury, Conn., afterwards of Danby, N. Y. She died August 4, 1831.
104 Noah,	born October 16, 1758.	Noah Webster, LL. D., author of Dictionary, married Rebecca Greenleaf, of Boston, October 26, 1789.
105 Charles,	born September 2, 1762.	Married 1. Betsey Woodruff. 2. Mrs. —— Wilkinson.

32

GOVERNOR THOMAS WELLES,

ONE OF THE

FIRST SETTLERS OF HARTFORD, CONN.

THOMAS WELLES, one of the first settlers of Hartford, Conn., and Wethersfield, Conn., and one of the early Governors of the Colony of Connecticut, was twice married. 1. To ————. She died ————. 2. To Elizabeth Foote, widow of Nathaniel Foote, one of the first settlers of Wethersfield, about 1646. She was sister of Hon. John Deming, who, likewise was one of the first settlers of Wethersfield.

Hon. Thomas Welles died at Wethersfield, January 14, 1659–60.

His widow, Mrs. Elizabeth Welles, alias Foote, died July 28, 1683, aged about 88 years.

FIRST GENERATION.

Children of Thomas Welles,—by his first wife.

I. John,	born		
II. Thomas,	born		
III. Samuel,	born		
IV. Mary,	born		Mary died before her father.
V. Ann,	born		Was married twice. 1. To Thomas Thompson, of Farmington, Conn., April 14, 1646. He died April 25, 1655. 2. To Anthony Hawkins, of Farmington.
VI. Sarah,	born	1631.	Was married to Capt. John Chester, of Wethersfield, February, 1653. John Chester, Esq., died February 23, 1698, aged 62. He was born in Watertown, Mass., August 3, 1635. His widow, Mrs. Sarah Welles, died December 16, 1698, aged 87.

Children of Thomas Welles, by his second wife,—none.

DESCENDANTS IN THE LINE OF JOHN WELLES, SON OF THOMAS WELLES, THE SETTLER.

SECOND GENERATION.

I.

JOHN WELLES, of Stratford, Conn., was married to Elizabeth

Curtis, sister of William Curtis, of Stratford, and daughter of John Curtis, one of the first settlers of that town, and of Elizabeth his wife, about 1647. [After his death, she was married to John Willcoxson, of Stratford, March 19, 1662–3, by whom she had children,—Patience, born February 1, 1663–4. Hannah, born February 14, 1664–5. Elizabeth, born July, 1666. Mary, born April, 1668. Mr. John Willcoxson died in 1690.]

Mr. John Welles died 1659.

Mrs. Elizabeth Welles, alias Willcoxson, died ⸺.

Children.

7 John,	born	1648.
8 Thomas, } twins	born	1651.
9 Robert, }		
10 Temperance,	born	1654.
11 Samuel,	born	1656.
12 Sarah,	born September 28,	1659.

THIRD GENERATION.

7.

JOHN WELLES, of Stratford, Conn., was married to Mary Hollister, daughter of John Hollister, of Wethersfield, Conn.

Mr. John Welles died March 24, 1713–14, aged about 66.

His widow, Mrs. Mary Welles, died ⸺.

Children.

13 Mary, born November 29, 1670. Married Jeremiah Judson, jun., of Stratford, Conn., April 24, 1695. He died in 1734. She died ⸺. Child, one only,—Eunice, born 1695, was married to Nathan Curtis, of Stratford. He died ⸺. She died ⸺. Perhaps married Sarah Stiles, August 31, 1710.

14 Thomas, born [no date.]

15 Sarah, born January 2, 1673–4.

16 John, born 1675–6. Married to Mary Judson, daughter of Isaac Judson, son of Jeremiah, of Stratford, December 15, 1698. Capt. John Welles died February 19, 1734–5. His widow, Mrs. Mary Welles, died ⸺. *Children,*—David, born October 16, 1699. Mary, born August 11, 1701. Elizabeth, born May 13, 1703. Sarah, born March 23, 1705. Phebe, born February 17, 1707. Isaac Judson, born April 28, 1709. Isaac Judson, born November 6, 1711. John, William, Hannah, Huldah.

17 Comfort, born Married to Abel Birdsey, of Stratford, June 8, 1704, who after her death was married to Mary ⸺.

18 Joseph, born June 21, 1679. Settled in Stratford. Was married to Sarah Preston, daughter of ⸺ Preston, of Stratford, February 3, 1714–15. He died January 21, 1765, in the 86th year of his age. She died October 16, 1760, aged ⸺. *Chil-*

dren,—Joseph, born December 15, 1716.

19 Elizabeth,   born   Was married to Joseph Curtis, jun., of Stratford, July 5, 1711. He died 1738. Children, named in his will. Mary Curtis, wife of Daniel Curtis. Elizabeth, Tabitha, Bethua, James, Joseph, Gideon, Robert.

20 Robert,   born September,   1688.   Was married to Eunice Curtis, daughter of Capt. Josiah Curtis, of Stratford, Conn., October 24, 1720. He died about 1758. Children, named in his will,—Samuel, Eunice, wife of Thomas Lewis. Sarah, wife of Edmund Curtis. Betsy, wife of Ephraim Burton. Abigail, widow of Samuel Southworth. Ruth Welles.

8.

THOMAS WELLES, of Stratford, Conn., was married to Eliza beth ———, daughter of ———.
Deacon Thomas Welles died January 7, 1720, aged about 70.
His widow, Mrs. Elizabeth Welles, died ———.

Children,—none.

9.

ROBERT WELLES, of Wethersfield, Conn., was twice married. 1. To Elizabeth Goodrich, daughter of Ensign William Goodrich, of Wethersfield, June 9, 1675. She died February 17, 1697–8, aged about 40. 2. To Mary ———.
Capt. Robert Welles died June 22, 1714, aged 66.
Mrs. Mary Welles died ———.*

Children,—by his first wife.

21 Thomas,   born May,   1676.   Settled in Wethersfield. Was twice married. 1. To Hannah Warner, daughter of Lieut. William Warner, of Wethersfield, September 28, 1699. She died September 18, 1738, aged 60. 2. To Sarah Robbins, widow of Capt. Joshua Robbins. Capt. Thomas Welles died September 21, 1741, aged 65. Mrs. Sarah Welles, alias Robbins, died December 3, 1744, aged 62.

22 John,   born June,   1678.   Died, before his father, unmarried, as is supposed, because none of his father's estate was distributed to him.

23 Joseph,   born September,   1680.   Settled in Wethersfield. Married Hannah Robbins, daughter of Joshua Robbins, of Wethersfield, January 6, 1708–9. He died 1744. She died ———. *Children,*—John, born November 13, 1710. Prudence, born

---

*Hartford Probate Records, Book 13, p. 72. Court September 2, 1740. Administration on the Estate of Mary Welles, late of Wethersfield deceased, widow of Robert Welles, of that town, deceased, granted to Michael Gibson, of Truro, Barnstable county, Mass., attorney to Dorathy Patman, and some of the rest of the heirs of said deceased Mary Welles, who gave bond with John Knowles, of Hartford.

February 12, 1712. Esther, born May, 1716. Hannah, born August 5, 1718. Joseph, born September 17, 1720, and died April 1, 1788. Eunice, born March 25, 1723. Joshua, born September, 1726. Christopher, born December, 1729, died young.

24 Prudence, born — Married to Rev. Anthony Stoddard, Pastor of the Congregational Church at Woodbury, Conn., October 20, 1700. She died May, 1714, aged —. After her death he was married to Mary Sherman, daughter of —— Sherman, of ——. She died January 12, 1720. He died September 6, 1760, aged 82.

25 Robert, born — Settled in Wethersfield. Was married to Sarah Wolcott, daughter of Samuel Wolcott, of Wethersfield, and of Judith his wife, daughter of the Worshipful Samuel Appleton, of Ipswich, Mass., December 12, 1706. Lieut. Robert Welles died ——. His wife died ——. *Children,—* Sarah, born February 1, 1708–9. Sarah was married to Jonathan Robbins, of Wethersfield, November 21, 1728. Robert, born September 7, 1710. Robert Welles settled in Newington, and there died February 3, 1786, aged 76. Appleton, born February 4, 1711–12. Abigail, born October 9, 1715. Elizabeth, born March 18, 1716–17. Mary, born June 23, 1719. Josiah, born March 9, 1720–21. Christopher, born May 29, 1724. Hezekiah, born December 9, 1725. Martha, born August 29, 1729. Judith, born March 4, 1730–31.

26 Gideon, born — Settled in Wethersfield. Was married to Hannah Chester, daughter of Major John Chester of Wethersfield, November 30, 1716. Capt. Gideon Welles died March 28, 1740. After his death, his widow was married to Jonathan Hale, Esq., of Glastenbury, Conn. His widow, Mrs. Hannah Welles, alias Hale, died ——. *Children,—*Chester, born October 8, 1718. Solomon, born October 6, 1721. Solomon Welles, son of Gideon Welles, married Sarah Welles, of Glastenbury, June 16, 1745, by whom he had 11 children, among whom, was Chester, his 9th child, born November 21, 1762, against whose time of birth on the Wethersfield Records, is entered, "and was the first child baptized in the brick meeting house." Eunice, born August 6, 1723. Sarah, born December 23, 1725. Gideon, born May 26, 1735.

Children,—by his second wife,—none.

10.

TEMPERANCE WELLES was married to Jonathan Pitman, of Stratford, Conn., November 21, 1681.

Mr. Jonathan Pitman died about 1727.

His widow, Mrs. Temperance Pitman, died ————.

Children,—recorded to them on Stratford Records.

27 Jonathan,	born November 4, 1682.	Died in infancy.
28 Jonathan,	born May 21, 1685.	
29 Robert,	born October 16, 1687.	
30 Samuel,	born February 1, 1691-2.	

11.

SAMUEL WELLES, of Stratford, Conn., was married to Abigail ————. Sergeant Samuel Welles, married to his third wife, Abigail, October 25, 1711. [Stratford Church Records.]

Mr. Samuel Welles died in 1729.

His widow, Mrs. Abigail Welles, died ————.

Children.

31 Samuel,	born October 15, 1686.	Married Mary Judson, daughter of ———— Judson, of Stratford. She died ————. He died April 16, 1750–51. *Children,*—Sarah, bap. December 21, 1712, married Nathan Blackman. Abigail, bap. December 21, 1712, married Samuel Prince, of Stratford, August 9, 1733. Prudence, born July 15, 1716. Esther, born ————. David, bap. July 20, 1718. Samuel, born ————. Jedediah, born ———— and perhaps Mary, 1714, married Andrew Hubbell, of Stratford, December 2, 1736. She was his 2d wife.
32 Ann,	born	Married John Hubbell, of Stratford, Stratfield Society, November 6, 1711.
33 Abigail,	born	Married to Thomas Turney, of Fairfield, November 24, 1709.
34 Elizabeth,	bap. January 31, 1693–4,	at Stratfield Parish. Married to John Cluckstone, of Stratford, June 13, 1718, at Stratfield Parish.

12.

SARAH WELLES was married to Benjamin Beach, of Stratford, Conn., February 1, 1678. [After his death it would appear that she was married to Ambrose Thompson.]

Mr. Benjamin Beach died April 10, 1715.

His widow, Mrs. Sarah Beach, died ————.

Children.

35 Sarah,	born May 4, 1679.
36 Hannah,	born September, 1681.

DESCENDANTS IN THE LINE OF THOMAS WELLES, SON OF THOMAS WELLES, THE SETTLER.

SECOND GENERATION.

II.

THOMAS WELLES, of Hartford, Conn., was married to Hannah Pantry, widow of John Pantry, of Hartford, and daughter of —— ——, June 23, 1654. [By her Pantry husband she had 2 children.]

Mr. Thomas Welles died 1668.

His widow, Mrs. Hannah Welles, died August 9, 1683, aged —.

Children.

37 Rebecca,	born	1655.
38 Thomas,	born	1657.
39 Sarah,	born	1659.
40 Ichabod,	born	1660.
41 Samuel,	born	1662.
42 Jonathan,	born	1664.
43 Joseph,	born	1667.

THIRD GENERATION.

37.

REBECCA WELLES was married to James Judson, of Stratford, Conn., August 18, 1680. [After her death, Mr. Judson was married to Ann Steele, widow of James Steele, deceased, of Wethersfield, November 20, 1718, by whom he had no issue.]

Mrs. Rebecca Judson died ——.

Capt. James Judson died February 25, 1721, aged 71, nearly.

Children.

44 Hannah,	born May	30, 1681.	Married James Lewis, of Stratford, Conn.
45 Sarah,	born February	16, 1683.	Married Rev. Nathaniel Chauncey, Pastor of the Congregational Church, Durham, Conn.
46 Rebecca,	born February	25, 1685.	Died February 26, 1698.
47 Joseph,	born January	10, 1687.	Married Hannah Hawley, of Stratford, Conn.
48 James,	born April	3, 1689.	Married Martha Lewis, daughter of —— Lewis, of Stratford, Conn.
49 Phebe,	born October	2, 1691.	Married Joseph Lewis, of Stratford, Conn.
50 David,	born August	7, 1693.	Was married to Phebe Stiles, daughter of Ephraim Stiles, of Stratford, Conn., October 29, 1713. He died May 5, 1761, aged 67. She died May 20, 1765, aged 69.

38.

THOMAS WELLES, of Hartford, Conn., was married to Mary Blackleach, jun., of Hartford, 1689. [After his death, she was married to John Olcott, of Hartford, 1695, by whom she had 4 children; and after the death of Mr. Olcott, which occurred in

1712, she was married to Capt. Joseph Wadsworth, of the same town, celebrated in History as the chief actor in the concealment of the Charter of the Colony of Connecticut in the time of Sir Edmund Andross, 1687.]

Mr. Thomas Welles died March 16, 1695, aged 38.
Mrs. Mary Welles, alias Olcott, alias Wadsworth, died ———.

Children of Thomas and Mary Welles.

51 Thomas, born October 16, 1690. Married Abigail ———. Supposed to have died August 25, 1750. *Children,*—Thomas, bap. September 14, 1718. Died before his father's estate was distributed, leaving children, Thomas and Hannah. Daniel, bap. August 25, 1722. John and Blackleach, twins, bap. August 23, 1724. Mary, bap. January 28, 1727. John, bap. April 6, 1730.

52 John, born December 16, 1693. Supposed the clothier and that he settled in Wethersfield.

39.

SARAH WELLES was married to John Bidwell, jun., of Hartford, Conn., November 7, 1678.

Mr. John Bidwell, jun., died before his wife.
His widow, Mrs. Sarah Bidwell, died about 1709.

Children.

53 John, born September 1, 1679.
54 Hannah, born August 31, 1680. Married Joseph Judd.
55 Sarah, born August 19, 1681. Married to Joshua Robbins, of Wethersfield, September 20, 1707.
56 Thomas, born December 27, 1682.
57 Jonathan, born March 15, 1684.
58 David, born 1687.
59 James, born 1691.

40.

ICHABOD WELLES, of Hartford, Conn., was married to Sarah Way, daughter of Eleazer Way, of the same town, September 4, 1684.

Children.

60 Mary, born April 15, 1686.
61 Jonathan, born September 17, 1689. Married Ruth Bull, daughter of ——— Bull, of Hartford, December 15, 1715. He died in 1752. *Children,*—Ruth, Jonathan, Ichabod, Joseph, Elisha, Sarah, Anna.
62 Ebenezer, born October 5, 1694. Married Rachel Skinner, daughter of John Skinner, of Hartford, May 19, 1726. He died December 27, 1737, aged 46. She died January 18, 1787, aged 92. *Children,*—Rachel, born January 30, 1727. Hannah, born November 4, 1728. Mary, born August 23, 1730. Ebenezer, July 22, 1732. Ashbel, born August 25, 1734, and Sarah, born January 30, 1737.

Ashbel Welles was married to Abigail ———, daughter of ——— of ———, by whom he had a number of children,—among them Abigail, born December 19, 1762, who was married to Henry Williams Dwight, of Stockbridge, Mass., June 8, 1796.

63 Sarah,	born December 1, 1701.	Died February 12, 1703.
64 Anna,	born	Married Eleazur Way, of Southold, L. I., formerly of Hartford.

41.

SAMUEL WELLES, of Hartford, Conn., (East side,) was married to Ruth ———.

Samuel Welles, Esq., died October 3, 1733, aged 70.

Mrs. Ruth Welles died May 2, 1744, in the 80th year of her age.

Children.

65 Hannah,	born November 22, 1689.	
66 Samuel,	born December 26, 1693.	Settled in East-Hartford, married to Esther Ellsworth, January 31, 1722. Capt. Samuel Welles died March 2, 1760, aged 66. His widow, Mrs. Esther Welles died November 3, 1791, aged 89. They had 8 children. Esther, born October 12, 1723. Samuel, born October 5, 1725. Ruth and Ann, twins, born December 17, 1727. John, born July 29, 1730. Jonathan, born February 20, 1733. Hannah, born April 25, 1736. Rebecca, born December 16, 1743.
67 Ruth,	born January 29, 1697.	
68 Sarah,	born December 16, 1700.	
69 Rebecca,	born October 3, 1704.	Married Thomas Pitkin, of East-Hartford. She died February 20, 1725, aged 21.
70 James,	born 1706.	Died February 10, 1725, aged 19.

43.

JOSEPH WELLES, of Hartford, Conn., was married to Elizabeth Way, daughter of Eleazer Way, of the same town.

Mr. Joseph Welles died 1698.

His widow, Mrs. Elizabeth Welles, died ———.

Children.

71 John,	born	Died in childhood.
72 Joseph,	born	Died in childhood.
73 Joshua,	born	Died in childhood.
74 Elizabeth,	born 1696.	Married William Powell, of Hartford, Conn. Their daughter Elizabeth was married to Fletcher Ranny, of Middletown, Conn., November 4, 1750, where, I believe, Mrs. Elizabeth Welles, the grandmother of said Elizabeth Ranny, died. Mr. Fletcher Ranny died December 14, 1772, aged 47. His widow, Mrs. Elizabeth Ranny, died January 14, 1785, aged 60.

33

DESCENDANTS IN THE LINE OF SAMUEL WELLES, SON OF THOMAS WELLES, THE SETTLER.

SECOND GENERATION.

III.

SAMUEL WELLES, of that part of Wethersfield, Conn., now called Glastenbury, was twice married. 1. To Elizabeth Hollister, daughter of John Hollister, of Wethersfield, 1659. She died ———. 2. To Hannah Lamberton, daughter of George Lamberton, of New-Haven, Conn. [After his death, she was married to "the Hon. Lieut. Colonel John Allyn, of Hartford." She was his second wife. Col. Allyn died November 6, 1696.]

Hon. Samuel Welles died July 15, 1675.

Mrs. Hannah Welles, alias Allyn, died ———.

Children,—by his first wife.

75 Samuel,	born April	13, 1660.	
76 Thomas,	born July	29, 1662.	
77 Sarah,	born September 29, 1664.		
78 Mary,	born November 23, 1666.		
79 Ann,	born	1668.	
80 Elizabeth,	born	1670.	

Children,—by his second wife,—none.

THIRD GENERATION.

75.

SAMUEL WELLES, of Glastenbury, Conn., was married to Ruth Rice, daughter of ——— Rice, of ———, June 20, 1683.

Capt. Samuel Welles died August 28, 1731, in the 72d year of his age.

His widow, Mrs. Ruth Welles, died March 30, 1742, in the 83d year of her age.

Children.

81 Mercy,	born October	15, 1684.	Died November 1, 1684.
82 Samuel,	born July	9, 1688.	Died October 16, 1688.
83 Samuel,	born December 24, 1689.		Died May 20, 1770. [Glastenbury Book.] Was ordained minister of Lebanon, December 5, 1710. Dismissed December 4, 1722. Removed to Boston and was grandfather of Hon. John Welles, Harvard College, 1782, who died September, 1855.
84 Thomas,	born February	14, 1693.	
85 Thaddeus,	born March	27, 1695.	
86 Silas,	born March	4, 1700.	Died September 17, 1754.

76.

THOMAS WELLES, of Wethersfield, Conn., was twice married. 1. To Thankful Root, daughter of John Root, deceased, of Northampton, Mass., January 7, 1697. She died November, 1704, aged —. 2. To Jerusha Treat, daughter of Lieut. James Treat, of Wethersfield, May 17, 1705. [After the death of Mr. Welles, she was married to Ephraim Goodrich, of Wethersfield, December 25, 1712. She was his second wife.]

"Capt. Thomas Welles died December 7, 1711, about 5 o'clock in the morning, and was buried on the 8th of December, in the evening, about 5 o'clock, aged 49 years and 5 months wanting a few days." [Wethersfield Records.]

Mrs. Jerusha Welles, alias Goodrich, died January 15, 1754, in the 76th year of her age.

Children,—by his first wife.

87 Thomas,   born January   10, 1698.
88 Hezekiah, born August   12, 1701, and died December 10, 1711.

Children,—by his second wife.

89 William,   born January   12, 1706.
90 Wait,   born January   4, 1708.
91 John,   born February   10, 1710.
92 Ichabod,   born April   26, 1712.

77.

SARAH WELLES was married to Ephraim Hawley, of Stratford, Conn., December 4, 1683, and after his death to Angur Tomlinson, of Stratford.

Ephraim Hawley, Esq., died ———.

Mrs. Sarah Hawley, alias Tomlinson, died about 1695.

Children,—by her first husband.

93 Daniel,   born September 20, 1684.
94 Gideon,   born January   30, 1687.
95 Abia,   born September 18, 1690.   (Posthumous.)

78.

MARY WELLES was married to Samuel Hale, jun., of Glastenbury, Conn., 1695. She was his second wife. [His first wife, to whom he was married June 20, 1670, was Ruth Edwards, daughter of Thomas Edwards, of Wethersfield. She died December 26, 1682, aged about 30. By her, he had children,—Ruth, born January 20, 1670, and died May 7, 1671. Samuel, born January 14, 1673, and died January 15, 1673. Mary, born June 13, 1675, married John Day, of Colchester, Conn., about 1715. She died November 2, 1749, aged 74. Samuel, born July 17, 1677. Ruth, born December 1, 1681, married Thomas Kimberly, of Glastenbury, son of Eleazer Kimberly, many years Secretary of the Colony of Connecticut, about 1704. He died January 29, 1730, aged 48. She died May 14, 1737, aged 55.]

Samuel Hale, Esq., died November 18, 1711, in the 67th year of his age.

His widow, Mrs. Mary Hale, died February 18, 1715, aged 48.

Children.

96 Jonathan,	born August	21, 1696.
97 David,	born January	7, 1700, and died March 31, 1718.
98 Joseph,	born July	10, 1702, and died August 4, 1702.
99 Benjamin,	born July	22, 1707.

79.

ANN WELLES was twice married. 1. To Capt. James Steele, of Wethersfield, Conn., July 19, 1687. He died May 15, 1713, aged —. 2. To James Judson, of Stratford, Conn., November 20, 1718. She was his second wife. [His first wife, to whom he was married August 18, 1686, and who died November 3, 1717, aged 62, was Rebecca Welles, daughter of Thomas Welles, Esq., of Hartford, Conn.]

Mr. James Judson died February 25, 1721, aged 71 nearly.

Mrs. Ann Judson, alias Steele, died at Wethersfield, 1739, aged 71.

Children,—by her first husband.

100 Samuel,	born October	1, 1688.	Married Anna Williams, daughter of Jacob Williams, of Wethersfield, June 23, 1714.
101 Joseph,	born September 27, 1690.	Married Elizabeth Hollister, daughter of John Hollister, of Glastenbury, Conn., February 16, 1715.
102 Prudence,	born January	17, 1693.	Married Josiah Deming, of Wethersfield, December 8, 1714.
103 Hannah,	born March	18, 1697.
104 Ann,	born October	28, 1702.
105 David,	born June	8, 1706.

80.

ELIZABETH WELLES was married to Daniel Shelton, of Stratford, Conn., merchant, April 4, 1692.

Mr. Daniel Shelton died at Ripton Parish in Stratford, about 1728.

His widow, Mrs. Elizabeth Shelton, died ———.

Children recorded to them on Stratford Records.

106 Elizabeth,	born January	2, 1693.
107 Sarah,	born January	2, 1695.
108 Joseph,	born June	24, 1698.

FOURTH GENERATION.

84.

THOMAS WELLES, of Glastenbury, Conn., was twice married, as is supposed. 1. To ———. 2. To Martha Pitkin, daughter of William Pitkin, Esq., of East-Hartford, Conn., December 28, 1715.

Mrs. Martha Welles died July 4, 1763, aged 72.

Hon. Thomas Welles died May 14, 1767, aged 75.

Children.

109 Ruth,	born April	4, 1717.
110 Mary,	born February 19, 1719.	Died April 22, 1733.
111 Thomas,	born November 23, 1720.	Died May 1, 1733.

112 Elizabeth, born November 15, 1722.
113 William,   born March   3, 1725. Died April 12, 1778.
114 Sarah,   born March   27, 1727.
115 John,   born August   11, 1729. Married Jerusha Edwards, daughter of
                                           Samuel Edwards, deceased, of Hart-
                                           ford, March 7, 1753. He died April
                                           16, 1764, aged 35. She died August
                                           15, 1778, aged 46. 6 children.
116 Jonathan,   born August   9, 1732. Died January 27, 1792.
117 Mary,   born March   30, 1735. Died June 7, 1814.

85.

THADDEUS WELLES, of Glastenbury, Conn., was married to
Elizabeth Cowles, daughter of Deacon Timothy Cowles, of East-
Hartford, Conn., and of Hannah his wife, daughter of Hon. Wil-
liam Pitkin, one of the early settlers of Hartford, Conn., and of
Hannah his wife, daughter of Ozias Goodwin, one of the first set-
tlers of Hartford.

Thaddeus Welles, Esq., died December 22, 1781, aged 86.

His widow, Mrs. Elizabeth Welles, died May 20, 1782, aged 85.

Children.

118 Samuel,   born   1727. Settled in Glastenbury. Was married
                                       to Lucy Kilbourn, daughter of Ebe-
                                       nezer Kilbourn, of Glastenbury, Au-
                                       gust, 1752. Deacon Samuel Welles
                                       died December 29, 1800, aged 73.
                                       His widow, Mrs. Lucy Welles, died
                                       March 15, 1812, aged 81. They raised
                                       a large family of children,—among
                                       them Samuel, born October 6, 1754,
                                       and married to Ann Hale, daughter
                                       of Gideon Hale, of Glastenbury, May
                                       2, 1783, and died November 12, 1834,
                                       aged 80, was the father of Gideon
                                       Welles, Esq., of Hartford, and of
                                       Thaddeus Welles, Esq., of Glasten-
                                       bury, (who resides on a farm that
                                       belonged to his first American an-
                                       cestors.)
119 Hannah,   born
120 Bathsheba, born   Died in early life.

87.

THOMAS WELLES, of Wethersfield, Conn., was married to Mary
Chester, daughter of Thomas Chester, of the same town, June 14,
1738.

Capt. Thomas Welles died in 1753.

His widow, Mrs. Mary Welles, died———.

Children.

121 Chester,   born March   22, 1739. Major Chester Welles died April 17,
                                           1815, aged 77.
122 Thomas,   born June   12, 1741.
123 Samuel,   born April   25, 1744.
124 Bille,   born April   26, 1747.

89.

WILLIAM WELLES, of Newington Society, Wethersfield, Conn., was married to Mary Hunn, daughter of Samuel Hunn, of Wethersfield, 1738.

Mrs. Mary Welles died August 19, 1756, in her 44th year.
William Welles, Esq., died December 7, 1783, aged 78.

Children.

125 Mary,	born August	7, 1739.	
126 William,	born January	16, 1741.	
127 Enos,	born November	2, 1742.	Died June 13, 1756.
128 Elijah,	born October	26, 1744.	
129 James,	born February	10, 1748.	
130 Martha,	born October	27, 1749.	
131 Simon,	born June	13, 1754.	

90.

WAIT WELLES, of Wethersfield, Conn., was married to Jerusha Treat, daughter of James Treat, of Wethersfield, January 10, 1734.

Children.

132 Samuel,	born February	4, 1735.	Died November 12, 1757.
133 John,	born August	25, 1736.	
134 Jerusha,	born September	12, 1738.	
135 Oliver,	born June	11, 1740.	Died September, 1741.
136 Oliver,	born October	31, 1742.	
137 Abigail,	born March	7, 1745.	
138 Prudence,	born July	16, 1747.	

92.

ICHABOD WELLES, of Wethersfield, Conn., was married to Abigail Bigelow, daughter of ——— Bigelow, of ———, January 3, 1751.

Mr. Ichabod Welles died in 1758, aged 46. Administration on his estate was granted to Benjamin Welles, of Bolton, March 7, 1758.

His widow, Mrs. Abigail Welles, died September 29, 1810, aged 82.

Children.

139 Abigail,	born October	29, 1751.
140 Mary,	born March	24, 1753.
141 Asa,	born September	16, 1755.

DESCENDANTS IN THE LINE OF ANN WELLES, DAUGHTER OF THOMAS WELLES, THE SETTLER.

SECOND GENERATION.

V.

ANN WELLES was twice married. 1. To Thomas Thompson, of Hartford, Conn., afterwards of Farmington, Conn., April 14, 1646. He died April 25, 1655, aged ——. Mr. Thompson removed from Hartford to Farmington, in 1652. 2. To Anthony Hawkins, of Farmington. She was his second wife. By his first wife he had three children, Mary, born July 16, 1644, Ruth, born 1649, and John, 1651.

Mr. Anthony Hawkins died ———, aged —.
Mrs. Ann Hawkins, alias Thompson, died in 1680.

Children,—by her first husband.

142 Beatrice,	bap. January	17, 1647, at Hartford.	
143 John,	born	1649, at Hartford.	
144 Thomas,	born	1651, at Hartford.	
145 Mary,	bap. June	7, 1653, at Farmington. Married ——— Holly.	
146 Esther,*	bap. June	17, 1655, at Farmington. (Posthumous.) Married ——— Gridley.	

Children,—by her second husband.

147 Sarah,	born	1657.	Died in 1678, unmarried.
148 Elizabeth,	born	1659.	Was married to ——— Brinsmade.
149 Hannah,	born	1661.	

DESCENDANTS IN THE LINE OF SARAH WELLES, DAUGHTER OF THOMAS WELLES, THE SETTLER.

SECOND GENERATION.

VI.

Sarah Welles was married to Capt. John Chester, of Wethersfield, Conn., February, 1653.

The worshipful John Chester, Esq., died February 23, 1698, in the 63d year of his age. He was born in Watertown, Mass., August 3, 1635.

His widow, Mrs. Sarah Chester, died December 16, 1698, aged 67.

Children.

150 Mary,	born December	23, 1654.	
151 John,	born June	10, 1656.	
152 Sarah,	born November,	1657.	
153 Stephen,	born May	26, 1660.	
154 Thomas,	born March	23, 1662.	
155 Samuel,	born May	23, 1664.	Died May 12, 1689, unmarried.
156 Prudence,	born December	10, 1666.	
157 Eunice,	born May	17, 1668.	

---

* I found a deposition, of which the following is a copy, enclosed in the Inventory of Anthony Hawkins.

"The deposition of Samuel Buckingham, of Milford, aged 34 years, saith, I being at my uncle, Mr. Anthony Hawkins, his house in Farmington, in the month called May, in the year 1664, my little cousins, [nieces, and nephews,] being going up and down before us, as my uncle and I sat together, I heard my uncle, Mr. Hawkins, say, concerning my cousin, [niece] Esther Thompson,—this little girl sucked when I married my wife, she being so small, I delighted much in her. Her father died before she was born, and she had no portion given her by him, but I have promised to give her twenty pounds. This above written was taken upon oath before me,
"Milford, August 10, 1674.   Robert Treat."

I notice on the Milford Records, that Samuel Buckingham, son of Thomas Buckingham was married to Sarah Baldwin, daughter of Timothy Baldwin, of Milford, December 14, 1663'

NICHOLAS WORTHINGTON.

NICHOLAS WORTHINGTON was the first, and probably the only Worthington that came early into New England. He settled in Hatfield, Mass., and was twice married. 1. To Sarah White, widow of John White, jun., of Hatfield, and daughter of Thomas Bunce, senior, of Hartford,* Conn., about 1668. She was born ———, and died June 20, 1676, aged —. 2. To Susanna ———, who, after his death, was married to Capt Jonathan Ball, of Springfield, about 1686, by whom she had several children. He died May 21, 1741.

Mr. Nicholas Worthington died September 6, 1683, aged —.

Mrs. Susannah Worthington, alias Ball, died March 9, 1727, aged —.

FIRST GENERATION.

Children of Nicholas Worthington,—by his first wife.

I. William,   born   1670.
II. Elizabeth, born   Married a Morton.
III. Mary,   born January 24, 1673-4. Died in early life.

Children,—by his second wife.

IV. Jonathan, born
V. John,   born August   17, 1679.

DESCENDANTS IN THE LINE OF WILLIAM WORTHINGTON, SON OF NICHOLAS WORTHINGTON, THE SETTLER.

SECOND GENERATION.

I.

WILLIAM WORTHINGTON, of Hartford, Conn., until about the year 1717, and afterwards of Colchester, Conn., was married to Mehitabel Morton, widow of Richard Morton, jun., of Hatfield, Mass. She was daughter of Isaac Graves, of Hatfield, was born October 1, 1671, and was married to Mr. Morton, in 1690. He died in 1691.

---

* By proceedings of the County Court of Hampshire County, Book I., p. 127, Court, March 28, 1670, it appears that at that date, Nicholas Worthington was called of Hartford.

Mrs. Mehitabel Worthington, alias Morton, died at Colchester, March 22, 1742, aged about 70.

William Worthington, Esq., died at Colchester, May 22, 1753, aged 83.

Children.

6 William,	born December	5, 1695, at Hartford.
7 Daniel,	born May	18, 1698, at Hartford.
8 Mary,	born September	23, 1701, at Hartford.
9 Mehitabel,	born July	18, 1706, at Hartford. Supposed to have deceased, unmarried, as no mention is made of her in her father's will.
10 Elijah,	born June	16, 1710, at Hartford.

THIRD GENERATION.

6.

REV. WILLIAM WORTHINGTON, first of Stonington, Conn., afterwards Pastor of the Church in that part of Saybrook, since and now known by the name of Westbrook, was twice married. 1. To Elizabeth Mason, daughter of Capt., afterwards Major Samuel Mason, of Stonington, and of Elizabeth his wife, October 13, 1720. She was born May 6, 1697, and died January 1, 1725, in the 28th year of her age. 2. To Temperance Gallup, daughter of William Gallup, of Stonington, and of Sarah his wife, September 20, 1726. She was born February 1, 1701. Rev. Mr. Worthington was graduated at Yale College, in 1716, and ordained at Saybrook, June 29, 1726.

Rev. William Worthington died November 16, 1756, in the 61st year of his age.

His widow, Mrs. Temperance Worthington, died at Durham, Conn., March, 1778, aged 77.

Children,—by his first wife.

11 Mary,	born August	18, 1721, at Stonington. Was married to Hon. Aaron Eliot, of Killingworth, Conn., son of Rev. Jared Eliot of that town, February 14, 1745. He was grandson of Rev. Joseph Eliot, minister of Killingworth, and great-grandson of the Apostolic John Eliot. He died December 27, 1785, in the 68th year of his age. She died June 28, 1785, in the 64th year of her age. His children were Hannah, born August 31, 1746. Mary, born July 11, 1751. Samuel Smithson, born July 2, 1753. William, born June 26, 1755. Aaron, born August 15, 1757. Joseph, born November 9, 1760. Benjamin and Elizabeth, twins, born December 9, 1762.
12 Sybil,	born November	9, 1723, at Stonington. Died February 23, 1724.

Children,—by his second wife.

13 Elizabeth,	born February	27, 1728, at Saybrook. Was twice married. 1. To Col. Samuel Gale of Saybrook, Conn. He died ———. 2. To Rev.

34

Elnathan Chauncey, of Durham,
Conn., February 6, 1760. Mrs. Elizabeth Chauncey, alias Gale, died
February 9, 1791, aged 63, nearly.
Rev. Elnathan Chauncey died May
4, 1796, aged 71. *Children,—by her
first husband*, Asa Worthington Gale,
born about 1756, died at Cape Francois, August 14, 1772. Benjamin
Gale, born about 1758, was in the
battle of Bunker Hill: he was washed overboard in a storm, from a ship
in which he had taken passage from
the East Indies to New York, in 1796
or 7. *Children,—by her second husband*,—Nathaniel William, born September 12, 1761, and died January
29, 1840. Catharine, born August 6,
1764; married to Reuben Rose Fowler, of Madison, Conn., March 14,
1790, and died in March, 1841,
by whom she had several children,
among them Rev. William C. Fowler,
Professor in Amherst College. Elnathan Elihu, born March 15, 1767,
and died April 8, 1773. Worthington Gallup, born March 22, 1772, and
now living in Durham.

14 Sarah,   born April 3, 1730, at Saybrook. Died June 15, 1732.
15 Temperance,born April 18, 1732, at Saybrook. She was twice married.
1. To Doct. Moses Gale, of Goshen,
Orange county, N. Y. He died
———. 2. To Rev. Cotton Mather
Smith, of Sharon, Conn., minister of
that town, May 31, 1758. The tradition is, that after the death of Doct.
Gale, being on her way from Goshen
to Saybrook, on horseback, to visit
her friends, she was overtaken by a
sudden shower near the boardinghouse of Rev. Mr. Smith, in Sharon,
and sought shelter there from the
storm. The acquaintance thus accidentally formed *ripened* into matrimony. Mrs. Temperance Smith,
alias Gale, died at Albany, N. Y., at
the house of her son-in law, Hon. Jacob Radcliff, one of the Judges of
the Supreme Court of that State, on
her return from Saratoga, June 26,
1800, aged 68. Rev. Cotton Mather
Smith died at Sharon, November 27,
1806, aged 75. *Children,—by her first
husband*,—Temperance, and perhaps
another. *By her second husband,
Rev. Mr. Smith*, she had Elizabeth
Smith, born June 29, 1759, married
Doct. Lemuel Wheeler, of Red-Hook,
N. Y., died January, 1788. Juliana
Smith, born February 12, 1761, married Hon. Jacob Radcliff, of Albany,
N. Y., one of the Judges of the Supreme Court of that State. Thomas
Mather Smith, born January 21, 1763,
died April 18, 1782. John Cotton
Smith, born February 12, 1765, died
December 7, 1845. Lucretia Smith,

born January 20, 1767, died 1773. Mary Smith, born February 16, 1769, married Rev. Daniel Smith, of Stamford, Conn., died January 10, 1801.

16 Sarah, bap. May 19, 1734, at Saybrook. Married Col. John Ely, of Saybrook, July 12, 1759. He died October 3, 1800, in the 63d year of his age. She died ——. *Children,*— Ethelinda, born 1764, married William Eliot. Annie Arnold, bap. July 13, 1766. Lucretia, bap. February 7, 1768. Died February 12, 1769. Lucretia, bap. April 18, 1770. Temperance, bap. October 10, 1772. Edward, bap. January 6, 1777.

17 Mehitabel, born September 11, 1736, at Saybrook. Married Michael Hopkins, of Saybrook, January 16, 1760. Supposed to have removed to Guilford. Capt. Michael Hopkins died ——. She died in 1771, leaving surviving children, Augustus, George, Silvia and Belinda.

18 William, born November 21, 1740, at Saybrook. Married Sabra ——. Some say Elizabeth Lyndes. He died in Hudson, N. Y. They had no children.

7.

DANIEL WORTHINGTON, of Colchester, Conn., was married to Elizabeth Loomis, daughter of Deacon Samuel Loomis, jun., of the same town, January 3, 1721. She was born November 13, 1702.

Mr. Daniel Worthington died March 1, 1784, in the 86th year of his age.

His widow, Mrs. Elizabeth Worthington, died December 3, 1789, in the 87th year of her age.

Children.

19 Elizabeth, born July 24, 1721. Married to Nehemiah Daniels, December 19, 1743.

20 Elias, born October 31, 1722.
21 Asa, born June 16, 1724. Died, unmarried, September 10, 1751.
22 Sibel, born April 19, 1727. Married to Elijah Smith, of South Hadley, Mass., November 8, 1750.

23 Samuel, born February 16, 1729.
24 Rhoda, born September 25, 1730. Married to Thomas Smith, of Hadley, Mass., October 15, 1754. She died in the 102d year of her age.

25 Mehitabel, born February 10, 1732. Died June 27, 1742.
26 Daniel, bap. August 19, 1733.
27 Sarah, born November 27, 1734. Married to Major Josiah Lyman, of Belchertown, Mass., January 9, 1759.

28 Jacob, born February 2, 1736.
29 Tabitha, (or Talitha,) born November 25, 1738. Married to Daniel Skinner, jun., of North-Bolton, Conn., November 9, 1758.

30 Abigail, born March 10, 1740. Married to —— Mather, of Lyme, Conn.
31 Amy, (or Amie,) born April 12, 1741. Married 1. To Noah Sexton, April 8, 1752, and after his death, 2. To a Mr. Walker, of Belchertown, Mass.

32 Mehitabel, born July 1, 1742. Married to Deacon Aaron Skinner, of Shelburne, Mass., April 12, 1764.
33 William, born October 20, 1743. Died March 4, 1744.

34 William, born January 29, 1745.
35 Amasa, born April 16, 1746. Died August 4, 1754.
36 Mary, (or
  Molly, born Married to Orlando Root, of Belchertown, Mass., November 24, 1761.

8.

MARY WORTHINGTON was twice married. 1. To Daniel Jones, of Colchester, Conn., October 13, 1720. He died June 18, 1740, in the 48th year of his age. 2. To Capt. Benjamin Lathrop, of Norwich, Conn., June 15, 1741. She was his second wife. [His first wife, to whom he was married November 13, 1718, was Mary Adgate, daughter of Thomas Adgate, of Norwich. She was born August 27, 1694, and died March 26, 1740.]

Mrs. Mary Lathrop, alias Jones, alias Worthington, died at Norwich, August 4, 1770, in the 69th year of her age.

Capt Benjamin Lathrop died ———.

Children,—by her first husband.

37 Mary, born May 26, 1724. Died June 13, 1729, in the 6th year of her age.

38 Amasa, born October 2, 1726. He was twice married. 1. To Elizabeth Chamberlain, daughter of William Chamberlain, of Colchester, July 12, 1749. She died September 23, 1753, aged —. 2. To Hope Lord, daughter of Epaphrus Lord, of Colchester, August 27, 1754. She was born at Middletown, Conn., November 22, 1726. Mr. Amasa Jones died at Hartford, Conn., February 24, 1785, aged 59. His widow, Mrs. Hope Jones, died at Hartford, December 11, 1798, aged 62.

39 Mary, born June 13, 1729. Died, unmarried.
40 Abigail, born May 1, 1732. Married, name unknown to me.
41 Ann, bap. October 5, 1735. Married Nun Clark, of Lyme, Conn., April 20, 1758.

42 Elizabeth, bap. September 24, 1738. Married Nathaniel Clark, of Colchester, Conn., October 25, 1757, as is said.

10.

ELIJAH WORTHINGTON, of Colchester, Conn., was married to Mary Welles, daughter of ——— Welles, of the same town, October 4, 1733.

Capt. Elijah Worthington died October 13, 1764, in the 55th year of his age.

She died ———

Children.

43 Elijah, born January 1, 1736.
44 Mary, bap. June 24, 1739. Married Capt. John Hopson, of Colchester, April 19, 1759. She died July 29, 1798. They had 5 children.

45 Judith, bap. January 24, 1742. Married John Bulokley, January 11, 1759. They had 13 children.

46 John, born February 17, 1744.
47 Gad, } twin. born June 11, 1747. Married Rebecca Robbins, of Colchester, September 25, 1774.
48 Dan, }

FOURTH GENERATION.

20.

ELIAS WORTHINGTON, of Colchester. Conn., was married to Rhoda Chamberlain, daughter of William Chamberlain, of the same town, September 19, 1744.

Mrs. Rhoda Worthington died ———

Col. Elias Worthington died September 23, 1811, in the 90th year of his age.

Children.

49 Lydia,	born April	15, 1745.	Died June 8, 1758.
50 Elias,	born December	25, 1749.	Married to Anna Morgan, of Colchester, October 24, 1770. He died September 23, 1811. The births of 3 children are on Record.
51 Rhoda,	born November	7, 1751.	Died June 12, 1758.
52 Joel,	born April	21, 1753.	Married to Eunice Newton, January 23, 1777. He died January 29, 1817, in the 64th year of his age. She died August 16, 1846. 4 children.
53 Asa,	born October	11, 1755.	
54 Elizabeth,	born August	14, 1757.	
55 Lydia,	born October	22, 1760.	Married Asa Newton, of Colchester, Conn., had a number of children, among them Rhoda, who married William Matson, of Lyme, Conn., father of Hon. William N. Matson, of Hartford, Conn.
56 Daniel,	born February	9, 1766.	

23.

SAMUEL WORTHINGTON, of Colchester, Conn., was twice married. 1. To Elizabeth Welles, daughter of ——— Welles, of the same town, December 26, 1749. She died ———. 2. To Affa Gilbert, daughter of ——— Gilbert, of ———.
He died ———.
She died ———.

Children—by his first wife.

57 David,	born May	19, 1750.	Died July 29, 1754.
58 Asa,	born June	23, 1752.	Died August 15, 1754.
59 David,	born July	19, 1755.	
60 Temperance,	born November	1, 1756.	

Children,—by his second wife.

61 Erastus,	born
62 Asa,	born
63 Samuel,	born
64 David,	born

28.

JACOB WORTHINGTON, of Colchester, Conn., and Mary Burchard, daughter of John Burchard, of Norwich, in the same state, were married May 29, 1760. She was born December 15, 1732.

Mr. Jacob Worthington died September 25, 1763, in the 28th year of his age.*

Child,—one only.

65 Mabel, (or
   Molly,)†   born July   10, 1761.

34.

WILLIAM WORTHINGTON, of Colchester, Conn., was married to Sarah Welles, daughter of Israel Wyatt Welles, of the same town, July 5, 1770. She was born May 14, 1747.

Mrs. Sarah Welles died at Pittsfield, Mass., August 5, 1822, aged 75.

Mr. William Worthington died at Pittsfield, Mass., January 1, 1825, aged 80 years, nearly.

Children.

66 Israel,	born March	20, 1771.	Died February 9, 1775.
67 Henry,	born May	27, 1773.	Died February 20, 1777.
68 Lydia,	born January	29, 1775.	
69 Sarah,	born December	2, 1776.	
70 Silena,	born September	14, 1779.	
71 Theodosia,	born October	13, 1781.	
72 William,	born July	24, 1784.	
73 Frank,	born November	29, 1787.	
74 Orra,	born June	24, 1790.	

43.

ELIJAH WORTHINGTON, of Colchester, Conn., was married to Anna Lovet, daughter of Rev. Joseph Lovet, a minister of the Episcopal Church, April 29, 1756.

Capt. Elijah Worthington died July 15, 1797, in the 62d year of his age. [Grave-stone.]

His widow, Mrs. Anna Worthington, died March 19, 1814, in the 76th year of her age. [Grave-stone.]

Children.

75 Elizabeth,	born January	15, 1757.	
76 Molly,	born October	16, 1758.	Died November 10, 1758.
77 Erastus,	born May	8, 1761.	
78 Elijah,	born December	6, 1765.	
79 Joseph,	born [no date in records.]		
80 Justin,	born [no date in records.]		
81 Anna,	born January	24, 1775.	
82 Artemas,	born December	11, 1777.	

46.

JOHN WORTHINGTON, of Colchester, Conn., was married to Abigail Wright, daughter of Dudley Wright, of the same town, January 4, 1770.

Mr. John Worthington died, as is said, July 15, 1797.

---

* November 3, 1763, administration on his estate granted to *Phebe* Worthington.

† Probably the latter.

His wife, Mrs. Abigail Worthington, died, as is said, September 28, 1795.

Children.

83 Dudley,	born August	18, 1770.
84 John,	bap. February	12, 1772.
85 Ralph,	born
86 George,	born
87 Elijah,	born		And perhaps others. My account of the family is very imperfect.

47.

GAD WORTHINGTON, of Colchester, Conn., was married to Rebecca Robbins, daughter of ——— Robbins, of the same town, September 25, 1774.

He died ———

She died September 21, 1821, as is said.

Children.

88 Joshua,	born August	20, 1775.
89 William Robbins,	born

48.

DAN WORTHINGTON, of Colchester, Conn., afterwards of Lenox, Mass., was married to Lois Foote, daughter of Charles Foote, of the same town, November 10, 1772.

Dan Worthington, Esq., died at Lenox, Mass., October 24, 1821, aged 74.

His widow, Mrs. Lois Worthington, died at Lenox, February 22, 1840, aged 89.

Children.

90 Molly,	born December	10, 1772.
91 Dan,	born September	22, 1774.
92 Jerusha,	born June	26, 1776.
93 Charles,	born August	27, 1778.
94 Judith,	born June	30, 1780.
95 Betsy,	born April	14, 1782.
96 John,	born May	2, 1784.
97 Gad,	born May	28, 1786.
98 Guy,	born April	5, 1788.
99 Robert,	born September	29, 1791.
100 Laura,	born August	14, 1793.
101 Louisa,	born December	9, 1795.

DESCENDANTS IN THE LINE OF JONATHAN WORTHINGTON, SON OF NICHOLAS WORTHINGTON, THE SETTLER.

SECOND GENERATION.

IV.

JONATHAN WORTHINGTON, of West-Springfield, Mass., was

married to Elizabeth Scott, daughter of John Scott, of the same
town, February 19, 1708.

Mrs. Elizabeth Worthington died September 18, 1743.

Mr. Jonathan Worthington died ———

Children.

102 Elizabeth,	born February	17, 1710.	
103 Margaret,	born February	2, 1712.	
104 Jonathan,	born June	17, 1715.	
105 Nicholas,	born July	26, 1717,	and died February 23, 1720.
106 William,	born January	16, 1720.	
107 Amy,	born November	3, 1725.	Died September 20, 1743.

DESCENDANTS IN THE LINE OF JOHN WORTHINGTON, SON OF NICHOLAS WORTHINGTON, THE SETTLER.

SECOND GENERATION.

V.

JOHN WORTHINGTON, of Springfield, Mass., was married to
Mary Pratt, daughter of John Pratt, Esq., of Saybrook, Conn.,
May 22, 1713.

Lieut. John Worthington died December 30, 1744, in the 66th
year of his age.

His widow, Mrs. Mary Worthington, died October 29, 1759, in
the 72d year of her age.

Children.

108 John,	born October	26, 1714.	Died March 1, 1717,—was scalded.
109 John,	born November	24, 1719.	
110 Timothy,	born July	1, 1722.	Died November 25, 1724.
111 Samuel,	born July	11, 1725.	Died of small pox, December 3, 1760.
112 Mary,	born March	8, 1728.	Died 1731.
113 Sarah,	born about	1731.	Married Rev. John Hooker, Pastor of the Congregational Church, Northampton, Mass., December 10, 1755. He died February 6, 1777, in the 49th year of his age. She died April 5, 1817, in the 86th year of her age.

THIRD GENERATION.

109.

JOHN WORTHINGTON, of Springfield, Mass., was twice married.
1. To Hannah Hopkins, daughter of Rev. Samuel Hopkins, second
Pastor of the First Church in West-Springfield, Mass., January 10,
1759. She died November 25, 1766, in the 36th year of her age.
2. To Mary Stoddard, daughter of Major John Stoddard, of
Northampton, Mass, and grand-daughter of Rev. Solomon Stoddard,
first minister of that town, December 7, 1768.

Hon. John Worthington, LL. D., died April 25, 1800, in the
81st year of his age.

His widow, Mrs. Mary Worthington, died July 12, 1812, in the
80th year of her age.

Children,—by his first wife.

114 Mary,	born March	7, 1760.
115 Hannah,	born June	17, 1761.
116 John,	born August	10, 1762. Died August 30, 1763.
117 John,	born September	2, 1763. Died November 10, 1765.
118 Frances,	born October	29, 1764.
119 Sophia,	born December	5, 1765.

Child,—by his second wife,—one only.

120 John,	born April	22, 1770. Died August 11, 1770.

FIFTH GENERATION.

114.

MARY WORTHINGTON was married to Jonathan Bliss, Esq., of the Province of New Brunswick, N. S., in 1790.

Children.

121 John Wor- thington,	born	Dead.
122 Lewis,	born	
123 William B.,	born	Now Chief Justice Queen's Bench, N. S.
124 Henry,	born	Now a lawyer in London.

115.

HANNAH WORTHINGTON was married to Thomas Dwight, Esq., of Springfield, Mass., in 1791.

"Hon. Thomas Dwight died January 2, 1819, aged 60. Behold, he taketh away, who can hinder him? Who will say unto him, what doest thou?" [Gravestone Springfield burying-ground.]

His widow, Mrs. Hannah Dwight, died July 10, 1833, aged 73.

Children.

125 Mary Stod- dard,	born January	26, 1792. Married John Howard, Esq., December 18, 1818, died July 20, 1836. Had children, Hannah Worthington, born August 12, 1821, and married William H. Swift, Esq., April 18, 1844. Margaret, born May 11, 1823. Frances Ames, born April 20, 1825. Eliza Wetmore, born May 3, 1826.
126 John Wor- thington,	born October	31, 1793. Died February 12, 1836.
127 Elizabeth Buckmin- ster,	born February	18, 1801. Married Charles Howard, June 1, 1824, and had children, Lucinda Orne, born March 8, 1825. Thomas Dwight, born December 25, 1826. Elizabeth Bridge, born December 17, 1828. Sophia Worthington, born January 26, 1831. Catharine Lathrop, born February 24, 1833. Mary Dwight, born October 12, 1835. Sarah Bancroft, born September 13, 1838. Emily Williams, born December 21, 1840. Amelia Peabody, born June 4, 1843, died January 21, 1844. John born June 28, 1845, died August 27, 1845.

35

118.

FRANCES WORTHINGTON was married to Fisher Ames, Esq.,
of Dedham, Mass., July 15, 1792.
Hon. Fisher Ames, LL. D., died July 4, 1808, aged 50.
His widow, Mrs. Frances Ames, died August 8, 1837, in the
73d year of her age.

Children.

128 John Wor- thington,	born October	23, 1793.	Died October 1, 1833.
129 Nathaniel,	born May	17, 1796.	Died January 18, 1835.
130 Hannah,	born March	1, 1799.	Died August 23, 1829.
131 William,	born October	3, 1800.	
132 Jeremiah Fisher,	born	1803.	Died January 3, 1829.
133 Seth,	born April	19, 1805.	
134 Richard,	born June	16, 1807.	

119.

SOPHIA WORTHINGTON was married to John Williams, Esq.,
of Wethersfield, Conn., September 25, 1799.
Mrs. Sophia Williams died May 15, 1813, aged 47.*
John Williams, Esq., died December 19, 1840, aged 78.

Children.

135 John Wor- thington,	born September 28, 1802.	Died October 4, 1802.
136 John Wor- thington,	born November 17, 1803.	
137 Hannah Hopkins,	born February 3, 1805.	Died.
138 Ezekiel Salter,	born November 11, 1806.	

* After her decease, Mr. Williams was married to Mary Silliman, widow of Rev. Ebenezer
Silliman, deceased, of Amsterdam, N. Y., January 1, 1817. She was Mary Dyer, of Windham, Conn., and was married to Rev. Mr. Silliman, May 30, 1815. He died in October, 1815,
aged 31. By his second wife, John Williams, Esq., had children, viz. :

Thomas Scott,	born November	20, 1818.	Died September 17, 1842; drowned.
Esther Sophia,	born May	19, 1820.	Died.
Mary Dyer,	born February	10, 1822.	
Henry Silliman,	born June	24, 1824.	Died August 29, 1825.
Elizabeth Byrne,	born March	10, 1828.	

APPENDIX.

JOHN CASE.

JOHN CASE married, 1. Sarah, daughter of William Spencer, of Hartford, Conn., about 1657. He resided in Windsor, Conn., until the spring of 1669, when he removed to Massacoe, (now Simsbury,) and settled in Weatogue. His first wife died November 3, 1691, aged 55, and he married Elizabeth, widow of Nathaniel Loomis, of Windsor, and daughter (as supposed) of John Moore, of Windsor. Mr. Case was appointed constable for Massacoe, by the General Court, October 14, 1669, being the first person that ever held office at that place. He represented his town at the General Court in 1670, and several times afterwards.

John Case died at Simsbury, February 21, 1703-4.

His widow, Mrs. Elizabeth Case, died at Windsor, July 23, 1728, aged 90.

FIRST GENERATION.

Children of John Case and Sarah his wife.

I. Elizabeth,	born about	1658.
II. Mary,	born June	22, 1660.
III. John,	born November	5, 1662.
IV. William,	born June	5, 1665.
V. Samuel,	born June	1, 1667.
VI. Richard,	born August	27, 1669.
VII. Bartholo-		
mew,	born October,	1670.
VIII. Joseph,	born April	6, 1674.
IX. Sarah,	born August	14, 1676.
X. Abigail,	born May	4, 1682.

DESCENDANTS IN THE LINE OF ELIZABETH CASE, DAUGHTER OF JOHN CASE.

SECOND GENERATION.

I.

ELIZABETH CASE married, 1. Joseph Lewis, of Simsbury, 1674. He died 1680. 2. John Tuller, of the same town, 1684.

Mrs. Elizabeth Tuller died October 9, 1718. "She was well and died in about six hours' time." [Simsbury Records.]

Mr. John Tuller died in 1742.

Children,—by her first husband.

11 Elizabeth,	born March	20, 1675.	Married —— Smith.
12 Joseph,	born March	15, 1676–7.	Settled in Waterbury, Conn.
13 John,	born January	8, 1680–1.	Married Abigail Bacon.

Children,—by her second husband.

14 Sarah,	born August	4, 1685.	Married John Moses, Jr.
15 William,	born June	10, 1687.	Married Damaris Cornish. Died September 22, 1749.
16 Mary,	born November	27, 1692.	Married Samuel Humphrey.
17 Jacob,	born May	22, 1694.	Married Mary Moses.
18 Mahabel,	born February	22, 1699.	Married Samuel Chedester, of Wallingford.

DESCENDANTS IN THE LINE OF MARY CASE, DAUGHTER OF JOHN CASE.

SECOND GENERATION.

II.

MARY CASE was twice married. 1. To William Alderman, of Simsbury, 1679. He died 1697. 2. To James Hillyer, of the same town, March 30, 1699.

Mr. James Hillyer died July 28, 1720, aged 76.

His widow, Mrs. Mary Hillyer, died August 22, 1725.

Children,—by her first husband.

19 Mary,	born September	22, 1680.	
20 Thomas,	born January	11, 1683.	
21 William,	born October	20, 1686.	Married Rebecca Osborn.
22 Sarah,	born	1692.	Married Thomas Moses.
23 John,	born	1695.	Married Sarah Case.
24 Joseph,	born	1697.	Married Mindwell Case.

Child,—by her second husband.

25 Elizabeth,	born		Married Daniel Palmer, of Branford, Conn.

DESCENDANTS IN THE LINE OF JOHN CASE, SON OF JOHN CASE.

SECOND GENERATION.

III.

JOHN CASE, eldest son of John Case, settled in Simsbury, and was twice married. 1. To Mary, daughter of Thomas Olcott, Jr., of Hartford, Conn., September 12, 1684. She died 1685. 2. To Sarah, daughter of Joshua Holcomb, of Simsbury, 1693.

Mr. John Case died May 22, 1733.

His widow, Mrs. Sarah Case, died ———.

Child,—by his first wife.

26 John,	born August	6, 1685.	Died in infancy.

Children,—by his second wife.

27 John,	born August	22, 1694.	
28 Daniel,	born March	7, 1695–6.	
29 Mary,	born about	1698.	Married Josiah Alford. Died about 1732.
30 Jonathan,	born April	15, 1701.	

31 Sarah,	born about	1703.	Married John Alderman.
32 Hannah,	born about	1709.	Married Capt. Noah Humphrey. Died September 23, 1799.

THIRD GENERATION.

27.

JOHN CASE married Abigail, daughter of Lieutenant Samuel Humphrey, January 24, 1716–17. He settled in Simsbury.

Mr. John Case died December 2, 1752.

His widow, Mrs. Abigail Case, died ———.

Children.

33 John,	born Feb'ry 19, 1718–19.		
34 Noah,	born October	4, 1720.	
35 Charles,	born July	1, 1723.	
36 Abigail,	born September 10, 1725.		Married Jonathan Case, Jr. Died August, 28, 1779.
37 Mary,	born December 29, 1727.		
38 Lucy,	born October	17, 1732.	Married William Wilcox.
39 Martha,	born July	31, 1735.	Married Thomas Barber, 4th.
40 Job,	born June	3, 1737.	
41 Lydia,	born September	1, 1741.	Married Jonathan Pinney.

28.

DANIEL CASE married Penelope, daughter of David Buttolph, May 7, 1719; she was born October 1, 1699. They resided in Terry's Plain, in Simsbury.

Sergeant Daniel Case died May 28, 1733.

His widow, Mrs. Penelope Case, died June 27, 1746.

Children.

42 Daniel,	born January	31, 1720.	
43 Mindwell,	born October	24, 1721.	Married Lieut. David Adams. Died February 16, 1813.
44 Dudley,	born November 23, 1723.		
45 Susannah,	born September 20, 1726.		Married Joseph Mills, 2d.
46 Zaccheus,	born	1728.	
47 Ezekiel,	born September 30, 1731.		

30.

JONATHAN CASE married Mary Beman, of Windsor, May 10, 1721. They resided in Simsbury.

Capt. Jonathan Case died ———.

His widow, Mrs. Mary Case, died ———.

Children.

48 Margaret,	born August	3, 1722.	Married Joseph Humphrey.
49 Jonathan,	born November 24, 1723.		
50 Elijah,	born		
51 Martin,	born	1730.	
52 Micah,	born		
53 Abel,	born		Died May 13, 1733.
54 Mary,	born		Married Joshua Marvin, of Sharon, July 4, 1758.
55 Abel,	born October	19, 1737.	
56 William,	born		
57 Sarah,	born	1746.	Married Elisha Tuller.

FOURTH GENERATION.

33.

JOHN CASE married Sarah, daughter of Samuel Barber, November 7, 1745. She was born April 1, 1722. They resided in Simsbury.

Capt. John Case died May 24, 1776.

His widow, Mrs. Sarah Case, died December, 19, 1805.

Children.

58 John,	born October	10, 1746.	Married Chloe Owen. Died November 16, 1776.
59 Giles,	born Febr'ary 20,	1747–8.	Died February 15, 1754.
60 Seth,	born September 29,	1749.	Married Eunice Tuller. Died 1820.
61 Sarah,	born July	27, 1751.	Married Dea. Elisha Cornish, Jr. Died August 20, 1827.
62 Asa,	born January	11, 1753.	Married Sarah Robe. Died March 21, 1830.
63 Mary,	born January	2, 1755.	Married 1. Silas Case. 2. Capt. Uriah Case. Died October 15, 1833.
64 Giles,	born May	24, 1757.	Married Dorcas Humphrey.
65 George,	born March	4, 1759.	Married Electa Moore.
66 Levi,	} twins. born December	14, 1760.	Married Polly Humphrey. Died April 23, 1802.
67 Judah,	}		Married Ruth Higley. Died 1821.
68 Abigail,	born November	8, 1763.	Married Asa Hoskins. Died March 25, 1844.

34.

NOAH CASE married Myriam Holcomb, May 5, 1740. She was born January 18, 1719–20. They resided in the extreme southwest part of what is now Granby.

Noah Case died December 17, 1797.

Mrs. Myriam Case died April 28, 1795.

Children.

69 Noah,	born January 10,	1740–1.	Married Mary Adams. Died September 1, 1807.
70 Amy,	born November	1, 1744.	Married Titus Reed.
71 Myriam,	born September	7, 1746.	Died August 23, 1750.
72 Roger,	born August	7, 1748.	
73 Abner,	born August	14, 1752.	Married Hannah Case. Died October 6, 1807.
74 Ruth,	born June	10, 1754.	
75 Darius,	born March	7, 1756.	Married Mary Giddings. Died December 19, 1801.
76 Lydia,	born		Married James Case.

35.

CHARLES CASE married Phebe ———. They dwelt in Simsbury.

Capt. Charles Case died October 17, 1808.

Children.

77 Charles,	born August	15, 1748.	Died October 1, 1750.
78 Phebe,	born October	24, 1751.	Married 1. ——— Griswold. 2. John G. Terry.
79 Charles,	born July	19, 1754.	

80 Chloe,   born July   19, 1756.
81 Shubael,   born February   25, 1759.   Died February 1, 1761.
82 Shubael,   born July   20, 1763.
83 Rosbick,   born January   19, 1769.

40.

Job Case married Joanna, daughter of Amos Wilcox. She was born in 1740. They lived in Terry's Plain, in Simsbury. Capt. Job Case died October 6, 1798. His widow, Mrs. Joanna Case, died December 17, 1812.

Children.

84 Job,   born July   27, 1758.
85 Joanna,   born August   9, 1760.   Married Israel Case.
86 Violet,   born October   19, 1762.
87 Ariel,   born June   28, 1765.   Married 1. Rachel ———. 2. Celia
                                            ———. Died September 17, 1827.
88 Lucy,   born February   14, 1767.
89 Asenath,   born June   12, 1770.
90 Luke,   born July   1, 1772.   Settled in Winsted, Conn.
91 Betsey,   born December   23, 1775.
92 Frederick,   born May   5, 1777.
93 Grove,   born June   29, 1779.
94 Friend,   born November   10, 1781.   Married Sarah ———. Died June 22,
                                            1840.

42.

Daniel Case married Mary Watson, of New Hartford, Conn., February 22, 1750. She was born in 1725. They removed from Terry's Plains to West Simsbury, (now Canton,) in 1743. Sergeant Daniel Case died May 24, 1801. His widow, Mrs. Mary Case, died May 25, 1807.

Children.

95 Daniel,   born April   19, 1752.   Married Elizabeth Humphrey. Died
                                            February 29, 1799.
96 Moses,   born March   27, 1754.   Married Eunice Case. Died 1782.
97 Mary,   born February   25, 1756.   Married John Garritt. Died 1832.
98 Abigail,   born January   8, 1758.   Married William Taylor. Died 1830.
99 Lois,   born September 15, 1760.   Died young.
100 Keturah,   born December   11, 1762.   Married James Humphrey, Esq. Died
                                            September, 1824.
101 Penelope,   born December   11, 1764.   Died June 17, 1781.
102 Ameri W.,   born October   23, 1767.   Married Betsey Harris. Died 1852.
103 Elam,   born May   10, 1772.   Married Phebe Case. Died July 8,
                                            1848.

44.

Dudley Case married Dorcas, daughter of Charles Humphrey, April 14, 1743. She was born in 1726. They removed from Terry's Plain to West Simsbury, in 1742. Lieut. Dudley Case died in 1792. His widow, Mrs. Dorcas Case, died June 17, 1805.

Children.

104 Dudley,   born October   28, 1744.   Married Susannah ———. Died No-
                                            vember 16, 1822.
105 Elisha,   born October   10, 1747.   Died in infancy.

106 Ozias,	born June	7, 1749.	Died in infancy.
107 Elias,	born March	5, 1753.	Died in infancy.
108 Elisha,	born April	30, 1755.	
109 Ozias,	born July	24, 1757.	Married —— Hills. Burnt to death.
110 Elias,	born April	15, 1759.	Married Lucretia Foote. Died March 20, 1809.
111 Dan,	born March	5, 1761.	Married 1. Rachel Foote. 2. Allice Hallock. Died 1815.
112 Dorcas,	born August	14, 1764.	Married 1. Benjamin Mills. 2. Noadiah Woodruff. Died 1849.
113 Truman,	born January	22, 1767.	Died 1836.
114 Emanuel,	born March	25, 1769.	Died 1782.

46.

ZACCHEUS CASE married Abigail, daughter of Thomas Barber. She was born February 10, 1730–31. They removed from Terry's Plain to West Simsbury, about 1749; resided there till 1792, and then removed to Whitestown, N. Y.

Capt. Zaccheus Case died in 1812.

Mrs. Abigail Case died in 1798.

Children.

115 Caleb,	born	1754.	Married 1. Sarah Case. 2. Rhoda Merrill.
116 Zaccheus,	born	1757.	
117 Abigail,	born	1759.	Married Charles Wilcox.
118 Mercy,	born	1761.	Married Col. William Wilcox. Died September 19, 1809.
119 Sarah,	born	1764.	Married 1. Jed. Wilcox. 2. Frederick Humphrey. 3. Wait Munson. Died 1830.
120 Thede,	born	1766.	Married 1. Benajah Humphrey. 2. Asa Case. Died April 15, 1851.
121 Rhoda,	born	1768.	Married Caina Mills. Died 1798.
122 Ruth,	born	1770.	Married Daniel Albertson. Died 1809.

47.

EZEKIEL CASE married Lucy, daughter of Capt. James Cornish, August 2, 1763; about which time he removed from Terry's Plain, to West Simsbury, and settled near the present site of Collinsville.

Children.

123 Lucy,	born February	17, 1755.
124 Ezekiel,	born April	15, 1756.
125 Violet,	born April	15, 1758.
126 Frederick,	born September	22, 1761.
127 Abigail,	born November	15, 1763.
128 Rachel,	born July	25, 1766.
129 Benoni,	born December	11, 1769.

50.

ELIJAH CASE, of Simsbury, married Hannah, daughter of Azariah Wilson, about 1750.

Mr. Elijah Case died ———.

Mrs. Hannah Case died ———.

Children.

130 Hannah,	born March	14, 1752.	Married Abner Case.
131 Reuben,	born September	5, 1755.	Married a daughter of Jonathan Pinney.
132 Deziah,	born February	9, 1757.	
133 Elijah,	born October	22, 1758.	
134 Gabriel,	born		
135 Asaph,	born		
136 Rosette,	born		

51.

MARTIN CASE, of Simsbury, married Lucy Adams, about 1756.
Mr. Martin Case died April 18, 1827.
Mrs. Lucy Case died January 6, 1801.

Children.

137 Martin,	born March	27, 1758.	Drowned June 2, 1774.
138 Roswell,	born January	20, 1760.	Married —— Adams. Died August 24, 1835.
139 Mary,	born April	8, 1763.	
140 Sybil,	born June	5, 1765.	
141 Lucy,	born October	20, 1766.	
142 Cleora,	born October	19, 1769.	

52.

MICAH CASE, of Simsbury, married Rhoda, daughter of William Wilson, November 7, 1751.
Mr. Micah Case died October 16, 1774.
Mrs. Rhoda Case died ——.

Children.

143 Rhoda,	born June	1, 1753.
144 Micah,	born July	10, 1756.
145 Rufus,	born January	8, 1761.
146 Lydia,	born May	10, 1763.
147 Daniel W.,	born January	8, 1769.
148 Seba,	born August	16, 1772.

FIFTH GENERATION.

108.

ELISHA CASE, of West Simsbury, married Delight, daughter of Samuel Griswold. She was born June 10, 1757.
Deacon Elisha Case died September 16, 1839.
His widow, Mrs. Delight Case, died April 28, 1842.

Children.

149 Almira,	born December 25, 1777.	Married David Wilmer. Died May 21, 1808.
150 Sally,	born September 23, 1779.	Married Thaddeus Mills. Died March 21, 1846.
151 Elisha,	born August 12, 1781.	Married Abiah Barber. Died July 21, 1824.
152 Delight G.,	born October 15, 1783.	Married John Barber, Jr. Died April 13, 1811.
153 Allen,	born August 2, 1785.	Married 1. Sally Higley. 2. Catharine Squires. Died March 25, 1849.
154 Juliana,	born August 7, 1787.	Died April 15, 1802.
155 Erastus,	born November 29, 1789.	Married Mary Pettibone. Resides in Auburn, N. Y.

156 Electa,	born December	1, 1791.	Married Reuben Hills.
157 Harvey,	born December	23, 1793.	Married Amelia Humphrey. Died March 21, 1853.
158 Fanny,	born January	16, 1796.	Died May 19, 1796.
159 John,	born June	10, 1797.	Married Susan Frisbie. Died August 24, 1854.
160 Emily,	born September	14, 1799.	Married Lemuel Whitman.
161 Fanny,	born August	6, 1802.	Married 1. Tracy Humphrey. 2. —— Hurlbut.
162 Edmund,	born January	14, 1806.	Married 1. Nancy C. Hinman. 2. Harriet R. King. Died Septemb'r 30, 1846.

DESCENDANTS IN THE LINE OF WILLIAM CASE, SECOND SON OF JOHN CASE.

SECOND GENERATION.

IV.

WILLIAM CASE married Elizabeth, daughter of Joshua Holcomb, in 1688. She was born April 4, 1670. [After the death of Mr. Case she was twice married. 1. To Deacon John Slater, of Simsbury, March 10, 1704. Deacon Slater died March 2, 1717. 2. To Deacon Thomas Marshall, of Windsor. Deacon Marshall died December 2, 1728.] They resided in Terry's Plain, in Simsbury.

Mr. William Case died March 31, 1700.

His widow, Mrs. Elizabeth Marshall, alias Slater, alias Case, died February 26, 1762.

Children.

163 Elizabeth,	born September,	1689.	
164 William,	born March	22, 1691.	Married a daughter of Andrew Robe. Died June 14, 1768.
165 James,	born March	12, 1693.	
166 Rachel,	born December	10, 1694.	Married Benjamin Adams.
167 Mary,	born August	23, 1696.	Married Joseph Adams.
168 Joshua,	born June	1, 1698.	
169 Mindwell,	born March	21, 1700.	Married Joseph Alderman.

THIRD GENERATION.

165.

JAMES CASE married Esther Fithin, of Newark, N. J., in 1715. She was born in 1701. He resided at his paternal homestead, in Terry's Plain.

Capt. James Case died September 26, 1759.

His widow, Mrs. Esther Case, died September 19, 1769.

Children.

170 James,	born March	5, 1716.	Died August 2, 1734.
171 Josiah,	born April	1, 1718.	
172 Esther,	born March	14, 1720.	
173 Rachel,	born August	14, 1722.	Married Deacon Abraham Case. Died about 1789.
174 Jeremiah,	born July	31, 1726.	Married Judith Humphrey.
175 Phebe,	born May	16, 1729.	Married Isaac Tuller. Died November 6, 1799.
176 Amasa,	born October,	18, 1731.	Married five wives. Died August 18, 1824.
177 Ruth,	born		Married Francis Garritt.

168.

JOSHUA CASE, of Simsbury, married Amie ———.
Mr. Joshua Case died February 15, 1764.
Mrs. Amie Case died ———.

Children.

178 Joshua,	born		
179 Naomi,	born May	12, 1725.	Married Noadiah Phelps.

FOURTH GENERATION.

171.

JOSIAH CASE married Esther, daughter of Brewster Higley, about 1740. She was born December 3, 1719. They removed from Terry's Plain, to West Simsbury, about 1743.
Capt. Josiah Case died November 21, 1789.
His widow, Mrs. Esther Case, died September 15, 1807.

Children.

180 Lois,	born	1741.	Died March 21, 1759.
181 James,	born April	2, 1744.	Married 1. Phebe Tuller. 2. Lydia Case. Died January 7, 1822.
182 Esther,	born May	16, 1745.	Married 1. Thomas Case, and two others after his death. Died 1791.
183 Anna,	born June	23, 1749.	Married Amos Wilcox. Died September 5, 1733.
184 Betty,	born April	20, 1752.	Married John Barber. Died May 26, 1817.
185 Fithin,	born September 17, 1758.		

174.

JEREMIAH CASE married Judith, daughter of Charles Humphrey, August 14, 1746. They resided in West Simsbury a few years, then removed to Onondaga, N. Y.
Mr. Jeremiah Case died ———.
Mrs. Judith Case died June 5, 1808.

Children.

186 Jeremiah,	born March	18, 1747.	Married —— Phelps.
187 Judith,	born May	13, 1749.	Married Capt. Elisha Case. Died September 1, 1805.
188 William,	born May	23, 1751.	Married Sarah Hickox.

176.

AMASA CASE married five wives. 1. Elizabeth, daughter of Robert Hoskins, in 1752; she died May 27, 1764. 2. Widow —— Viets, about 1766; she died about 1785. 3. Widow Abigail Griswold, daughter of David Phelps; she died October 4, 1798. 4. Widow Charity Cornish, daughter of John Pettibone, 3d; she died October 5, 1803, aged 53. 5. Widow Sarah Graham, daughter of Benajah Humphrey; she was his fifth wife, and he was her fourth husband. They resided in Terry's Plain, in Simsbury.
Deacon Amasa Case died August 18, 1824.
Mrs. Sarah Case died ———.

Children,—by his first wife.

189 Amasa,	born October	29, 1753.	
190 Aaron,	born June	16, 1755.	Married —— Meacham. Died March 24, 1811.
191 Elizabeth,	born August	15, 1756.	Died December 21, 1822.
192 Stephen,	born October	6, 1758.	
193 Mary,	born January	2, 1760.	
194 Mehitabel,	born March	8, 1762.	

Children,—by his second wife.

195 Apollos,	born August	1, 1768.	Married Polly Frazier. Died June 15, 1827.
196 Ruth,	born September	30, 1770.	
197 Julius,	born February	20, 1773.	Died May 17, 1773.
198 Enoch,	born May	10, 1774.	Died July 27, 1797.
199 Salome,	born December	6, 1777.	
200 Chloe,	born August	1, 1781.	

178.

JOSHUA CASE married Lydia Griswold, (or Palmer,) of Windsor, October 10, 1748. Resided in that part of Simsbury which now belongs to Bloomfield.

Mr. Joshua Case died about 1777.

Mrs. Lydia Case died ————.

Children.

201 Oliver,	born May	13, 1749.	
202 Elisha,	born September	29, 1750.	
203 George,	born February	1, 1752.	
204 Mary,	born January	12, 1755.	
205 Alexander,	born November	9, 1756.	Died May 12, 1763.
206 Rhoda,	born October	21, 1758.	
207 Lydia,	born October	27, 1761.	
208 Sabra,	born August	24, 1763.	
209 Rosittee,	born August	16, 1764.	
210 Medad,	born May	2, 1766.	
211 Alexander,	born February	18, 1768.	

FIFTH GENERATION.

185.

FITHIN CASE married Amrilla Humphrey, September 20, 1780; she was born in 1764. They resided on the paternal homestead on Chestnut Hill, West Simsbury, (now Canton.)

Capt. Fithin Case died August 25, 1829.

His widow, Mrs. Amrilla Case, died May 31, 1845.

Children.

212 Maria,	born May	28, 1781.	Married Moses Case, Jr.
213 Fithin,	born July	22, 1784.	Married Statira Phelps. Died 1853.
214 Mamre,	born March	23, 1786.	Married Abia Tuller.
215 Amrilla,	born February	12, 1788.	Married Chauncey Eno.
216 Josiah W.,	born February	12, 1790.	Married Agnes, daughter of Levi Case. Died June 26, 1830.
217 Salma,	born August	25, 1792.	Died August 4, 1794.
218 Charity,	born November	15, 1794.	Married Col. Salmon Merrill.
219 Jasper,	born December	15, 1796.	Married Flora Humphrey.
220 Melissa,	born February	18, 1799.	Married Ithuel Gridley; she was his second wife.

221 Jarvis,
    [Gen.]   born September 10, 1801.   Married Lucia Adams.
222 Julia,   born March   1, 1805.   Married Ithuel Gridley.   Died October
                                    24, 1845.

189.

AMASA CASE married Mercy Hillyer; she was born in 1763. They resided in Westover's Plain, in Simsbury.
Mr. Amasa Case died June 23, 1834.
Mrs. Mercy Case died September 3, 1809.

Children.

223 Amasa,	born February	17, 1780.	Died June 8, 1847.
224 Philetus,	born February	2, 1782.	Married Lucinda Reed.
225 Stephen,	born January	17, 1784.	
226 Mercy,	born July	13, 1785.	Married Peter Mason.
227 Charlotte,	born September	28, 1787.	Married Dr. Timothy Phelps.
228 Julius,	born May	22, 1790.	Married Mary Phelps.
229 Nathaniel,	born		Married Anna Maria Case.
230 Salome,	born		Married Alpheus Chafee.
231 Buckland,	born	1800.	Married Sally Holcomb. Died May 8, 1845.

232 Chauncey, born

DESCENDANTS IN THE LINE OF SAMUEL CASE, THIRD SON OF JOHN CASE.

SECOND GENERATION.

V.

SAMUEL CASE married 1. Mary, daughter of Jonah Westover, sen., of Simsbury; she died September 27, 1713. 2. Elizabeth, widow of Samuel Thrall, of Windsor, and daughter of Josiah Owen, of Windsor, November 8, 1721. They resided a few years at Weatogue, then removed to that part of Simsbury now included in Bloomfield.
Mr. Samuel Case died July 30, 1725.
Mrs. Elizabeth Case died ———.

Children.

233 Samuel,	born January	24, 1696.	
234 Mary,	born November	15, 1697.	Married John Drake, April 20, 1721.
235 Hannah,	born January	30, 1699.	Married Benjamin Holcomb, October 4, 1727.
236 Mercy,	born January	12, 1700.	Married Thomas Barber, January 16, 1726.
237 Abigail,	born February	4, 1701.	Died in infancy.
238 Nathaniel,	born April	26, 1703.	
239 Eunice,	born July,	1704.	Married Jeremiah Stratton, December 12, 1728.
240 Jonah,	born August,	1705.	
241 Caleb,	born about	1707.	
242 Azrikrim,	born February	16, 1709.	Resided in Newark, N. J., in 1739.
243 Benjamin,	born	1710.	
244 Pelatiah,	born		Died in 1733.
245 Irenia,	born January	12, 1724.	Married Samuel Buell, Jr., May 28, 1740.

THIRD GENERATION.

233.

SAMUEL CASE married Eunice, daughter of John Burr, of Farmington, July 5, 1728; she was born in 1704. They lived near the paternal homestead.

Deacon Samuel Case died September 23, 1768.

His widow, Mrs. Eunice Case, died August 31, 1775.

Children.

246 Eunice,	born July	17, 1731.
247 Sarah,	born August	25, 1733.
248 Samuel,	born August	11, 1736.

238.

NATHANIEL CASE married Myriam, daughter of John Burr.

Mr. Nathaniel Case, died June 8, 1753.

Mrs. Myriam Case died September 24, 1752.

Children.

249 Silas,	born March	11, 1731-2.	Died May 9, 1732.
250 Myriam,	born June	23, 1733.	
251 Nathaniel,	born Feb'ary	11, 1737-8.	
252 Silas,	born August	1, 1740.	

240.

JONAH CASE married ——— Phelps. Removed to Goshen, Conn., in 1745.

Children,—born in Simsbury.

253 Jonah,	born	
254 Martha,	born August	8, 1736.

241.

CALEB CASE married ——— ———. Died ———. His will was exhibited in Court, September 2, 1746.

Children.

255 Samuel,	born	Died May 2, 1739.
256 Benjamin,	born	Married Hannah Drake.

FOURTH GENERATION.

248.

SAMUEL CASE married Violet Burr, April 7, 1757.

Mr. Samuel Case died August 27, 1775.

Mrs. Violet Case died ———.

Children.

257 Violet,	born January	29, 1759.
258 Eunice,	born January	12, 1763.
259 Lois,	born January	28, 1767.
260 Pelittiah,	born August	28, 1768.
261 Samuel,	born September	21, 1770.
262 Rosittee,	born June	8, 1773.

256.

BENJAMIN CASE, of Simsbury, married Hannah Drake, November 9, 1743.

Mr. Benjamin Case died ———.

Mrs. Hannah Case died July 9, 1760.

Children.

263 Zenas, born November 30, 1740.
264 Benjamin, born

FIFTH GENERATION.

263.

ZENAS CASE, of Simsbury, married Mary Loomis, March 2, 1769.

Mr. Zenas Case died ———.

Mrs. Mary Case died ———.

Children.

265 William M., born September 22, 1769.
266 Zenas, born September 21, 1771.
267 Shadrich, born October 26, 1773.
268 Polly, born July 22, 1776. Died October 15, 1778.
269 Nathaniel, born September 28, 1778.
270 Polly, born March 31, 1781.
271 Elizabeth, born July 2, 1787.
272 Timothy, born February 9, 1789.

DESCENDANTS IN THE LINE OF RICHARD CASE, FOURTH SON OF JOHN CASE.

SECOND GENERATION.

VI.

RICHARD CASE married Amy, daughter of Dr. Philip Reed, of Concord, Mass., September 1, 1701. Resided in Weatogue, in Simsbury.

Capt. Richard Case died about 1746.

Mrs. Amy Case died ———.

Children.

273 Amy, born about 1702. Died February 22, 1703.
274 Amy, born about 1703. Married Jonathan Holcomb, Jr. Died after 1740.
275 Richard, born 1710.
276 Timothy, born about 1711.
277 Margaret, born about 1713. Married Jacob Holcomb. Died after 1740.
278 Edward, born March 5, 1715. Died June 1, 1746.
279 Lydia, born March 15, 1718. Died after 1740.
280 Mary, born January 30, 1722. Died after 1740.

THIRD GENERATION.

275.

RICHARD CASE married Mercy Holcomb, May 4, 1733. They

removed from Weatogue to Chestnut Hill, in West Simsbury, (now Canton,) in 1737, and were the first settlers there.

Mr. Richard Case died April 12, 1769.

His widow, Mrs. Mercy Case, died June 20, 1780, aged 68.

Children.

281 Richard,	born June	7, 1734.	Married 1. Ruth Case. 2. Mary Case. Died April 7, 1805.
282 Joab,	born December	16, 1735.	Died in 1738.
283 Sylvanus,	born July	31, 1737.	Married 1. Caroline Humphrey. 2. Hepzibah Humphrey. Died April 5, 1817.
284 Simeon,	born July	4, 1739.	Married Mary Case. Died October 19, 1823.
285 Eli,	born May	2, 1741.	
286 Uriah,	born January	16, 1744.	
287 Edward,	born April	15, 1748.	
288 Phineas,	born March	8, 1750.	Married Sarah, daughter of Elijah Tuller. Died July 19, 1798.
289 Mercy,	born June	2, 1752.	Married Abraham Moses. Died May 22, 1818.
290 Naomi,	born October	30, 1755.	Married David Pettibone. Died 1822.
291 Timothy,	born February	2, 1759.	Married Esther Brown. Died November 14, 1750.

276.

Timothy Case married Sarah, daughter of Nathaniel Holcomb, about 1730. Resided in Simsbury about ten years, then removed to Berkshire County, Mass.

Children,—born in Simsbury.

292 Philip,	born Feb'ary 12, 1731-2.
293 Sarah,	born October 18, 1734.
294 Timothy,	born December 5, 1736.
295 Martha,	born May 25, 1739.

FOURTH GENERATION.

285.

Eli Case married Athildred, daughter of Peter Curtiss; she was born in 1745. They resided upon Chestnut Hill, in West Simsbury.

Mr. Eli Case died March 26, 1804.

His widow, Mrs. Athildred Case, died March 13, 1805.

Children.

296 Athildred,	born January	16, 1766.	Married Ephraim B. Case. Died September, 1804.
297 Eli,	born January	16, 1768.	Married Hannah Alford. Died November 12, 1795.
298 Riverious,	born March	20, 1770.	Married Abigail Case. Died October 22, 1822.
299 Zabad,	born April	4, 1772.	Married Sarah Merrett. Died October 21, 1836.
300 Giles,	born August	23, 1776.	
301 Orange,	born January	15, 1779.	Married Sarah Jones. Died March 17, 1814.
302 Thede,	born February	11, 1781.	Married Ozias Woodford.
303 Calvin,	born		Married 1. Dianthe Humphrey. 2. Sarah Case.

| 304 Chestnia, | born | | 1785. | Married David Ackert. Died April 25, 1826. |
| 305 Harriet, | born | | 1788. | Married Truman Allen. Died April 5, 1845. |

286.

URIAH CASE married 1. Susannah, daughter of Lieut. Samuel Lawrence, March 21, 1765; she was born in 1741, and died January 17, 1776. 2. Eunice, daughter of Solomon Dill, about 1777; she was born December 6, 1753, and died May 18, 1815. 3. Mary, widow of Silas Case, and daughter of Capt. John Case, 4th, December 27, 1815; she was born January 2, 1755. They resided near the paternal homestead upon Chestnut Hill, in West Simsbury.

Capt. Uriah Case died December 23, 1826.

His widow, Mrs. Mary Case, died October 15, 1833.

Children,—by his first wife.

306 Zilpah,	born March	17, 1766.	Married Isaiah Taylor.
307 Sylvia,	born June	13, 1768.	Married 1. Amos Tuller. 2. David Sutleff.
308 Uriah,	born July	2, 1771.	Married Sarah Nobles.
309 Susannah,	born	1774.	Married Jared Mills, Jr. Died May 21, 1808.

Children,—by his second wife.

310 Joab,	born January	31, 1779.	Married Sarah Case. Died January 18, 1818.
311 Eunice,	born March	19, 1780.	Married Roswell Reed.
312 Watson,	born June	8, 1781.	Married Sylvia Case. Died August, 1853.
313 Elizabeth,	born August	3, 1783.	Died May 24, 1808.
314 Holcomb,	born December	27, 1784.	
315 Lorenda,	born October	1, 1786.	Died May 23, 1808.
316 Clara, } twins.	born May	9, 1788.	
317 Laura, }			Married Charles Humphrey. Died July 11, 1842.
318 Lydia,	born September	1, 1791.	Died October 27, 1822.
319 Cynthia,	born May	9, 1793.	Married Ruggles Case.
320 Lucinda,	born September	19, 1796.	Married Francis H. Case.

Children by his third wife,—none.

287.

EDWARD CASE married Zeruah, daughter of Lieut. Samuel Lawrence, about 1774; she was born May 20, 1754. They resided at the eastern extremity of Chestnut Hill.

Mr. Edward Case died December 2, 1822.

His widow, Mrs. Zeruah Case, died February 24, 1832.

Children.

321 Edward,	born about	1775.	Died about 1780.
322 Zurah R.,	born August	25, 1777.	Married 1. Thomas Hayes. 2. Levi Lattimer. Died May 5, 1847.
323 Chloe,	born February	2, 1780.	Married Solomon Case, Jr. Died March 22, 1847.
324 Edward,	born April	11, 1782.	Married Rhoda, daughter of Asa Case.
325 Sarah,	born July	16, 1784.	Died quite young.

37

326 Bigelow,   born October   20, 1786. Died April 22, 1809.
327 Anna,   born November 11, 1788. Married Watson Garrett. Died June
                                                  1, 1832.

FIFTH GENERATION.

300.

GILES CASE married Polly, daughter of Silas Case, in 1799 ;
she was born January 12, 1781. They resided upon Chestnut
Hill, now in Canton.

Mr. Giles Case died May 22, 1852.

Mrs. Polly Case died May 9, 1850.

Children.

328 Betsey,   born January   22, 1800. Died October, 1805.
329 Mary,   born April   20, 1802. Married John Curtiss.
330 Achsah,   born April   15, 1804. Died March 12, 1823.
331 Eli,   born January   25, 1806. Married Rosanna Bandle.
332 Betsey,   born August,   1806.
333 Electa,   born November,   1810. Married Norton Case.
334 Pliny,   born January   20, 1813. Married Susan Terry.
335 Amos,   born September,   1816. Married Nancy Alderman.
336 Eveline, born February 29, 1820. Married Amos Hosford.

314.

HOLCOMB CASE married Jane, daughter of Silas Case, November 27, 1811 ; she was born January 12, 1792. They resided
upon Chestnut Hill.

Mr. Holcomb Case died April 26, 1854.

Children.

337 John,   born August   20, 1813. Married Tirzah Hosford.
338 Lorenda, born April   3, 1816. Married Harvey Barber.
339 Zilpah,   born April   14, 1819. Married Nelson L. Barber.
340 Jane,   born April   3, 1822. Married Cyrus W. Harvey.
341 Sylvia,   born August   9, 1825. Married Irving Case.
342 Uriah,   born March   17, 1828. Married Adeline M. Johnson.
343 Susannah, born August   28, 1834. Died December 8, 1839.

DESCENDANTS IN THE LINE OF BARTHOLOMEW CASE, FIFTH SON OF JOHN CASE.

SECOND GENERATION.

VII.

BARTHOLOMEW CASE married Mary, daughter of Lieut. Samuel Humphrey, December 7, 1699; she was born November 16,
1681. They resided on the paternal homestead in Weatogue, in
Simsbury.

Mr. Bartholomew Case died October 25, 1725.

Mrs. Mary Case died ———.

Children.

344 Mary,   born   1701. Died April 23, 1701.
345 Thomas,   born June   28, 1702.
346 Mary,   born November 8, 1704.
347 Elizabeth, born before   1710. Died July 12, 1742.

348 Amos,	born in	1712.	
349 Sarah,	born in	1715.	Married Joseph Higley.
350 Isaac,	born October	23, 1717.	Married Bathsheba Humphrey. Died January 3, 1796.
351 Abraham,	born August	20, 1720.	
352 Abigail,	born in	1721.	

THIRD GENERATION.

345.

THOMAS CASE married Elizabeth Woodford, October 4, 1727.
Resided on the paternal homstead, Weatogue.
Deacon Thomas Case died September 3, 1770.
Mrs. Elizabeth Case died ———.

Children.

353 Thomas,	born October	4, 1728.	Died February 20, 1736-7.
354 Elizabeth,	born October	1, 1730.	Married Abel Pettibone.
355 Mary,	born August	5, 1732.	Married 1. Dea. Hosea Case. 2. Richard Case. Died July 29, 1817.
356 Roger,	born August	3, 1734.	
357 Lydia,	born March	7, 1735-6.	Married Solomon Buell.
358 Thomas,	born January	21, 1740.	Married Esther Case. Died March 27, 1773.
359 Bartholo-mew,	born June	20, 1746.	Married 1. Ruth Owen. 2. Mary Humphrey. Died January 16, 1808.
360 Eunice,	born February	29, 1747-8.	Married Elias Vining. Died January 8, 1832.
361 Susannah,	born June	16, 1750.	
362 Sarah,	born		Married Haskell Bacon.

348.

AMOS CASE married Mary Holcomb, August 15, 1739. Removed to Chestnut Hill, (West Simsbury,) about 1740.
Mr. Amos Case died May 24, 1798.
His widow, Mrs. Mary Case, died January 27, 1802.

Children.

363 Mary,	born March	6, 1740.	Married Simeon Case. Died 1834.
364 Ruth,	born April	26, 1742.	Married Richard Case. Died February 29, 1794.
365 Huldah,	born March	18, 1744.	Died September 5, 1774.
366 Amos,	born February	8, 1746.	Married Betsey Ward. Died March 29, 1798.
367 Abel,	born January	13, 1748.	
368 Silas,	born December	29, 1749.	
369 Lucy,	born February	22, 1752.	Married 1. Ruggles Humphrey. 2. Solomon Buell. Died May 10, 1837.
370 Pliny,	born November	2, 1754.	Married Rhoda Merrill. Died January 25, 1780.
371 Rhoda,	born April	20, 1757.	Married Hosea Case, Jr. Died June 12, 1786.
372 Seth,	born June	3, 1760.	Died September 3, 1776.

350.

ISAAC CASE, of Simsbury, married Bathsheba Humphrey,
March 19, 1741.
Mr. Isaac Case died January 3, 1796.
His widow, Mrs. Bathsheba Case, died May 4, 1803.

Children.

373 Mehetabel, born November 13, 1741.
374 Isaac,   born May   19, 1743.   Married two wives.
375 Bathsheba, born January   1, 1745.   Died October 13, 1751.
376 Elizabeth, born September   19, 1747.
377 Mercy,   born December   23, 1749.
378 Bathsheba, born October   27, 1751. Married Ezekiel Phelps, Jr.
379 Joanna,   born October   13, 1752. Married 1. David Russell. 2. Jared
                                               Mills. Died July 4, 1820.
380 Lydia,   born December   14, 1755.
381 Israel,   born November   18, 1757. Married Joanna, daughter of Capt. Job
                                               Case.
382 Azuba,   born March   28, 1760.
383 Aaron,   born May   29, 1762. Married Abigail Case.
384 Cleopatra, born July   29, 1764.
385 Myriam,   born about   1766. Married Thias Garritt. Died December
                                               17, 1747.

351.

ABRAHAM CASE married 1. Rachel, daughter of Capt. James Case, May 6, 1740; she was born August 14, 1722, and died about 1789. 2. Anna, daughter of Deacon Joseph Case, Jr., and widow of Joseph Webster, in 1790; she was born January 28, 1728. They removed from Weatogue to Chestnut Hill, in West Simsbury, about 1740.

Deacon Abraham Case died March 13, 1800.

Mrs. Anna Case died ————.

Children.

386 Rachel,   born January   6, 1741. Died April 6, 1759.
387 Abraham,   born March   18, 1743. Married Sarah Humphrey   Died April
                                            10, 1776.
388 Rosanna,   born May   8, 1745. Married Ezra Wilcox, Jr.   Died Janu-
                                            ary 15, 1807.
389 Elisha,   born   1747. Married 1. Judith Case. 2. Elizabeth
                                            Case. Died May 19, 1808.
390 Sarah,   born   1752. Married Caleb Case. Died February
                                            26, 1781.
391 Eunice,   born   1753. Married 1. Moses Case. 2. Ebenezer
                                            Cowles.
392 Hannah,   born   1757. Married Charles Humphrey.   Died
                                            May 28, 1808.
393 Elizabeth, born   1757. Married Giles Humphrey.
394 Phebe,   born about   1760. Married Jeremiah Griswold. Died in
                                            1798.

FOURTH GENERATION.

356.

ROGER CASE, of Simsbury, married Mindwell Buell, August 10, 1760.

Mr. Roger Case died ————.

Mrs. Mindwell Case died ————.

Children.

395 Ephraim,   born November   8, 1761. Married Athildred Case.
396 Mercy,   born November 30, 1763.
397 Mindwell, born December   31, 1766.
398 Eunice,   born November   15, 1768.

399 Dorothy,   born March   4, 1770.
400 Roger,   born April   7, 1772.
401 Asenath,   born July   25, 1777.
402 Sarah,   born October   11, 1780.
403 Lois,   born October   20, 1786.

359.

BARTHOLOMEW CASE married 1. Ruth, daughter of John
Owen, Esq., about 1771 ; she was born in 1754, and died May 14,
1782.   2. Mary, daughter of Hezekiah Humphrey ; she was born
in 1753. They resided on the paternal homestead, in Weatogue.
Capt. Bartholomew Case died June 16, 1808.
His widow, Mrs. Mary Case, died May 19, 1818.

Children,—by his first wife.

404 Bartholo-
     mew,   born October   27, 1772.   Married Rachel Phelps. Died June 10,
                                           1833.
405 Philander, born November   7, 1774.   Married Caroline Humphrey. Died
                                           November 18, 1815.
406 Ruth,   born May   10, 1778.   Married Asaph Tuller, Esq. Died
                                           March 15, 1838.
407 Grandison, born about   1781. Married 1. Dorcas Humphrey. 2. Sa-
                                           lome Marks.

Children,—by his second wife.

408 Horace,   born December   1, 1785.   Married —— Stebbins. Removed to
                                           Aurora, N. Y.
409 Aurora,   born March   20, 1787.   Married Betsey, daughter of Aaron
                                           Case.
410 Harvey,   born June   28, 1790.   Died March 5, 1854.

367.

ABEL CASE married Huldah Higley, July 8, 1777 ; she was
born February 1, 1750. Resided on the paternal homestead, on
Chestnut Hill.
Mr. Abel Case died April 29, 1834.
Mrs. Huldah Case died August 12, 1840.

Children.

411 Huldah,   born August   19, 1778.   Married Jabez Hamblin.
412 Abel,   born April   12, 1783.   Married Rachel Humphrey. Died Sep-
                                           tember 29, 1831.
413 Dinah,   born April   1, 1786.   Married Ira Case. Died September 3,
                                           1848.
414 Tirzah,   born September   4, 1788.   Married Dora Case.
415 Carmi,   born July   20, 1793.   Died July 8, 1815.

368.

SILAS CASE married 1. Jane Kelly about 1776 ; she died May
5, 1777.   2. Mary, daughter of Capt. John Case, September,
1780; she was born January 2, 1755. Resided near the paternal
homestead, on Chestnut Hill.
Mr. Silas Case died June 20, 1809.
His widow, Mrs. Mary Case, died October 15, 1833,

Child,—by his first wife.

416 Kelly,   born April   10, 1777. Married 1. Roxy Hoskins. 2. Meheta-
                                             bel Steele.

Children,—by his second wife.

417 Polly,	born June	20, 1781.	Married Giles Case. Died May 9, 1850.
418 Ira,	born December	7, 1782.	Married 1. Mary Humphrey. 2. Dinah Case. Died September 17, 1848.
419 Silas,	born February	24, 1785.	Died October 13, 1816.
420 Levi,	born August	8, 1787.	Married Keturah Bandle.
421 Ruggles,	born September	28, 1789.	Married Cynthia Case.
422 Jane,	born January	12, 1792.	Married Holcomb Case.
423 Lucy,	born March	9, 1794.	Married Everest Case.
424 Gad,	born May	5, 1796.	Married Tirzah Gibbons.
425 Ruth,	born January	18, 1799.	Married Case Braman.

FIFTH GENERATION.

409.

COL. AURORA CASE married Betsey, daughter of Aaron Case, November 3, 1812; she was born April 19, 1790. Resides on the paternal homestead in Weatogue, being the place where John Case, Sen. settled, and having been kept in the family ever since.

Children.

426 Aurora,	born August	22, 1813.	Married Abigail Tryon. Removed to Indiana.
427 Averitt,	born May	19, 1815.	Died April 27, 1851.
428 Albert,	born February	17, 1817.	Died January 4, 1819.
429 Harvey E.,	born April	19, 1820.	
430 Seth E.,	born December	23, 1825.	Married Minerva E. Wilcox. Is an Attorney at Law; residence, New Britain, Conn.

DESCENDANTS IN THE LINE OF JOSEPH CASE, SIXTH SON OF JOHN CASE.

SECOND GENERATION.

VIII.

JOSEPH CASE married Anna, daughter of James Eno, of Windsor, Conn., April 6, 1699; she was born April 10, 1682. They resided in Meadow Plains, in Simsbury.

Mr. Joseph Case died August 11, 1748.

His widow, Mrs. Anna Case, died June 10, 1760.

Children.

431 Joseph,	born February	2, 1700.	
432 Jacob,	born March	19, 1702.	
433 A son,	born in	1705.	Died August 19, 1705.
434 Benajah,	born about	1710.	Died after 1748.
435 Josiah,	born February	1, 1716.	
436 Hezekiah,	born April	26, 1719.	Died before 1748.
437 David,	born about	1722.	Died after 1748.
438 Joel,	born May	30, 1724.	

THIRD GENERATION.

431.

JOSEPH CASE married Hannah, daughter of Deacon John Humphrey, December 7, 1721; she was born March 17, 1701. Resided on the paternal homestead in Meadow Plain.
Deacon Joseph Case died March 12, 1782.
Mrs. Hannah Case died ———.

Children

439 Joseph,	born November	30, 1722.	Married 1. Mary Tuller. 2. Sarah Reed. Died February 13, 1801.
440 Hannah,	born March	25, 1725.	Married 1. ——— Nearing. 2. ——— Fuller.
441 Anna,	born January	28, 1728.	Married 1. Joseph Webster. 2. Dea. Abraham Case.
442 Asahel,	born March	23, 1729.	Married ——— Phelps. Settled in Norfolk, Conn.
443 Hosea,	born March	23, 1731.	
444 Jedediah,	born March	30, 1733.	Married Mary Hart. Died January 11, 1818.
445 Solomon,	born March	11, 1735.	
446 Benajah,	born August	10, 1738.	Married Lydia Woodruff.
447 Sarah,	born	1743.	Married Timothy Phelps. Died 1795.

432.

JACOB CASE married Abigail Barber, October 28, 1728; she was born in 1706. Removed from Meadow Plain to Cases' Farms, in Simsbury, about 1730, and was the pioneer of that place.
Mr. Jacob Case died July 23, 1763.
His widow, Mrs. Abigail Case, died January 8, 1779.

Children.

448 Abigail,	born January	12, 1730.	Married Daniel Hoskins. Died June 20, 1806.
449 Sarah,	born June	5, 1733.	Married Elijah Tuller. Died December 20, 1798.
450 Jacob,	born June	19, 1735.	
451 Jesse,	born May	19, 1738.	
452 Anna,	born April	9, 1740.	Married Deacon Solomon Case. Died April 6, 1817.
453 Martha,	born May	21, 1743.	Died December 30, 1748.
454 Moses,	born September	8, 1746.	
455 Martha,	born April	12, 1749.	Died April 5, 1834.

435.

JOSIAH CASE married Mary Hoskins, July 22, 1742. Removed from Meadow Plain to Cases' Farms, about 1743.
Mr. Josiah Case died ———.
Mrs. Mary Case died ———.

Children.

456 Hezekiah,	born August	11, 1743.	Died December 25, 1761.
457 Mary,	born September	30, 1745.	Married David Goodhue.
458 Ezra,	born September	15, 1747.	Settled in Barkhamsted, Conn.
459 Andrew,	born July	10, 1749.	Died August 19, 1749.
460 Andrew,	born August	15, 1750.	Settled in Barkhamsted.

461 Josiah,	born February	19, 1753.	
462 Ozias,	born November	2, 1755.	Settled in Burlington, Conn.
463 Abel,	born November	3, 1758.	Married Anna ———. Died December 10, 1844.
464 Oliver,	born June,	1761.	Settled in Barkhamsted.

438.

JOEL CASE married Thankful Hoskins, October 28, 1746.
Removed from Meadow Plain to Cases' Farms about 1746.
Mr. Joel Case died ———.
Mrs. Thankful Case died ———.

Children.

465 Thankful,	born September	23, 1747.	Married Michael Moses.
466 Elizabeth,	born February	24, 1749.	Married 1. Abijah Reed. 2. Isaac Case, Jr. Died March 4, 1816.
467 Isabel,	born January	16, 1751.	Married Roderick Adams.
468 Joel,	born March	3, 1753.	Died January 4, 1754.
469 Susannah,	born October	20, 1754.	
470 Joel,	born September	20, 1756.	Died November 8, 1758.
471 Luther,	born March	30, 1759.	
472 Rositte,	born May	10, 1761.	Married Joel Barber.
473 Lois,	born April	10, 1763.	
474 Calom,	born April	10, 1765.	
475 Joel,	born January	30, 1770.	

FOURTH GENERATION.

443.

HOSEA CASE married Mary, daughter of Deacon Thomas Case,
April 11, 1751 ; she was born August 5, 1732. [After the death
of Dea. Hosea Case, she married Richard Case.] They removed
from Meadow Plain to Chestnut Hill, in West Simsbury, about
1752.
Deacon Hosea Case died May 7, 1793.
His widow, Mrs. Mary Case, died July 29, 1817.

Children.

476 Mary,	born April	8, 1752.	Married John Hills, of Burlington.
477 Elizabeth,	born June	26, 1754.	Married Reuben Barber. Died June 9, 1826.
478 Hosea,	born October	6, 1756.	Married 1. Rhoda Case. 2. Sarah Buell. Died October 11, 1834.
479 Asa,	born December	9, 1758,	
480 Dora,	born April,	1761.	Died October 12, 1778.
481 Lydia,	born August	25, 1763.	Married Benjamin Barber.
482 Rosanna,	born May	6, 1766.	Married Peter Buell. Died October 21, 1839.
483 Titus,	born February	14, 1769.	Married 1. Sarah Eggleston. 2. Phebe Tuttle. Died July 20, 1845.
484 Eunice,	born August	20, 1771.	Married Arba Alford.
485 Lodamia,	born July	31, 1774.	Married Aaron, son of Asahel Case.
486 Phebe,	born July	14, 1776.	Married 1. Philemon Andrus. 2. Elam Case. Died December 14, 1845.

444.

JEDEDIAH CASE married Mary Hart, of Farmington, May 10,
1758. Resided on the paternal homestead in Meadow Plain.

Mr. Jedediah Case died January 11, 1818.
Mrs. Mary Case died ———.

Children.

487 Jedediah,	born July	13, 1759.	Married 1. Lettice Tuller. 2. Roxana Case. Died April 28, 1828.
488 Elihu,	born January	16, 1761.	Married Faithy Case. Died January 13, 1832.
489 Humphrey,	born August	29, 1762.	Married ——— Harrington. Settled in Barkhamsted, Conn.
490 Phebe T.,	born August	12, 1765.	Died February 18, 1823.
491 Hezekiah,	born March	11, 1769.	Married Cynthia Eno.
492 Elizabeth,	born February	21, 1771.	Married Elisha Tuller, Jr.
493 Horatio G.,	born September	21, 1777.	Married Hepzibah Cornish. Died July 2, 1853.

445.

SOLOMON CASE married Anna, daughter of Jacob Case, May 11, 1758; she was born April 9, 1740. Removed from Meadow Plain to Cases' Farms, in Simsbury, about 1758.
Deacon Solomon Case died July 3, 1811.
His widow, Mrs. Anna Case, died April 6, 1817.

Children.

494 Anna,	born April	29, 1759.	Married Jonathan Allen.
495 Hannah,	born June	28, 1761.	Married Allen Smith.
496 Abigail,	born May	6, 1763.	Married Aaron Case.
497 Chloe,	born March	8, 1769.	Married Abel Barber. Died April 15, 1820.
498 Solomon,	born	1771.	Married Chloe Case. Died January 28, 1831.
499 Faithy,	born	1774.	Married Elihu Case. Died February 10, 1850.
500 Wealthy,	born	1776.	Died August 31, 1850.
501 Dianthe,	born about	1778.	Married Zephaniah Ames.
502 Jacob,	born January	1, 1781.	

450.

JACOB CASE married Elizabeth Hoskins, April 13, 1758. Resided in West Simsbury, one mile west of Cases' Farms.
Mr. Jacob Case died September 27, 1807.
Mrs. Elizabeth Case died November 22, 1804.

Children.

503 Elizabeth,	born January	22, 1759.	Married Jehiel Lattimer. Died April 22, 1831.
504 Jacob,	born July	3, 1761.	Died September 15, 1779.
505 Mary,	born February	15, 1763.	Married Abraham Humphrey. Died November 28, 1828.

451.

JESSE CASE married Sarah, daughter of Capt. Noah Humphrey, November 20, 1766; she was born in 1743. Resided in West Simsbury, one mile west of Cases' Farms.
Mr. Jesse Case died October 3, 1807.
His widow, Mrs. Sarah Case, died March 13, 1818.

38

Children.

506 Jesse,   born July   20, 1767.
507 Sarah,   born December   4, 1768. Married Samuel Leet.
508 Augustus, born May   31, 1770. Married Hannah Hoskins. Died March
                                         17, 1855.
509 Asenath, born June   30, 1772. Died 1776.
510 Abigail, born October   13, 1774. Married Riverious Case. Died August
                                         5, 1825.
511 Asenath, born August   26, 1777. Died January 19, 1845.
512 Gideon,   born February   26, 1779. Married Persis Seward. Died May 11,
                                         1822.
513 Hannah,   born September 19, 1781. Married Edmund O'Sullivan.
514 Charlotte, born January   24, 1785. Married Allen Barber.
515 Salome,   born about Nov.,   1786. Died January 10, 1788.

454.

MOSES CASE married 1. Lucy Wilcox about 1770; she was
born 1754, and died June 17, 1779. 2. Abigail, daughter of Elisha Wilcox, about 1781. Resided on the paternal homestead in
Cases' Farms.

Moses Case, Esq., died December 18, 1794.

Mr. Abigail Case died ———.

Children,—by his first wife.

516 Lucy,   born   1772. Married Rufus Humphrey. Died Au-
                                 gust 17, 1826.
517 Roxana, born about   1774. Married 1. Israel Graham. 2. Jededi-
                                 ah Case, Jr.
518 Moses,   born May 11, 1776. Married Maria Case. Died October 16,
                                 1848.
519 Martha, born about   1778. Married Walter Robe.

Children,—by his second wife.

520 Abigail, born   1783. Married Reuben Tuller. Died January
                                 13, 1843.
521 Chloe,   born about   1785. Married Luther Smith.
522 Violet, born about   1787. Married James Smith.

FIFTH GENERATION.

479.

ASA CASE married 1. Lois, daughter of Solomon Dill, January
28, 1781; she was born March 29, 1759, and died August 5, 1812.
2. Thede, widow of Benajah Humphrey, and daughter of Capt.
Zaccheus Case; she was born in 1766. Resided on Chestnut Hill.

Mr. Asa Case died February 26, 1837.

His widow, Mrs. Thede Case, died April 15, 1851.

Children.

523 Lois,   } ⸠ born October 25, 1782. Died September 23, 1783.
524 Lorenda,   } twins   Died May 31, 1787.
525 Asa,   born December   1, 1786. Married Hepzibah Buell.
526 Dosa,   born March   7, 1788. Married Tirzah Case.
527 Bera,   born July   22, 1790. Married Sarah Humphrey.
528 A daughter, born May   25, 1793. Died June 22, 1793.
529 Hosea,   born June   13, 1794. Married 1. Thede M. Humphrey. 2.
                                          Charlotte Mills. Died August 29,
                                          1827.

530 Lois,   born December 23, 1796.   Married Solomon V., son of Solomon
                                      Case, Jr.
531 Lorinda,   born March   24, 1799.   Married Orson Reed. Died January
                                        30, 1833.
532 Milton,   born February 19, 1801.   Married Eunice Reed.

502.

JACOB CASE married Sally H. Montague, January 1, 1806 ; she was born May 10, 1781. Resides on the paternal homestead, in Cases' Farms.

Children.

533 Emeline,   born October   21, 1806.   Died January 21, 1811.
534 Sarah Ann, ⎰ born March   20, 1808.   Married Dr. John C. Howe.
535 Mary Ann, ⎱   Married Whiting Wadsworth.
536 Juliette E.,   born April   4, 1810.   Married Amos G. Tuttle.
537 Susan M.,   born December 31, 1811.   Married James F. G. Andrews.
538 Lucia D.,   born September 17, 1815.   Married Luke S. West. Died August
                                        9, 1852.
539 Jacob B.,   born September 11, 1817.   Married Julia Stannard.
540 Theodore D.,born September 8, 1819.   Married Elvira Whiting.
541 Emily S.,   born February 27, 1822.   Married William Weeks.

506.

JESSE CASE married 1. Sarah, daughter of Dea. Elisha Cornish, Jr., October 3, 1791 ; she was born April 20, 1773, and died June 6, 1815. 2. Lydia, daughter of Rev. Aaron Church, January 11, 1816 ; she was born June 22, 1778. Resided near the paternal homestead in West Simsbury, (now Canton.) Deacon Jesse Case died February, 1842.

Children,—by his first wife.

542 Jesse O.,   born October   29, 1792.   Married Chloe Gleason.
543 Justin,   born January   4, 1795.   Died June 22, 1802.
544 Everest,   born December 19, 1796.   Married Lucy Case.
545 Sarah,   born October   31, 1798.   Married Ezekiel H. Case.
546 Newton,   born June   7, 1801.   Died April 12, 1807.
547 Elmira,   born April   15, 1803.
548 Justin,   born March   11, 1805.   Married Rachel H. Talcott. Died Oc-
                                      tober 1, 1841.
549 Newton,   born March   12, 1807.   Married Lemira B. Hurlburt.
550 Rowena,   born November 27, 1809.   Died January 31, 1834.
551 Abigail,   born August   21, 1812.

Children,—by his second wife.

552 Lydia C.,   born December 5, 1817.   Died April 9, 1820.
553 Lydia,   born April   25, 1820.

DESCENDANTS IN THE LINE OF SARAH CASE, DAUGHTER OF JOHN CASE.

SECOND GENERATION.

IX.

SARAH CASE married Joseph Phelps, Jr., of Simsbury, November 6, 1699 ; she was his second wife. [His first wife, by whom he had three children, viz., Joseph, born October 9, 1689 ; Hannah, born October 25, 1693, and Mary, born October 17, 1696, was daughter of Joseph Collyer, of Hartford, Conn., and her mother was sister of Zachariah Sanford, of the same town ; she died in 1697.]

Mrs. Sarah Phelps, died May 2, 1704.

Joseph Phelps died January 20, 1750.

Children.

554 Sarah,	born August	11, 1700.	Died June 14, 1714.
555 Damaris,	born March	5, 1702.	Married John Mills.

DESCENDANTS IN THE LINE OF ABIGAIL CASE, YOUNGEST DAUGHTER OF JOHN CASE.

SECOND GENERATION.

X.

ABIGAIL CASE married Jonah Westover, Jr., September 1, 1701.

Jonah Westover, Jr., died June 3, 1714.

His widow, Mrs. Abigail Westover died ———.

Children.

556 Nathaniel,	born about	1704.
557 Jonah,	born	1709.
558 John,	born	1712.
559 Abigail,	born about	1714.

EDWARDS FAMILY.

[NOTE to p. 49. The name of the first wife of Richard Edwards would be perhaps with more propriety spelled Tuttle and not Tuthill. See MSS. in State Library, at Hartford; Private Controversies I., Nos. 146 and 148, where are the signatures of Benjamen Tutell, brother, and of Elizabeth Tuttle mother of the wife of Richard Edwards.]

FIFTH GENERATION.

71. p. 54.

ELIZABETH HUNTINGTON, daughter of Jabez Huntington, Esq., of Windham, Conn., was married to Abraham Davenport, Esq., of Stamford, Conn., son of the Rev. John Davenport, Pastor of the Church in that place, November 1, 1750. [After her death, Mr. Davenport was married to Martha Fitch, widow of Perez Fitch, deceased, of Stamford, August 8, 1776, and daughter of ——— Coggeshall. She survived him.

Mrs. Elizabeth Davenport died December 17, 1773, aged 48.

Hon. Abraham Davenport died November 20, 1789, in the 74th year of his age.

Children.

1 John,   born January   16, 1752.*
2 Abraham,   born October   21, 1753.   Died October 25, 1754.
3 Elizabeth, born September 16, 1756.†
4 James,   born October   12, 1758.‡
5 Huntington, born April   18, 1761.   Died October 22, 1769.

72. p. 54.

SARAH HUNTINGTON, daughter of Jabez Huntington, Esq., of Windham, Conn., was twice married. 1. To Hezekiah Wetmore, Esq., of Middletown, Conn., August 22, 1748. He died ———. 2. To Samuel Beers, Esq., of Stratford, Conn., February 19, 1758.

Mrs. Sarah Beers, alias Wetmore, died December 4, 1784, in the 58th year of her age. [Gravestone, Stratford burying-ground.]

Mr. Samuel Beers died October 17, 1798, aged 70 years and 4 months. [Gravestone.]

---

* See No. 1 of Sixth Generation of this Appendix.

† See No. 2 of Sixth Generation of this Appendix.

‡ See No. 3 of Sixth Generation of this Appendix.

Children,—by her first husband.

6 Tryphena, bap. July   8, 1750.
7 Hezekiah, bap. March   3, 1754.

Children,—by her second husband.

8 Lucy,   born September 10, 1760. Married George Smith, of Smithtown,
                                           L. I.
9 Sarah Ann, born June   6, 1762.   Married David Beers, of Fairfield,Conn.
10 William Pitt,born April   2, 1766.   Married Anna Sturgis, daughter of Hon.
                                           Jonathan Sturgis, of Fairfield, Conn.,
                                           June 9, 1793. He died September
                                           18, 1810, aged 44. His remains were
                                           interred at Fairfield. He settled in
                                           Albany, N. Y., and was an eminent
                                           Attorney and Counsellor at Law.

76. p. 54.

SOLOMON ELLSWORTH, of East Windsor, Conn., was married
to Mary Moseley, daughter of Abner Moseley, Esq., of Glastenbury, Conn., December 27, 1758.

Solomon Ellsworth, Esq., died October 19, 1822, aged 85.

His widow, Mrs. Mary Ellsworth, died February 16, 1823,
aged 85.

Children.

11 Mary,   born September 14, 1759.
12 Ann,   born March   13, 1761. Died.
13 Solomon,   born December 12, 1762.
14 Elizabeth,   born January   16, 1765.
15 Stoddard,   born April   14, 1767.
16 Abigail,   born January   6, 1769.
17 Abner Mose-
     ley,   born January   4, 1771.
18 John,   born February 13, 1773.
19 Marilda,   born December 27, 1774.
20 Timothy,   born December 12, 1776. Died December 22, 1776.
21 Timothy,   born April   17, 1778. Married Miss Mather.
22 Joseph,   born March   6, 1780.
23 Ann,   born April   30, 1784.

78. p. 55.

ANN ELLSWORTH was married to Lemuel Stoughton, of East
Windsor, Conn., 1769.

Col. Lemuel Stoughton died March 4, 1793, in the 62d year of
his age.

His widow, Mrs. Anna Stoughton, died November 8, 1819,
aged 77.

Children.

24 Anna,   born November 7, 1770.
25 John,   born February 2, 1772.
26 Lemuel,   born March   27, 1774.
27 Ruth,   born May   12, 1776.
28 Martha,   born November 15, 1777.
29 Eunice,   born November 20, 1779.

90. p. 56.

CLORINDA BACKUS was married to Zebadiah Lathrop, of Norwich, Conn., about 1740.

Mr. Zebadiah Lathrop died November 14, 1793, aged about 68.

His widow, Mrs. Clorinda Lathrop, died October 25, 1803, aged 73.

Children.

30 Joseph,	born about	1755.	Died at West Point, during the Revolutionary War aged 23.
31 Zebadiah,	born about	1758.	Married ——— Starr, daughter of William Starr, of Middletown, Conn., December 11, 1783, and settled in that town. She was born May 1, 1759. He died about 1798, aged about 40. She died in June, 1849, aged 93 years, nearly. 6 children are recorded to them on Middletown Records.
32 Simon Backus,	born	1760.	Married Molly Culver, of Norwich, March 1, 1792. He died December 14, 1805, aged 45. They had children.
33 Asa,	born		Married a daughter of Ebenezer Jones, of Norwich. He died in Norwich, October 29, 1808. She died at St. Marys, in Georgia. They had no children.
34 Eunice,	born		Died, unmarried, in New Canaan, N. Y., in 1820.
35 Nathaniel,	born	1768.	Died at Stockbridge, Mass, in 1848, aged 80.

92. p. 56.

ELIZABETH BACKUS was married to David Bissell, Jun., of East Windsor, Conn., February 25, 1761.

Mr. David Bissell died December 16, 1799.

His widow, Mrs. Elizabeth Bissell, died ———.

Children.

36 Noadiah,	bap. November 22, 1761.	Married Sibil Enos, of Vermont; and after her death, Betsy Shuttleworth, of Dedham, Mass. They settled in East Windsor, but subsequently removed to Windsor, Vermont. *Children,*—one by his first, and four by his last wife.
37 David,	born June 6, 1764	Married Heart Wickam, of Pomfret, Conn., where he settled. From Pomfret, he removed to East Windsor, Conn., and from East Windsor, to Hartford, Conn., where he died in or about 1816, leaving 6 children, 3 sons and 3 daughters. After his death, she was married to Dr. Edward Tudor, of Middlebury, Ver., where she died. Dr. Tudor was a native of East Windsor.
38 Mary,	born November 14, 1766.	Died November 7, 1771.
39 Simon Backus,	bap. January 22, 1769.	Married a daughter of Gen. Morey, of

Orford, N. H., where he settled; afterwards removed to Cincinnati, O. *Children*,—4, all sons, one of which, as I have been informed, was educated at West Point, under the patronage of General, afterwards President Harrison, and is a Lieutenant in the navy of the United States, and resides in Philadelphia.

40 Mary,	born April	10, 1774.	Married Nathan Lyman, of Coventry, Conn. He settled in East Windsor, and died March 3, 1826, aged 58. They had 13 children.
41 Child,	born	1776.	Died August 27, 1776.

93. p. 56.

REV. SIMON BACKUS, pastor, first, of the Church in Granby, Mass., and afterwards of the Church in Guilford, Conn., was married to Rachel Moseley, daughter of Abner Moseley, of Glastenbury, Conn., February 7, 1763.

Rev. Simon Backus died in Stratford, Conn., August 7, 1823, in the 86th year of his age. His remains were interred at Bridgeport, Conn.

His widow, Mrs. Rachel Backus, died in Stratford, Conn., July 28, 1825, aged 79 years, 9 months and 4 days. Her remains were also interred at Bridgeport.

Children.

42 Joseph,	born December	26, 1764.	Married Huldah Burroughs, daughter of Stephen Burroughs, Esq., of Stratford, October 15, 1797, and settled in Bridgeport. Joseph Backus, Esq., died ————. His widow, Mrs. Hul dah Burrows, died December 15, 1851, aged 83.
43 Simon,	born September	1, 1766.	Died.
44 Simon,	born February	27, 1768.	Died September 2, 1775.
45 Clarina,	born June	25, 1770.	
46 Abner Moseley,	born May	30, 1772.	Died August 21, 1775.
47 Mary,	born July	1, 1774.	Died, unmarried, in Newbern, N. C.
48 Dilecta,	born September	15, 1776.	Died May 4, 1800.
49 Simon,	born January	6, 1779.	Died December, 1836, in N. York city.
50 Eunice,	born February	18, 1781.	
51 Abner Moseley,	born June,	1783.	Died November, 1818, in Ithica, N. Y.
52 Rachel,	born October	13, 1785.	
53 Thomas Moseley,	born November,	1787.	

94. p. 56.

ESTHER BACKUS was married to Benjamin Ely, of that part of West Springfield, Mass., now called Holyoke, June 1, 1758.

Mr. Benjamin Ely, died December 25, 1802, aged 72.

His widow, Mrs. Esther Ely, died September 19, 1820, aged 81, nearly.

Children.

54 Lois,	born March	14, 1759.
55 Esther,	born November	23, 1760.
56 Robert,	born February	28, 1763.
57 Elihu,	born July	13, 1765.
58 Eunice,	born October	15, 1767. Died March 13, 1772.
59 Benjamin,	born January	30, 1770.
60 Elijah,	born March	1, 1772.
61 Eunice,	born January,	1782.

96. p. 56.

JERUSHA BACKUS was married to Smith Bailey, of East Windsor, Conn., afterwards of the eastern part of Connecticut, (town not ascertained,) about 1765.

Mr. Smith Bailey died ———.

Mrs. Jerusha Bailey died ———.

Children.

62 Child, (not named,) born 1766. Died in infancy.

63 Child, (not named,) born 1768. Died in infancy.

64 Tertius, born 1770. Married and settled in Stonington, Conn.

65 Polly, born May 16, 1773. Married Jonathan Birge, of East Windsor, December, 1791. She died September 5, 1793, aged 21. He died December 12, 1820, aged 52. *Child,—one only,* Bailey Birge, born August 4, 1793. After the death of Mrs. Birge, Mr. Jonathan Birge was married to Sally Warner, daughter of Doct. Ichabod Warner, of Bolton, Conn., May 8, 1794, by whom he had 7 children; the first child, Backus Birge, born February 8, 1795, and died ———, was the first husband of Mrs. Roderick Terry, of Hartford. Mrs. Birge, the second wife of Jonathan Birge, died at South Windsor, Conn., April 21, 1855, aged 80.

103. p. 57.

LUCY WETMORE was married to Chauncey Whittlesey, of Wallingford, Conn., afterwards of Middletown, in the same State, February 17, 1770.

Chauncey Whittlesey, Esq., died March 14, 1812, aged 66.

His widow, Mrs. Lucy Whittlesey, died January 23, 1826, aged 78.

Children.

66 Lucy, born October 4, 1773. Married Capt. Joseph W. Alsop, of Middletown, Conn., November 5, 1797. He died October 16, 1844, aged 73. His widow, Mrs. Lucy Alsop, is alive at this date, September 24, 1850. *Children,*—7; among them, Joseph Wright, born November 22, 1804, died ———; favorably known as a poet.

39

67 Hannah,	born May	10, 1775.	
68 Elizabeth,	born May	24, 1780.	Married Capt. Josiah Williams, of Middletown, Conn., May 25, 1817, being his second wife. She died October 16, 1828, aged 48. He died October 5, 1835, aged 56. No children.
69 Chauncey,	born June	18, 1783.	Married Sarah Lathrop Tracy, daughter of Doctor Ebenezer Tracy, of Middletown, Conn., April 14, 1818. They have 6 children.

104. p. 57.

OLIVER WETMORE, of Middletown, Conn., was married to Sarah Brewster, daughter of Elisha Brewster, of the same town, and Lucy Yeomans his wife, October 13, 1774.

Deacon Oliver Wetmore died December 1, 1798, in the 47th year of his age.

His widow, Mrs. Sarah Wetmore, died July 5, 1827, in the 73d year of her age.

Children.

70 Oliver,	born December	1, 1774.	Died at Utica, N. Y., January 1, 1852, aged 77. He was a preacher.
71 Elisha,	born October	1, 1776.	Married Polly Bacon.
72 Sarah,	born October	1, 1778.	Married John Stoughton, of East Windsor.
73 Timothy,	born August	2, 1780.	
74 Lucy,	born May	9, 1782.	Died unmarried.
75 Hannah,	born August	8, 1784.	
76 Clarissa,	born July	5, 1786.	Married Stephen Dodge.
77 Sophia,	born May	25, 1788.	Married Giles Southmayd.
78 Chauncey,	born June	5, 1790.	
79 Emily.	born January	4, 1795.	

SIXTH GENERATION.

1.

JOHN DAVENPORT, of Stamford, Conn., son of Abraham Davenport, of that place, and grandson of Jabez Huntington, of Windham, Conn., was married to Mary Sylvester Welles, daughter of the Rev. Noah Welles, Pastor of the Church in Stamford, May 7, 1780, by Abraham Davenport, Esq., assistant.*

Hon. John Davenport died November 28, 1830, in the 79th year of his age. He sustained many civil offices, was member of Congress, &c.

His widow, Mrs. Mary Sylvester Davenport, died June 25, 1847, in the 94th year of her age.

Children.

80 Elizabeth Huntington,	born March	4, 1781.
81 John Alfred,	born January	21, 1783.
82 Mary Welles,	born September	12, 1785.
83 Theodosia,	born January	31, 1789.

* Rev. Noah Welles, was son of Noah Welles, of Colchester, Conn., and was born September 25, 1718.

84 Theodore,	born January	26, 1792.
85 Rebecca,	born July	7, 1795.
86 Matilda,	born April	7, 1798.

2.

ELIZABETH DAVENPORT, daughter of Abraham Davenport, of Stamford, Conn., and granddaughter of Jabez Huntington, of Windham, Conn., was married to Doct. James Cogswell, of Preston, Conn., May 4, 1775.

Mrs. Elizabeth Cogswell died at Stamford, November 15, 1779, aged 23.

Doct. James Cogswell died ———.

Child,—one only.

87 Alice,	born June	15, 1777.

3.

JAMES DAVENPORT, of Stamford, Conn., son of Abraham Davenport, Esq., of that town, and grandson of Jabez Huntington, Esq., of Windham, Conn., was twice married. 1. To Abigail Fitch, daughter of Doct. Perez Fitch, of Stamford, May 7, 1777. She died November 11, 1779, aged 22 years. 2. To Mehitabel Coggeshall, daughter of ——— Coggeshall, of ———, November 6, 1790.

Hon. James Davenport died August 3, 1797, in the 38th year of his age.*

His widow, Mrs. Elizabeth Davenport, died November 30, 1804, aged 41.

Children,—by his first wife.

88 Elizabeth Cogswell,	born January	27, 1778.	Married Charles Apthrop, Esq., of Boston, merchant. She is mother of the wife of Rev. Dr. Bushnell, of Hartford, Conn.
89 James Huntington,	born November 11, 1779.		Died in infancy.

Children,—by his second wife.

90 Abigail Fitch,	born November 17, 1791.	Married Rev. ——— Whelpley, of the City of New York.
91 Mary Ann,	born November 11, 1793.	Married Rev. Matthias Bruen, of the City of New York. He died September 6, 1829, aged 36.
92 Frances Louisa,	born November 10, 1795.	Married Rev. Dr. Thomas H. Skinner, of the City of New York.

---

* " Called in early life to the important offices of a Judge of the Court of Common Pleas, a Member of the Council of the State, and Representative to the Congress of the United States, he discharged the respective duties of these offices, as well as the various duties of private life, with honor to himself, and fidelity to his country."

[Tombstone, Stamford burying-ground.]

WILLIAM GOODRICH.

67. p. 79.

ELIZUR GOODRICH, born October 18, 1734, settled in Durham, Conn., married Katharine, daughter of Hon. Elihu Chauncey, February 1, 1759; she was born April 11, 1741.

Rev. Elizur Goodrich, D. D., died November 21, 1797.

Mrs. Katharine Goodrich, died April 8, 1830.

Children.

1 Chauncey,	born October	20, 1759.	U. S. Senator, and Lieut. Governor of Connecticut. Died August 18, 1815.
2 Elizur,	born March	24, 1761.	
3 Samuel,	born January,	12, 1763.	
4 Elihu,	born September	16, 1764.	Died unmarried.
5 Charles Augustus,	born March	2, 1768.	Died unmarried.
6 Nathan,	born August	5, 1770.	Died young.
7 Catharine,	born December	2, 1775.	Married Rev. David Smith, D. D., of Durham, Conn. Died in 1845.

2.

ELIZUR GOODRICH married Anne Willard Allen, only daughter of Daniel and Esther Allen, September 1, 1785.

Hon. Elizur Goodrich died at New Haven, Conn., November 1, 1849.

Mrs. Anne Willard Goodrich died November 17, 1818.

Children.

8 Elizur,	born October	3, 1787.	Married Eliza, daughter of Gen. Henry Champion, October 25, 1818. Residence, Hartford.
9 Chauncey Allen,	born October	23, 1790.	Married Julia, daughter of Noah Webster, LL. D.
10 Nancy,	born January	1, 1793.	Married Hon. Henry L. Ellsworth. Died January 15, 1847.

3.

SAMUEL GOODRICH married Elizabeth, daughter of Col. John Ely, July 29, 1784.

Rev. Samuel Goodrich died at Berlin, April 19, 1835.

Mrs. Elizabeth Goodrich died at Berlin, March 3, 1837.

Children.

11 Sarah Wor-
thington, born August   7, 1785.   Married 1. Amos Cooke. 2. Hon. Fred-
eric Wolcott. Died ———.
12 Elizabeth, born April   26, 1787.   Married Rev. Noah Coe.
13 Abigail, born November 29, 1788.   Married Rev. Samuel Whittlesey.
14 Charles Au-
gustus, born August   19, 1790.   Married Sarah Upson.
15 Catharine, born December   4, 1791.   Married Daniel Dunbar, of Berlin.
16 Samuel
Griswold, born August   19, 1793.   Married 1. Adaline Bradley. 2. Mary
Boot.
17 Elihu
Chauncey, born November 18, 1795.   Died June 9, 1797.
48 Mary Ann, born May   29, 1799.   Married Hon. N. B. Smith, of Woodbury.
19 Emily
Chauncey, born November 25, 1801.   Died October 22, 1803.
20 Emily
Chauncey, born November 13, 1805.   Married Rev. Darius Mead. Died ———.

WILLIAM SPENCER.

WILLIAM SPENCER, brother of Thomas and Jared, had been at Cambridge, in 1631, and was a representative in 1634–5. He was one of the first settlers of Hartford, Conn., and in 1639, a selectman of that town; was married (in England probably) to Agnes ———, about 1633. [After his death, she was married to William Edwards, who, likewise, was one of the first settlers of Hartford.]

Mr. Spencer was one of the deputies in the General Court in 1639, and appointed with Mr. Wyllis, and Mr. Webster to prepare the first revisal of the laws in that year.

William Spencer, Esq., died in 1640.

Mrs. Agnes Spencer, alias Edwards, died ———.

FIRST GENERATION.

Children of William Spencer and Agnes Spencer his wife.

I. Samuel,	born	
II. Sarah,	born	1636. Married John Case, of Windsor, and Simsbury, Conn.
III. Elizabeth,	born	

DESCENDANTS IN THE LINE OE SAMUEL SPENCER, SON OF WILLIAM SPENCER, THE SETTLER.

SECOND GENERATION.

I.

SAMUEL SPENCER, of Hartford, Conn., was married to Sarah, daughter of ———, of ———.

Mrs. Sarah Spencer died April 24, 1706.

Mr. Samuel Spencer died about 1716.

Children.

4 Samuel,	born	1668.
5 Sarah,	born	
6 Hannah,	born	
7 Elizabeth,	born	
8 Rachel,	born	
9 Mary,	born	1681.
10 Abigail,	born	
11 Agnes,	born	

THIRD GENERATION.

4.

SAMUEL SPENCER, first of Hartford, Conn., then of Colchester, Conn., afterwards of Bolton, in the same State, was married to Hepzibah Church, daughter of Deacon Edward Church, of Hatfield, Mass., son of Richard Church, one of the first settlers of Hartford, September 16, 1696, at Hatfield.

Mrs. Hepzibah Spencer died at Bolton, September 13, 1745, in the 66th year of her age. [Gravestone, Bolton burying-ground.]

Mr. Samuel Spencer died at Bolton, March 26, 1748, in the 80th year of his age. [Gravestone, Bolton burying-ground.]

Children.

12 William,	born February	9, 1698.	Died September 28, 1702.
13 Hepzibah,	born December	28, 1701.	
14 Samuel,	born March	8, 1705.	
15 William,	born August	9, 1708.	
16 Edward,	born April	29, 1711.	
17 Sarah,	born September	4, 1714.	Married —— Downer. They removed to Susquehannah Co., Penn., where they both died; they had one child only, a son, who died in infancy.
18 Caleb,	born June	28, 1718.	
19 Job,	born	1722.	
20 Phillip,	born April	30, 1724,	in Bolton. [Bolton Records.]

5.

SARAH SPENCER was married to Joseph Easton, of Hartford, Conn., son of Joseph Easton, of Hartford, and grandson of Joseph Easton, one of the first settlers of the same town, 1694.

Mr. Joseph Easton died ——.

His widow, Mrs. Sarah Easton, died ——.

Children.

21 Timothy,	bap. August	11, 1695.
22 Joseph,	bap. October	16, 1697.
23 Sarah,	bap. January	2, 1700.
24 Samuel,	bap. February	14, 1702.
25 Elisha,	bap. March	11, 1704.
26 Elijah,	bap. [no date.]	

6.

HANNAH SPENCER was married to Caleb Stanley, Jr., Esq., of Hartford, Conn., May 13, 1696.

Mrs. Hannah Stanley died December 5, 1702.

Caleb Stanley, Esq., died January 4, 1712, aged 37.

Children,—none.

7.

ELIZABETH SPENCER was married to Nathaniel Marsh, of Hartford, Conn.

Lieut. Nathaniel Marsh, died in 1748.

His widow, Mrs. Elizabeth Marsh, died ——.

Children.

27 Hannah,   born
28 Nathaniel,   born
29 Daniel,   bap. October,   30, 1709.
30 Lemuel,   bap.

8.

RACHEL SPENCER was married to Joseph Cook, of Hartford, Conn., October 8, 1705.

Mr. Joseph Cook, died November 1, 1747, aged 67.

His widow, Mrs. Rachel Cook, died ———.

Children,—none.

9.

MARY SPENCER was married to Cyprian Nichols, of Hartford, Conn., May 24, 1705. She was his second wife. [His first wife, to whom he was married ———, was Helena Talcott, daughter of the " Hon. Lieutenant John Talcott," of Hartford, and of Helena, his wife, daughter of the Rev. John Wakeman, of New Haven. She died about 1703. By this marriage, Mr. Nichols had one child only, a daughter, Elizabeth, bap. January, 14, 1700 ; who was married to William Davenport, of Hartford, being his second wife.]

Capt. Cyprian Nichols died January 2, 1756, aged 84.

His widow, Mrs. Mary Nichols, died February 15, 1756, aged 75.

Children.

31 Cyprian,   bap. February 14, 1706.   Was married to Agnes Humphreys, daughter of Nathaniel Humphreys, of the same town, 1732. [After his death she was married to Isaac Seymour of Hartford, by whom he had two children, Isaac and Lydia. Mr. Isaac Seymour died January 14, 1755, in the 32d year of his age.] Mr. Cyprian Nichols died 1745, aged 39. Mrs. Agnes Nichols, alias Seymour, died of small-pox, December 29, 1793, aged 82. *Children,*—Rachel, bap. November 18, 1833 ; George, bap. December 13, 1741, married Eunice ———. She died April, 1794, aged 48.

32 James,   bap. February 2, 1708.   Married Mary Wadsworth, of Hartford, January 22, 1738. She died July 26, 1783, aged 69. He died December 18, 1785.

33 William,   bap. January, 1710.   Was married to Mary Farnsworth, daughter of Joseph Farnsworth, of the same town, February 5, 1739. Capt. William Nichols died of fever, on his passage from Ireland to Antigua, September 3, 1767, in the 56th year of his age. His widow, Mrs. Mary Nichols, died October 13, 1771, aged 52. *Children,*—Rachel, bap. February 17, 1740; William, bap. October 4, 1741, died October 12, 1792,

aged 51; Mary, bap. April 10, 1743; Abigail, bap. April 7, 1745, died August 5, 1750; Cyprian, bap. June 18, 1749, died December 28, 1749; Abigail, bap. May, 1751, died February 8, 1753; Caty, bap. February 24, 1754; Anna, bap. January 16, 1756; James, bap. July 10, 1757, died September 14, 1790, aged 33; Hannah, bap. March 2, 1760.

34 Helena, bap. December, 1711. Was twice married. 1. To James McIlroy, of Hartford, Conn., formerly of Northampton, Mass., December 12, 1736. He died September 30, 1751, aged —. 2. To Thomas Long, of Hartford, 1754. Mrs. Helena Long, alias McIlroy, died February 10, 1762, aged 51. Mr. Thomas Long died ——. *Children,*—none.

35 Mary, born October 4, 1713. Was married to Moses Griswold, of Windsor, Conn., June 26, 1740. He was son of Benjamin Griswold, of Windsor, and of Elizabeth Cook, his wife. Mrs. Mary Griswold died December 27, 1775, in the 63d year of her age. Capt. Moses Griswold died January 4, 1776, in the 62d year of his age. *Children,*—Moses, born ——, married Anna Holcomb, daughter of —— Holcomb, of ——. He settled in Windsor, but subsequently removed to Herkimer, N. Y., and had children, born in Windsor, Anna, born February 17, 1766; Moses Nichols, born January 4, 1768; Anson, born September 30, 1769; Vashti, born April 1, 1774. Mary, born 1742, married Augustin Drake, of Windsor, Conn. He died May 6, 1777, aged 53; she died January 22, 1816, aged 73; they had children, Mary, born September 3, 1761; Elihu, born September 24, 1763; Martha, born September 20, 1765; Job, born August 23, 1767, he was father of Richard G. Drake, Esq., of the firm of Chapman & Drake, of Hartford, Attornies at Law; Rhoda, born ——; Lucy G., born ——. Hannah, born ——, married Abijah Enos, of Windsor, where they settled; removed thence to Rutland, Ver., and afterwards, from Rutland to Western New York. Lucy, born 1753, married Joseph Alford, of Windsor, 1772. He died November 1, 1826, aged 79; she died April 10, 1835, aged 82; they had children, Lucy, born December 17, 1772; William born May 3, 1774; Joseph, born May 16, 1776; Mary, born August 19, 1778. Rowel, born July, 1781; Moses, born April, 1783; Alamathea, born September 17, 1785; Sophia, born 1788; Eleanor, born May, 1791.

36 Rachel, born June 10, 1726. Died in childhood.

40

37 Sarah,   bap. June   8, 1718.   Married Return Strong, of Windsor,
                                            Conn., January 19, 1744.
38 Hannah,   bap. May   8, 1720.   Was married to Elisha Bigelow, of Hart-
                                            ford, Conn., 1747. Mrs. Hannah Big-
                                            elow died September 26, 1795, aged
                                            75. Mr. Elisha Bigelow died June
                                            22, 1796, aged 73. *Children*,—James,
                                            bap. May 8, 1848, died in childhood;
                                            William, bap. May 21, 1749; Elisha,
                                            bap. December 23, 1750, died Octo-
                                            ber 23, ——; Cyprian, bap. Decem-
                                            ber 17, 1752; Normand, bap. October
                                            13, 1754, died October 16, 1758; Rod-
                                            erick, bap. September 5, 1756; Sam-
                                            uel, bap. June 18, 1758, died October
                                            21, 1758; Normand, bap. May 27,
                                            1759; Samuel, bap. February 22,
                                            1761; Edward, bap. January 30, 1763;
                                            Hannah, bap. May 5, 1765.
39 Thankful,   bap. July   22, 1722.   Was married to Ebenezer Barnard, of
                                            Hartford, Conn., July 17, 1747, at
                                            Wethersfield. [Wethersfield Church
                                            Records.] After her death, he was
                                            again married to ——, by whom
                                            he had two children. Mrs. Thankful
                                            Barnard died August 25, 1780, aged
                                            58. Mr. Ebenezer Barnard died April
                                            19, 1799, aged 73. *Children*,—Thank-
                                            ful, bap. March 24, 1751, married
                                            Rev. Allyn Mather, of New Haven,
                                            and after his death, Ebenezer Town-
                                            send, Esq., of New Haven. He died
                                            ——; she died in Middletown, Conn.,
                                            at the house of her son-in-law, Na-
                                            than Starr; she had children, by her
                                            first husband, Increase, died in in-
                                            fancy; Allyn, was a lawyer, but
                                            left his profession, and went to sea
                                            as commander of a ship employed
                                            in the European trade, and was lost
                                            in the English channel, in a storm;
                                            Sophia; the children by her sec-
                                            ond husband, were Elihu, settled in
                                            the city of New York, died 1853,
                                            was of the late firm of Nevins &
                                            Townsend, of that city, brokers;
                                            Grace, married Nathan Starr, of Mid-
                                            dletown. Cyprian, bap. September
                                            2, 1753, settled in Hartford, died No-
                                            vember, 1832; had several children,
                                            among them, Edwin Barnard, of Wa-
                                            terville, Wis., merchant.   Timothy,
                                            bap. June 20, 1756, settled in Hart-
                                            ford, but subsequently removed to
                                            Mendon, Munroe Co., New York,
                                            married Phebe Dewey, daughter of
                                            Daniel Dewey, of Sheffield, Mass.;
                                            he died March 29, 1847; she died
                                            ——; they had ten children, among
                                            them, Hon. Timothy Barnard and E.
                                            Henry Barnard, both of Mendon,
                                            and Hon. Daniel D. Barnard, of Al-
                                            bany, N. Y. Daniel, bap. July 13,
                                            1760, died October 7, 1763. Ebene-
                                            zer, born 1761, settled in Hartford,
                                            married Elizabeth Lane; she died
                                            ——; he died May 8, 1827, aged 78;

they had no children. Charles, bap.
August 28, 1763, died February 20,
1765.

10.

ABIGAIL SPENCER was married to Joseph Symonds, of Hartford, Conn., March 3, 1708.

Mrs. Abigail Symonds died ———.

Mr. Joseph Symonds died February, 1756.

Children.

40 Abigail,	bap. July	10, 1709.	
41 Joseph,	bap. February	25, 1711.	Died in childhood.
42 Mary,	.bap. June	29, 1712.	Died in childhood.
43 Joseph,	bap. January	31, 1714.	
44 Samuel,	born		
45 Benjamin,	born		
46 William,	born		
47 Agnes,	born		
48 Sarah,	born		

11.

AGNES SPENCER was twice married. 1. To Nathaniel Humphries, of Hartford, Conn., March 14, 1709. He died December, 1711, aged ——. 2. To John Hubbard of the same town, October, 1715. He was the son of Samuel Hubbard, of Hartford, and was born in August, 1691.

He died ———.

She died ———.

Children,—by her first husband.

49 Dosetheus,	born December	4, 1709.	
50 Agnes,	born	1711.	Married Cyprian Nichols, Jr., of Hartford.

Children,—by her second husband.

51 Hannah,	born December	25, 1716.
52 Abigail,	born January	29, 1719.
53 John.	born April	25, 1721.

FOURTH GENERATION.

13.

HEPZIBAH SPENCER was twice married. 1. To ——— Smith, of Haddam, Conn. He died ———. 2. To Azariah Dickinson, Jun., of the same town, November 30, 1732. He was born June 5, 1709, at Haddam, and was son of Azariah Dickinson, of Haddam, formerly of Deerfield, Mass.

Mrs. Hepzibah Dickinson, alias Smith, died July 18, 1754, in her 47th year.

Mr. Azariah Dickinson died ———.

Children,—by her first husband,—none found.

Children,—by her second husband.

54 Azariah,	born July	17, 1733.
55 Mary,	born September	2, 1735.
56 John,	born December	27, 1737.

```
57 Dan,      born January  14, 1740.
58 Ruth,     born March    10, 1742.
59 Agnes,    born March    21, 1745.
```

14.

SAMUEL SPENCER, first of Bolton, Conn., then of Suffield, Conn., and afterwards of Salisbury, in the same State, was married to Hannah Shailor, daughter of Abel Shailor, of Bolton, April 26, 1735.

Mrs. Hannah Spencer died ———.

Mr. Samuel Spencer died at the house of his brother, Deacon Job Spencer, in Salisbury, February 2, 1796, aged 92.

Children.

```
60 Rachel,    born November 17, 1736, in Bolton, Conn.
61 Hannah,    born December  1, 1738, in Bolton, Conn.
62 Miriam,    born February   8, 1741, in Bolton, Conn.
63 Hepzibah,  born November 17, 1743, in Bolton, Conn.
64 Samuel,    born March      8, 1746, in Bolton, Conn.
65 John,      bap. August    21, 1748, in Bolton, Conn.
```

15.

WILLIAM SPENCER, first of Bolton, Conn., then of Suffield, Conn., then of Salisbury, in the same State, and afterwards of Sheffield, Mass., was married to Hannah Copeley, daughter of Matthew Copeley, of Suffield, June 12, 1734.

Mr. William Spencer died at Suffield, 1782, aged 74.

His widow, Mrs. Hannah Spencer, died ———.

Children.

```
66 Hannah,    born June     24, 1735, in Bolton. Died in childhood.
67 Tryphena,  born November  4, 1736, in Suffield. Died September 21, 1754,
                                 in Salisbury.
68 Eliphaz,   born April    27, 1738, in Suffield.
69 Hannah,    born October  23, 1739, in Suffield. Died in infancy.
70 Hannah,    born August   26, 1741, in Suffield.
71 Irena,     born June     16, 1743, in Suffield.
72 Alpheus,   born February 11, 1745, in Suffield.
```

16.

EDWARD SPENCER, first of Bolton, Conn., afterwards of Susquehanna county, Penn., was married to Sarah Chapman, daughter of Jabez Chapman, Esq., of East Haddam, Conn., April 8, 1737.   She was born September 8, 1720.

Mrs. Sarah Spencer died in Susquehanna county, September 13, 1786, in her 66th year.

Mr. Edward Spencer died at Hanover, Susquehanna county, March 26, 1790, in his 80th year.

Children.

```
73 Mehitabel,  born March    17, 1739, in Bolton.
74 Edward,     born December  3, 1741, in Bolton. Died December 13, 1750.
75 Ann,        born June     27, 1744, in East Haddam.
76 Beaumont,   born January  25, 1747, in East Haddam.  Died in February,
                                 1779.
77 Simeon,     born August   19, 1749, in Bolton.
```

78 Edward,   born May   17, 1752, in Bolton.
79 Esther,   born December   7, 1754, in Bolton.
80 Josiah,   born June   16, 1757, in Bolton. Went to Wyoming, with a
                                 view to settle there, but was killed
                                 in battle, July 3, 1778.
80½ Sarah,   born December   5, 1761. Married Abraham Lines, April 26, 1784.
                                 Died without children, April 5, 1845.

18.

CALEB SPENCER, of Bolton, Conn., until 1774, then of Wilkes-
Barre, Penn., until about 1793, when he removed to Kentucky,
was married to Hannah Hebard, widow of Ebenezer Hebard, deceased, and daughter of Andrew Downer, of Norwich, Conn.,
about 1760.

"Doct. Avery Downer, the last survivor of the battle of Fort
Griswold, died at Preston, on Saturday, July 15, 1854, aged 91
years and 8 months. He was at Fort Griswold with his father,
who also was a physician at the time of the massacre, and assisted
to dress the wounds of the soldiers." [Connecticut Courant, Saturday, July 22, 1854.] Doct. Avery Downer was a son of Doct.
Joshua Downer, of Preston, born August 6, 1735, son of Andrew
Downer, of that place, and brother of Hannah Downer, who married Ebenezer Hebard, and after his death, Caleb Spencer.

Mrs. Hannah Spencer, alias Hebard, died at Wilkes-Barre, in
the spring of the year 1779, of small-pox, aged 55.

Mr. Caleb Spencer died ———.

Children.

81 Walter,   born April   14, 1761, in Bolton. Settled in Wilkes-Barre.
                                 Was in the battle of that place, July
                                 3, 1778, and escaped unhurt. Mar-
                                 ried Sally Johnson about 1779. Re-
                                 moved from Wilkes-Barre to Ken-
                                 tucky, in company with his father,
                                 about the year 1793, and at the time
                                 of his removal, had several children,
                                 smart and promising.
82 Hannah,   born   1763. Married Richard Inman, of Wilkes-
                                 Barre, about 1779. He was one of
                                 several brothers, two of whom were
                                 killed on the battle-field, July 3,
                                 1778, and two more by skirmishing
                                 parties of Indians, in the same year.
                                 Mrs. Hannah Inman died in March,
                                 1835, aged 73. Mr. Richard Inman
                                 died in July, 1831, aged 77. They
                                 had a numerous family of children,
                                 who are all removed to the "western
                                 country."

19.

JOB SPENCER, first of Bolton, Conn., then of East Haddam,
Conn., and afterwards of Salisbury, in the same State, was mar-
ried to Rebecca Chapman, daughter of Jabez Chapman, Esq., of
East Haddam, November 13, 1746. She was born May 16, 1725,

Mrs. Rebecca Spencer died in Salisbury, July 22, 1792,
aged 67.

Deacon Job Spencer died in Salisbury, February 20, 1800, in his 78th year.

Children.

83 Asa,	born September	1, 1747.
84 Samuel,	born October	5, 1749.
85 Eliphaz,	born March	23, 1752.
86 Thankful,	born November	28, 1753. Died July 24, 1754.
87 Tryphena,	born June	22, 1756.
88 Thankful,	born March	22, 1759.
89 Job,	born October	10, 1761.
90 Esther Selden,	born January,	1764. Died at an advanced age, unmarried.

20.

PHILIP SPENCER, first of Bolton, Conn., then of Salisbury, in the same State, and afterwards of the town of North-East, Dutchess county, N. Y., was twice married. 1. To Abigail Moore, daughter of Jonathan Moore, of Salisbury, formerly of Simsbury, Conn., and of Hannah his wife, and daughter of Thomas Long, of Hartford, Conn., afterwards of Windsor, in the same State, September 25, 1751, " by Jonathan Lee, Pastor."* She died December 18, 1787, aged 53.† 2. To Sarah Hopkins, widow of Michael Hopkins, and aunt of Luther Holley, of North-East.

Mrs. Sarah Spencer, alias Hopkins, died March 1, 1808, " over 80."

Philip Spencer, Esq., died May 8, 1815, in the 86th year of his age.‡

Children,—by his first wife.

91 Abigail,	born May	8, 1752, in Salisbury.
92 Tryphena,	born May	1, 1755, in Salisbury.
93 Diademia,	born June	27, 1759, in Salisbury.
94 Philip,	born September	26, 1763, in Salisbury.
95 Ambrose,	born December	13, 1765, in Salisbury.
96 Alexander,	born June	16, 1769, in North-East.

Children,—by his second wife,—none.

FIFTH GENERATION.

83.

ASA SPENCER, first of Salisbury, Conn., then of Vermont, and afterwards of Western New York, was married to Polly Peck, daughter of Abner Peck, of East Haddam, Conn.

---

* Thomas Long married Sarah Willcox, daughter and only child of John Willcox, of Hartford, afterwards of Middletown, by his first wife Sarah Wadsworth, daughter of William Wadsworth, Esq., one of the first settlers of Hartford—ancestor of the late Rev. Daniel Wadsworth, of Hartford, of the late Hon. Col. Jeremiah Wadsworth and Daniel Wadsworth, Esq., of Hartford, Gen. William Wadsworth and Hon. James Wadsworth, of Genesee, N. Y., and of a long line of other distinguished men of his name.

† In Memory of Mrs. Abigail Spencer, consort of Philip Spencer, Esq., who died December 18, 1787, aged 53. This stone is erected by her son Ambrose Spencer, to record his filial love for one of the best of mothers, who in her religion was sincere ; in her morals, pure ; and in her life, irreproachable. [Gravestone, North-East burying-ground.]

‡ In Memory of Philip Spencer, Esq., who died May 8, 1815, in the 86th year of his age. This stone is erected by his son, Ambrose Spencer, as a testimonial of the filial love which he bore to a parent who exhibited through life the tenderest affection for his children ; who lived an honest man, and died a Christian. [Gravestone, North-East burying-ground.]

Mrs. Polly Spencer died in Vermont.

Mr. Asa Spencer died in Western New York, at an advanced age, at the house of his eldest son.

Children,—recorded to him on Salisbury town records.

97 Betsey,	born March	31, 1777.
98 James,	born April	26, 1780.
99 Polly,	born April	15, 1782.
100 Olivia,	born June	23, 1784.
101 Abner		
Peck,	born April	17, 1786.
102 Laura,	born May	18, 1788.

84.

SAMUEL SPENCER, first of Salisbury, Conn., afterwards of Sunbury, Geo., was married to Love Yates, of Sunbury, about 1776. After his death, she is said to have married Benjamin Terry, who subsequently removed to the State of New York.

Mr. Samuel Spencer died at Sunbury, July 5, 1786, in his 37th year.

His widow, Mrs. Love Spencer, died ———.

Children.

103 John,	born March,	1777.
104 Esther,	born October,	1780.
105 Love,	born	1782.

85.

ELIPHAZ SPENCER, first of East Haddam, Conn., afterwards of Salisbury, of the same State, was married to Statira Hall, daughter of Thomas Hall, of East Haddam, 1777. She was born June 19, 1755.

Mr. Eliphaz Spencer died June 8, 1833, aged 81.

His widow, Mrs. Statira Spencer, died September 12, 1833, aged 77.

Children.

106 Achsah,	born April	13, 1778, in East Haddam.
107 Gurdon,	born March	26, 1781, in East Haddam. Died February 24, 1788, in Salisbury.
108 Lovina,	born October	4, 1785, in Salisbury. Died August 18, 1786.
109 Gurdon,	born April	29, 1789, in Salisbury.
110 Statira,	born March	29, 1791, in Salisbury.

87.

TRYPHENA SPENCER was married to Gideon Buckingham, of ———. After his death, she was married to a Mr. Weare, of Renssellaerville, N. Y.

Mr. Gideon Buckingham died June 19, 1792; killed by the fall of a tree.

His widow, Mrs. Tryphena Buckingham, died ———.

Child,—one only.

111 Tryphena, born	Married James Ware, of Rensellaerville, N. Y.

88.

THANKFUL SPENCER was married to Seymour Selleck, first of Salisbury, Conn., afterwards of Middlebury, Ver.

Mr. Seymour Selleck died ———.

His widow, Mrs. Thankful Selleck, died at an advanced age.

Children.

112 Rebecca,   born
113 Sally,   born
114 Seymour,   born

89.

JOB SPENCER, of Salisbury, Conn., was thrice married. 1. To Rachel Hurlburt, daughter of Amos Hurlbut, of Chatham Conn., 1785. She died January 30, 1807, aged 47. 2. To Hannah Moulton, daughter of ——— Moulton, of Castleton, Ver., April, 1810. She died April 5, 1815, aged 44. 3. To Elizabeth Bingham, widow of Jabez Bingham, deceased, of Salisbury, and daughter of Daniel Brewster, of ———, 1822.

Mr. Job Spencer died February 18, 1840, aged 78.

Mrs. Elizabeth Spencer, alias Bingham, was alive in 1850.

Children,—by his first wife.

115 Lavinia,   born July   21, 1786.   Married Chauncey Reed, of Salisbury, January 4, 1809. They have had 6 children.
116 Sally,   born November 21, 1788.   Died November 1, 1795.
117 Thankful, born November 27, 1791.   Married Julius Hollister, of Salisbury, November 29, 1810. They had 3 children —all sons.

Children,—by his second wife.

118 Sally,   born November 21, 1813.   Died at the age of 7 years.
119 Hannah,   born March   23, 1815.   Married Aden W. Coburn, of Windsor, N. Y., where they now dwell.

Child,—by his third wife,—one only.

120 Job B.,   born January   19, 1823,   Lives in Salisbury, unmarried.

91.

ABIGAIL SPENCER was married to Ezra St. John, of Sharon, Conn. He settled in Salisbury, Conn., from which place, about sixty years ago, he removed to Stillwater, N. Y., and from thence to Butternuts, in the same State.

Ezra St. John, Esq., died at Butternuts, about 1814.

His widow, Mrs. Abigail St. John, died at Butternuts, about 1839.

Children,—names not found.

92.

TRYPHENA SPENCER was twice married. 1. To Medad Parker, of Salisbury, Conn. He died ———. 2. To Rev. John Barnet, first settled minister of the Presbyterian Church, Middle-

bury, Ver., Chaplain in the army of the Revolution, and afterwards Pastor of the Church, at Amenia, N. Y.

Mrs. Tryphena Barnet, alias Parker, died at Amenia, March 9,
1812, in her 61st year.

Rev. John Barnet died at New Durham, N. Y., December 5,
1837, aged "about 87."

Children,—by her first husband.

121 Ralph,   born September 17, 1772.   Dwelt some time in Rochester, N. Y.
122 Tryphena, born September 14, 1774.
123 Philip,   born September 7, 1776.   Settled in Albany, N. Y.; was many
                                           years recorder of that city.

Children,—by her second husband.

124 John,   born February   4, 1787, at North-East, where he settled, and now
                                         dwells.
125 William, born December,   1791, at Middlebury, Ver.
126 Alma,   born   1794.

93.

DIADEMIA SPENCER was married to Doct. William Wheeler,
first of Salisbury, Conn., afterwards of Red Hook, N. Y. After
her death, he was again married.

Mrs. Diademia Wheeler died January 13, 1781, in her 22d year.

Doct. William Wheeler died ———.

Child,—one only.

127 Diademia, born December 3, 1780.

94.

PHILIP SPENCER, first of Poughkeepsie, N. Y., afterwards of
the State of Louisiania, was married to Susan Bull, daughter of
Doct. Daniel Bull, of North-East, and sister of Doct. John Bull,
of the same town.

95.

AMBROSE SPENCER, of Albany, N. Y., was thrice married. 1.
To Laura Canfield, daughter of John Canfield, Esq., of Sharon,
Conn., February 18, 1784. She died May 18, 1807, aged 39.
2. To Mary Norton, widow of Burrage Norton, Esq., of England,
deceased, daughter of Gen. James Clinton, of the city of New
York, and Mary De Witt, his wife, and sister of Hon. De Witt
Clinton. She died September 4, 1808, in the 36th year of her
age. 3. To Catharine Norton, widow of Samuel Norton, Esq.,
deceased, of England, and sister of his second wife.

Mrs. Catharine Spencer, alias Norton, died September, 1838.

Hon. Ambrose Spencer died at his house in Lyons, N. Y.,
March 13, 1848, in the 83d year of his age.

Children,—by his first wife.

128 Son, (not
     named,) born September,   1786. Died in infancy.

41

129 John Can- field,	born January	3, 1788.	Married Eliza S. Smith.
130 Abigail, (or Abba,)	born January	12, 1790.	Married John Townsend. She died August 17, 1839.
131 William Augustus, born January		7, 1793.	Married 1. A daughter of William Hill, of Albany; after her death, 2. E. Lorillard, and after her death, 3. Catharine Lorillard, daughters of Pe- ter Lorillard, Esq., of New York. William A. Spencer, Esq., Capt. U. S. N., died in New York, March 3, 1854, aged 61. As Lieutenant in the battle of Lake Champlain, under Commodore McDonough, he won distinction.
132 Ambrose,	born July	18, 1795.	Died August 5, 1814, on the Niagara River, of wounds received in the bat- tle of Lundy's Lane.
133 Theodore,	born August	20, 1797.	Died July 12, 1798.
134 Theodore,	born April	24, 1800.	Married Catharine Vosburg.
135 Laura Isa- bella,	born September	24, 1803.	Married Robert Gilchrist, of New York.

96.

ALEXANDER SPENCER, of North-East, N. Y., was married to
Olive Harrison, daughter of Jared Harrison, of Salisbury, Conn.
[After his death, she was married to Rev. Dr. Lee, pastor of
the Congregational Church in Colebrook, Conn., by whom she had
several children.]

Alexander Spencer, Esq., died March 18, 1802, being at Albany,
N. Y., as a member of Assembly from Dutchess County, aged 33.

Mrs. Olive Spencer, alias Lee, died ———.

Children.

136 Alexander, born
137 Laura,   born

DESCENDANTS IN THE LINE OF ELIZABETH SPENCER, DAUGHTER OF WILLIAM SPENCER, THE SETTLER.

SECOND GENERATION.

III.

ELIZABETH SPENCER was twice married. 1. To William
Wellman, one of the first settlers of New London, Conn., afterwards of Killingworth, in the same State, 1649. He died in
Killingworth, August 9, 1671. 2. To Jacob Joy, of Killingworth,
formerly of Fairfield, Conn., May 23, 1672.

He died ———.
She died ———.

Children,—by her first husband.

138 Mary,	born	1650.	
139 Martha,	born	1652.	
140 Benjamin,	born	1654.	"Left home unmarried, when a young man, and never, thereafter, heard from."

141	Elizabeth,	born	1657.
142	William,	born	1661.
143	Sarah,	born October	16, 1665, in Killingworth. Died in childhood.
144	Samuel,	born January	19, 1667, in Killingworth. Died in or before, 1682.
145	Rachel,	born [no date.]	Died in 1692, leaving a will.

Children,—by her second husband.

146 Deborah, born February 23, 1673. Married Andrew Ward, of Killing worth, afterwards of Guilford, Conn., November 19, 1691. She died February 22, 1752, aged 79 years, " wanting a day." Capt. Andrew Ward died August 7, 1756, " at noon," aged 86. They had 9 children.

147 Jacob, born March 14, 1675. Supposed to have died young.
148 Walter, born August 14, 1677. Died, before 1690.
149 Mary, born September 17, 1680. Married Peter Ward, of Killingworth, brother of the husband of her sister Deborah, March 30, 1699. She died before her husband. Capt. Peter Ward, died December 18, 1763, aged 37. *Children,*—Pelatiah, born December 22, 1699; Ira, born August 30, 1704; Ichabod, born April 2, 1707; Peter, born October 11, 1709; Mary, born April 20, 1713; Matteniah, born March 24, 1718.

THIRD GENERATION.

138.

MARY WELLMAN was twice married. 1. To Thomas Howard, of Norwich, Conn., January, 1666. He died ———. 2. To William Moore, of the same town, afterwards of Windham, Conn., August, 1677. [After her death, Mr. Moore was married, 1. To Mary Allen, widow of Joshua Allen, deceased, of Windham, July 17, 1700. She died September 18, 1727. 2. To Tamerron Simmons, of Windham, June 10, 1728. She survived Mr. Moore. No issue by his two last wives.]

Mrs. Mary Moore, alias Howard, died April 3, 1700, aged 50. Mr. William Moore died April, 1729.

Children,—by her first husband.

150 Mary, born December, 1667.
151 Sarah, born February, 1669. Married Joseph Gere, of Preston, Conn., January 7, 1693. He died July, 1743. Children are recorded to them on the Preston records.

152 Martha, born February, 1672. Died about one month after.
153 Thomas, born March, 1673. Died in childhood.
154 Benjamin, born June, 1675. Settled in Windham. Married, and had 4 children born to him in Windham. Removed from Windham, and afterwards removed again. His last place of abode not discovered.

Children,—by her second husband.

155 Elizabeth, born July 20, 1679. Married Daniel Edwards, of Windham, Conn., February 27, 1701. He died 1756. 7 children recorded to them.

156 Experience, born May 12, 1680.
157 Martha, born February 22, 1681.

158 Joshua,	born	1683.	Settled in Mansfield, Conn. Married Dorothy Badcock, daughter of Jonathan Badcock, of Windham, Conn., March 3, 1714. He died October 2, 1756, in the 73d year of his age. [Gravestone, South Mansfield.] She died January 9, 1783, in the 94th year of her age. [Gravestone, South Mansfield.]
159 William,	born	1685.	Died, unmarried, January 23, 1700.
160 Abigail,	born	1687.	Married Caleb Badcock, of Windham, Conn., January 21, 1713. He was born June 30, 1667. [After her death, he was married to Mirriam Simmons, widow of Jonathan Simmons, deceased, of Windham, May 7, 1728.] Mrs. Abigail Badcock died April 21, 1719, in the 31st year of her age. Mr. Caleb Badcock died August 6, 1741, aged 64. They had 3 children.

139.

MARTHA WELLMAN was married to Clement Miner, of New London, Conn., formerly of Gloucester, Mass., 1678. She was his second wife. [After her death he was married to Joanna ———, but had no issue by her. She died October, 1700. His first wife, to whom he was married in 1662, was Frances Willie, widow of Isaac Willey, Jun., deceased, of New London. She died January 6, 1673. By her he had children,—Mary, born January 19, 1665; Joseph, born August 6, 1666; Clement, born October 6, 1668; William, born November 6, 1670; Ann, born November 30, 1672.]

Mrs. Martha Miner died July 5, 1681, aged 29.

Deacon Clement Miner died October, 1700.

Child,—one only.

| 161 Phebe, | born April | 13, 1679. | Married John Stebbins. |

141.

ELIZABETH WELLMAN was married to John Shethar, of Killingworth, Conn., January 9, 1678.

Mrs. Elizabeth Shethar died February 5, 1718, aged 61.

Sergeant John Shethar died May 12, 1721, aged —.

Children.

162 Elizabeth,	born November	20, 1679.
163 Hannah,	born November	25, 1681.
164 John,	born March	23, 1685.
165 Rachel,	born [no date.]
167 Susannah,	born [no date.]

142.

WILLIAM WELLMAN, of Killingworth, Conn., was twice married. 1. To Elizabeth ———. She died January 5, 1729, aged 68.

2. To Elizabeth Griswold, widow of Isaac Griswold, deceased, of Killingworth, June 25, 1730.

Mrs. Elizabeth Wellman, alias Griswold, died October 27, 1732, aged —.

Sargeant William Wellman died August 23, 1736, aged 75.

Children,—by his first wife.

167 Mary,	born March	26, 1692.	Married to Jonathan Lane, of Killingworth, Conn., February 1, 1711. [After her death, he was married to Patience ——, by whom he had two children.]¹ Mrs. Mary Lane died November 13, 1727, in the 36th year of her age. Jonathan Lane, Esq., died, 1759. They had 3 children.
168 William,	born May	2, 1694.	
169 Gideon,	born March	8, 1696.	
170 Benjamin,	born December	26, 1697.	

FOURTH GENERATION.

168

WILLIAM WELLMAN, of Killingworth, Conn., was married to Ruth Hurd, daughter of —— Hurd, June 14, 1722. [After his death, she was married to Samuel Kelsey, of Killingworth. He was a descendant of Stephen Kelsey, one of the first settlers of Hartford, Conn.]

Mr. William Wellman died November 12, 1753, aged 57.

Mrs. Ruth Wellman, alias Kelsey, died ——.

Children.

171 Elizabeth,	born March	18, 1723.	
172 Zadock,	born February	12, 1725.	
173 Benjamin,	born January	12, 1727.	
174 Ruth,	born February	27, 1729.	
175 Jerusha,	born April	1, 1732.	
176 Gideon,	born June	17, 1735.	Died December 31, 1836.
177 Gideon,	born September	30, 1737.	Died December 7, 1762, unmarried.
178 Hannah,	born December	27, 1744.	

169.

GIDEON WELLMAN, of Killingworth, Conn., was twice married. 1. To Concurrence Hull, daughter of Nathaniel Hull, of the same town, April 14, 1720. She died February 14, 1740, aged —. 2. To Rebecca Doud, daughter of —— Doud, February 13, 1741.

Capt. Gideon Wellman died —— 1760.

His widow, Mrs. Rebecca Wellman died ——.

Children,—by his first wife.

179 Samuel,	born April	22, 1721.
180 Mary,	born December	11, 1722.
181 Elihu,	born December	19, 1724.
182 Mercy,	born October	6, 1726.
183 William,	born August	11, 1728.
184 Barnabas,	born June	17, 1730.
185 Concurrence, 186 Lydia,	twins	born September	8, 1733.

170.

BENJAMIN WELLMAN, of Killingworth, Conn., until 1782, and after that year of Sunderland, Ver., was twice married. 1. To Patience Griswold, daughter of ——— Griswold, of Killingworth, February 28, 1754. She died November 30, 1754, aged ———. 2. To Molly Divall, daughter of ——— Divall. He died ———.
She died ———.

Child,—by his first wife,—one only.

187 Ruth, born November 16, 1754.

Children,—by his second wife.

188 Patience,	born September 28, 1756.
189 Temperance,	born August 7, 1758.
190 Mercy,	born November 28, 1759.
191 John,	born April 8, 1761.
192 Gideon,	born May 21, 1763. Died September 9, 1763.
193 Gideon,	born October 5, 1764.
194 Jerusha,	born January 27, 1767.
195 Molly,	born January 14, 1769.
196 Lydia,	born September 24, 1771.

FIFTH GENERATION.

172.

ZADOCK WELLMAN, of Killingworth, Conn., was twice married. 1. To Sarah Spencer, daughter of Caleb Spencer, of Westbrook Society, Saybrook, Conn., and descendant of Sargeant Jared Spencer, one of the first settlers of Haddam, in the same State, December 11, 1754. She died August, 1788, aged 54. 2. To Martha Chatfield, widow of John Chatfield, deceased, of Killingworth, 1789.
Mr. Zadock Wellman died December 1794, aged 69.
Mrs. Martha Wellman, alias Chatfield, died ———.

Children,—by his first wife.

197 William, } twins. 198 Sarah, }	born March 7, 1756.
199 Jemima,	born December 9, 1758.
200 Zadock,	born September 2, 1760.
201 Jonathan,	born July 4, 1762.
202 Hannah,	born January 26, 1764.
203 Lemuel,	born November 26, 1766.
204 Samuel,	born October 12, 1767.
205 John Spencer,	born January 9, 1769.
206 Phebe,	born November 2, 1770.
207 Benjamin,	born February 18, 1772.
208 Elizabeth,	born May 4, 1774.
209 David,	born January 4, 1776.

183.

WILLIAM WELLMAN, Jun., of Killingworth, Conn., was married to Margaret Stevens, daughter of ——— Stevens, December 17, 1750.
He died ———.
She died ———.

Children,—recorded to them on the Killingworth records.

210 Grace,   born October   20, 1752.
211 Samuel,   born August   14, 1754.
212 William,   born September   5, 1756.
212 Joel,   born September   2, 1758.

184.

BARNABAS WELLMAN, of Killingworth, Conn., was married to Sarah Ward, daughter of ——— Ward, April 7, 1752.

Capt. Barnabas Wellman died 1766, aged 36.

His widow, Mrs. Sarah Wellman, died ———.

Children.

214 Freelovè,   born May   22, 1753.
215 Molly,   born March   15, 1755.
216 Barnabas,   born
217 Paul,   born
218 Sarah,   born
219 John,   born
220 James,   born

RICHARD TREAT.

II. p. 229.

Children of Hon. Robert Treat.

1 Samuel,	born	1648.	Harvard College, 1669; settled in the Ministry in 1672, at Eastham, Mass. He died March 18, 1717, aged 69, leaving a numerous family. One of his daughters was the mother of Robert Treat Paine, one of the signers of the Declaration of Independence.
2 John,	born	1650.	Settled in Newark, N. J.
3 Robert,	born	1654.	Settled in Milford, Conn.
4 Abigail,	born	1659.	Married Rev. Samuel Andrew, pastor of the Congregational Church at Milford, and afterwards rector of Yale College. She died December 25, 1727, in the 68th year of her age. Rev. Samuel Andrew died January 24, 1727-8, lacking five days of eighty-two years of age.
5 Hannah,	born	1661.	Married Rev. Samuel Mather, of Windsor, Conn. She died March 18, 1727-8, aged 77.
6 Joseph,	born	1662.	Settled in Milford. Married Frances Bryan, daughter of Richard Bryan, of Milford. She was born February 13, 1668.
7 Jane,	born		
8 Anna,	born		

WILLIAM WHITING.

WILLIAM WHITING, one of the early settlers of Hartford, is mentioned in the histories of this country as early as 1632 or 3. Between 1631 and 1633, " The Bristol men had sold their interest in Piscataqua, to the Lords Say and Brooke, George Wyllys and William Whiting, who continued Thomas Wiggin their agent, &c." Mr. Whiting retained his interest in Piscataqua till his death.

He was "one of the most respectable of the settlers in 1636"— " one of the civil and religious Fathers of Connecticut," a man of wealth and education, styled in the records "William Whiting, Gentleman." In 1642 he was chosen one of the Magistrates; 1641, Treasurer of the Colony, which office he retained till his death. In 1646 "a plot was laid by Sequasson, Sachem of the Naticks, to kill Governors Haynes and Hopkins and Mr. Whiting, on account of the just and faithful protection which these gentlemen had afforded to Uncas. The plot was made known by a friendly Indian and the danger averted."

He bore the title of Major in 1647.

William Whiting died July, 1647.*

[His widow, Susannah, married, 1650, Mr. Samuel Fitch, of Hartford, by whom she had two sons. Mr. Fitch died 1659, and she married 3. Mr. Alexander Bryan, of Milford. She died at Middletown, at the house of her daughter, Mrs. Collins, and was buried there July 8, 1673.]

FIRST GENERATION.

Children,—of William Whiting and Susannah.

I. William,	born		Died, 1699, in London.
II. John,	born	1635.	Died, 1689, in Hartford.
III. Samuel,	born		
IV. Sarah,	born about	1637.	Married 1. Jacob Mygatt. 2. John King. Died, 1704.
V. Mary,	born		Died October 25, 1709.
VI. Joseph,	born October	2, 1645.	Died 1717.†

---

* The will of William Whiting may be seen in Trumbull's Colonial Records of Connecticut, Vol. I., page 493.

† It appears by Trumbull's Colonial Records, Vol. I., page 495, that there was also a son born after the death of his father.

DESCENDANTS IN THE LINE OF WILLIAM WHITING, SON OF WILLIAM WHITING.

SECOND GENERATION.

I.

WILLIAM WHITING, eldest son of William Whiting, was probably born in England, before his parents came to this country. He went to England, and was a merchant in London where he died in 1699. His son Joseph was appointed administrator of his estate. In 1686 the Assembly of Connecticut appointed him their "agent to present their petition (in reference to the Charter) to the King." He exerted himself in behalf of the colony and received the thanks of the Assembly for his services, and was requested to continue them.

DESCENDANTS IN THE LINE OF JOHN WHITING, SON OF WILLIAM WHITING.

SECOND GENERATION.

II.

JOHN WHITING, second son of William Whiting, was born 1635; graduated at Harvard College, 1653; preached several years in Salem, Mass. He was there in 1659, March 8, when "the selectmen, together with the deacons and Mr. Gedney, are desired to treat with Mr. Whiting to know his mind about staying with us." [Salem Town Records.] He removed with his family "from the Bay" to Hartford, and was ordained over the First Church in 1660. In 1669, in consequence of the discussions which agitated the church at that time, Mr. Whiting and others presented a petition to the Assembly "for their approbation, for a distinct walking in Congregational Church Order," which was granted, and in 1670, a new Church was formed, of which Mr. Whiting was chosen pastor, and so continued till his death, September 8th, 1689.

Rev. John Whiting was twice married. 1. To Sybil Collins, daughter of Deacon Edward Collins, of Cambridge, Mass., by whom he had 7 children. 2. In 1673, to Phebe Gregson, daughter of Thomas Gregson, of New Haven, (who was lost at sea, 1646, in the Phantom ship.) She was born 1643. Died September 19, 1730. [She married again, 1692, Rev. John Russell, of Hadley, and after his death went to New Haven, and died there.]

Children,—by his first wife.

7 Sybil,	born	1655.	
8 John,	born	1657.	Died young.
9 William,	born	1659.	Baptized February 19, 1660.
10 Martha,	born	1662.	

11 Sarah,	born	1664.
12 Abigail,	born	1666.
13 Samuel,	born April	22, 1670. Settled in Windham.

Children,—by his second wife.

14 Thomas,	born	1674. Died in infancy.
15 Mary,	born	1676. Died September 30, 1689.
16 Elizabeth,	born	1678. Married Nathaniel Pitkin. Died in Hadley, Mass.
17 Joseph,	born	1680. Settled in New Haven.
18 Nathaniel,	born	1683. Died young.
19 Thomas,	born	1686. Died young.
20 John,	born	1688. Died 1715, unmarried.

THIRD GENERATION.

7.

SYBIL WHITING married Alexander Bryan, of Milford, son of
Richard Bryan, and grandson of Hon. Alexander Bryan, one of
the first settlers of that town.

Children.

21 Ann,	born September	8, 1674.
22 Alexander,	born June	15, 1677.
23 John,	born July	12, 1680.
24 Alexander,	born November	24, 1682.
25 Ebenezer,	born February	2, 1690.
26 Augustina-tha,	born April	25, 1694.

9.

WILLIAM WHITING represented Hartford in the General
Court from 1710 to 1715, and was Speaker in 1714. In 1693,
he went as Captain of a company of Whites and Indians to
Maine. In 1705 he held the rank of Major. In 1709 he bore
the rank of Colonel, and led a body of horse and infantry into the
county of Hampshire, Mass., to repel the French and Indians.
In 1710 he was in command of the troops at Port Royal, and in
1711, in the expedition against Canada. Col. Whiting was Sheriff
of Hartford county in 1722. He removed to Newport, R. I., late
in life, and probably died there. He married October 6, 1686,
Mary Allyn, daughter of Col. John Allyn, and great-granddaughter of Hon. William Pynchon. She was born April 3, 1657, and
died December 14, 1724.

Children.

27 Mary,	born April	1, 1688. Died November 6, 1714, unmarried.
28 Charles,	born July	5, 1692.
29 William,	born February	15, 1694.

10.

MARTHA WHITING was married December 25, 1683, at Hartford, by Col. John Allyn, to Samuel Bryan, of Milford, son of
Richard Bryan, of that town.

Children.

30 Mary,	born	1685.
31 Martha,	born	1689.
32 Susanna,	born	1691.
33 Abigail,	born	1693.
34 Sybil,	born June	9, 1695.
35 Jerusha,	born July	4, 1697.

11.

SARAH WHITING was married March 19, 1685, to Jonathan Bull, of Hartford, merchant, son of Capt. Thomas Bull, the Pequot officer, and grandson of Thomas Bull, one of the first settlers of the same town.

Major Jonathan Bull died August 17, 1702, aged 53.

Children.

35½ Susanna,	born December	26, 1685.
36 Sarah,	born August	25, 1687.
37 Sybil,	born April	13, 1690.
38 Ruth,	born April	21, 1692.
39 Abigail,	born July	24, 1694.
40 Jonathan,	born July	14, 1696, about 1 o'clock in the morning.
41 Moses,	born May	18, 1699.
42 Ebenezer,	born August	27, 1701.

12.

ABIGAIL WHITING was married to Rev. Samuel Russell, of Deerfield, Mass., afterwards second minister [of Branford, Conn., son of Rev. John Russell, second minister of Wethersfield, Conn., and afterwards first minister of Hadley, Mass.

Rev. Samuel Russell died June 24, 1731, at Branford, in the 71st year of his age, and 34th of his ministry.

Mrs. Abigail Russell died May 7, 1733, in her 67th year.

Children.

43 John,	born January	24, 1686.
44 Abigail,	born August	16, 1690.
45 Samuel,	born September	28, 1693.
46 Timothy,	born November	18, 1695.
47 Daniel,	born June	19, 1698.
48 Jonathan,	born August	21, 1700.
49 Ebenezer,	born May	4, 1703.

13.

SAMUEL WHITING received his early education from his father, and afterwards finished his education for the ministry under the direction of Rev. James Fitch, of Norwich, there being no College in Connecticut. He was the first minister of Windham, Conn. In a record kept by him, (now in possession of one of his descendants in Hartford,) he says, "I preached my first sermon at Windham, from the first verse of Genesis, on the first day of January, 1692–3." "I was ordained at Windham, on the 4th day of December, 1700. Rev. Mr. Whiting died at Enfield, while on a visit to his cousin, Rev. Nathaniel Collins, September 27, 1725.

(Mr. Collins was also his brother-in-law, having married Alice Adams the sister of his wife.)

He married at Norwich, September 14, 1696, Elizabeth Adams, daughter of Rev. William Adams, of Dedham. She was born at Dedham, February 21, 1681, and died December 21, 1766. Her mother was Alice Bradford, daughter of Deputy Governor William Bradford, and granddaughter of Governor Bradford of the Mayflower.

The widow of Rev. Samuel married in 1737, the Rev. Mr. Niles of Braintree, Mass., and on becoming again a widow, May 1, 1762, went to New Haven to live with her son, Col. Nathan Whiting, and died there December 21, 1766.

Children.

50	Anne,	born January	2, 1698.	Married Joseph Fitch.
51	Samuel,	born February	20, 1700.	Lost at sea, 1718.
52	Elizabeth,	born February	11, 1702.	Died September, 1730, unmarried.
53	William,	born January	22, 1704.	Lived in Norwich.
54	Joseph,	born February	17, 1705.	Died, unmarried.
55	John,	born February	20, 1706.	Lived in Windham.
56	Sybil,	born May	6, 1708.	
57	Martha,	born March	12, 1710.	Died June 29, 1719.
58	Mary,	born November	24, 1712.	
59	Eliphalet,	born April	8, 1715.	Died August 9, 1736, unmarried.
60	Elisha,	born January	17, 1717.	
61	Samuel,	born May	15, 1720.	Lived in Stratford.
62	Nathan,	born May	4, 1724.	Died April 9, 1771, in New Haven.

17.

JOSEPH WHITING settled in New Haven. He was elected to the General Court in 1716, 1722 and 1724, and was clerk of the House. He was elected to the upper House in 1725, where he continued 21 years. He married January 30, 1709–10, Hannah Trowbridge, daughter of Thomas Trowbridge.

Hon. Joseph Whiting died April 4, 1748.

Mrs. Hannah Whiting died August 9, 1748.

Children.

63	Hannah,	born February	21, 1712.	Married Jared Ingersoll.
64	Mary,	born February	5, 1714.	Married Stephen Alling, 1744.
65	Elizabeth,	born June	8, 1717.	Married Rev. Chauncey Whittlesey, 1745. Died 1751.
66	Phebe,	born October	23, 1720.	Married Enos Alling, 1749.
67	John,	born March	1, 1721.	Married Sarah Ingersoll. Died 1786.
68	Sarah,	born April	15, 1725.	Married Daniel Lyman, 1748.
69	Joseph,	born January	28, 1727.	
70	Elisha,	born July	29, 1729.	Married Esther Harpin. Died 1766.

20.

JOHN WHITING settled in Hartford, as a merchant. He died unmarried, in 1715, and administration was granted to his brother, Capt. Joseph Whiting, of New Haven.

FOURTH GENERATION.

28.

CHARLES WHITING married, January 10, 1716–17, Elizabeth, daughter of Samuel Bradford, of Duxbury, Mass., and great-granddaughter of Gov. Bradford, of Plymouth. Her mother was Hannah Rogers, daughter of John Rogers and Elizabeth Paybodie, and Elizabeth Paybodie was the granddaughter of John Alden and Priscilla Mullins, two passengers in the Mayflower in 1620. Elizabeth Bradford was born December 15, 1696. [After the death of Mr. Whiting, she married, March, 1739, Deacon John Noyes, of Stonington, and had one daughter, Dorothy, born March, 1740.]

Lieut. Charles Whiting, died at Montville, March 7, 1738.

Mrs. Elizabeth Noyes, alias Whiting, died May 10, 1777.

Children.

71 Mary,	born January,	1717.	Married ——— Gardiner, of Hingham, Mass.
72 John,	born August	3, 1719.	
73 Sybil,	born July,	1722.	Married Willian Noyes. Died April 27, 1790.
74 Charles, }twins 75 Elizabeth, }	born August,	1725.	Married ——— Goodrich.
76 Gamaliel.	born September	17, 1727.	
77 William Bradford,	born April	15, 1731.	
78 Berenice,	born March,	1733.	
79 Ebenezer,	born May,	1735.	

50.

ANNE WHITING, eldest daughter of Rev. Samuel Whiting, of Windham, married, December 29, 1721, Joseph Fitch, son of Rev. James Fitch, of Norwich, Conn. He was born in 1681.

Joseph Fitch died at Lebanon, Conn., May 7, 1741.

Mrs. Anne Fitch died in 1778.

Children.

80 Samuel,	born January	16, 1723.	Settled in Boston, Mass. Was Attorney General of Massachusetts. Married Elizabeth Lloyd, of Boston, and died in England.
81 Eleazer,	born August	27, 1726.	Colonel of the 4th Regiment of Connecticut troops in 1758–60. Married Amy Bowen.
82 Asael,	born November	7, 1728.	
83 Ichabod,	born May	7, 1734.	
84 Ann,	born July	12, 1737.	
85 Thomas,	born		
86 Joseph,	born		
87 Mason,	born		

53.

WILLIAM WHITING married in 1724. 1. Ann, daughter of Joshua Raymond, of Block Island. She died November, 1773. 2. Widow Alithea Woodworth. He was Lieut. Colonel at the seige of Louisburg and at Lake George, under Sir William Johnson. His son John, who was with him, was murdered by the Indians near Lake George.

Children.

88 John,	born	1725.	Killed by the Indians.
89 Samuel,	born	1727.	Married Sarah Dyer, of Canterbury.
90 Caleb,	born	1729.	
91 William,	born	1730.	
92 Anna,	born	1738.	Married James Dyer, of Canterbury. Died 1799.

55.

JOHN WHITING, Yale College, 1726, was for some time a preacher; licensed 1727, but left the ministry, and was judge of probate and colonel of a regiment. He married 1. ——— ———. 2. Widow Mary Clark; he was her third husband. [Her maiden name was Tracy, and she married 1. James Luce. 2. ——— Clark.]

Col. John Whiting died August 28, 1786.

Children.

93 Amos,	born	
94 Mary,	born	Married 1. Harding Jones, of North Carolina. 2. ——— Ellis. Her daughter, Mary Jones, married Abner Nash, Governor of North Carolina, 1779.
95 Wealthy,	born	Married Dr. Gideon Welles, of Canterbury.

56.

SYBIL WHITING married, May 12, 1725, John Backus, Jr., of Windham, Conn.

John Backus died ———

Mrs. Sybil Backus died August 17, 1755.

Children.

96 Lucretia,	born	1733.	Married John Benjamin, of Stratford.
97 Polly,	born		Married Benjamin Lathrop, of Windham.
98 Lydia,	born	1736.	Married Aaron Fish, of Lebanon.
99 Sylvanus,	born	1738.	Married Elizabeth Gamble.
100 Ebenezer,	born	1740.	Married 1. Mercy Edwards. 2. Mrs. Maria Ketchum.
101 DeLucena,	born	1744.	Married 1. Electa Mallory. 2. Tempé Waters.
102 Whiting,	born	1747.	Married Sally Bingham.
103 Charles,	born	1753.	
104 Nathaniel,	born		Died young.
105 Sybil,	born		Died young.
106 Elizabeth,	born		Died young.

58.

MARY WHITING married November 23, 1727, Rev. Thomas Clap, her father's successor in the ministry at Windham, and afterward president of Yale College. She died August 9, 1736.

[After her death he married February 5, 1741, Mrs. Mary Saltonstall, widow of Roswell Saltonstall, of Branford.]

Children.

107 Mary,	born April	25, 1729.	Married March 6, 1745-6, Gen. David Wooster, who lost his life in the service of his country May 1, 1777.
108 Temperance,	born April	26, 1731.	Died June 3, 1731.
109 Temperance,	born April	29, 1732.	Married August 9, 1753, Rev. Timothy Pitkin, of Farmington, Conn., who was son of Gov. William Pitkin; she died May 19, 1772. *Children*,—Samuel, born May 17, 1754, died 1777; Catharine, born February 22, 1757, married Rev. Nathan Perkins, D. D.; Charles, born August 13, 1759, married Cynthia Wells; Elizabeth, born September 19, 1761, married Rev. Timothy Langdon; Anna, born February 19, 1764, married Enoch Perkins; Timothy, born January 20, 1766, (the historian,) married Elizabeth, daughter of Rev. Bela Hubbard, D. D.; Mary, born October 4, 1769, married Rev. Asahel Norton; Temperance, born May 3, 1772, married Bissell Hinsdale.
110 Anna,	born May	13, 1734.	Died May 2, 1735.
111 Child,	born July	25, 1736.	Died same day.

61.

SAMUEL WHITING was a Colonel in the French War, and served also in the Revolution. Four of his sons served in the army ; three, if not all, as officers. He married Elizabeth ———.
Col. Samuel Whiting died at Stratford, February 15, 1803.
Mrs. Elizabeth Whiting died December 5, 1793.

Children.

112 Samuel,	born	Yale College, 1765; a surgeon in the army. Died at Greenwich, Conn., 1832.
113 John,	born	A captain.
114 Judson,	born	An ensign. Died in the old Jersey Prison-ship.
115 David,	born	
116 William,	born	
117 Seymour,	born	

62.

NATHAN WHITING, Yale College, 1743, married July 12, 1750, Mary Saltonstall, daughter of Capt. Roswell Saltonstall, of Branford, Conn. Her mother was Mary Haynes, (widow of Elisha Lord,) granddaughter of Gov. John Haynes of Hartford. [After the death of Mr. Whiting, she married Rev. Warham Williams, of Northford, Conn.] He was a colonel in the French War.
Col. Nathan Whiting died April 9, 1771.

Children.

118 Mary,	born June	6, 1751.	Married Col. Elisha Hale, of Glasten-bury, Conn.
119 Eliphalet,	born June	17, 1753.	
120 A daughter,	born October	4, 1754.	Died an infant.
121 A son,	born	1756.	Died an infant.
122 Nathan Haynes,	born November	6, 1759.	
123 Elizabeth,	born July	21, 1761.	Died an infant.
124 Elizabeth,	born October	14, 1763.	
125 Gurdon Saltonstall,	born September	10, 1766.	
126 Samuel,	born February	22, 1768.	

FIFTH GENERATION.

72.

JOHN WHITING was a colonel in the French war, and had principal command of the troops raised in the colony of Rhode Island, where he then resided. He married ———— Cogswell.

Col. John Whiting died in New London, December 17, 1770.

Children.

127 James,	born	A Physician. Died without issue.
128 Elizabeth,	born	Married —— Leffingwell, of Norwich.
129 Philena,	born	Married —— Haughton, of Montville.
130 Polly,	born	Married —— Root.

74.

CHARLES WHITING married May 18, 1749, Honor Goodrich, daughter of Hezekiah Goodrich, Esq., of Wethersfield. [After the death of Mr. Whiting, his widow married November 14, 1774, Rev. Joshua Belden, of Newington, and had a son, Hezekiah Belden, born February 17, 1778. Died in 1849.]

Children.

131 Charles,	born April	5, 1751.	Died in Great Barrington, Mass., un-married; was an officer in the Revolution.
132 Honor,	born July	5, 1753.	Married —— Goodrich.
133 Hezekiah,	born June	2, 1755.	Lost at sea, unmarried.
134 Mary,	born October	7, 1757.	Married, 1778, Capt. John Ducasse, a French officer in our Revolution. He died in 1780, and she married —— Willis, of North Carolina. She died October 27, 1799.
135 Elizabeth,	born May	29, 1760.	Married —— Romans. Died May 12, 1848.
136 Jeffrey,	born December	18, 1762.	Died at Bath, N. C., unmarried.

76.

GAMALIEL WHITING married June 18, 1752, Anna Gillett; she was born February 18, 1738. He held a commission in the Revolution from John Hancock, and had command of a company in the neighborhood of Boston, soon after the Battle of Lexington. Two or three of his sons who were old enough to carry a musket, served in the army.

43

Gamaliel Whiting died November 27, 1790.
Mrs. Anna Whiting died February 27, 1808.

Children.

137 Elizabeth,	born May	19, 1753.	Died November 11, 1772.
138 Anna,	born November	8, 1754.	Married Rev. Mr. Hopkins, of Great Barrington, Mass.
139 William,	born February	16, 1757.	
140 Mary,	born December	11, 1758.	Married —— Kellogg, of Great Barrington.
141 Ebenezer,	born July	30, 1760.	Died in Canada in 1836.
142 Sarah,	born April	26, 1762.	Died 1838.
143 Gamaliel,	born February	7, 1764.	Died February, 1844.
144 Charles,	born January	6, 1766.	Died 1816.
145 Berenice,	born April	14, 1769.	Died April 1, 1845.
146 John,	born January	3, 1771.	Died January 13, 1846.
147 Elizabeth,	born March	17, 1773.	Married Rev. Mr. Wheeler. Died 1848.

77.

WILLIAM BRADFORD WHITING married 1. 1754, Abigail Carew, and had one daughter; both mother and child died 1756. 2. Amie Lathrop, daughter of Nathaniel Lathrop, of Norwich, July 24, 1757; she was born September 8, 1735. He was a Colonel in the Revolution, and was a member of the Senate of the State of New York for 20 years, and a Judge of the County Court for many years.

Col. William B. Whiting died in Canaan, N. Y., October 13, 1796.

Mrs. Amie Whiting died January 20, 1815.

Children.

148 William,	born May	29, 1758.	Died 1759.
149 Abigail,	bap. February	4, 1760.	Married February 25, 1783, Jason Warner. Died March 31, 1810.
150 Anne,	born February	8, 1762.	Married June 4, 1789, Isaiah Tiffany. She died May 17, 1830. He died December 12, 1800. *Children,—5.*
151 John,	born February	4, 1764.	
152 William B.,	born April	17, 1766.	
153 Daniel,	born May	23, 1768.	
154 Hannah,	born May	8, 1770.	Died 1781.
155 Nathan,	born May	16, 1772.	
156 Samuel,	born October	16, 1776.	
157 Harriet,	born September	14, 1779.	Died July 13, 1804.
158 Charles,	born January	13, 1783.	Died the same year.

79.

EBENEZER WHITING married Ann Fitch, daughter of Col. Eleazer Fitch, of Windham. He resided in Norwich, Conn., and was an officer in the Revolution with the title of Major.

Major Ebenezer Whiting died at Westfield, Mass., September 6, 1794.

His widow, Mrs. Ann Whiting, died June 27, 1827, aged 80.

Children.

159 Augustus,	born	Married Betsey Hoes.
160 Edward,	born	Married Nancy Perkins.
161 Henry,	born	Was a Major U. S. A. Married Nancy Goodwin.

162 Nancy,	born	Married —— Gordon.
163 Charles,	born	Married Margaret Regis; lived in Kinderhook, N. Y.
164 Bowen,	born	Married Nancy McKinstry; lived in Geneva, N. Y.
165 Betsey,	born	Unmarried.
166 Charlotte,	born	
167 Berenice,	born	

90.

CALEB WHITING married in 1756, Lois Lyon. He was a farmer, and resided in Bozrah, Conn.

Caleb Whiting died ———.

Children.

168 Nancy,	born	1756.
169 Lucy,	born	1759.
170 Martha,	born	1761.
171 Ebenezer,	born	1763.
172 Abigail,	born	1766.
173 William,	born	1768.
174 Caleb, ?	born	
175 Raymond,	born	1771.

91.

WILLIAM WHITING "was a learned and distinguished physician, and a devoted patriot in the Revolutionary War." He married in 1759, Anna Mason, daughter of Jeremiah Mason, of Franklin, Conn. He resided in Hartford after his marriage till 1766, when he removed to Great Barrington, Mass., where he died.

Dr. William Whiting died December 8, 1792.

Mrs. Anna Whiting died ———.

Children.

176 Samuel,	born August	14, 1762, at Hartford.
177 William,	born November	7, 1764, at Hartford.
178 Mary Anna,	born October	19, 1767.
179 Abraham,	born September	1, 1769.
180 Elizabeth,	born January,	15, 1772.
181 Mason,	born May	8, 1774.
182 Fanny,	born December	1, 1778. Married Frederic Abbot, of Ohio.

122.

NATHAN HAYNES WHITING, Yale College, 1777, married Ruth Hooker, of Farmington, Conn., and lived on the Haynes farm at West Hartford.

Nathan H. Whiting died in 1801.

Child,—one only.

183 Nathaniel H.,	born	Now living in West Hartford,

125.

GURDON SALTONSTALL WHITING married Elizabeth Wells, of West Hartford, Conn.

Gurdon S. Whiting died July 9, 1804.

Mrs. Elizabeth Whiting died March 17, 1802, aged 34.

Children.

184 Samuel, born September 25, 1794. Married Sophia Kilbourn, of Glastenbury, Conn. She was born January
23, 1796. They are still living.
(1856.)

185 Jason, born May 19, 1796. Married June 5, 1828, Sarah G. Clark,
of Litchfield, Conn., where they now
reside.

SIXTH GENERATION.

139.

WILLIAM WHITING married, May 4, 1779, Lois Andrews.

William Whiting died March 11, 1838.

Mrs. Lois Whiting died January 17, 1729, aged 68.

Children.

186 Sophia, born July 10, 1780. Married Eleazer Valentine. She died
September 2, 1810, and after her
death, Mr. Valentine married for his
second wife, her sister, Lois Whiting.

187 Horace, born September 7, 1782.

188 Charlotte, born August 8, 1784. Married 1. March 25, 1805, Joseph
Mills. He died February, 1813, and
she married 2. August 10, 1817, Luther Gale.

189 Polly, born March 12, 1787. Married 1810, William S. Smith.

190 Wealthy, born January 27, 1789. Married 1. June, 1810, Seth Judd, who
died in 1811. 2. In 1814, Joseph
Belcher.

191 Lois, born March 16, 1790. Married E. Valentine. (2d wife.)

192 Gamaliel, born July 31, 1793.

193 Berenice, born April 14, 1796.

194 Sally, born December 9, 1798.

195 Betsey, born July 23, 1801. Married James Whiting. Died April
7, 1834.

196 William, born December 18, 1803. Died October 5, 1804.

197 William, born October 4, 1804. Died October 16, 1805.

146.

JOHN WHITING married 1. March 4, 1800, Hannah, daughter of Col. Aaron Kellogg; she died March 23, 1823. 2. May 24, 1831, Lucy Allen. He was an eminent lawyer, and a Major General in Berkshire county, Mass.

Gen. John Whiting died at Great Barrington, Mass., January 13, 1846.

Children,—by his first wife.

198 John, born December 4, 1800. Died May 7, 1834.

199 Lucy, born February 24, 1803. Died August 16, 1824.

200 Nancy, born September 29, 1805. Died August 4, 1827.

201 Francis, born March 27, 1808. Married Harriet W. Curtiss.

202 Richard, born June 14, 1811. Died November 26, 1848.

203 Martha, born July 1, 1813. Married David Allen.

204 Hannah, born September 4, 1815.

205 Edward, born January 11, 1818. Died February 29, 1844.

Child,—by her second husband.

206 Isabella, born August 6, 1833.

151.

JOHN WHITING married 1. February 5, 1793, Lydia Leffing-well, of Norwich, Conn. 2. July 24, 1809, Rheua Ellsworth. They lived in Canaan, N. Y.
John Whiting died in 1844.

Children,—by his first wife.

207 John L.,	born November 28, 1793.	Married 1821, Harriet Talman.
208 William S.,	born November 9, 1795.	Married 1820, Mary Starr.
209 Eliza C.,	born	1799.	Married Henry Warner. Died 1831.
210 George B.,	born	1801.	He was for 26 years, missionary of the American Board, and died at Beirut, Syria, November 8, 1855. He married a daughter of Dr. John Ward, of Newark, N. J.
211 Lydia,	born	1803.	Married ——— Grey.
212 Christo-pher,	born	1806.	Married 1831, S. Hamilton.

Children,—by his second wife.

213 Joanna,	born	1810.	Died young.
214 Samuel,	born	1812.	Died young.
215 Henry,	born	1816.	Married Eleadar Warner.
216 Harriet,	born	1820.	Married George Tracy.

152.

WILLIAM B. WHITING married February 5, 1793, Abby Lathrop, of Norwich, Conn.
William B. Whiting, died January 26, 1810.

Children.

217 William,	born	Married Mary Pearce.
218 Charlotte,	born	Married L. Winchester.
219 Edward,	born	Died in Montreal.
220 Mary S.,	born	

153.

DANIEL WHITING married January 4, 1804, Betsey Powers.
Daniel Whiting died in Philadelphia, June 12, 1855.

Children.

221 Elizabeth,	born	1804.	
222 Mary,	born	1806.	Married Rev. Thomas Brainard.
223 Daniel,	born	1808.	Capt. U. S. A. Married Indiana Sanford.
224 Angelica,	born	1810.	
225 William B.,	born	1813.	Lieut. U. S. N. Married Mary L. Nichols.
226 Harriet,	born	1818.	Married George Young.
227 Henry,	born	1821.	Engineer U. S. Coast Survey.

155.

NATHAN WHITING married 1. October 27, 1801, Lydia Backus, of Norwich, Conn. 2. 1835, Mrs. N. B. Williams, of Norwich.
Nathan Whiting died in New Haven, February 19, 1848.
Mrs Lydia Whiting died December 1, 1832.

Children.

228 Daniel W., born December 28, 1802. Died March 2, 1832.
229 Harriet B., born September 6, 1804. Married Hon. A. N. Skinner, of New Haven.
230 Elizabeth, born June, 1806. Died October 16, 1810.
231 Nathan C., born February 13, 1808. Married Mary, daughter of E. Bryan.
232 Esther, born May 30, 1810. Died May 7, 1831.
233 Albertus, born June 22, 1812. Married Katharine De Witt.
234 Alexander, born March 8, 1814. A physician in New York.

156.

SAMUEL WHITING married 1. Fanny Leffingwell, of Norwich, Conn., 1802; she died in 1804. 2. Mrs. Hannah Kinsley, 1806. Samuel Whiting died in New York, in 1834.

Children,—by his second wife.

235 Isabella, born 1806. Died 1833.
236 Hannah, born 1808. Died 1827.
237 Frances, born 1810.
238 Samuel, born 1816.
239 Harriet, born 1821. Married ——— Brooks.

176.

SAMUEL WHITING married 1803, Sarah Betts, daughter of Stephen Betts, of Reading, Conn. Samuel Whiting died January 29, 1832.

Children.

240 William, born Married 1833, Amelia Sherman.
241 Stephen, born May, 1806. Died October 14, 1833.
242 Maria, born Married 1840, Rev. Thomas Dutton.

178.

MARY ANNA WHITING married September 25, 1792, Hon. Elijah Boardman, of New Milford, Conn.

Hon. Elijah Boardman, died ———.

Mrs. Mary Anna Boardman, died at New Milford, June 24, 1848.

Children.

243 William W.,born October 10, 1794. Residence New Haven.
244 Henry M., born January 4, 1797. Married Sarah Benham. Died December, 1829.
245 George S., born October 7, 1799. Died January 18, 1825.
246 Caroline, born Married Rev. Mr. Schroeder.
247 Mary Ann, born November 19, 1805. Died April 7, 1822.
248 Cornelia, born

179.

ABRAHAM WHITING married 1793, Currence Wheeler; was a physician in Great Barrington, Mass.

Children.

249 Harriet, born
250 Emma, born
251 Theodore, born Married 1820, Amelia Ann Robbins.
252 Truman, born Died in Illinois.
253 Huldah, born Married Edward Hills.
254 Gideon, born Married 1833, Louisa Rood.

181.

MASON WHITING married April 26, 1800, Mary Edwards.
Mason Whiting died at Binghampton, N. Y., January 11, 1849.

Children.

255 Mary,	born	Married John T. Doubleday, Brooklyn, N. Y.
256 William,	born	Married Ann Post, New York.
257 Caroline,	born	Married Richard Mather, Binghampton.
258 Rhoda,	born	Married Ralph Lester, Rochester, N. Y.
259 Frances,	born	Married Henry Mather, Binghampton, N. Y.
260 Mason,	born	Married Eliza Vandewater, Binghampton, N. Y.
261 Catharine,	born	Married U. M. Stowers, Binghampton, N. Y.
262 Amelia,	born	Married William S. Tyler, Amherst, Mass.

SEVENTH GENERATION.

187.

HORACE WHITING married May, 1803, Clarissa Miller; lived
at Mount Morris, N. Y.
Horace Whiting died August 11, 1820.

Children.

263 Orpha,	born April,	1806.	Married 1826, Alfred B. Adams.
264 William,	born May	11, 1808.	Married 1832, Catharine Stanley.
265 Nancy,	born February	17, 1809.	Married 1833, Moses Gregory.
266 Charles,	born February	27, 1811.	
267 Hannah,	born March	20, 1813.	Married 1838, Andrew J. McNair.
268 Horace,	born December	20, 1820.	Died 1821.

192.

GAMALIEL WHITING married 1821, Betsey Lawrence.
Gamaliel Whiting died August 1833.

Children.

269 Horace,	born	1822.	Married 1. Harriet Clifford. 2. Elizabeth Wilcox.
270 Gamaliel,	born	1824.	Married Sarah Ireland.
271 Cornelia,	born	1826.	Died in infancy.
272 Alonson,	}born	1827.	
273 Alonzo,			
274 William,	born	1829.	Died an infant.
275 Sophia,	born	1831.	

DESCENDANTS IN THE LINE OF MARY WHITING, DAUGHTER OF WILLIAM WHITING.

SECOND GENERATION.

V.

MARY WHITING was married August 3, 1664, to Rev. Nathaniel Collins, Harvard College, 1660, pastor of the Church in Middletown, Conn., and son of Deacon Edward Collins, of Cambridge, Mass.

Rev. Nathaniel Collins died December 28, 1684, aged 42.
His widow, Mrs. Mary Collins, died October 25, 1709.

Children.

276 Mary, born May 11, 1666. Married John Hamlin, of Middletown, January, 1684; he was a son of Giles Hamlin; she died May 5, 1722.

277 John, born January 31, 1668. Married Mary Dixwell, of New Haven, December 24, 1707; she was daughter of the regicide, Judge Dixwell.

278 Susanna, born November 26, 1669. Married William Hamlin, of Middletown, son of Giles Hamlin, May 26, 1692.

279 Sybil, born August 20, 1672.
280 Martha, born December 26, 1674. Married Thomas Hurlburt, of Middletown, December 15, 1705.

281 Nathaniel, born June 13, 1677. First minister of Enfield, Conn.; married Alice Adams, daughter of Rev. William Adams, of Dedham, January 7, 1701. She died February 19, 1735. He died in 1757.

282 Abigail, born July 13, 1681. Married Captain Samuel Wolcott, of Wethersfield, Conn. He died September 15, 1734. She died February 6, 1758.

283 Samuel, born April 16, 1683. Died April 23, 1683.

DESCENDANTS IN THE LINE OF JOSEPH WHITING, SON OF WILLIAM WHITING.

SECOND GENERATION.

VI.

JOSEPH WHITING was a merchant, first of Westfield, Mass., but returned to Hartford in 1675 or 6. He was Treasurer of Connecticut, from 1678 till his death, (39 years,) when his son John succeeded him, and continued in the office 32 years. He married 1. October 5, 1669, Mary, daughter of Hon. John Pynchon, and granddaughter of Hon. William Pynchon, the founder of Springfield, Mass.; her mother was Anna, daughter of Hon. George Wyllys. 2. In 1676, Anna, daughter of Col. John Allyn, son of Matthew Allyn; (her mother was daughter of Henry Smith, of Springfield, and granddaughter of Hon. William Pynchon.) She was born August 18, 1654, and died March 3, 1735.

Children,—by his first wife.

284 Mary, born August 19, 1672. Married 1. Joseph Sheldon. 2. John Ashley.

285 Joseph, born October 5, 1674. Died young.

Children,—by his second wife.

286 Anna, born August 28, 1677. Died April 18, 1684.
287 John, born November 13, 1679. Died young.
288 Susannah, born June 18, 1682. Married 1. Sam'l Thornton. 2. Thomas Warren.

289 William, born March 14, 1685. Died September 6, 1702.
290 Anna, born August 18, 1687.
291 Margaret, born January 5, 1690. Married Rev. Jonathan Marsh.
292 John, born December 15, 1693.

THIRD GENERATION.

289.

ANNA WHITING married November 14, 1706, Nathaniel Stanley, son of Nathaniel Stanley and Sarah Boosey, his wife, and grandson of Timothy Stanley, one of the first settlers of Hartford.

Mrs. Anna Stanley died August 9, 1752, aged 66.

Hon. Nathaniel Stanley died August 15, 1755, aged 72, nearly.

Children.

293 Nathaniel,	born August	11, 1707.	Yale College, 1726; settled in Windsor, Conn.
294 Sarah,	born January	18, 1709.	Married Hon. Andrew Burr, of Fairfield, Conn.
295 Joseph,	born January	4, 1711.	Died August 14, 1712.
296 Augustus,	born March	31, 1713.	
397 Anna,	born June	22, 1715.	Died December 17, 1722.
298 Susanna,	born June	26, 1717.	Married Aaron Day, of New Haven, September 18, 1745, being his second wife, by whom she had six children. He died at Southington, Conn., September 9, 1778, aged 78; she died April 1, 1805, aged 88.
299 Abigail,	born July	24, 1719.	Married Rev. Elnathan Whitman, pastor of the Second Church, in Hartford.
300 Mary,	born June	20, 1721.	Died December 27, 1722.
301 Joseph,	born June	18, 1723.	Died August 21, 1723.
302 William,	born	1724.	Died December 31, 1786, aged 63; left no children, surviving him. He gave the perpetual use of his large estate to the Second Church in Hartford.

291.

MARGARET WHITING married Rev. Jonathan Marsh, pastor of the First Church in Windsor, July 13, 1710. Mr. Marsh was the son of John Marsh, of Hartford, and grandson of John Marsh, one of the first settlers of that town, afterward of Hadley, Mass. He graduated at Harvard College, 1705.

Rev. Jonathan Marsh, died September 8, 1747, aged 63. [Gravestone.]

His widow, Mrs. Margaret Marsh, died December 8, 1747.

Children.

303 Margaret,	born June	10, 1711.	Married Rev. Nathaniel Roberts, of Torrington; she died October 1, 1747. Rev. Mr. Roberts died February 6, 1783.
304 Jonathan,	born January	1, 1714.	Yale College, 1735; minister of New Hartford, Conn.
305 Mary,	born July	19, 1716.	Married Rev. Stephen Heaton, minister of Goshen, Conn.; he died suddenly December 29, 1788, aged 78, leaving his widow and one daughter.
306 Dorcas,	born August	31, 171–.	Married Jabez Bissell, of Windsor, Conn.
307 Hannah,	born May	28, 1723.	
308 Joseph,	born November	10, 1727.	
309 Ann,	born January	28, 1730.	

44

292.

JOHN WHITING married Jerusha Lord, daughter of Richard Lord, of Hartford, who was grandson of Thomas Lord, one of the first settlers of the town. She was born February 25, 1699.
Col. John Whiting died February 14, 1766.
Mrs. Jerusha Whiting died October 21, 1776, at Windsor.

Children.

310 Jerusha,	born	1720.	Married Daniel Skinner. Died July 6, 1803.
311 Ann,	born	1723.	Married October 27, 1746, Lieut. Benjamin Colton, of West Hartford, Conn. Died May 31, 1762.
312 John,	born		
313 Mary,	born	1730.	Married November 27, 1748, John Skinner.
314 Susanna,	bap. March	19, 1732–3.	
315 William,	born		
316 Allyn,	born	1738.	Died February 9, 1818, aged 79.
317 Sarah,	born		
318 Elizabeth,	bap. June	26, 1743.	Died August 14, 1750.

FOURTH GENERATION.

312.

JOHN WHITING married 1. Sarah ———, who died July 22, 1760, aged 29.   2. ——— ———, who died September 23, 1766.

Children,—baptized at West Hartford.

319 Sarah,	bap. June	25, 1749.	
320 Elizabeth,	bap. May	14, 1752.	
321 John,	bap. November	30, 1755.	
322 Jerusha,	bap. February	19, 1758.	Died September 13, 1759.
323 Abigail,	bap. September,	1759.	Died March 23, 1764.
324 ———,	born July	21, 1760.	Died the same day.

THOMAS LORD.

[NOTE. The following genealogy of the descendants of Thomas Lord was undoubtedly intended by Mr. Goodwin to be included in the book but was not found among his papers till too late to be placed in its proper alphabetical order.]

THOMAS LORD, of Hartford, Conn., and one of the first settlers of that town, was married in England, to Dorothy ———, about 1610.

Mr. Thomas Lord died ———.

His widow, Mrs. Dorothy Lord, died in 1676 aged about 87.

FIRST GENERATION.

Children of Thomas Lord and of Dorothy, his wife.

I. Richard, born	1611.	
II. Thomas, born	1619.	
III. Ann, born	1621.	
IV. William, born	1623.	
V. John, born	1625.	Married Adrean Basey, of Hartford, May 15, 1648, soon after which he removed to parts unknown to the compiler.
VI. Robert, born	1627.	
VII. Aymie, born	1629.	
VIII. Dorothy, born	1631.	Married John Ingersoll, of Hartford, about 1651; she died at Northampton, January, 1657, aged about 26.

DESCENDANTS IN THE LINE OF RICHARD LORD, SON OF THOMAS LORD, THE SETTLER.

SECOND GENERATION.

I.

RICHARD LORD, of Hartford, was married to Sarah ———, about 1635.

Capt. Richard Lord died at New London, Conn., May 17, 1662, aged 51.*

His widow, Mrs. Sarah Lord, died ———.

Children.

9 Richard,	born	1636.
10 Sarah,	born	1638.
11 Dorathy,	born	1640.

THIRD GENERATION.

9.

RICHARD LORD, of Hartford, Conn., was married to Mary Smith, daughter of Mr. Henry Smith, of Springfield, Mass., and of Ann his wife, daughter of Hon. William Pynchon, the principal founder of that town, April 25, 1665. [After his death she was married to Doct. Thomas Hooker, of Hartford, son of Rev. Samuel Hooker, second minister of Farmington, Conn., and grandson of Rev. Thomas Hooker, first minister of Hartford, about 1686, by whom she had no children.]

Richard Lord, Esq., died November 5, 1685, aged 49.

Mrs. Mary Lord, alias Hooker, died May 17, 1702, aged 59.

Child,—one only.

12 Richard,   born February 1, 1669.

10.

SARAH LORD was married to Rev. Joseph Haynes, third pastor of the First Church in Hartford, about 1668. He was son of Rev. John Haynes, of Hartford, first Governor of the colony of Connecticut.

---

* At a General Court holden at Hartford, October 11, 1643, "Richard Lord, for his miscariedge in draweing his sowrd and useing threatning speeches in contending with Tho : Stanton about tradeing for indean corne, is fyned to pay to the County five pound." Mr. Stanton had married Ann Lord, sister of Richard Lord.

At a General Court holden at Hartford, January 28, 1646, "Richard Lord, for transgressing the Order against selleing lead out of this Jurisdiction, is fyned seaven pound."

Tho : Staynton, for the like transgression is fyned 5l. five pound.

At a General Court holden at Hartford, March 11, 1658, "The listed persons for Troopers, presented to this Court their choice of Officers, wch the Court did confirme : Richard Lord, Capt. ; Daniell Clarke, Lieftent. ; John Allin, Cornett ; Nicho : Olmsted, Corporall ; Richard Treat, Corporall ; Sam : Marshall, Corporall ; Mr. Tho : Wells, Junior, Quartr. Mr."

Mr. Lord was a Deputy to the General Court, in March, 1659.

Both father and son of this name, merchants of Hartford, had commercial dealings in New London. The senior Mr. Lord, died in the place, and was interred in the old burial-ground. A table of red sandstone covers his grave, on which is the following inscription, in capitals :

AN EPITAPH ON CAPTAINE RICHARD LORD, DECEASED, MAY 17, 1662, ÆTATIS SUÆ, 51.

The bright Starre of our Cavallrie lyes here ;
Unto the State, a Counselour full Deare,
And to ye Truth a Friend of Sweet Content,
To Hartford Towne a silver Ornament.
Who can deny to Poore he was Releife,
And in composing Paroxysmes was Cheife.
To Marchantes, as a Patterne he might stand,
Adventring Dangers new by Sea and Land.

Miss Caulkins' History of New London.

Rev. Joseph Haynes died May 14, 1679, aged 38.
His widow, Mrs. Sarah Haynes, died November 15, 1705, aged 67.

Children.

13 John,	born	1669.	Settled in Hartford. Assistant and Judge; married Mary Glover, daughter of —— Glover, of Springfield, Mass. He died November 27, 1713, aged 44. She died August 19, 1726, aged 54.
14 Mabel,	born		
15 Sarah,	born		Married Rev. James Pierpont.
16 Mary,	born		

FOURTH GENERATION.

12.

RICHARD LORD, of Hartford, Conn., was married to Abigail Warren, daughter of John Warren, of Boston, Mass., and of Elizabeth, his second wife, January 14, 1692. She was born May 10, 1676. [After the death of Mr. Lord, she was married to Rev. Timothy Woodbridge, sixth pastor of the First Church in Hartford, about 1716. She was his second wife. By him she had one child only, a son, Theodore, born June 23, 1717. The first wife of Rev. Mr. Woodbridge was Mehitabel Foster, widow of his predecessor in the ministry, Rev. Isaac Foster, alias Russell, widow of Rev. Daniel Russell, of Charlestown, Mass., and daughter of Hon. Samuel Wyllys, of Hartford, and of Ruth his wife, daughter of Gov. Haynes. Rev. Daniel Russell died January 4, 1679. Rev. Isaac Foster died in 1683.]

Richard Lord, Esq., died January 29, 1712, in his 43d year.
Mrs. Abigail Lord, alias Woodbridge, died January 1, 1754, aged 77.

Children.

17 Abigail,	born March	15, 1694.	Died May 22, 1694.
18 Richard,	born August	16, 1695.	Died December 16, 1699.
19 Abigail,	born January	19, 1698.	Died April 19, 1698.
20 Jerusha,	born February	25, 1699.	Married John Whiting, of Hartford. She died at Windsor, Conn., October 21, 1776. Children, 9.
21 Elisha,	born March	15, 1701.	
22 Mary,	born February	20, 1703.	
23 Richard,	born February	18, 1705.	
24 Elizabeth,	born August	3, 1707.	
25 Epaphras,	born December	26, 1709.	
26 Ichabod,	born March	16, 1712.	

FIFTH GENERATION.

21.

ELISHA LORD was married to Mary Haynes, daughter of John Haynes, Esq., of Hartford, Conn., and granddaughter of Gov. Haynes, May 2, 1723. [After his death, she was married to Rosewell Saltonstall, of Hartford, afterwards of Branford, Conn., son of Gov. Saltonstall, April 6, 1727, and after *his* death, which occurred October 1, 1738, to Rev. Thomas Clap, President of Yale College, being his second wife, February 5, 1741. President Clap died at Scituate, Mass., his birth-place, January 7, 1767, aged 63.]

Mr. Elisha Lord died April 15, 1725, aged 24.

Mrs. Mary Lord, alias Saltonstall, alias Clap, died ———.

Child,—one only.

27 John Haynes
Lord,   born January   12, 1725. Died March, 1796, aged 72.

22.

MARY LORD was married to Joseph Pitkin, of East Hartford, Conn., February 20, 1724. [After her death, Mr. Pitkin was married to Eunice Chester, daughter of Major John Chester, of Wethersfield, Conn. And after *her* death which took place June 25, 1756, at the age of 55, to Eunice Law, widow of Gov. Jonathan Law, of Milford, Conn., alias Eunice Andrew, widow of Samuel Andrew, of Milford, son of Rev. Samuel Andrew, minister of that town. She was the only daughter of Hon. John Hall, of Wallingford, Conn, and aunt to Lyman Hall, one of the signers of the Declaration of Independence from the State of Georgia. She died at New Haven, Conn., June 23, 1774, aged 75.]

Hon. Joseph Pitkin, died November 3, 1762, aged 67.

Mrs. Mary Pitkin, died October 10, 1740, aged 38.

Children.

28 Mary,	born	1727.	Married David Hills, of East Hartford. He died July 2, 1785, aged 60. She died December 9, 1793, aged 66. They had 12 children.
29 Abigail,	born	1730.	Died unmarried, November, 1781.
30 Elisha,	born	1733.	Settled in East Hartford. Married Hannah Pitkin, daughter of Samuel Pitkin, of East Hartford. She died June 23, 1811, aged 86. He died March 11, 1819, aged 86. They had 11 children.
31 Jerusha,	born	1736.	Married John Welles, of East Hartford. She died July 12, 1800, aged 64. He died March 15, 1801, aged 71. They had 9 children.
32 Richard,	born	1738.	Settled in East Hartford. Married Dorothy Hills, daughter of David Hills, of East Hartford. He died August 22, 1799, aged 61. She died ———. They had 8 children.
33 Joseph,	born	1739.	Settled in East Hartford. Married Anna Hills, daughter of David Hills, of East Hartford. She died July 4, 1758, aged 25. He died October 30, 1770, in his 42d year. They had 3 children.

23.

RICHARD LORD, of Wethersfield, Conn., was married to Ruth

Wyllys, daughter of Hezekiah Wyllys, Esq., of Hartford, Conn.,
and of Elizabeth his wife, daughter of Rev. Jeremiah Hobart,
pastor of the Congregational Church, Haddam, Conn., December
31, 1724. She was born February 22, 1705 ; after his death, she
was married to ———— Belden, of Wethersfield.
Mr. Richard Lord died ————.
Mrs. Ruth Lord, alias Belden, died ————.

Children.

34	Elizabeth,	born October	9, 1725, at Hartford.	
35	Elisha,	born February	24, 1727, at Wethersfield.	Died June 7, 1727.
36	Elisha,	born March	25, 1728, at Wethersfield.	Died January 10, 1729.
37	Ruth,	born December	28, 1729, at Wethersfield.	
38	Richard,	born December	14, 1731, at Wethersfield.	
39	Mary,	born February	22, 1734, at Wethersfield.	
40	Samuel Wyllys,	born February	27, 1735, at Wethersfield.	Died July 13, 1736.
41	George,	born July	8, 1736.	

24.

ELIZABETH LORD was married to John Curtis, of Wethersfield, Conn., afterwards of New Haven, in the same State, October 21, 1728.

25.

EPAPHRUS LORD, first of Wethersfield, Conn., then of Middletown, Conn., and afterwards of Colchester, Conn., was twice
married. 1. To Hope Phillips, daughter of Capt. George Phillips, of Middletown, March 17, 1731.* She was born March 17,
1711, and died December 1, 1736, in her 25th year. 2. To
Eunice Bulckley, daughter of Rev. John Bulckley, first minister

---

* The mother of Hope Phillips, was Hope Stow, granddaughter of Rev. Samuel Stow, the
first " Preacher of the Word " at Middletown, Conn. A trace of her descent from her first
American ancestor, follows:
REV. SAMUEL STOW, of Middletown Conn., was married to Hope Fletcher, daughter of
William Fletcher, of Chelmsford, Mass., about 1649.
Mrs. Hope Stow died ————.
Rev. Samuel Stow died May 8, 1704.

Children,—seven,—among them,

John, born June 16, 1650, at Charlestown.

JOHN STOW, of Middletown, Conn., son of Rev. Samuel Stow, of that town, was married
to Esther Willcox, widow of John Willcox, of the same town, 1678. She was Esther Cornwell, daughter of Sargeant William Cornwell, of Middletown, and was married to Mr. Willcox in 1671. He died May 24, 1676.
Mr. John Stow died June 30, 1732, in the 83d year of his age.
His widow, Mrs. Esther Stow, alias Willcox, died May 2, 1733, " being about 83 years
of age."

Children,—two. Their first child,

Hope, born September 10, 1679.

HOPE STOW, daughter of John Stow, was married to George Phillips, of Middletown,
Conn., September 29, 1707.
Mrs. Hope Phillips died March 18, 1747, in her 68th year.
Capt. George Phillips died October 8, 1747.

Children,—five,—among them, their second child,

Hope, born March 17, 1711. Married Epaphras Lord, March 17, 1731.

of Colchester, November 25, 1742. Epaphras Lord was graduated at Yale College, in 1729.

Epaphras Lord, Esq., died November 25, 1799, in the 90th
year of his age.

His widow, Mrs. Eunice Lord, died May 10, 1800, in the 81st
year of her age.

Children,—by his first wife.

42 Epaphrus,	born October	1, 1732.	Died in childhood.
43 Samuel			
Phillips,	born October	28, 1734.	Settled in East Haddam, Conn.
44 Hope,	born December	1, 1736.	Married Amasa Jones, of Colchester, August 27, 1754.

Children,—by his second wife.

45 Epaphras,	born December	22, 1743.	
46 Elisha,	born March	18, 1745.	
47 Dorathy,	born April	27, 1746.	Died May 26, 1752.
48 Theodore,	born May	18, 1747.	Capt. Theodore Lord died February 11, 1845, in the 98th year of his age. Sarah his wife died June 26, 1834, aged 85.
49 Lucy,	born August	26, 1748.	
50 Jerusha,	born November	7, 1749.	
51 Bulckley,	born January	15, 1751.	Died January 25, 1751.
52 Dorathy,	born May	26, 1752.	Died April 16, 1753.
53 Dorathy,	born September	16, 1753.	
54 John Bulck-			
ley,	born November	5, 1754.	
55 Eunice,	born July	26, 1756.	
56 Caroline,	born March	2, 1758.	
57 Lydia,	born November	4, 1759.	
58 Abigail,	born June	3, 1761.	
59 Ichabod,	born June	12, 1762.	Died February 11, 1840, aged 73. His widow, Mrs. Elizabeth Lord, died August 11, 1842, aged 81.

26.

ICHABOD LORD, of Colchester, Conn., that part of ancient
Colchester, now called Marlborough, was married to Patience
Bulckley, daughter of Rev. John Bulckley, first minister of Colchester, December 14, 1743. She was born March 21, 1714,
" about noone." [Colchester Records.]

Ichabod Lord, Esq., sickened and died of fever, in Colchester,
(where his remains were buried,) December 18, 1762, aged 50.

His widow, Mrs. Patience Lord, died ———.

Children.

60 Abigail,	born November	22, 1744.	
61 Patience,	born February	7, 1746.	Died, unmarried, February 25, 1836, in her 90th year.
62 Mary,	born May	12, 1748.	
63 Sarah,	born November	28, 1749.	
64 Elizabeth,	born October	7, 1751.	
65 Anna,	born September	19, 1753.	
66 Jerusha,	born February	5, 1755	
67 Lydia,	born July	4, 1756.	

DESCENDANTS IN THE LINE OF THOMAS LORD, SON OF THOMAS LORD, THE SETTLER.

SECOND GENERATION.

II.

THOMAS LORD, first of Hartford, Conn., afterwards of Wethersfield, in the same State, was married to Hannah ——. [After his death she was married to an Olmsted, as says Wm. S. Porter. Mr. Thomas Lord died in 1662, aged about 43. He appears to have been a physician.* Mrs. Hannah Lord, alias Olmsted, died ———.

Children.

68 Dorothy,	born August	17, 1653.
69 Hannah,	born	1656.
70 Mary,	born	1659.
71 Sarah,	born	probably. See wlil of Sarah Lord, wife of Richard Lord, brother of Thomas Lord.

DESCENDANTS IN THE LINE OF ANN LORD, DAUGHTER OF THOMAS LORD, THE SETTLER.

SECOND GENERATION.

III.

ANN LORD was married to Thomas Stanton, first of Hartford, Conn., afterwards of Stonington, in the same State, about 1637. Mr. Thomas Stanton, died in 1678. His widow, Mrs. Ann Stanton, died in 1688.

Children.

72 Thomas,	born about	1638. Settled in Stonington. Married and had a family of children. Died April 11, 1718, aged 80.
73 John,	born about	1641. Settled in Stonington. Married and had several children. Was a captain in Philip's war. Died October 3, 1713, aged 72.
74 Mary,	born	Married Samuel Rogers, November 17, 1662.

---

* At a Session of the General Court, this 11th day of October, 1648. Present, Mr. Hopkins, Governor, Mr. Ludlow, Deputy,—several Magistrates, and Deputies.
" Thomas Lord was called upon for selling lead to an Indian, and he is to answer the next Courte."
At a Session of the General Court in Hartford, the 30th of June, 1652. Present, John Haynes, Esq., Deputy Governor, and the several Magistrates and Deputies. " Thomas Lord, having ingaged to this Courte to continue his abode in Hartford, for the next ensuing yeare, and to improve his best skill amongst the inhabitants of the Townes uppon the River within this Jurissdiction, both for setting of bones and otherwise, as at all times occasions or necessityes may or shall require ; This Court doth graunt that hee shall bee paid by the Country the sum of fifteene p unds for the said ensuing yeare, and they doe declare that for every visitt or journye that he shall take or make, being sent for to any house in Hartford, twelve pence is reasonable ; to any house in Wyndsor, five shillings ; to any house in Wethersfield, three shillings ; to any house in Farmington, six shillings ; to any house in Mattabeseck, eight shillings ; (he having promised that he will require no more ;) and that hee shall be freed for the time aforesaid from watching, warding and train - ing ; but not from finding armes, according to lawe."

45

75 Hannah,	born	Married Nehemiah Palmer, son of Walter Palmer, November 20, 1662. Nehemiah Palmer, Esq., died February 17, 1718. His widow, Mrs. Hannah Palmer, died October 17, 1727. They had several children.
76 Joseph,	bap. March	21, 1646, at Hartford. Three children are recorded to him on the Records of Westerly, R. I.
77 David,	born	Named in a list of " Free Inhabitants," of Westerly, May 18, 1669. Died at Barbadoes shortly after 1681.
78 Dorathy,	born	1652. Married Rev. James Noyes, minister of Stonington, September 11, 1674. He was son of Rev. James Noyes, of Newberry, Mass. Rev. James Noyes died December 30, 1719, in his 80th year. His widow, Mrs. Dorathy Noyes, died January 19, 1743, in her 91st year. A number of children are recorded to them on Stonington records.
79 Robert,	born	1653. Settled in Stonington. Married Joanna Gardner, September 12, 1677. He died October 25, 1724, aged 71. Nine children are recorded to them on Stonington records.
80 Samuel,	born	Married Boradell Denison, daughter of Capt. George Denison, and of Anna [Boradell] Denison, his wife, June 15, 1680. Children are recorded to them.
81 Sarah,	born about	1654. Married William Denison. She died in 1713, aged 59.

DESCENDANTS IN THE LINE OF WILLIAM LORD, SON OF THOMAS LORD, THE SETTLER.

SECOND GENERATION.

IV.

WILLIAM LORD, of that part of ancient Saybrook, Conn., now called Lyme, was married to ———.

Mr. William Lord died May 17, 1678 aged about 68.

His widow, Mrs. ——— Lord, died ———.

Children.

82 William,	born October,	1643. Settled in East Haddam, Conn. Married Mary Shayler. He died December 4, 1696. They had eight children. After his death, she married Samuel Ingram.
83 Thomas,	born December,	1645. Settled in Lyme. Died June 27, 1730, in his 86th year.
84 Richard,	born May,	1647. Settled in Lyme. Died August 20, 1727, aged 80.
85 Mary,	born May,	1649.
86 Robert,	born August,	1651.
87 John,	born September,	1653.
88 Joseph,	born September,	1656.
89 Benjamin,	born	
90 Daniel,	born	
91 James,	born	
92 Samuel,	born	

And three daughters whose names are unknown to the compiler.

DESCENDANTS IN THE LINE OF ROBERT LORD, SON OF THOMAS LORD, THE SETTLER.

SECOND GENERATION.

VI.

ROBERT LORD was a " sea-captain," and is supposed to have been in life in 1670, and to have died abroad, after that year, unmarried. In her will, which is dated February 8, 1670, his mother says,—" I give unto my son Robert Lord, if he live after my decease, so long as to have notice of this my will, three acres of my upper meadow lot, adjoining that I have given to my daughter Gilbert. * * * * * And in case my son Robert shall depart this life before he hath notice of this my last will, then that three acres of land given to him shall be divided between my son William and my grandson Richard Lord."

DESCENDANTS IN THE LINE OF AYMIE LORD, DAUGH-TER OF THOMAS LORD, THE SETTLER.

SECOND GENERATION.

VII.

AYMIE LORD was married to John Gilbert, of Hartford, Conn., May 6, 1647.

Corporal John Gilbert died December 29, 1690.

His widow, Mrs. Aymie Gilbert, died January 8, 1691, aged about 62.

Children.

93 John,	born January	16, 1648,	Died in infancy.
94 John,	born February	19, 1652.*	
95 Elizabeth,	born February	12, 1655.*	
96 Thomas,	born September	4, 1658.	Died in 1706.
97 Dorathy,	born [no date.]		Married a Palmer.
98 Aymie,	born April	3, 1663.*	
99 Joseph,	born April	3, 1666.*	
100 James,	born [no date.]		Died in 1697.

* This child is not named in its father's will, neither is a trace of it to be found; supposed therefore, to have died in early life.

ERRATA.

Page 30, line 15, for *Henry*, read *George*.

Page 61, line 9 from bottom, *November*, 1837, manifestly wrong, though unable to correct it.

Page 65, line 16, for *He*, read *She*.

Page 79, line 9 from bottom, for BELDEN, read GOODRICH.

Page 94, line 26, for 56, read 60.

Page 95, line 3, for 57, read 61.

 Line 32, for 65, read 69.

 Line 33, for 66, read 70.

Page 96, line 7 from bottom, for 67, read 71.

Page 101, line 18, *Hollister*, evidently an error, though unable to correct it.

Page 104, line 40, for 3, read 113.

 Line 44, for 4, read 114.

 Line 47, for 5, read 115.

Page 105, line 1, for 6, read 116.

 Line 7, for 10, read 120.

 Line 13, for 11, read 121.

Page 135, line 23, for *Hooper*, read *Hooker*.

Page 151, line 36, 1716, should perhaps read 1706.

Page 161, line 9, for 1700, read 1800.

Page 176, line 30 of note, for 1665, read 1655.

Page 187, line 27, strike out *one only is recorded to them on Boston Records*, for *Child*, read *Children*, and add, 100½ William, born June 9, 1676.

Page 187, line 28, for 1667, read 1677.

Page 199, line 17, for *Timothy*, read *Samuel*.

Page 211, line 10 of note, for *Judge* read *Hon. James*.

Page 212, line 4, for 1670, read 1646.

 Line 5, for *bap.*, read *born*.

Page 233, line 9 from bottom, for *Jacob*, read *Joseph*.

Page 237, line 5 from bottom, strike out *Harvard College*, 1690.

 Line 7 from bottom, strike out *Yale College*, 1738.

Page 238, line 34 for *daughter*, read *widow*, and see page 323.

Page 242, strike out line 24.

Page 279, line 2, for *February*, read *January*.

 Line 8, for *October*, read *December*.

Page 280, line 36, for 1763, read 1753.

Page 281, line 3 from bottom, for *Juliana*, read *Julima*.

 Line 13 from bottom, for *Wilmer*, read *Wilmot*.

Page 282, line 11, for *R.*, read *K.*

Page 288, line 10, for *Hepzibah*, read *Hepzibeth*.

 Line 23, for 1750, read 1850.

Page 291, line 28, for *Haskell*, read *Maskell*.

Page 292, line 1 from bottom, for *November*, read *February*.

 Line 16 from bottom, for 1757, read 1755.

Page 293, line 11, for *June*, read *January*.

 Line 40, for 1788, read 1787.

Page 294, line 27, for *December* 23, read *December* 3.

Page 296, line 13 from bottom, for *Dora*, read *Dosa*.

Page 297, line 6, for *January* 16, read *January* 15.

 Line 13, for *Hepzibah*, read *Hepzibeth*.

Page 299, line 32, for *Ezekiel H. Case*, read *Ezekiel H. Wilcox*.

 Line 34, for *Elmira*, read *Elmina*.

Page 314, line 8, for 1848, read 1748.

Page 317, line 25, fill the blank by inserting *April 5, 1782*.

INDEX.